IRA INTERNMENTS AND THE IRISH GOVERNMENT
SUBVERSIVES AND THE STATE 1939–1962

IRA INTERNMENTS AND THE IRISH GOVERNMENT

*Subversives and the State
1939–1962*

By
JOHN MAGUIRE

Foreword by
Ruán O'Donnell

IRISH ACADEMIC PRESS
DUBLIN • PORTLAND, OR

First published in 2008 by Irish Academic Press

44 Northumberland Road,
Ballsbridge,
Dublin 4, Ireland

920 NE 58th Avenue, Suite 300
Portland, Oregon,
97213-3786

www.iap.ie

copyright © 2008 John Maguire

British Library Cataloguing in Publication Data
An entry can be found on request

ISBN 978 0 7165 2943 9 (cloth)
ISBN 978 0 7165 2944 6 (paper)

Library of Congress Cataloging-in-Publication Data
An entry can be found on request

All rights reserved. Without limiting the rights under copyright reserved alone, no part of this publication may be reproduced, stored in or introduced into a retrieval system, or transmitted, in any form or by any means (electronic, mechanical, photocopying, recording or otherwise) without the prior written permission of both the copyright owner and the above publisher of this book.

Printed by Biddles Ltd., King's Lynn, Norfolk

For Oonagh,
Mo grá go daingean thú

Also for my parents, and
my grandparents, Norah, Larry and Maura

Contents

Acknowledgements	ix
List of abbreviations	xi
Foreword	xiii
1. Introduction	1
2. 'Liquidating the Irish Separatist Movement': Internment, 1939–1945	21
3. 'A Tireless, Ceaseless Effort': IRA Reorganization, 1948–1956	54
4. 'The National Revolutionary Resurgence': Campaign and Reaction, December 1956	85
5. 'The Nettle Had At Last Been Gripped': Forkhill and the Reintroduction of Internment, July 1957	117
6. 'The Powers of Detention Should Not Again Be Exercised': the Lawless Case, 1957–1961	143
7. 'This is not an Abandonment of the Campaign, but a Strategic Retreat': Closing Stages, 1957–1962	173
8. Conclusion	202
Notes	210
Appendix 1: Organizational structure of the IRA	244
Appendix 2.1: Variation in the number of internees, May 1940 – February 1946	245
Appendix 2.2: Prisoners and Internees in Military Custody on Hunger Strike, 1939–1946	245
Appendix 3: Activities in Northern Ireland, from 1 December 1956–3 March 1958	248
Bibliography	255
Index	267

Acknowledgements

The completion of this book has been a long and rewarding process that would not have been possible without the assistance and support of a large number of individuals. First of all I am deeply indebted to the Irish Research Council for the Humanities and Social Sciences, who kindly agreed to fund and support my PhD research. I would like to thank my PhD supervisor, Dr Ruán O'Donnell, for his direction, advice and insight. Lisa Hyde of Irish Academic Press also deserves a special mention for her invaluable input as I endeavoured to convert my PhD thesis into something more publishable. I am grateful to the staff of the National Archives of Ireland, the Military Archives of the Irish Defence Forces, particularly Commandant Victor Laing, the staff of the National Library of Ireland, the University College Dublin Archives Department, the Public Record Office in London and the Public Record Office of Northern Ireland. I would also like to express my gratitude to Mr Ken Bergin and Ms Jean Turner of the Special Collections Library at the University of Limerick. I wish to acknowledge the assistance of Ms Catriona Lawlor and Mr Declan Costello in providing access to the private papers of Seán MacBride and John A. Costello.

I would also like to express my thanks to Mr Tony Hayde, Mr Noel Kavanagh and Mr Patrick O'Regan for sharing their experiences, which have served to enrich this work. I wish to acknowledge the assistance of Mr Des Long in the latter stages of this project. I am grateful to Mr Pierce James Moore for his sharp eye and exemplary proof reading skills. I would also like to thank my PhD examiners, Dr Donal Ó Drisceoil and Dr Bernadette Whelan. I wish to take this opportunity to express my profound thanks to all of my friends and former colleagues in the Department of History, University of Limerick, especially: Dr John Logan, Dr Pádraig Lenihan, Dr Angus Mitchell, Dr John O'Brennan, Dr Liam Chambers, Dr Catherine Lawless, Professor Anthony McElligott, Dr Ciara Breathnach, Mr Declan Jackson, Mr John O'Callaghan, Miss Jennifer Moore, Mr

David Meeres, Miss Ailbhe O'Flaherty, Miss Mairéad Conneely, Dr Máiréad Moriarty, Dr Íde O'Sullivan, Dr Catherine O'Connor and Ms Lorna Moloney. I am deeply indebted to my parents, Tony and Debra Maguire, for all of their love, encouragement and support throughout the past twenty-seven years. I would also like to make special mention of my deceased grandparents, Laurence and Norah Maguire and Maura Bermingham, who inspired my love of history. Lastly, but by no means least, I owe a profound debt to Miss Oonagh Nash, without whose unwavering love and constant encouragement and support I would not be here today.

List of Abbreviations

ACA	Army Comrades Association
ADM	British Admiralty
A/G	Adjutant-General
AGO	Attorney General's Office
Air	Air Ministry
APL	The Anti-Partition League
BBC	British Broadcasting Corporation
CAB	Cabinet Office
CID	Criminal Investigation Division
C/S	Chief of Staff
DEA	Department of External Affairs
DJ	Department of Justice
DO	Dominions Office
DORA	Defence of the Realm Act, 1914–1918
DT	Department of An Taoiseach
DVP	Éamon de Valera Papers
ECHR	The European Convention for the Protection of Human Rights and Fundamental Freedoms
EPA	The Emergency Powers Act, 1939
FBI	Federal Bureau of Investigation
FCA	*An Fórsa Cosanta Áitiúil* (Reserve of the Irish Defence Forces)
FLN	National Liberation Front (Algeria)
FO	Foreign Office
GAA	Gaelic Athletic Association
GLP	Gerard Lawless Papers
HA	Department of Home Affairs (Northern Ireland)
HO	Home Office
IRA	Irish Republican Army
IRB	Irish Republican Brotherhood
IRPB	Irish Republican Publicity Bureau

JACP	John A. Costello Papers
MA	Military Archives, Irish Defence Forces
MCP	MacMillan Cabinet Papers
MP	Member of Parliament
NAI	National Archives of Ireland
NATO	The North Atlantic Treaty Organization
NAUK	National Archives, UK
NCO	Non Commissioned Officer
NCCL	The National Council for Civil Liberties
NIO	Northern Ireland Office
NLI	National Library of Ireland
OASA	The Offences Against the State Act, 1939
O/C	Officer Commanding
PM	Provost Marshal's Office (Irish Defence Forces)
PREM	Prime Minister's Office
PRONI	Public Record Office of Northern Ireland
QMG	Quartermaster General
RAF	Royal Air Force
RIC	Royal Irish Constabulary
ROIA	Restoration of Order in Ireland Act
RUC	Royal Ulster Constabulary
RPRA	Republican Prisoners Release Association
SMP	Seán MacBride Papers
SPA	The Civil Authorities (Special Powers) Act (Northern Ireland), 1922
TD	Teachta Dála (Member of the Irish Parliament)
UCDA	University College Dublin Archives Department
UN	The United Nations
UNESCO	The United Nations Education, Scientific and Cultural Organization
US	The United States
UUP	Ulster Unionist Party
WHO	The World Health Organization
WO	War Office

Foreword

The history of the Irish Republican Army (IRA), engine of political change during Ireland's years of revolution, remains largely unwritten. There are major gaps in the historiography of the War of Independence and Civil War and subsequent IRA campaigns have received very little attention from historians. If often helpful, the works published by political scientists, journalists and occasional protagonists, do not constitute history. Satisfactory historical analysis requires the declassification of state archives and the cooperation of former activists, factors which have only recently come into play in relation to the IRA in modern Ireland. This book draws upon new sources to reassess the nature of militant republicanism during the tumultuous 1940s and 1950s.

In selecting the years under review, Dr John Maguire has spanned a period normally considered, if at all, in isolation. The 'Forties Campaign' of Tom Williams and Sean McCaughey presaged the 'Fifties Campaign' of Sean South and Fergal O'Hanlon. That the two efforts were profoundly different was not simply a matter of immediate political conditions and the passage of a few years. In fact, the republican movement was essentially re-founded with a view to breaking the organization out of the demoralizing 'Twilight Years' and into a new progressive role in 1948–50. The last vestiges of the Civil War were laid to rest in order to focus attention on the continued existence of partition and its much resented consequences for northern nationalists and Irish republicans. This intriguing process is fully explored by Maguire.

The IRA was not the only entity to respond to the changing times. The bedding down of the Free State and its re-emergence as a Twenty-Six County Republic entailed far more than a mere modification of nomenclature. Republicans were subject to severe repression in the 1940s from a vibrant political force, Fianna Fáil, which many had actively supported in the late 1920s and early 1930s. Stormont and Unionists within the disputed Six Counties in Ulster, in the meantime, received renewed assurances of aid from Westminster. This had bearings on their dealings with the resurgent IRA. Stormont moved with decision in their efforts to crush republicanism in the 1940s and 1950s and the recourse to coercion in both decades was mirrored by the Dáil. The use of internment in both jurisdictions, a vital counter-insurgency tool, is detailed by Maguire in unprecedented detail.

Examining the 1950s in the light of the 1940s enables the reader to trace previously hidden developments that were sufficiently serious to oblige the Dáil to intern its citizens. The legal repercussions were not inconsiderable and effectively prevented any subsequent rush to intern republicans. By looking at the manner in which the IRA moved from outright opposition to the Irish government into a form of realistic co-existence, Maguire has raised important questions as to the nature of subversion in modern Ireland. Hitherto concealed material is brought into the public domain in a book which makes a strong contribution to illuminating the true character of Ireland in the mid-twentieth century.

DR RUÁN O'DONNELL
University of Limerick

1

Introduction

Singularly neglected in the historiography of the Irish republican movement, the Irish Republican Army's (IRA) 'border campaign' of 1956–1962 has left an indelible mark on the development of modern counter-insurgency policy within the jurisdiction of the Republic of Ireland. Portrayed by republicans as a campaign of 'organised resistance to British rule' in Northern Ireland, 'Operation Harvest', as it was called, envisaged the widespread use of guerrilla tactics 'to break down the enemy's administration' until 'he is forced to withdraw his forces'.[1] Skirmishes began on 11 December 1956, when a number of self-styled 'flying columns' infiltrated Northern Ireland with the intention of perpetrating a series of attacks against various military, administrative and infrastructural targets. Impelled by a revival in republican fortunes arising from a series of audacious arms raids in Northern Ireland and Britain during the early 1950s, this campaign was inspired by the widely held perception that the Ireland Act of 1949 precluded the border issue from being reopened by constitutional means.[2] Initially, IRA activities generated a certain measure of public enthusiasm, particularly following the deaths of Seán South and Fergal O'Hanlon during an abortive attack on Brookeborough Royal Ulster Constabulary (RUC) barracks in January 1957. This campaign quickly disintegrated, however, not least because of the efforts of both Irish governments in implementing internment. It was eventually abandoned in February 1962 due to a lack of public support.

Often dismissed as a self-indulgent political irrelevancy, the border campaign heralded a new departure for the republican movement, with its emphasis on tackling the perceived root of partition at its source – the British presence in Northern Ireland. Wedded to this, the simultaneous eschewal of militant activity within the boundaries of the Irish Republic implied a more pragmatic acceptance of the growing legitimacy of the Irish State. For a government already grappling with an intense economic crisis, the use of its territory as a staging post for the IRA's cross-border forays aroused the spectre of a damaging diplomatic confrontation with Britain at a time when it was to be most avoided. News of the attacks was greeted with alarm by the serving Fine Gael Taoiseach, John A. Costello, who described it as 'a challenge of the gravest kind to the democratic rights of the Irish people and to the authority of the Oireachtas'. The receipt of a 'stiffly' worded *aide-mémoire* from London served to underline his misgivings by calling for a more proactive response from the Irish government in tackling the IRA.³ Ultimately, the border campaign was to precipitate a general election in March 1957 in which a Fianna Fáil government was returned with an impressive parliamentary majority. From the IRA's perspective, the campaign's eventual collapse accelerated a growing impetus towards a fundamental reappraisal of the movement. Encompassing a wide-ranging strategic review, this reappraisal had a bearing on fomenting the subsequent split within republicanism in the early 1970s.⁴

In many respects, the border campaign's most enduring legacy is inextricably bound up with a definitive shift away from the use of internment by the Irish government in the late 1950s. Provision for the use of this measure had been extensively legislated for in the past as it became established as an integral part of the state's strategy against subversives. In 1923 the Public Safety (Emergency Powers) Act authorised the detention of 11,000 republicans who had been interned during the Civil War. These powers were renewed in 1924 by the Public Safety (Powers of Arrest and Detention) Temporary Act, before being made permanent in 1926.⁵ With the ratification of Bunreacht na hÉireann in 1937, the way was paved for the enactment of updated security legislation as embodied by the Offences Against the State Act, 1939 (OASA). Described as the 'zenith of coercive legislation in Ireland', this statute provided for the treatment of any organization deemed to be illegal by the government and greatly increased Garda powers of search and arrest.⁶ The main purpose of this act, however, was to provide for a new statutory mechanism allowing for the discretionary use of internment in order 'to secure the preservation of public peace and order'.⁷ In August 1939 these powers were formally invoked as part of a concerted crackdown against the IRA after it had embarked on a widespread bombing campaign in Britain a number of months previously.⁸

The outbreak of the Second World War in September 1939 encouraged a fundamental re-evaluation of the IRA threat to the Irish state, as official policy was motivated by a desire to ensure that Ireland, as a neutral state, should not give any belligerent power cause for complaint. In light of international circumstances largely beyond governmental control, it remained to be seen if such a policy could be successfully executed. In the event of a protracted war, occasioning a substantial interruption in international trade, the economic survival of Ireland would rest entirely on the continued goodwill of the British government.[9] Within this context the Taoiseach, Éamon de Valera, who was understandably wary of antagonising London, quickly set about reining in his erstwhile comrades within the republican movement.[10] For their part, the British authorities recognised that de Valera had been placed in a very embarrassing position as the IRA's campaign had effectively sabotaged his own peaceful efforts against partition. The situation was further complicated by a series of revelations concerning alleged republican links with German *Abwehr* agents, which in turn had the potential to either encourage prospective Nazi designs on Ireland or provoke a pre-emptive British strike.[11] As such, there was an urgent need in de Valera's mind to reassure London that the IRA would not pose a significant threat to British interests by acting as a sort of 'fifth column of the Third Reich'.[12]

In facing this threat to the security of the state, the Irish government elected to pursue a ruthless and multifaceted strategy aimed at neutralizing the militant republican movement. Between 1940 and 1945 over 1,100 IRA volunteers were detained in a custom-built internment facility in the Curragh camp, where the combination of a harsh disciplinary regime, miserable conditions and the psychological strain of indefinite internment exacted a heavy toll on volunteer morale.[13] The IRA's organizational infrastructure collapsed and by 1944 the republican movement was practically moribund, being forced into an extended period of retrenchment and consolidation. In light of this evident success, the government showed little hesitation when reactivating its powers of detention in July 1957 in order to contain a reinvigorated IRA, emboldened by its ongoing border offensive in Northern Ireland. On this occasion, however, the authorities opted for a more restrained approach in the application of these powers, detaining approximately 150 internees over an eighteen-month period.[14] For an organization with limited manpower resources, the detention of such a large number of its activists effectively disrupted the momentum of its campaign and fatally prejudiced the chances of its successful conclusion.[15]

A relatively benign and permissive regime was immediately implemented within the internment camp, standing in stark contrast to the hostile and mutually antagonistic atmosphere that prevailed there during the 1940s. Given that a significant cohort of the contemporary IRA leadership had served their republican apprenticeships while interned during the war, most would have witnessed first hand the demoralization of their comrades occasioned by the failure of repeated attempts to defy the military authorities running the camp. Informed by previous experience and motivated by a desire to preserve morale and foster an element of *esprit de corps*, the republican leadership chose to adopt a strict policy of cooperation and non-confrontation in respect of their dealings with the camp guards. For its part, the government was quick to reciprocate and encouraged a more convivial attitude on behalf of the military authorities. In contrast to the war years, when internment was effected in concert with a policy of strict censorship, the detention of republicans in 1957 was also widely reported in the press. From the government's perspective, then, it comes as little surprise to note that the development of a less repressive atmosphere within the Curragh internment camp was to be encouraged in an attempt to offset much of the negative publicity generated by the reintroduction of internment.

Despite the fact that the IRA remained doggedly intent on pursuing its flagging campaign in Northern Ireland, the Curragh was abruptly closed in March 1959. In many ways, this was to herald the end of internment as the customary response to political violence in Ireland. When faced with a brief resuscitation of the IRA's campaign in 1961, the government chose to reconstitute the Special Criminal Court rather than revert to internment.[16] As a non-jury court, this format was successfully used to obtain a large number of convictions against key republicans, prompting the IRA to abandon its campaign in February 1962.[17] In spite of the significance of these developments, the abrupt abandonment of what had previously been the mainstay of the Irish state's counter-insurgency policy has yet to be fully addressed. In contrast to 1940, the detention of unconvicted republicans within the more transparent political climate pertaining in 1957 was a significant liability. Just as the Irish State was attempting to position itself as a non-aligned liberal democracy within an international domain polarized by Cold War ideological divisions, the growing publicity afforded the plight of republican internees was proving to be a substantial embarrassment for the government. The closure of the camp was also effected against the backdrop of an ongoing legal challenge initiated by former internee Gerard Lawless, with a view to securing compensation for his own internment in 1957.

Although unsuccessful, this application was remarkable for the fact that Lawless managed to litigate his case to the newly established European Court of Human Rights (ECHR), becoming in the process the first private citizen to prosecute a lawsuit against a state.[18] From the government's perspective, initial domestic proceedings taken by Lawless created a number of unanticipated difficulties with the effective operation of the various statutory mechanisms regulating its powers of detention.[19] Moreover, the final judgement as laid down by the European Court of Human Rights fundamentally restricted its right of recourse to this measure in the future.[20] Following the termination of the border campaign in 1962, a root and branch re-evaluation of established counter-insurgency policy was implemented, as the decision in the Lawless case was influential in determining how successive Irish governments chose to deal with armed subversive organizations. Certainly the progression of this case was a decisive factor in prompting the closure of the Curragh camp in 1959. In the long term, however, the restrictions applied by the decision of the European Court certainly contributed to the official drift away from the use of this measure as an acceptable defence against subversives.

By exploring the ramifications arising out of the use of internment during this period, it is anticipated that this study will serve as a significant addition to Irish historiography. To date, the most striking feature of the academic study of Irish republicanism is the near exclusive preoccupation with the IRA's participation in the revolutionary period of 1919–1923 and its role in the outbreak of the Northern conflict in the 1970s. While this narrow focus is important in terms of developing a comprehensive understanding of the complex political factors at play during these periods, the existence of a number of research gaps in the history of twentieth-century Irish republicanism is problematic. In an effort to justify the armed struggle, the ideology of republicanism is characterized by the exposition of a history emphasising a linear tradition of rebellion against British rule in Ireland. As a result, republicanism has become what Fearghal McGarry has termed 'an introspective political tradition'.[21] Given the role of the past in dictating the evolution of the IRA and its legitimating ideology, the establishment of a more expansive scholarly approach, encompassing all aspects of republican history, is of fundamental import to the continued development of the discipline. As the first full-length academic treatment of the border campaign and its immediate antecedents, it is intended that this book will go some way towards filling this gap by incorporating this period into the canon of Irish historical discourse.

Although generally concerned with the detention of republicans within the jurisdiction of the southern Irish state throughout the period 1939–1962, this study will pay particular attention to the application of internment against the backdrop of the border campaign. In doing so, it will trace the origins of this offensive out of the IRA's post-war resurgence in the early 1950s and will explore the various issues arising from the outbreak of the campaign in December 1956. It will assess the effectiveness of internment as a means of containing the border campaign by suppressing the militant republican threat to the state. This book will also address some of the issues arising from the use of internment during the Second World War, particularly its role in prompting the near total collapse of the contemporary IRA organization. A comparative case study of the internment experience of the 1940s and 1950s will be used as a device to elucidate the development of the complex dynamic within the Curragh camp at this time. In effect, this will facilitate a more comprehensive exploration of the divergent perspectives of the Irish government and the republican movement, leading, for the first time, to a more objective and nuanced treatment of the subject of internment in Ireland. The multitude of overlapping legal and political considerations arising from the Lawless case will also be considered as perhaps the key factor in motivating a major realignment in Irish counter-insurgency policy. Consequently, in drawing on a wide variety of sources, this study will offer a new perspective on a neglected period of republican history and its role in promoting a new approach to the problem of curbing subversive organizations in the Republic of Ireland.

INTERNMENT IN IRELAND: THE HISTORICAL CONTEXT

The precedent for the use of internment in Ireland as a means of protecting the civil authority of the state from subversion had long been established prior to the advent of independence. Throughout the eighteenth and nineteenth centuries the British government in Ireland routinely provided for detention without trial during times of emergency with the temporary suspension of *habeas corpus*.[22] In 1797, a procedure for preventative detention by order of the Privy Council was laid down by the *Habeas Corpus* Suspension Act as a counter to the growing threat of the United Irishmen. In some cases, however, it appears that the military authorities were already practising their own dubious form of long-term preventative detention, without making any attempt to operate the relevant mechanisms within this legislation.[23]

The Insurrection Act of 1796 effectively abolished trial by jury and endowed local magistrates with sweeping powers of search and arrest.[24] Although it remained in force until 1802, and was reintroduced with modifications in 1807–1810, 1814–1818 and 1822–1825, it was superseded in 1833 by a new type of 'coercion' act as the standard response to ongoing Irish disorders. Like its predecessors, the Suppression of Disturbances Act empowered the Lord Lieutenant to proclaim a district as disturbed and permitted the introduction of a curfew. Crucially, it also allowed for a period of detention without trial for up to three months.[25]

During the course of the nineteenth century, parliament also enacted a series of statutes, popularly but misleadingly known as *habeas corpus* suspension acts. There were fifteen such acts in all. While these statutes did not completely suspend the operation of *habeas corpus*, they indirectly superseded the right of a state prisoner to submit a petition for trial. In effect, this legislation empowered the Lord Lieutenant to detain persons suspected of treason or treasonable practices without any requirement to institute a criminal prosecution.[26] Such measures were most effectively employed in the face of the Young Ireland rising in 1847 and the Irish Republican Brotherhood (IRB) insurrection of 1867.[27] By 1887, the introduction of the Criminal Law and Procedure (Ireland) Act was to ensure that the phenomenon of nineteenth-century style coercion was at an end. Passed in order to counteract the ever-present difficulties in enforcing the criminal law in Ireland, this act made permanent provision for the invocation of special powers by proclamation.[28] Thereafter, new inspiration for the suppression of political violence in Ireland derived from the wartime Defence of the Realm Acts, 1914–1918 (DORA), which bestowed upon the government extensive regulation-making powers for the purposes of securing the public safety.[29] In 1916, special powers promulgated within this legal framework were widely employed in order to dispose of the large number of insurgent prisoners that had been detained in the wake of the Easter rising.

As a military enterprise the rising was a gallant but ultimately hopeless operation in the face of a superior force, as the insurgents managed to hold out for over a week before being overwhelmed. In its aftermath martial law was proclaimed and capital sentences were imposed on fifteen of the rebels by secret field general courts martial of dubious legality.[30] (A sixteenth, Sir Roger Casement, who had been captured in Kerry, was tried for treason by a London jury and hanged on 3 August.) Irish politics was instantly polarized by the rising and initial popular hostility to the insurgents was quickly converted into widespread sympathy by the protracted and semi-secret manner in which the executions were conducted.³¹ Coupled with the prospect of the extension of conscription to Ireland, this was to arouse much anti-British feeling, leaving Sinn Féin, a radical nationalist party, to reap the benefits of this wave of popular revulsion.³² In the meantime, the minds of the British authorities were firmly fixated with the problem of containing the burgeoning mass of Irish prisoners, many of whom had already been dispatched to overcrowded military prisons in England. In most cases the insurgents had been arrested 'red-handed either as a result of the storming of certain strongholds or capitulation or surrender', while the remainder had been rounded up on the basis of 'a strong suspicion of complicity'. The problem from a legal standpoint arose when it was noted that proper records had not been kept, and even with those taken 'red-handed' it was

> ... fairly certain that it would be practically impossible to ascertain either the particular overt acts alleged against them or even the names of the particular military officers or men by whom they were made amenable.³³

While the release of these prisoners was obviously out of the question, it was also noted that it would be 'practically useless to bring them back to Ireland with a view to being disposed of by Courts Martial'. To circumvent this problem, the Home Office proposed to invoke Defence of the Realm Regulation 14b, which had been promulgated under the DORA regulation-making framework in October 1915 to allow for the internment of any person of alleged 'hostile origin or association'.³⁴ An exercise in semantics was now required to justify the detention of the Irish prisoners, as they could not reasonably be classified as enemy aliens given that their status as British citizens was firmly entrenched in law. To overcome this difficulty, the Home Office suggested that the phrase 'hostile origin or association' could be reinterpreted to cover the rebels because of the 'known connection of the Sinn Féin movement with Germany'.³⁵ In the end, the British cabinet approved these measures and regulation 14b was formally used to justify the internment of 1,800 insurgent prisoners in Frongoch, Wales.³⁶ On 9 June 1916 the first Irish detainees arrived, just as the previous occupants of the camp – German prisoners of war – were speedily removed.³⁷ Their internment was relatively short-lived, however, as the majority of prisoners were unconditionally released in December following an amnesty by the Irish Chief

Secretary, Henry Duke. Politicized by their detention, the former internees quickly set about reorganizing the Irish Volunteers, thereby setting the stage for a renewal of military hostilities.[38]

In the 1918 general election, Sinn Féin successfully supplanted the Irish Parliamentary Party when it secured 73 out of a possible 106 seats. Under the leadership of Éamon de Valera, it quickly moved to set up an alternative Parliament in Dublin in 1919, known as Dáil Éireann.[39] Concurrently the Volunteers, now increasingly known as the IRA, began to engage in displays of public disobedience that quickly broadened into a more concerted campaign of violence and intimidation against the Royal Irish Constabulary (RIC).[40] By October 1920, some 492 vacated barracks had been destroyed and 117 RIC men had been killed. This police retreat from the countryside ceded partial control to republicans, who subsequently attempted to substitute their own legal and administrative structures in order to actualize their claim to the governance of Ireland. When the emergency legislative regime of the First World War was legally terminated in 1920, new powers to contain the deteriorating situation in Ireland emerged under the Restoration of Order in Ireland Act, 1920 (ROIA). Heavily influenced by the wartime code, it also relied extensively on regulation-making powers that in substance provided a panoply of counter-measures to combat the IRA. When these measures proved to be insufficient, martial law was declared in parts of the south and west of Ireland in December 1920.[41]

As the violence intensified throughout this period, the civil authority of the British government was undermined to the extent that it was now forced to rely on more coercive measures to suppress the IRA. In the spring of 1920 two undisciplined paramilitary style police forces, known colloquially as the 'Black and Tans' and the 'Auxiliaries', were introduced in order to reinforce the RIC. Atrocities committed by these forces shocked British liberal opinion and alienated the civilian population. As the guerrilla tactics of the IRA made it ever more difficult to detect and destroy its military capacity, it became apparent that the only way to extinguish this insurgency was through the wholesale subjugation of Ireland. This was an unappealing course of action, as the British government did not wish to be cast more fully into the role of colonial oppressor.[42] Fearful of alienating public opinion, the British authorities instead sought a truce in order to pave the way for a negotiated resolution to the conflict. The resultant settlement, which was eventually signed in December 1921, historically established the Irish Free State as a self-governing dominion within the

British Commonwealth.⁴³ The Anglo-Irish Treaty, as it was known, also made provision for the exclusion of the six northeastern counties of Armagh, Antrim, Down, Fermanagh, Derry and Tyrone from the Irish Free State and, most controversially, maintained the monarchy as the head of that Free State.⁴⁴

The embittered and divisive debate that followed the signing of the Treaty violently split the republican movement over the issue of its acceptance. For the advocates of the Treaty, the way was now paved for elections to a new Free State parliament, and while it may not have delivered the much-desired republic, it did establish full internal autonomy over fiscal and social policy, provided for the evacuation of British forces and established the basis for the creation of a national army. For Michael Collins, the architect of the IRA's military campaign against Britain, the Treaty was a 'stepping stone', which Ireland could harness to extricate itself from British domination.⁴⁵ Its detractors, however, remained unconvinced as acceptance of the Treaty amounted to a renunciation of the symbolic republic for which they had fought. In the minds of IRA leaders like Liam Lynch and Ernie O'Malley this symbolic republic was very real and tangible, an actuality that had been established by the elected representatives of the Dáil in 1919.⁴⁶ Many of those who opposed the Treaty also favoured the continuation of violence in furtherance of their aims – even if it meant entering into armed conflict with their former pro-Treaty comrades.⁴⁷

REPUBLICANS AND THE IRISH FREE STATE: 1922–1939

Following the Dáil's ratification of the Treaty in January 1922 a new provisional government was established in order to prepare for the handover of power from the British authorities.⁴⁸ From the onset the new administration faced a number of difficulties, especially within the key areas of defence and public order. The IRA had divided on the Treaty, just as the Dáil had done, with the anti-Treaty majority repudiating the authority of the government. Between January and June 1922 continuous efforts were made to produce an acceptable political compromise, while at the same time both the government and the IRA began to prepare for hostilities.⁴⁹ In February 1922 a new police force known as An Garda Síochána came into being, together with the introduction of a number of plain-clothes units collectively known as the Criminal Investigation Department (CID). Initially tasked with tackling armed crime in Dublin, the activities of the CID quickly expanded to include intelligence work against the anti-Treaty IRA.⁵⁰

During the same period, the government set about organizing its national defence and in January 1922 established an army headquarters at Beggar's Bush barracks in Dublin.⁵¹ Under the guidance of Michael Collins, the pro-Treaty elements of the IRA quickly transformed into a formally organized paid national army under government control. Given the imperative of enforcing the government's writ throughout the country, this body quickly expanded and was readily furnished with weapons and supplies by the British army.⁵²

In a defiant gesture, in April 1922 the anti-Treaty IRA occupied the Four Courts building in Dublin. Hostilities commenced on 28 June, when the provisional government, under pressure from the British Colonial Secretary, Winston Churchill, attacked this garrison with artillery borrowed from the British army.⁵³ In less than two weeks all fighting in Dublin was over, and by August the government was in control of all urban areas. Crucially, in the face of such civil unrest the government's policy was clear and inflexible. It would not tolerate armed resistance to its rule and would introduce and operate draconian laws in an effort to restore order. In September 1922, the provisional government introduced the Army (Emergency Powers) Resolution, which sanctioned the establishment of military courts and committees to try offences of a political nature. Significantly, these bodies were empowered to issue capital sentences for a wide range of proscribed offences, including the illegal possession of arms. Following the formal constitution of the Free State government in December 1922, this system was amended to provide for a more summary administration of military rule on a decentralized basis.⁵⁴ As a result, there were seventy-seven executions in all, including the controversial summary execution of four unconvicted IRA leaders in December 1922.⁵⁵ There were also widespread internments during this period, with the detention of over 11,000 republicans. Thereafter, the republican campaign, which now reverted to the guerrilla tactics employed during the War of Independence, was hastily improvised and poorly coordinated. By December, the IRA was virtually defeated and, following the death of Liam Lynch, the IRA's intransigent Chief of Staff (C/S) in May 1923, republicans declared a unilateral ceasefire.⁵⁶

In the immediate aftermath of the Civil War, the government became concerned that the use of internment might be illegal, particularly as the Free State constitution neither expressly permitted nor forbade it. It was subsequently decided to legislate temporarily for this eventuality with the passage of the Public Safety (Emergency Powers) Act in August 1923.⁵⁷ Providing for the continued detention of republican internees, the act also conveyed upon the Gardaí wide powers of arrest and made provision for dealing with a raft of politically motivated offences, including the unlawful possession of arms, ammunition and explosives.[58] As the political situation began to stabilize throughout 1923 and 1924, it was formally decided to begin the release of internees in small groups once they had given written undertakings not to resume subversive activities.[59] In 1924 the Public Safety (Powers of Arrest and Detention) Temporary Act renewed the government's powers of detention for another year.[60] With the expiry of this act in 1925, it was felt prudent, in light of continuing republican militancy, to enact a permanent statute that would confer upon the government powers of detention during times of emergency. The Public Safety (Emergency Powers) Bill, 1926, was introduced in the Dáil that November, where it was justified by W.T. Cosgrave on the grounds that it would 'provide for the preservation of public safety and the protection of persons and property during national emergencies'.[61]

The use of temporary emergency statutes to quell political violence in Northern Ireland was no less pronounced during this period, as the unionist government sought to enact a series of measures aimed at consolidating its control of the province. Introduced in 1922 as a response to the outbreak of mass sectarian rioting in Belfast and an extension of the IRA campaign across the border, the Civil Authorities (Special Powers) Act (SPA) empowered the Northern Ireland parliament to: impose curfews; proscribe organizations; censor printed, audio and visual material; ban meetings, processions and gatherings; restrict the movement of individuals within specified areas; and detain and intern suspects without proffering criminal charges. Moreover, the statute provided the Royal Ulster Constabulary (RUC) with extensive powers of entry, search and seizure, and, most importantly, authorized the civil authority to 'take all such steps and issue all such orders as may be necessary for preserving the peace and order'.[62] Initially intended as a temporary expedient to establish peace and maintain order, the SPA gradually became viewed as a necessity for maintaining Northern Ireland's constitutional position, and in 1928 the incumbent unionist government called for its permanent entrenchment. In 1933 the Northern Ireland parliament formally enacted the SPA on an indefinite basis and in 1943 it introduced a second act that made minor amendments to the original 1922 statute. Ultimately, the continued operation of the SPA became one of the central grievances of the civil rights movement of the late 1960s, eventually leading to the collapse of the Stormont administration in 1972.[63]

South of the border, the republican movement witnessed a dramatic parting of the ways in May 1926 when Sinn Féin's continued refusal to abandon its abstentionist policy prompted Éamon de Valera and his supporters to leave the party and found Fianna Fáil. By taking this course of action, de Valera committed himself to taking his seat in the Dáil, provided the oath of allegiance to the British monarch was abolished. His delicate political calculations were upset, however, with the unsanctioned assassination of the Minister for Justice, Kevin O'Higgins, by three members of the IRA in July 1927.[64] The Free State government, fearful of a renewed republican campaign, quickly responded with the introduction of a new Public Safety Act. This statute not only empowered the executive to declare an association to be unlawful if it fulfilled a number of specified criteria, it also allowed for the establishment of special courts comprised solely of military officers.[65] Although the sentences and convictions imposed by these tribunals were subject to confirmation by a confirming authority, they were authorized to issue capital sentences from which there was no right of appeal.[66] In concert with this, the passage of the Electoral Amendment Act compelled de Valera and his colleagues to dispense with their ideological objections and take the oath of allegiance. Fianna Fáil's ensuing entry into the Dáil was significant in that a large majority of those who had rejected the Treaty now accepted their lot as a defeated minority and agreed to work within the constitutional framework of the Irish Free State.[67]

While no one was ever convicted of O'Higgins' murder, once the immediate clamour had passed, the government thought it reasonable, 'in view of the altered circumstances', to limit the duration of the Public Safety Act.[68] It was repealed in December 1928.[69] Despite its limited arsenal, however, the IRA remained a serious irritant to the government. When faced with the erosion of its support base by the rising popularity of Fianna Fáil, a group of left-wing republicans headed by Peadar O'Donnell and George Gilmore attempted to broaden the appeal of the movement by hitching the nationalist standard to socialist policies that addressed popular grievances.[70] This dalliance in the field of social agitation led to the establishment in 1931 of a short-lived republican socialist organization known as Saor Éire.[71] As the architect of this initiative, O'Donnell's political outlook was inspired by the writings of James Connolly, who sought to link the idea of national revolution with the concept of a simultaneous social revolution. Through his experience of organizing a systematic campaign against the payment of land annuities in his native County Donegal during the late 1920s, O'Donnell articulated the first serious attempt since partition to create a project of social and political transformation. Through the formation of Saor Éire, O'Donnell hoped to push the broad front of contemporary republican organizations, including the IRA and Fianna Fáil, towards the idea of 'national re-conquest' based on the ideals of social justice.[72]

Many within the IRA, including Seán MacBride and Moss Twomey, were certainly receptive to policies that not only addressed social injustices, but might also reinvigorate a stagnant organization.[73] For them, O'Donnell's recoding of republicanism in the language of class struggle held out the possibility of enlisting new masses for traditional republican objectives. For the Irish government, the existence of Saor Éire was immediately taken as evidence that the IRA was involved in a communist conspiracy to undermine the Free State, and used this to discredit the militant republican movement.[74] In October 1931 the Irish Catholic bishops denounced Saor Éire as 'frankly communistic' and declared it and the IRA to be 'sinful and irreligious'.[75] The intensity of this condemnation immediately forced a rethink among the IRA leadership about association with such an openly socialist body. Following the collapse of Saor Éire a series of politically inspired killings prompted the government to act decisively with the introduction of legislation, by means of a constitutional amendment, as a comprehensive response to every difficulty the Free State had experienced with the IRA.[76] The ensuing Constitution (Amendment No. 17) Act, 1931, inserted into the constitution the substantive provisions of a new public safety bill as a schedule to a new article – 2(a).[77]

This measure created a new range of Garda powers such as obliging suspects to account for their movements, as well as several new offences including membership of an 'unlawful association'. This act also made provision for the creation of a new kind of military court solely designed to try cases of a political nature. Known as the Constitution (Special Powers) Tribunal, it was to consist of a three-member panel of army officers not below the rank of commandant, who were removable at will by the government. By ending the reliance on juries for convictions, the government hoped to remove the uncertainty in trying members of illegal organizations. As such, this tribunal was to have the jurisdiction to try persons charged with offences under the Treasonable Offences Act, 1925, the Juries (Protection) Act, 1929, the Firearms Act, 1925 and the Explosives Act, 1875. It was also empowered to impose capital sentences that were not open to appeal, it was not required to adopt fixed procedures, and was not bound by the normal rules of evidence.[78] Although heavily criticized by Fianna Fáil, the tribunal undeniably proved effective with a 91 per cent conviction rate for IRA members tried before it between 1931 and 1937.

The election of Ireland's first Fianna Fáil administration in 1932 was to result in a more tacit toleration of the activities of the IRA, especially when de Valera moved to suspend the Constitutional Tribunal.[79] In this regard, Fianna Fáil policy towards the republican movement was animated by a desire to ensure that the IRA was effectively neutralized by being brought under its control.[80] Nevertheless, growing impatience with Fianna Fáil's insistence on constitutional methods and its apparent failure to realise a thirty-two county Irish Republic led the IRA to become more openly critical of the government.[81] When it became apparent that the IRA Army Council had rejected de Valera's overtures regarding the establishment of a 'national front' in 1932 and was determined to remain as an independent body, the government instead focused its attention on reducing the IRA's support base. In particular, the Irish government identified the lure of IRA membership for young men, bored with the tedium of life in 1930s Ireland, and set about diverting the energies of these prospective young recruits into other more fruitful and lawful avenues of occupation.[82]

In 1933 de Valera sanctioned the swearing in of hundreds of former anti-Treaty IRA men as armed, plain-clothes Gardaí. Dubbed the 'Broy Harriers', after the incumbent Garda Commissioner Éamonn Broy, the government contended that these men were an overdue influx needed to fortify the Gardaí in order to counter the growing Blueshirt threat (see below). This move, which was correctly interpreted by the IRA Army Council as a device to wean activists away from the IRA, was further compounded by the launch of an ostensibly republican reserve of the army in 1934.[83] Accusing it of being a 'Free State militia', the Army Council immediately set its face against any attempts to infiltrate this body for use against the British army in a military confrontation.[84] Of course this played directly into the government's hands as much of the army reserve's target constituency signed up, with a commensurate effect on IRA recruiting. Boasting an estimated membership of over 8,000 in 1934, the number of IRA volunteers had been dramatically reduced to around 3,000 by November 1936.[85] Notwithstanding this rapid decline, the IRA continued to assume a very public role, particularly when it became embroiled in a series of violent clashes with the Army Comrades Association (ACA).

Formed in 1932, the ACA was notable for the prominent role played by members of Cumann na nGaedhael, who were horrified at the perceived government tolerance of the IRA. Throughout 1933, the ACA engaged in a significant trial of strength with the government and quickly began to adopt the trappings of continental fascism, including the wearing of a distinctive shirt which gave rise to the movement's popular name – 'The Blueshirts'.[86] In managing this public order crisis, de Valera played an adroit hand by portraying the government as the sole and legitimate defender of democracy and the rule of law in Ireland.[87] Repeated entreaties to the IRA to lay down its arms and embrace constitutional politics were offset by the forcible suppression of the Blueshirts. In 1933, article 2(a) was reactivated and the Constitutional Tribunal was deployed against the ACA, thereby making its subsequent invocation against the IRA more palatable to the Fianna Fáil rank and file.[88] The initiation of a republican campaign against English imports was to provide the government with the pretext to bring the IRA to heel, when the destruction of several stocks of the English-manufactured Bass beer in September 1933 led to increasing violence and clashes with the Blueshirts. The robbery of the film 'Gallipoli' from a travelling cinema proprietor by armed IRA members on 18 September 1933 was to be the first offence involving republicans to be tried by the tribunal under a Fianna Fáil government.[89]

Although the full force of the law was now being brought to bear on the IRA, and Fianna Fáil–IRA relations were rapidly beginning to sour, the final break with the government was still some way off. Renewed attempts by Peadar O'Donnell to fashion a new socialist forum prompted the Minister for Justice, Gerald Boland, to propose that the government reconsider its previous policy towards the IRA.[90] At the 1934 IRA Army Convention O'Donnell and his supporters proposed a resolution that the IRA should mobilize a 'united front' campaign for a republican congress that would 'wrest the leadership of the National Struggle from Irish Capitalism'.[91] While O'Donnell and his allies had been quietly canvassing delegates in advance, the IRA leadership, mindful of the Catholic Church's condemnation of Saor Éire and the growing anti-communist trend within Irish society, voted to defeat the motion. O'Donnell and his supporters immediately withdrew from the IRA and, in April 1934, organized a meeting in Athlone attended by various former IRA officers, socialists and trade unionists at which a manifesto was issued denouncing capitalism as an obstacle to independence. For the first time the inherent ideological contradictions of contemporary Irish republicanism were exposed as the IRA was characterized by 'an unfocused radicalism ... complimented [sic] by an explicit anti-communism'.[92]

Predictably, the IRA leadership rejected all the implied criticism of its own policies and condemned O'Donnell's congress initiative as the beginnings of a new constitutionalist political party that would ultimately follow Fianna Fáil into Leinster House.[93] This organization, known as Republican Congress, was a short-lived initiative that ruptured at its first major conference in Rathmines in September 1934. During this meeting, a number of delegates, led by Michael Price, began to agitate for the aim of a 'Workers' Republic' as a means of foisting upon the organization a more openly socialist agenda. When this move was successfully resisted by O'Donnell, Price's immediate withdrawal from the organization fatally undermined its long-term chance of survival.[94] Despite its failure, Republican Congress is important in that it represented the unsurpassed limit of republican radicalism until the 1970s.[95] During its brief existence it was vigorously opposed by the IRA, and a series of violent clashes ensued between these two organizations throughout 1934 and 1935.[96] While this unrest was seized upon by Fianna Fáil as evidence of the IRA threat to public order, the split precipitated by the formation of Congress was to have more profound implications for the IRA's relationship with the government. The IRA's growing disillusion with Fianna Fáil, coupled with the failure of the movement's socialist excursions, reinforced the perception that the political road was a profitless one to travel and concentrated power within the movement solely in the hands of a hard-line militarist coterie.[97]

As the entente between Fianna Fáil and the IRA began to unravel, the adoption of a more provocative stance by these hard-liners served to alienate the last strands of sympathetic opinion within Fianna Fáil, thereby providing de Valera with a free hand to take more decisive action. In conceding that republicans had failed to develop 'a sense of respect for the law', de Valera subsequently moved to authorize the government's first major clampdown, following the IRA's intervention in the Dublin transport dispute of 1935.[98] The ensuing arrests failed to have the desired effect and only served to provoke further militancy from the republican movement. In February 1935 the IRA became embroiled in a land dispute in Edgeworthstown, County Longford, by attempting to intimidate Maria Saunderson, the village landlord, and the local estate agent, Gerald More O'Farrell. Following an altercation at More O'Farrell's home, his son Richard was shot by a band of IRA men posing as policemen and died eleven days later.[99] Although the attack was denounced by de Valera, who warned that he had no intention of tolerating the existence of a private army within the state, the IRA remained undeterred and was implicated in two other assassinations.[100]

The first of these occurred in March 1936, when the elderly Vice-Admiral Henry Boyle Somerfield, a referee for local youths seeking to join the British navy, was shot dead on his doorstep in Castletownshend, County Cork.[101] This was quickly followed by a second incident when John Egan, a former member of the IRA, was killed in Dungarvan, County Waterford, after allegedly providing the Gardaí with the location of an arms dump.[102] Many within Fianna Fáil were appalled, and the party made great play of how these 'callous and cowardly murders' made nonsense of the IRA's claim to patriotism.[103] In the Dáil, Boland denounced the murder of Vice-Admiral Somerfield as 'a cowardly crime' and reiterated the government's determination to bring those responsible to justice.[104] A 'sensational round up' of individuals with 'IRA affiliations' quickly ensued, resulting in the detention of several senior figures in Counties Dublin and Cork.[105] The conviction of Moss Twomey, the IRA C/S, and his Adjutant-General (A/G), Jim Killeen, by the Constitutional Tribunal proved to be a clear statement of intent on de Valera's behalf. Acting under the provisions of article 2(a), the government prepared an order formally proscribing the IRA as an 'unlawful association' in June 1936.[106]

In spite of this, de Valera still harboured the hope that republicans would become reconciled to the Irish state following the introduction of the new constitution in 1937. Unsurprisingly, the IRA dismissed it out of hand. However, some republicans, including Seán MacBride, felt that it was significant as it allowed for the election of a parliament that 'did not owe allegiance to the British government'.[107] With the lapse of the Free State constitution in December 1937, all powers conveyed upon the government by article 2(a) were now rendered invalid. In obvious anticipation of the IRA's rejection, the architects of Bunreacht na hÉireann drafted a constitution containing several emergency provisions designed to deal primarily with subversive organizations. A new definition of treason was included in order to more appropriately encompass the aims and activities of the IRA as the act of 'levying war against the state ... or attempting by force of arms or other violent means to overthrow the organs of government'.[108] Great care was also taken to make provision for the operation of a Special Criminal Court in circumstances where the ordinary courts were deemed to be 'inadequate to secure the effective administration of justice and the preservation of public peace and order'.[109] It also envisaged the establishment of military tribunals during time of 'war or armed rebellion'.¹¹⁰

With the inclusion of these measures within the constitution the way was now paved for the enactment of updated security legislation as embodied in the proposed new Offences Against the State Bill. Drafted as a successor to article 2(a) and intended as a replacement for the Treasonable Offences Act, 1925 and the Public Safety Act of 1926, this bill was to represent in many respects a substantial diminution of civil liberties.¹¹¹ The act formally became law on 14 June 1939 following a lengthy debate in the Oireachtas that concentrated primarily on procedural rather than substantive amendments. The act increased the powers of the Gardaí by authorizing them to circumvent established procedures in issuing search warrants if it was deemed necessary. Suspects under arrest could be detained for a period of up to twenty-four hours without charge, which could be extended by a further twenty-four on the authority of a Garda 'not below the rank of Chief Superintendent'.¹¹² Provided part five of the act was brought into operation by a proclamation from the government, it was also lawful for a Garda to demand a full account of a person's movements.¹¹³ As with article 2(a), the government continued to enjoy the power to issue suppression orders against 'unlawful organizations', thereby making membership of such proscribed associations a criminal offence.¹¹⁴

Crucially, the act also allowed for the establishment of Special Criminal Courts in order to facilitate the trial of treasonous and subversive offences when internment was felt to be insufficient.¹¹⁵ Like the Constitutional Tribunal before it, the Special Criminal Court was to consist of a minimum three-member panel, which was removable at the will of the government. Membership of the court was no longer restricted to army officers, and was broadened to include judges of the High Court or Circuit Court, district justices, and solicitors and barristers of at least seven years' standing. The trial procedure, in so far as was possible, was to be the same as that of the Central Criminal Court, with those under indictment enjoying the right to silence. Persons who were convicted by the Special Criminal Court were entitled to appeal their convictions or sentences to the Court of Criminal Appeal.¹¹⁶ In many respects, however, the prime function of the OASA was to restore the government's powers of internment. With the activation of part six of the act, a minister of state was empowered to order the arrest and detention of an individual when satisfied that he was engaged in activities 'calculated to prejudice the preservation of the peace, order or security of the State'.[117] A person arrested in these circumstances would be detained in a prison or internment camp according to regulations issued under the act.[118]

In light of the deteriorating international political situation and the consequent drift towards war, the government wasted little time in bringing the full measure of the OASA to bear against the IRA. On 23 June 1939, the IRA was declared unlawful under section nineteen of the act, followed by a series of proclamations on 22 August which established a Special Criminal Court and activated the government's powers of internment. The government then moved to appoint the former members of the Constitutional Tribunal to sit on the panel of the Special Criminal Court – Colonel Francis Bennett, Colonel Daniel McKenna, Major John Vincent Joyce, Major Cornelius Whelan and Major Patrick Tuite. Commandant Richard Feely was appointed as court registrar.[119] In taking this action, the government was attempting to prepare itself for the myriad of security problems with which it would inevitably be faced while trying to pursue a neutral policy in the upcoming European conflict. While many technical matters, such as the control of communications and the supervision of people into and out of the country, were considered, the continued existence of the border and the activities of the IRA were to remain an unpredictable variable in the government's calculations.[120] It was within this context that the simmering confrontation between Fianna Fáil and the IRA was to escalate dramatically, becoming manifest in de Valera's unequivocal commitment to the wholesale extirpation of the republican movement.

2

'Liquidating the Irish Separatist Movement':[1] Internment, 1939–1945

In many respects the advent of the late 1930s was to signal the growing stagnation of the IRA's ideological standpoint in the face of the pragmatic republicanism of Fianna Fáil. While de Valera's efforts to undermine its support base had already paid dividends with the creation of the Broy Harriers and the army reserve, the public endorsement of Bunreacht na hÉireann was to strike at the heart of the IRA's position and its avowed aim of overturning the Treaty settlement. Moreover, the evaporation of the Blueshirt threat and the dissolution of Peadar O'Donnell's republican socialist faction were to reveal an organization lacking in direction and uncertain about the means with which to achieve its goals. While the IRA remained fundamentally wedded to the utility of physical force, questions abounded as to how and in what circumstances it should be applied.[2] Despite recent setbacks, however, the IRA still maintained 'a tight skeletal organization in all of Ireland's thirty-two counties' and retained the power 'to make itself felt'.[3] With the increasing prospect of a European war looming on the horizon this was to lead certain elements within the IRA to consider the possibility of renewed action. Nevertheless, this ignored the fundamental problem faced by the IRA of what to do and where to act in order to advance the interests of the 'Republic'. The resolution of this dilemma was further complicated by a number of factional disputes within the leadership, leading to the formulation of a set of contradictory and conflicting policies.[4]

THE S-PLAN BOMBING CAMPAIGN

As early as 1926, there had been suggestions that the central thrust of the IRA's military activities should be concentrated in Britain rather than against the Irish Free State. Central to this position was the belief that this was the logical place to prosecute the 'war', given the perception of the British government as the 'real enemy' bent on maintaining partition in Ireland. This was not a new proposition, as the IRA had previously engaged in a number of limited operations in various English cities during the latter stages of the War of Independence. Based on a vague and ill thought out strategy, it was hoped that a concerted and sustained campaign of violence within the United Kingdom would prove to be a more efficient means of precipitating a British withdrawal from Ireland. By the mid-1930s, the chief advocate of such an approach was the IRA Quartermaster-General (QMG), Seán Russell, a firebrand militarist who had become disillusioned by the movement's recent flirtation with socialist policies. Seeking to draw a parallel with the Fenian dynamiters of the 1880s, Russell believed that more could be achieved through a campaign of 'raw violence' directed against public facilities in the United Kingdom, which would put ordinary British people in the firing line, rather than the army or police. If prosecuted correctly, Russell also felt that such a campaign would invariably persuade de Valera to throw in his lot with the IRA, thus restoring the unity of the republican movement in the fight for Irish independence.[5]

For the pragmatists within the IRA this was an outlandish supposition and many leading figures, including the C/S, Seán MacBride, were among his most vocal opponents. Undaunted and determined to press through his plans, Russell publicly censured the Army Council for being too involved in 'politics', and defied MacBride by departing on a fundraising tour of the USA in late 1936.[6] He was enthusiastically received in New York by the influential leader of Clan na nGael, Joseph McGarrity, with whom he reached a 'complete understanding'.[7] At his behest, Russell made a controversial approach to the German embassy in Washington in order to solicit financial aid for his scheme.[8] Ever the self-publicist, Russell concluded his trip by circulating a statement through the tabloid press alluding to 'an amazing plot' by 'skilled IRA pilots ... to rain bombs on England'. He returned to Ireland in November after having 'secured a considerable amount of money for employment on IRA work'.[9] Needless to say, Russell's unilateralism did not sit well with MacBride, who had him expelled from the IRA on a technicality. Russell did not take dismissal lightly and his supporters quickly began a campaign to lobby the Army Council in favour of his proposals. For his part, after being called to the Bar MacBride resigned his position as C/S in order to concentrate on his burgeoning legal practice. Together with Noel Hartnett, he was to spend the next several years representing many of his former colleagues at trial.[10]

His successor, Tom Barry, was even more unenthusiastic about Russell's proposals and likened the bombing of innocent English civilians to the indiscriminate tactics employed by the 'Black and Tans'. He commented: 'Leave a bomb in a cloak room, leave a bomb in a hotel, and be forty or sixty miles away with a time bomb, and you blow to pieces someone who is working for £3.10 or £3.30 a week'.[11] During the course of a fiery address to the 1936 Army Convention', Barry put forward his own alternative for a campaign in Northern Ireland, which envisaged a concerted series of attacks on various army barracks across the province.[12] This bold offensive failed to materialise, however, and at a meeting of the IRA Army Council in 1937 Barry was forced to tender his resignation when a motion in favour of Russell's scheme was carried by a single vote.[13] In April 1938, Russell's triumphant election as C/S by an Army Council dominated by a cadre of hard-line physical force advocates was to signal the final and visceral rejection of 'politics' in favour of the philosophy of unadulterated militarism.[14] This new direction was given virtually undiluted expression with the formal adoption of a proposal for a bombing campaign in England.

Wasting little time in implementing his agenda, Russell quickly persuaded Seamus O'Donovan, the IRA's former Director of Chemicals, to come out of retirement in order to plan this campaign. The resultant framework, known as the 'Sabotage Plan' (S-plan), revolved around the destruction of numerous strategic targets, including military installations and communications centres, as well as a sustained attack on various public services such as the post office, the electrical grid, and the transportation system. Much of this was to be effected by IRA operatives in Britain who had received instruction on how to construct rudimentary explosive devices using gelignite, paraffin wax and potassium chlorate. The loss of civilian life was to be avoided at all costs, and the campaign was to be complemented by the employment of propaganda designed to build a broad and solid support network in Britain, based on sympathy to the cause.[15] Mindful of the weakness of the IRA organization in the United Kingdom, the Army Council also decided to send a number of volunteers from Ireland, including Seán MacNeela, who was appointed to serve as Officer Commanding (O/C) the campaign.[16] With preparations complete, the IRA, acting as the self-styled 'government of the Republic of Ireland', issued an ultimatum to the British authorities on 12 January 1939. It stated that:

> A period of four days is sufficient notice for your government to signify its intentions in the matter of the military evacuation and for the issue of your declaration of abdication in respect of our

country. Our government reserve(s) the right of appropriate action without further notice if upon the expiration of this period of grace, these conditions remain unfulfilled.[17]

Despite the lofty rhetoric, the campaign as it subsequently unfolded bore little resemblance to what was originally intended and proved to be a graphic illustration of the IRA's paucity of strategic planning, induced by a loss of internal political guidance. If the campaign was designed to cause sufficient panic and fear within British society to force the government to open negotiations on the ending of partition, it severely backfired, as it merely served to arouse strong anti-Irish feeling.[18] The first setback came on the opening night when a number of explosions aimed at disrupting the electrical network in London, Manchester, Birmingham and Alnwick resulted in three unintended civilian fatalities, including the death of a twenty-seven-year-old fish porter named Albert Ross.[19] In the wake of the bombings, an intensive police operation in London uncovered 'a clearing house for explosives' and resulted in the arrest of fourteen men on arms and explosives charges.[20] In February, two explosions at Tottenham Court Road and Leicester Square underground stations were followed by a series of fires in Coventry and an attempt to bomb the outside wall of Walton Jail in Liverpool.[21] In response, the British authorities visibly tightened security on various public buildings across the country, while simultaneously keeping watch on all major Irish communities in British cities.

To combat this threat, the British government passed the Prevention of Violence (Temporary Provisions) Act in July 1939, which empowered the Home Secretary to issue expulsion and prohibition orders and demand the registration of all Irish living in Britain.[22] This did not prove to be a sufficient deterrent, however, as the IRA responded on 25 August by detonating a bomb in one of the main shopping thoroughfares in Coventry. Five people were killed instantly and up to sixty were injured.[23] The British government immediately condemned the attack and announced its intention to take more steps to counter '[this] IRA plot'.[24] A number of arrests ensued, including those of Peter Barnes and James McCormick, who were members of the IRA's Coventry unit.[25] Although they disclaimed all involvement in the affair, both were sentenced to death for their alleged part in the bombing.[26] Despite a substantial reprieve campaign spearheaded by the Irish government, the executions went ahead as scheduled and both were hanged on 7 February 1940.[27] In light of the widespread opprobrium occasioned by the Coventry bombing, the death of these men was greeted with a muted response. Coming under increased police pressure and overshadowed by the outbreak of war in Europe, the IRA decided to quietly abandon the campaign.[28] As a result, Russell, finding his return to Ireland barred after undertaking yet another fundraising tour in the USA, made his way to Germany, where he attempted to solicit aid for the republican cause.[29]

Acting in the belief that the aims of the IRA and those of Nazi Germany represented a natural synergy, he was received in Berlin in May 1940 as a registered representative of the 'Irish Republic', and accorded all the privileges of a diplomat. Throughout his stay, Russell repeatedly urged the Nazi government to make use of the IRA to strike at British forces stationed in Northern Ireland and authorized the incorporation of this scheme into Operation Sealion.[30] In August, Russell was to return to Ireland to oversee the implementation of this scheme, but died *en route* in mysterious circumstances aboard a German U-boat.[31] Despite this setback, republican contact with Germany was stepped up as a number of *Abwehr* operatives were landed in Ireland during late 1940 and early 1941.[32] Of these agents, Herman Görtz proved to be the most successful, remaining at liberty for over eighteen months.[33] In any event, while the extent of republican collusion with Nazi agents was relatively limited, the public disclosure of these links was to constitute a significant threat to the neutrality of the state, given the strategic importance of Ireland during a period of unprecedented crisis for the British government.

THE INTRODUCTION OF INTERNMENT

Despite the formal proscription of the IRA by the Irish government in June 1939, the republican movement in Ireland still managed to enjoy a certain degree of impunity with which to prosecute its campaign in Britain. Although de Valera exhibited few qualms about cooperating with the British authorities, in his mind the likelihood of republican violence seemed remote, provided the IRA was preoccupied with its entanglements in the United Kingdom. With the passage of the Prevention of Violence Act, the situation was radically altered as the government was now faced with the spectre of dealing with large numbers of militant republicans who had been deported from Britain.[34] With the threat of war looming ever closer, de Valera could ill afford to ignore the destabilizing influence of the IRA, particularly in light of London's increasing displeasure with the *fait accompli* of

Irish neutrality. On 22 August 1939, three days before the Coventry bombing, de Valera moved to play his first hand against the IRA with the establishment of a Special Criminal Court and the activation of the internment provisions of the OASA. Nevertheless, these events were quickly overshadowed when the German invasion of Poland on 1 September heralded the start of the Second World War in Europe.[35]

In anticipation of the outbreak of war, the Irish government had spent the previous two years drafting emergency legislation aimed at protecting the state and ensuring its survival during this crisis.[36] On 2 September, the Dáil sat in emergency session in order to introduce an amendment to the constitution, which was silent as to the ramifications of a war taking place in which the Irish state was not a belligerent. This amendment was tabled in order to extend the definition of 'time of war' contained in the constitution to make it clear that this phrase could also be interpreted to apply to a situation in which 'there are hostilities and conflict about us'.[37] The passage of this amendment provided the necessary legal basis for the enactment of the Emergency Powers Act (EPA), by allowing the Oireachtas to declare a state of emergency for the purpose of introducing such legislation.[38] In concert with the OASA, the EPA effectively suspended civil rights and conveyed upon the government the authority to act by emergency order in almost every aspect of Irish life. The act also made provision for the internment of persons who were not natural born Irish citizens and empowered the government to authorize the search of any person or place without a warrant. Under section two, the Gardaí were also authorized to arrest, without a warrant, any individual upon suspicion of having committed or being about to commit an offence specified by a government order.[39]

Now armed with what the government believed were the necessary legislative provisions with which to tackle the IRA, de Valera quickly moved to implement 'the rule of order' with a new ruthless authoritarianism.[40] On 8 September 1939, he appointed the uncompromising Gerald Boland as the new Minister for Justice and established a committee on internal security.[41] Boland wasted little time and immediately ordered the arrest of those believed to be the most important and active members of the IRA. A Garda raid in Dublin the following day netted most of the IRA leadership and the bulk of its liquid assets, though Stephen Hayes, Russell's replacement as C/S, escaped.[42] By the end of the month, there were ninety-three republicans in custody, of whom sixty-seven were being held in Arbour Hill prison with another fifteen awaiting trial.[43] In addition, a strict regime of press censorship was introduced and quickly extended to minimize the impact of actions taken by the republican movement. In an attempt to 'keep the temperature down' and deny the IRA 'the life blood of publicity', reports relating to IRA killings, hunger strikes and blanket protests, as well as coverage of Easter Rising commemorations, were suppressed.[44]

Citing the need to take steps to prevent a serious 'disturbance of the peace', Boland moved on 15 September to issue a number of internment warrants for those engaged in activities 'prejudicial to the security of the state'.[45] In deciding on this course of action, the government was then required to discharge its legal obligations under the OASA by setting up a 'Detention Commission'. Provided for by section fifty-nine of the OASA, this Commission, which was to be set up once the government had activated its powers of internment, was designed as a mechanism to protect the civil rights of internees. Being fully removable at the will of the government, this body was to consist of a three-member panel of whom one was required to be either a judge of the Supreme Court, High Court or Circuit Court, a district justice, or a solicitor or barrister of at least seven years' standing. Once established, it was open to all internees to apply to this body to have the reason for their detention considered. If it was found that there were no reasonable grounds for the individual's continued detention, the government was obliged to either release him forthwith, or charge him with an offence under the law.[46] In accordance with the act, the commission was duly established on 17 September, when the government appointed the barrister Hugh McGann, Major Michael Touhy and Major Felix Devlin as its members.[47]

Not content to rely solely on the expedient of internment, the government also began to seek the prosecution of republicans before the Special Criminal Court. On 16 October, Myles Heffernan earned the unwelcome distinction of being the first person to be convicted by this court when he received a three-month sentence for possessing incriminating documents and for being a member of an unlawful organization.[48] The government crackdown continued throughout the autumn with widespread arrests in Dublin, Dundalk, Limerick and Tipperary.[49] By December, over thirty members of the IRA had been tried by the Special Criminal Court, while seventy-six were interned in either Mountjoy Prison or Arbour Hill military barracks.[50] Pressurised by the Irish government and faced with the collapse of its bombing campaign, the focus of IRA activity, as in the past, now shifted towards the prisons. Republican prisoners began to agitate for political status and sought the right to exercise freely and walk around the prison rather than being confined to their cells at 4 p.m. each day.[51] In October, these protests were ratcheted up when several republicans began refusing food and demanding their release. These hunger strikes subsequently elicited widespread public debate and, in the case of such as Patrick McGrath, a disabled War of Independence veteran, many private representations to de Valera.[52]

Much to his subsequent regret, de Valera relented and ordered the release of Charles McCarthy on 12 October and Jeremiah Lynch and Richard McCarthy on 18 November 1939. Patrick McGrath was transferred to hospital on 15 November and, following his subsequent release, a *nolle prosequi* was entered in his case before the Special Criminal Court.[53] This was not the only setback to be encountered by the government as its powers of internment came under significant legal challenge in the High Court following the application of internee James Burke to serve for a motion of *habeas corpus*. The case was heard in November 1939 with Seán MacBride, who was acting for Burke, contending that his internment under the OASA should be deemed to be invalid as it was repugnant to the constitution.[54] After two days of turgid legal argument, Justice Gavin Duffy delivered his reserve judgement, in which he held for Burke, on the grounds that the relevant sections of the OASA conferred on the government the authority to act judicially. Not only was the government empowered to administer criminal justice, it could also condemn an alleged offender without charge or hearing. In his view these were not the appropriate functions of government and therefore a law that endowed the executive with such powers was illegal.[55]

The government appealed the ruling to the Supreme Court, which concluded by a majority decision that it did not have the jurisdiction to entertain the appeal.[56] In effect all of the previous internment orders issued by the government were now deemed to be illegal, necessitating the immediate release of fifty-three detainees. In the short term the government was content to let the situation lie, given the effectiveness of the Special Criminal Court in encouraging a lull in republican activity. In any case, de Valera was yet to suffer his greatest political embarrassment at the hands of the IRA, when on Christmas Eve 1939 a raiding party managed to infiltrate the Irish army's magazine fort, before escaping with over a million rounds of ammunition.[57] While the ammunition was quickly recovered, the Dáil was summoned to meet in emergency session, during which Boland declared the government's intention of proceeding with the widespread internment of republicans under the EPA.[58] This was a prudent course of action as the EPA was not open to judicial scrutiny. Consequently, an amendment to the act was passed on 4 January 1940, removing the prohibition on interning natural born Irish citizens.[59]

These new powers formally came into operation on 6 January, when de Valera signed the Emergency Powers (No. 20) Order, 1940. However, the government was not content to leave the issues raised by Justice Gavin Duffy unresolved, and Boland also informed the Dáil that a more permanent measure legislating for internment would be needed.[60] The Offences Against the State (Amendment) Bill, 1940, which was designed as a replacement for part six of the OASA, was promptly introduced. Virtually identical to the original act, in line with Justice Gavin Duffy's judgment, the wording of section four was altered to avoid the interpretation that the executive was acting in a judicial manner by issuing internment warrants. In effect, a minister of state would no longer be required to be 'satisfied that any particular person is engaged in activities calculated to prejudice the preservation of the peace, order or the security of the state'; he would simply have to form 'an opinion'.[61]

To activate these powers the government was obliged to publish a proclamation declaring that it was desirable that part two of the Offences Against the State (Amendment) Act should come into force immediately. Provision was also made for the creation of a Detention Commission along previously established lines and a supervisory role for parliament was incorporated as the government would be compelled to furnish the Oireachtas every six months with the particulars of those under detention.[62] In enacting this legislation the government was attempting to determine whether or not it had the right to intern persons outside of wartime by obtaining from the Supreme Court an opinion as to its constitutionality.[63] As de Valera explained to the Council of State, 'the government believed that such powers were not contrary to the Constitution, and I suppose that this is such an important question that it must be resolved authoritatively.' Once it had passed all stages in the Oireachtas, the President duly submitted the bill to the Supreme Court on 6 January 1940. Without specific reference to the Burke case, it was held that internment was not punitive, but preventative justice, and did not take away a citizen's right to *habeas corpus*.[64] As the bill was declared to be constitutional it was now, crucially, beyond judicial review. Although it was signed into law on 9 February 1940, the provisions of this act would not be activated until after the war and only then following the expiry of the EPA.

Encouraged by its previous successes the IRA began to step up its campaign in the prisons and on 24 February informed the governor of Mountjoy that unless republican prisoners were removed to military custody and granted political status, a hunger strike would commence. When this notice was ignored, Tomás MacCurtain, Thomas Grogan, Michael Traynor, Tony D'Arcy, Jack McNeela and John Plunkett began refusing food.[65] In contrast to the situation of six months earlier, the resolve of the government had unmistakably stiffened and de Valera announced that prisoners would not be allowed to dictate the conditions under which they were kept in detention.[66] All reports of the strike were suppressed in the media and, on 24 March, McNeela, Plunkett, D'Arcy and Traynor were transferred to St Bricin's Hospital, to be followed in the coming days by Grogan and MacCurtain.[67] Several days later, in a show of solidarity with their comrades, a number of prisoners informed the governor at Arbour Hill that they also intended to join the strike. This abortive protest proved to be short lived, however, when those involved were reported by the military authorities to have partaken in breakfast just two days after their dramatic announcement.[68] As the strike progressed, efforts by republican activists to intercede on behalf of the protesters were stepped up, particularly in the wake of Josephine Plunkett's emotive appeal to Cardinal McRory to exercise his 'paternal solicitude' to save her son, whom she believed to be inappropriately imprisoned with 'sexual degenerates'.[69]

Following a number of preliminary enquiries from the cardinal as to the veracity or otherwise of these claims, de Valera moved to diffuse the situation with the issue of a detailed rebuttal designed to assuage the fears of the Catholic primate. While he conceded that republican prisoners were allowed to associate freely with each other while at work, as a group they were segregated from all the other categories of inmates, thereby removing the risk of 'moral contamination' from contact with 'depraved types'.[70] All republican prisoners were authorized to wear their own clothing and, contrary to established government policy, were housed primarily in Mountjoy Prison. In de Valera's mind this was an obvious sop to republican sensibilities as the usual practice was to transfer those sentenced to terms of penal servitude to Portlaoise Prison. Therefore, any attempt by these individuals to extract further concessions from the government could not be countenanced. Given the entrenched position of both sides, it was now becoming increasingly obvious to all concerned that the protesters would be forced to bring the strike to its obvious conclusion. The death of D'Arcy on 16 April was to dispel any remaining doubts about the government's determination to face down the remaining protesters.[71]

During the inquest into his death the jury publicly censured the government for its handling of the whole affair by adding a rider appealing for immediate action to be taken 'with regard to the five men at present on hunger strike'.[72] Two days later, a private appeal by Kathleen Clarke, the Lord Mayor of Dublin, urging de Valera to dispense with the 'petty technicalities' at issue elicited a forceful restatement of the government's position:

> To allow the hunger strike to be used to dictate to the government would be for the government to surrender the only means at its disposal for preserving order and restraining or deterring those who claim a moral right to make war on the community. Were the government to surrender in this way and abandon the punishment of imprisonment they would be left with no sanction for the protection of the community except the death penalty.[73]

Although he expressed regret at the death of D'Arcy, de Valera was unmoved by the appeal of the Lord Mayor and called on all public representatives to give their support to the legitimately elected government. The increased sense of urgency following the death of D'Arcy was now given a more powerful resonance, as it was evident to all concerned that the government was prepared to let the remaining protesters die.

In an effort to prevent further fatalities, Father John O'Hare, a Carmelite priest, attempted to intercede on the protesters' behalf by presenting himself as a neutral intermediary in the affair. On 8 April, he wrote to de Valera and proposed that the military authorities be put in charge of the 'political prisoners' wing' at Mountjoy. Needless to say this was rejected and on 11 April he arranged to have an interview with the Minister for Justice, where it was expected that he might present a more reasoned proposal to bring the strike to an end. Such hopes were quickly dashed when he arrived with a demand from the prisoners, who insisted on being detained in military custody. By now doubting the impartiality of Fr O'Hare, the government began to refuse his requests to visit Mountjoy on the grounds that they could serve no useful purpose, particularly in light of the visit of Senator Seán Campbell, who had 'informed himself of the treatment being given to prisoners there'.[74] On 19 April, despite the critical nature of McNeela's condition, the whole dynamic of the strike was changed when Boland received a visit from a delegation of women headed by Mrs Austin Stack and Mrs George Lawlor.

During the course of the interview the delegation held out the possibility that the strike may be terminated if the conditions in Mountjoy were improved. While Boland responded reasonably positively to this suggestion, he did inform the delegation that he was not prepared to consider this proposal 'under pressure of hunger strike tactics'. This was interpreted by the delegation to mean that if the protest was called off an improvement in the conditions in Mountjoy would necessarily follow and they publicly reproached the minister for not holding out this inducement at an earlier date. Incorrect as this interpretation was, it did serve as a useful 'face-saver' for the protesters in the event of the strike collapsing, as they could now establish the pretence that they had not surrendered unconditionally. In light of this, Fr O'Hare contacted the government and again sought permission to visit Mountjoy in order to provide the prisoners there with the opportunity to tell their comrades in St Bricin's if they wished the strike to be called off. In the view of the minister this was a gamble worth pursuing and during the course of a recorded telephone conversation with the priest he issued the requisite authorization for the visit.[75]

That evening Fr O'Hare arrived in Mountjoy and informed the governor that his visit to the prison was now a 'mere formality' as he had a written document from the IRA Army Council ordering the termination of the strike. He subsequently declined the governor's offer to speak with all of the republican prisoners within the prison, insisting instead on a brief interview with a man named MacDermott, who was 'the spokesperson for the lot'. During his brief consultation with MacDermott he was instructed to inform the hunger strikers in St Bricin's that the republican prisoners in Mountjoy wanted an end to the protest. Significantly, he did not mention the written order from the IRA.[76] O'Hare then proceeded to St Bricin's, where he had a private conversation with the hunger strikers during which he persuaded them to abandon their protest. This proved to be too late for the gravely ill McNeela, however, and he died a few hours afterwards.[77] The ensuing inquest proved to be politically humiliating for the government when Boland was called to the stand in order to refute allegations made by Fr O'Hare that the strike could have been called off much earlier if he had been granted permission to visit Mountjoy. Boland was subjected to a severe cross-examination by Seán MacBride, resulting in an adverse finding when the jury censured the government for not allowing Fr O'Hare to visit the prisoners at an earlier date.[78]

In spite of this, the prevailing mood in Dublin was remarkably subdued, as there was very little public anger directed at the government, which was now resolutely opposed to conceding any form of political status to IRA prisoners.[79] In many ways, this was to represent a significant victory for de Valera, as he had succeeded, for the first time, in undermining the power of the hunger strike as a weapon of political confrontation. Previous to this, the authorities routinely conceded to the demands of republican hunger strikers in an understandable bid to avoid creating martyrs. In doing so, the government was not only facilitating the short-term objectives of the IRA, it was also encouraging further resort to this tactic in the future.[80] When faced with a further hunger strike in 1943, the government again held firm and refused to accede to republican demands.[81] The ensuing collapse of this protest proved to be a graphic illustration of the limitations of the hunger strike weapon in the face of an unyielding government and an unsympathetic populace. In retaliation, the IRA detonated a bomb at the Special Criminal Court headquarters in Dublin Castle and shot at two unarmed detectives in an attempt to redirect the focus of activity in its escalating struggle with the government.[82] This again proved to be counter-productive as the Gardaí were now seeking to severely disrupt, if not destroy, the IRA.

As was to be expected, this only served to provoke further confrontation and in May 1940 a number of republicans were involved in a gun fight with armed detectives who had been carrying diplomatic mail, three days before a raid on the safe house of Herman Görtz. Although Görtz managed to evade arrest on this occasion, Gardaí seized documents of a military character, linking the IRA with Germany.[83] The discovery of these documents shocked the political establishment and led to the convening of an all-party 'Defence Conference' designed to assist the government in dealing with this renewed subversive threat. Several days later, Boland moved to issue 400 internment warrants after consulting with the Gardaí as to who might be regarded as a danger to the peace.[84] In order to cope with such a large number of internees and an ensuing increase in the number of convicted republican prisoners, the government decided to make provision for the construction of a dedicated internment facility. In doing so it was following the precedent established during the Civil War when two custom-built internment camps, known colloquially as 'Tintown No. 1' and 'Tintown No. 2', were established in the Curragh, County Kildare. For the republicans who had been convicted of the most serious offences it was decided to transfer them to Portlaoise, where they would be subjected to a harsh regime.[85]

Once these arrangements had been put in place, the government introduced an amendment to the EPA allowing for the trial of civilians by a military tribunal, equipped with the sole sanction of execution upon conviction.[86] In August 1940, this tribunal, staffed by three of the sitting members of the Special Criminal Court, was established following the death of two Gardaí during a gunfight with an IRA party in Rathgar.[87] Both Tom Harte and Patrick McGrath were convicted by the military tribunal and, following the muted response engendered by their executions, it became apparent that as long as a repressive censorship regime was maintained, republicans could be executed without any adverse effect on public opinion.[88] In July 1941 Richard Goss was executed for shooting and wounding a soldier in a bank raid in County Longford, followed by Maurice O'Neill in November and George Plant in 1942, who was executed for the murder of an informer.[89] In the face of widespread public apathy the government, now equipped with a willingness to execute, was in a position to entirely eliminate the IRA as an armed force.

THE OPERATION OF INTERNMENT

In deciding to pursue a policy of widespread internment the government was immediately faced with a number of significant logistical problems, given the anticipated volume of detainees. In line with previously established Civil War practice, the burden of the day-to-day implementation of internment fell squarely on the shoulders of the defence forces, as the internees were placed under the responsibility of the military police corps under the command of a provost marshal. Initially, they were billeted in three of the army's military detention barracks, which were situated in Arbour Hill, the Curragh and Cork military barracks. As internee numbers increased, however, it was felt prudent to centralize them in a single purpose-built camp. In order to expedite the construction of this new facility the government decided to utilize the infrastructure that was already *in situ* at the site of the former internment camp at Tintown No. 1. As the camp had fallen into a severe state of disrepair after 'fifteen years of disuse', it was decided to issue a tender for the reconstruction of this facility.[90] In September 1939 the contract for this project was awarded to Richard Macken, a building contractor based in Synge St, Dublin, who agreed to undertake the redevelopment of the site at a cost of £15,665.

Once these technicalities had been resolved the Department of Defence sought the sanction of the Department of Finance to start the construction of an outer boundary fence, as well as a bathhouse, a dining hall, a small assembly hall and accommodation for 300 men.[91] The scheme was formally approved on 25 September, whereupon work at the site promptly began.[92] Initially, construction progressed to schedule and by January 1940 the cooking and dining facilities were complete and 'entirely satisfactory', as well as sleeping accommodation, night latrines and the ablution facilities. However, according to Major Kinneen, the main bathhouse was only 'half finished', while work on the church and recreation room had yet to begin. In addition, a search hut, meeting room and interview room were only partially built, 'to be rushed to completion', along with the construction of two extra sentry posts, a guard room and an administration block.[93] While these teething difficulties were eventually overcome, the scale of the project at No. 1 Tintown was quickly becoming apparent.

On 31 May 1940, ninety-seven internees were assigned to the camp, followed quickly by nearly all of the 400 republicans who had been arrested in the government crackdown in June.[94] Transfers of convicted prisoners followed soon afterwards, including the playwright Brendan Behan, as well as a number of other prominent republicans including Thomas Grogan, Christopher Querney and Seamus Murphy.[95] Ultimately, over 1,100 internees were to pass through the gates of the Curragh camp, which at it peak, in March 1943, was home to 550 detainees.[96] The Irish government also sought to intern a number of notable communist and socialist activists, the most important of whom were Neil Goold-Verschoyle, Johnny Powers and Diarmaid Breathnach. Although there appeared to be minimal conflict between these men and the rank and file of the IRA, several members of the IRA leadership, unhappy at Goold-Verschoyle's insistence on conducting lectures on communism, were successful in having him removed from the Curragh.[97] Under the immediate command of the camp commandant, Captain James Guiney, No. 1 Tintown was described by republicans as 'a concentration camp', where conditions were at best 'miserable', and at worst 'primitive'.[98] Writing in 1951, an anonymous former internee went so far as to claim that this internment camp was 'conceived and designed with the sole purpose of liquidating the Irish separatist movement'.[99] Men were confined sixty to each of the huts, which were in most cases 'cold and draughty'.[100] Beds were often placed directly on the concrete or timber floor of the hut and the stifling atmosphere within was often augmented by the fact that there were no partitions or private cubicles erected where the men could retire to 'read, rest or write'.[101]

As the camp had no dedicated sewerage system, sanitary arrangements were rudimentary and it has been claimed that the 'receptacles in use were unchanged throughout the whole period of internment'.[102] Consumables such as tea, cigarettes, butter and sugar were rationed and while the diet, though monotonous, was 'reasonably good at the start', standards quickly fell.[103] Supper in the main consisted of 'a half-pint of cold milk and one slice of bread', while the usual dinner was 'one large and one small potato, a small spoonful of vegetable and one or two slices of boiled beef'.[104] Internees were required to take all of their meals in the dining hall, which was characterized by the almost total lack of hygiene and described by Tom Doran as 'a terrible looking dive'.[105] Life was bleak in the camp, particularly in winter where the open plains of the Curragh exposed the internees to the vagaries of inclement weather. While conditions in the Curragh were often described as 'quite nice in the summer', many internees recalled the cold winter ('the wind used to howl through the huts') despite the fact that they were notionally heated by fires and stoves.[106] For Liam Burke, the overriding memory of his incarceration at the Curragh was of 'hunger and the severity of the wind'.[107]

Given the close proximity in which internees were confined, outbreaks of dysentery were common and the spread of lice from individual to individual was endemic.[108] Regulations relating to personal hygiene were heavily enforced in order to avoid an outbreak of disease. All internees were required to shower or bathe at least once a week and clothing was to be washed in the 'wash house', where large sinks with hot and cold running water were provided. Psychologically, the sudden and complete loss of privacy that this type of confinement entailed took a serious toll on many, as a growing number of minor disagreements increased tensions and frustrations among internees. The monotony of long-term and indefinite detention also increased the rate of depression, with John McCormack describing how it was especially 'rough on the men married with kids … it went on … for so long … not knowing when you were going to be released'.[109] Upon his arrival in the camp, Tom Doran was struck by the dishevelled appearance of several of his comrades, whom he described as being 'dapper and trendy' on the outside. Many had beards, some had their heads shaved and their clothing looked 'crumpled and shabby'.[110] While internees were permitted to wear their own clothing, they were issued with replacements from army stocks when their garments became threadbare.[111] More often than not, this clothing was of poor quality and in the view of Eddie Keenan served to add to the 'gloomy' and 'depressing' atmosphere of the Curragh.[112]

Upon arrival in the camp internees were assigned to a specific hut and quickly settled in to the established daily routine. Following the conventions established at Arbour Hill detention barracks, internees were permitted to exercise and associate freely between the hours of 9 a.m. and 9 p.m. in the summer and from 9 a.m. to 5.30 p.m. in the winter.[113] On wet days, however, it was claimed that 'the compound in which we had to exercise was a sea of mud and water. Many ... were barefooted and therefore there could be no exercise.'[114] In the afternoons, if the sports field was unplayable, internees engaged in craftwork, making belts, crosses and harps, while in the evenings many would retire to their huts where there would often be a concert, a debate or 'a laugh around the fire'.[115] Detainees were also granted the privilege of writing one letter a week, which was often revoked when camp discipline was breached.[116] Closed visits with friends and relatives were permitted but in many cases internees declined on principle and agitated for the right to have open visits.[117] Internees established their own bank and a mobile shop used to call to the camp on a weekly basis.[118] In order to pass the time, Irish classes were often organized by Martin Ó Cadhain, and several internees managed to establish their own Gaelic football competition where 'you played a league then you got so far to semi-final'.[119] Card playing also proved to be a popular pastime, with many playing a 'bit of pontoon ... but we wouldn't be playing for money ... we'd have no money to play for'.[120] The spiritual welfare of the detainees was also catered for by a resident chaplain, who celebrated Mass once a week.[121]

As a matter of common practice most republicans who were interned during this period were detained following the expiation of existing prison sentences. In most cases, individuals were simply transferred from prison directly to the Curragh, where they were immediately presented with a written order empowering the Minister for Justice to intern them indefinitely.[122] Several release mechanisms were made available to these internees, including the device of 'signing out'. Instituted in the wake of the Civil War, established government policy was to let internees go provided they gave a written undertaking to respect the Irish constitution and not to resume subversive activities.[123] Few republicans availed themselves of this measure as it entailed an implicit recognition of the legitimacy of the Irish state. Those who did sign out were often regarded as being unprincipled and were ostracized by their comrades.[124] To avoid this, many internees, under the guise of leaving their hut to tidy up, would put on a pair of shoes with a signed undertaking concealed inside. They would then make their way outside and surreptitiously pass the undertaking to the relevant authorities, who would discreetly arrange for their release.[125] On rare occasions exceptions were made, particularly in the case of those suffering ill health. In some instances, certain internees were even ordered to sign out, as in the case of Liam Burke, whose expertise relating to the location of arms dumps was urgently required by the Army Council.[126]

To provide for the running and defence of the camp, Commandant Guiney issued a set of standing orders outlining the duties and responsibilities of his staff. By doing so, this document provided for the establishment of a number of posts, including that of an adjutant, a quartermaster, a censor, a purchase and accounts officer and a medical officer. In his instructions to the military police, Guiney outlined how it was their responsibility to keep the internees under strict observation and to take note of how they occupied their time. They were to ensure that the buildings within the camp were only to be used for the purpose for which they were originally intended and were advised to keep a constant watch for signs of tunnelling or other 'unlawful activities'. They were also forbidden to converse with internees 'except on a point of duty' and were not allowed to supply them with 'tobacco, cigarettes, matches, drink, books, or newspapers'.[127] While the military police were authorized to fire live ammunition in a number of specific circumstances, their position in respect of the internees was unclear and proved to be a matter of significant debate within the government.[128]

At the outset, the Minister for Justice, Gerald Boland, did consider the desirability of seeking an amendment to these regulations, but felt it would not be possible to justify the use of firearms unless the escape was accompanied by a forceful attempt to disarm the military police. The Minister for Defence, Oscar Traynor, was unhappy with this imprecision and consulted with the Attorney-General, Kevin Haugh, as to the desirability of introducing an Emergency Powers Order to clarify the situation. In his view, the use of any kind of force was problematic as it would, in most cases, lead to 'a searching enquiry' that may encourage the 'institution of criminal proceedings'. He dismissed the need for an Emergency Powers Order on the grounds that 'the justification for the use of firearms in any such case will lie in the need of the action for such an extreme step and not in any precise form of words contained in the order'.[129] This did not resolve the matter to the satisfaction of the Department of Defence, however, and in June 1940 the cabinet acquiesced in the introduction of the Emergency Powers (No. 28) Order, authorizing the application of reasonable force, including the use of firearms, in preventing the escape of internees.[130] In October, Commandant Guiney proceeded to issue a new set of standing orders empowering the military police to employ the use of lethal force in order to quell serious disturbances or riots within camp only in circumstances where 'less extreme measures will [not] suffice'.[131]

When it came to the enforcement of camp discipline, the military police were afforded a degree of discretion, and accounts of beatings at the hands of the authorities are commonplace among former internees. In many cases, it appeared that being threatened with 'The Mahogany' (a reference to the hardwood batons carried by the military police) was a common means of pacifying recalcitrant individuals, while Tomás Ó Broin recalled how internees were often 'battered … with batons just to make sure who was the boss'.[132] Major breaches of discipline were punishable by internees being lodged in solitary confinement in the military detention barracks in the Curragh, which was colloquially known as 'the Glasshouse'. It was often alleged that the standard practice in the Glasshouse consisted of beatings with wooden batons. Usually the prisoner was beaten on the arms until they became numb, so that he was unable to defend himself. Blows to the head were avoided 'as this would have rendered him lifeless too quickly' and it was claimed that the internee was then beaten around his cell until his 'assailants got tired'.[133] Furthermore, the military police were also authorized to use tear gas in the case of emergency, where it was deemed to be 'a preferable method' of controlling riotous and disorderly internees, especially 'where conditions render its use effective'.[134]

Needless to say relations between the internees and the military police were often strained and best summarized by Christy Querney, who described how 'we weren't falling over each other or throwing our arms around each other in friendship'. Notably, as appeared to be the case with most internees, he did not harbour any long-term resentment because in his mind the beatings administered by the military police were considered to be 'part and parcel with their job'.[135] As a result, when addressed by military police, internees were often 'sarcastic and insolent', but on the whole refrained from overtly aggressive and emotive outbursts.[136] Exceptions were known to occur and on 1 December 1944, a group of prisoners lead by Brendan

Behan and Patrick Martin verbally abused Captain Michael Connolly when he attempted to take the nightly roll.[137] Although this incident was dismissed as 'impulsive in character brought about by the fact that feeling was running high due to the impending execution of their comrade Charles Kerins', Commandant Guiney did recommend that some form of collective punishment be administered.[138] In most cases, internees had little interaction with the military police, as they rarely entered the camp. Patrols were confined to the perimeter and at night they 'used to come into every hut and check that we were all there'. When they did enter, apart from the batons that they carried as standard issue, they were not armed:

> They didn't walk around the place with guns and rifles, that would be daft, a couple of hundred of us there and five or six of them come in and if they were carrying arms they would lose them pretty quick ... they might get shot.[139]

The most notable feature of life in the camp was the fact that the internees, in defiance of the military authorities, had begun to organize themselves along military lines with a hierarchical chain of command. An elected camp staff headed by an O/C was established with responsibility for the control and discipline of all republicans within the Curragh. Each hut was represented by its own subordinate O/C, or 'hut leader', who was in turn supported by an adjutant.[140] In September 1940, Colonel Dan Bryan of G2 military intelligence inadvertently uncovered the existence of this organization while visiting the camp during the course of an investigation into ongoing IRA activity.[141] On this occasion, Bryan, accompanied by an aide, approached a non commissioned officer (NCO) on duty within the compound, with a view to retrieving internee Liam Walsh for the purpose of conducting an interview. After several minutes the NCO emerged from the compound without Walsh and discreetly approached Bryan's aide. Following a brief exchange between the two he re-entered, leaving Major Bryan and his associate to wait for another ten minutes before Walsh was finally produced. Bryan considered the whole episode to be highly unusual and formed the impression that Walsh's O/C had to be informed before he was interviewed.[142]

Bryan proceeded to make further enquiries, leading to the disclosure of a number of unorthodox practices that had become tolerated within the camp. In particular, Bryan was surprised to learn of the latitude afforded to 'the "internees' camp staff"' to dictate the running of the compound and the influence that this body was allowed to exercise over the day-to-day lives of the internees. After some investigation, he was satisfied that the IRA leadership within the camp was running a system of censorship aimed at preventing written applications for release. Mail and personal correspondence was particularly singled out and all letters had to be screened by hut leaders before dispatch. Any material not presented in this manner was automatically regarded as an application for release and the individual involved was publicly shunned after being subjected to an 'ostracization parade'. As part of this ritual, the 'offender' would be formally paraded into the compound and ordered to perform an 'about turn' before being marched away by two 'policemen'.[143] Such parades were highly intimidating affairs and it appears that the 'offender' would often be physically threatened. On one occasion Daniel Conroy was seized by the throat by William Mulligan, the incumbent camp O/C, and told that 'if he dared recognize the court[s] or give bail drastic reprisals would follow'.[144] Unsurprisingly, most quickly repented for the alleged offence and resubmitted to the control of the camp staff.

From Bryan's perspective the toleration of this 'illegal exercise of authority' was an unacceptable practice as

> the Minister for Justice would hardly be satisfied to find that persons who were interned with a view to preventing their indulgence in illegal activities outside could still exercise authority and pressure, presumably technically illegal, within an internment camp.[145]

To counteract this he recommended that the camp commandant be given power to severely punish persons who refused to obey instructions and that a report be compiled on the demeanour and conduct of an internee whose application for release was being considered. This was to be done to ensure that the relevant authorities were made aware that an applicant may be suffering some form of persecution for his actions. Invariably, the implementation of these proposals was resisted as the military authorities tasked to run the camp sought to downplay the extent of these allegations. A detailed rebuttal was prepared by Commandant M.J. Cummins, who dismissed claims of censorship as a complaint that had been much 'exaggerated'. He assured his superiors that he had received guarantees from the internees that the holding of ostracization parades would no longer take place and maintained that there was no need to treat the matter too seriously or make any amendments to existing regulations.[146]

Colonel Archer of G2 remained unimpressed and was convinced that 'a virile prisoners' organization' was in existence that had 'supplemented to a large extent the functions of the [military authorities] in matters of discipline'.[147] His superiors were inclined to agree and an internal enquiry was established to examine the matter. After a thorough investigation, the chairman of the enquiry, Col. T. McNally, emphatically confirmed that:

> the prisoners [are given] a great deal more control than would appear to be warranted by statutory orders. The general attitude ... would appear to be to keep down trouble and complaints at all costs even to sacrifice, to some extent, control ... [as] the staff wanted to get through the day's work without giving any cause for offence to the internees and are actually prepared to be excessively tolerant with that end in view.[148]

McNally recommended a tightening of discipline and advised that internees should be divided into groups, 'allocating a number of men and huts to individual officers ... to ensure that the occupants of such huts are known individually'.[149] Nevertheless, it appears from the oral testimony of former internees that these recommendations were not taken on board as the situation within the camp was allowed to remain largely unchanged until after December 1940.[150]

Escape attempts within the camp were common and on one occasion a large number of internees endeavoured to affect a mass escape by cutting through the barrier fence of the camp. While this was thwarted by the reinforcement of the sentries on duty, it appears a similar escape was attempted in 1943, albeit on a smaller scale.[151] In this instance, internee Michael Dunne was found in bed 'fully dressed' with his face and arms blackened. Upon further investigation it was found that the wire covering one of the windows on the north side of the hut in which he was billeted had been forced away 'from the wood' and it appeared Dunne was awaiting the cover of darkness before trying to escape.[152] In order to discourage this kind of behaviour the military authorities resorted to leaving the lights in the internees' huts on all night. While it was admitted that this was not an ideal solution, it was stated that the psychological effects of having the lights continually on had the desired effect as the prisoners did not know when or where the military police were peering at them from the outside darkness.[153] Inevitably, the internees objected to this practice and after considering the matter the Minister for Defence was inclined to agree. Alternative arrangements were instituted whereby

> one diffused light will be permitted in each hut for night lighting. Care will be taken to make sure the light is not of a 'dazzling' type, but needless to say it must be of such strength as would permit of observation of the occupants from the outside.[154]

As a result of this, the only other avenue of escape open to internees was the clandestine excavation of tunnels and shafts designed to breach the outer perimeter of the camp. The most ambitious attempt was instituted sometime in late 1940, when the camp council devised a complicated and elaborate scheme to dig a network of small passageways beneath the camp in order to service a main outgoing tunnel.[155] In doing so, the internees hoped to link up several huts with the main tunnel, thereby providing for a mass escape as well as affording numerous outlets for the surreptitious disposal of waste clay.[156] In designing the camp, the authorities had obviously not anticipated that such a sophisticated operation would be undertaken, as several huts had wooden floors. Work commenced on the project in the autumn of 1940, with the construction of six tunnels, each of which was 2 feet in diameter. In a painstaking effort, these tunnels, some of which were up to 13 feet in length, were hollowed out using an extraordinary array of improvised tools and equipment. While the main implement for excavation was a pick fashioned from the leg of a table trestle, other instruments included a series of butcher's knives, with the edge formed into a saw, scrapers fashioned from spoons and forks as well as claw hammers, parting chisels and mallets. In places the tunnels were skilfully lined with timber to prevent their collapse, and clay was transported out in tin basins and homemade wooden barrows with the help of an ingenious pulley system constructed out of discarded clothing, ropes and tapes. In order to illuminate the tunnels candles were made by filling cigarette tins with stones and grease, and a piece of fabric was attached as a wick.[157]

As work continued on the tunnels throughout October and November, relations between the internees and the authorities deteriorated drastically as Thomas Grogan, the prisoners' O/C, began to agitate for improved camp conditions. Matters came to a head on 13 December when the internees were informed that their butter ration was to be cut by ½ oz per man daily.[158] The following morning Grogan issued an ultimatum to Commandant Guiney that if the butter ration was not restored 'he would not accept responsibility for what might happen next'. This was passed on to Colonel McNally, the O/C at the Curragh, and he immediately arranged to have the military police in the camp form into 'stand to' parties in the event that the internees were to become riotous.[159] At 12.50 p.m., Commandant Guiney was suddenly interrupted in his administrative duties by Sergeant Fitzpatrick, who informed him that there was 'trouble in the compound'. Guiney immediately rushed out, where he noticed that there were 'black smoke and flames issuing from the direction of the internment camp'. Apparently, in a deliberate act of arson the internees had attempted to burn down a number of huts by scattering hot coals used in the heating stoves to set fire to the wooden floors. Blankets were then suspended from the wooden roof trusses and the interior lining of bed mattresses was placed in cavities along the walls in order to act as wicks in an effort to spread the flames. In order to hamper the fire-fighting effort, all the extinguishers in the huts were set off and used to smash the windows of the burning structures.[160]

Owing to a stiff wind, the blaze unintentionally spread to several other huts, including those that had been involved in the tunnelling operation. Upon his arrival at the camp, Major Kinneen, the Director of Military Engineering, observed that 'huts were on fire in all three lines of the camp and were blazing furiously'. In an effort to contain the fire, the military's own fire brigade, which was stationed in the Curragh, was called to the scene. Kinneen then proceeded to issue instructions to abandon the huts that were already ablaze, so that all efforts could be directed at preventing the further spread of the blaze. By the late afternoon the situation was brought under control following the intercession of a private fire-fighting force from the nearby town of Newbridge, County Kildare.[161] In the interim, Commandant Guiney proceeded to assemble a company of armed military police, who were authorized to open fire in the event of being charged down by any of the prisoners. Upon entering the camp, Guiney and his men were confronted by a large group of internees wielding various improvised weapons, including bed boards, handles of brushes, iron piping and trestle legs of tables. After firing a series of warning shots the group dispersed and Guiney ordered his men to herd the internees towards the camp's main sports field, where they would be held until the situation was brought under control.[162]

In the ensuing mêlée, Guiney found himself detached from his company and threatened by a lone internee who was 'endeavouring to push [a] burning mattress through the roof of [an] unoccupied hut'. Guiney challenged the individual before firing two shots. He immediately sprinted towards the sports field and did 'not indicate in any way that he had been shot'. The situation threatened to escalate as a number of shots were then fired in an attempt to quell the disorder. Reinforced by a group of military policemen armed with batons, Guiney proceeded to the western side of the camp and continued his efforts to herd internees towards the sports field:

> Every internee that we met we drove towards the sports field. Some resisted and I got the men with batons to ... [drive] them off ... They had to strike a number of them as they resisted violently. They were also throwing burning blankets and mattresses on to the roofs and trying to push lighted mattresses through the broken windows. During this time the internees threw a good deal of what appeared to be bricks and stones at us. Some of the stones found their mark and injured two of my policemen.[163]

The situation was only alleviated with the arrival of a company of infantry into the compound with orders to gather all the internees in the sports field. Faced with fixed bayonets and a mounted Lewes machine gun, the internees' rebellion collapsed and order was restored.[164]

In the aftermath of the fire, six and a half huts lay in ruins and an opening into one of the escape tunnels had been exposed. After a thorough search of the compound, the full extent of the escape plot quickly became apparent as the entire network of tunnels was uncovered and sealed.[165] As the search for further tunnels continued into the night it became necessary to detain the internees in the sports field until the early hours of the morning. Owing to the shortage of accommodation the internees were removed in batches of twenty under armed guard to a disused dining hall 'with a bare concrete floor'.[166] The following day, a Sunday, normal routine within the camp was suspended, as Mass was cancelled and the internees remained locked in their huts. Tensions remained high within the camp and on Monday morning the prisoners were permitted to leave their huts in order to receive their breakfast. In accordance with their own established practice, the prisoners proceeded to line up in military fashion and parade towards the cookhouse. The armed guards who were overseeing the entire situation seemed to panic, and as the prisoners drew near they opened fire, mortally wounding internee Barney Casey. Several others were injured, including Martin Staunton, Bob Flanagan, Art Moynihan and Walter Mitchell.[167]

While the authorities later maintained that they had informed the prisoners that they would not be allowed to line up in military fashion, John McCormack, a former internee, disputes this and attributes the shooting to the fact that: '[the military police] were trigger happy, they were vexed with us of course I suppose for burning the camp and some of their fellows did get injured.'[168] All details of the shooting were suppressed in the media and the coverage of Barney Casey's funeral was restricted to giving the names of the priest and chief mourners.[169] In order to identify the chief ringleaders it was claimed that informal identification parades were held by the military police within the internment camp. Selected individuals were then made to 'run the gauntlet' of military police who had 'lined both sides of the road from the doors of the huts to the gate of the camp', where they were beaten with 'revolver butts or batons' until 'they fell senseless'.[170] They were then lodged in solitary confinement in the Glasshouse where they faced a ten-week wait before being returned for trial.[171] In all, forty-nine internees were charged before the Special Criminal Court for their part in the affair and thirty-seven convictions were obtained.[172]

Despite the fire, the internees remained undeterred in their attempts to escape and in 1943 a new plot was discovered during a routine inspection of the old tunnel network. Although this network was not completely filled in, it had been 'effectively blocked up to prevent its use by internees attempting escape'. During a scheduled inspection of this system of tunnels, Guiney and his officers became suspicious after noticing fresh deposits of clay. Following a thorough search of the camp, a new tunnel was discovered that ran the whole way under the wire and trench surrounding the camp. Stretching to over 83 feet in length, the tunnel, upon discovery, was within a few feet of the surface, leading to speculation that a mass escape could have taken place within forty-eight hours from the time it was found. As on the previous occasion an array of improvised tools was uncovered as well as a system of wooden trays connected with strips of blanket, which was used to transport the clay out of the tunnel. It subsequently emerged that these strips had been obtained when a number of old blankets had been given to internees in order to facilitate the holding of a concert the previous St Patrick's Day. Although Guiney admitted that the tunnel was quite advanced, he praised the vigilance of his staff for its discovery in time and urged that no further action be taken.[173]

In the immediate aftermath of the fire, life in the internment camp quickly reverted back to its established routine. In light of the death of Casey this was resented by some of the internees, who believed that normality was restored with indecorous haste.[174] Overt displays of militarism were no longer permitted, while indefinite internment, exacerbated by close confinement, began to take its toll as an increasing number of demoralized prisoners relented and signed out.[175] In the eyes of many, the prestige of the camp leadership had been irreparably damaged by the whole affair as the internees had lost more than they had gained. A humiliating nightly roll call became a permanent feature of camp life, while the internees were also deprived of sheets and pillow covers for their beds.[176] In fact, in the immediate aftermath of the fire the internees' beds were temporarily removed, forcing some to 'sleep on the wide shelf over the toilet area' in an effort to keep warm at night. According to Joe Dolan, the military authorities objected to this practice and he recalls how on one occasion 'the staters ... well tanked up I suppose ... started firing into our hut, riddling it with bullet holes'.[177] The prisoners' organization also began to break down and, with the departure of Grogan, Liam Leddy of Cork was appointed O/C.[178]

Leddy's tenure was dogged by controversy as his style of leadership proved to be 'so narrow as to exclude any form of thought or prospect of progress'.[179] Late in 1941, tensions among the internees boiled over when a group of individuals, centred on Tadhg Lynch, defied Leddy during a protest over an arbitrary 50 per cent reduction in each hut's turf ration. During this protest, Leddy had implemented a ban on accepting any turf from the military authorities until the full ration was restored. Given the adverse weather conditions, the Lynch faction refused to accept this and proceeded to accept the reduced ration.[180] As a reprisal, the camp council ordered the ostracization of Lynch, whose mutiny had attracted several others who were dissatisfied with Leddy's leadership. In an effort to resolve this situation, Pearse Kelly, who was one of the Lynch faction, circulated a document proposing the election of a new camp council. Leddy's reaction was overwhelmingly negative, leading to the establishment of a rival organization when a large body of internees declared support for Kelly's position.[181] Over time Kelly's organization became the larger of the two as his relaxed style of leadership proved to be an attraction, in contrast to Leddy's rigid approach.

Caught between these two mutually antagonistic groups, several internees attempted to remain neutral, only to be openly ostracisized by both sides. Many internees privately disliked this practice, particularly when there was 'no great point of principle involved'. Over the following weeks the formation of a separate 'neutral' faction headed by Seamus Dowling was to confirm for Tom Doran that he was not alone in his views when he stated that:

> The way I looked at it we were all in for the same cause. I was not going to walk by a comrade of mine because some fellow instructed me. I did not know the rights and wrongs and I was not going to condemn any man.[182]

Upon arrival in the camp, all new internees were given three weeks to decide which faction they wished to join. Like Tom Doran and Eddie Keenan, most were unconcerned with the internal politics of the split and joined a particular grouping on the basis of friendship.[183] Therefore, in order to provide for the peaceful running of the camp, the military authorities arranged for all groups to be accommodated separately and, from time to time, the camp commandant found himself approached by internees requesting a transfer from one group to another.[184]

Matters came to a head in March 1942, when a group of ostracized internees announced their intention of going on hunger strike in an attempt to pressurise Leddy into re-admitting them into the mainstream camp organization. Headed by Jeremiah Daly, this group had been housed in a separate hut since the burning of the camp in 1940 and had suffered significant hardship as a result of their ostracization. According to Daly their life in the camp had been made 'impossible' and their decision to embark on this course of action was motivated by a desire to exonerate themselves from the allegation that they were informers.[185] During the course of a private interview, Daly assured Guiney that the matter was purely an internal one and that the internees had 'no grievances against the camp authorities'.[186] Guiney maintained a watching brief on the strike and made preliminary arrangements to move the protesters to the camp hospital should the need arise. Six days into the protest, Leddy, who was under pressure to resolve the situation, announced his intention to re-admit the protesters on the condition that Daly made a public apology to the camp council. Daly initially refused this offer, despite the fact that the majority of his group were now willing to terminate the strike.[187] When faced with an increasingly isolated position Daly reluctantly relented and the strike was terminated after ten days.[188]

The situation within the camp was to deteriorate even further, when the IRA Army Council issued a directive in October 1942 ordering that all internees within the camp were to be reunited. This proved to be a highly counter-productive intervention, when a number of individuals headed by Seán McCool voted in its favour during the course of a meeting organized by Leddy to discuss the matter. Faced with this opposition, Leddy responded by expelling them, prompting them to approach the camp commandant to inform him of their new status as 'a distinct party' within the camp.[189] Farcically, a fifth grouping was to emerge in June 1944, when a number of prisoners from Arbour Hill were transferred to the camp. Refusing to attach themselves to any of the pre-existing groups within the camp, it was noted that:

> Generally speaking there appears to be a general disunity amongst all the groups and the arrival of the Arbour Hill prisoners seemed to be very much resented by the internees, while the prisoners, on the other hand, have expressed their disapproval on having to leave Arbour Hill.[190]

It was by now obvious that the factional nature of the IRA organization within the camp was having a long-term effect on internee morale.[191] The trauma of the splits was a deeply disheartening experience that persuaded most, upon their release, to sever their connection with the IRA and attempt to 'pick up the pieces of their lives'.[192]

Mindful of this, the first releases from the camp began in the autumn of 1943 as the threat of belligerent invasion decreased and the collapse of the republican movement became more manifest.[193] As was standard practice, internees were released in small groups over an extended period of time, often 'in threes in case we'd cause a riot going out'.[194] In pursuit of this leisurely release policy, the number of internees declined steadily throughout 1943 and 1944. With the defeat of Nazi Germany in May 1945 it was felt prudent to expedite this process and release the remaining 142 internees as quickly as possible. Irrespective of the concerns of the Department of Justice, the Gardaí were able to report that there was 'no crime attributable to the members of the [IRA] since July 1943'. As a result, the government formally ordered the release of all internees in June in order to 'give them a chance to get back to normal lives'.[195] Within two months the camp was emptied, although it was not officially closed until the government divested itself of the powers of internment in 1947. In order to smooth the process, internees were only informed of their impending release in the early morning and ordered to gather up their meagre possessions, before being issued with clothing from army stores in order to disguise their dishevelled appearance.[196] For those requiring transportation to their homes, money for train and bus fares was also provided.[197] Despite in some cases enduring up to five years' incarceration, release was then granted with the minimum of fanfare, as many took the option presented by the government and retired back into private life.

THE DISINTEGRATION OF THE IRA

From the Irish government's perspective, the application of internment had the desired effect as the arrest and incarceration of large numbers of republicans was pivotal in quickly dispersing the IRA threat. In the long term, the instigation of a harsh regime within the camp also had an adverse effect on republican morale, as the internees' experiment in organized opposition to the military authorities disintegrated amid protracted feuding and factionalism. Outside the confines of the Curragh, the remnants of the IRA fared little better as government repression was stepped up. Between 1940 and 1945 the Special Criminal Court was used to obtain 438 convictions for politically motivated offences, while the military tribunal was used to obtain nine. In addition, six IRA members were executed and two others were flogged following conviction for armed robbery. Increased Garda vigilance also resulted in the seizure of over 300 rifles and over 700 short arms. A total of 171 machine guns were also recovered as well as 180 lbs of gelignite and over 600 grenades.[198] The republican movement was also to suffer its own self-imposed setbacks as several members of the IRA in Northern Ireland concluded that Stephen Hayes, the IRA C/S, was a Garda agent.

In June 1941, Seán McCaughey and several of his comrades on the IRA Army Council abducted Hayes and proceeded to interrogate him over the course of several weeks, managing to extract a detailed confession. In this document, apparently written to stave off his impending execution, Hayes claimed that all of the events that the IRA had been involved in since 1935 had been elements of an elaborate conspiracy designed by the government to discredit and destroy the IRA. However, before he could be executed for his 'crimes', McCaughey was arrested following Hayes' escape to a local Garda station, where he demanded protective custody. Although Hayes vigorously protested his innocence of the charges and claimed that the confession was a complete fabrication, the affair remained a matter of controversy within the IRA and served to highlight the growing ineptitude of the organization's leadership.[199] The confession also appeared to have led the Gardaí to the body of Michael Devereux, who had been shot in 1940 upon suspicion of being an informer. Four men were charged with the murder and three were convicted, though only George Plant was executed. In the wake of this affair the IRA continued to fare badly as members of the organization continued to become embroiled in running gun battles with members of the Gardaí. In 1942 three Gardaí were killed, including Sergeant Denis O'Brien, which led to the arrest of the IRA's new C/S, Charles Kerins, in June 1944.[200]

While the authorities were sure he was not directly involved in the murder, they were certain that Kerins had given the order to kill O'Brien. In an effort to finally extinguish the IRA the Irish government sought his execution for the killing. This may not have been entirely necessary however, given the organizational state of the IRA at this time:

> [Kerins was] virtually a lone operator – 'chief of staff of a one man army'. Units across the country had disintegrated and the long-lived IRA infrastructure was broken, disillusionment, disorganization and state repression having taken their toll.[201]

Found guilty and sentenced to death by the Special Criminal Court, a reprieve campaign was immediately mounted under the auspices of Kerry County Council. The Irish authorities immediately clamped down on this campaign, viewing it as a front for an IRA reorganization, and all mention of it was suppressed in the media.[202] The execution went ahead as scheduled and the death of Kerins proved to be a crushing blow to the IRA. With his execution, the position of C/S was vacated as the Army Council fell into abeyance. It was not to be resurrected again until 1948.

The republican movement in Northern Ireland fared little better during this interlude as the unionist government responded to the discovery of an IRA plot to carry out a series of attacks on public property by introducing internment in November 1938.[203] Although only thirty-four men were detained on this occasion, it was enough to prevent any serious attempts at a campaign in Northern Ireland from getting off the ground. That was not to say that the IRA was completely inactive during this period. With the outbreak of war, the organization's northern command, under the leadership of Hugh McAteer from Derry, resolved to take action 'by sabotage of war industries and enemy military objectives by a semi-military force'.[204] What followed in April and May 1940 was a series of thirteen bomb attacks, seven of which were in Belfast, and a number of bank raids the following July. To contain the situation, the Northern Ireland government decided to step up the use of internment and purchased the hulk of an old merchant ship, the *Al Rawdah*, in order to house the increasing number of prisoners. Moored in Strangford Lough, conditions aboard the *Al Rawdah* were so bad that, by November 1940, the bulk of the internees who had been initially housed there had already been transferred to Derry Prison and Crumlin Road Prison in Belfast.[205]

For those who were interned, this period was a particularly dispiriting time, as there was no active campaign organized to press for their release. Owing to wartime privations, food shortages were common and relations between the republican internees and the prison warders were strained. In protest, the internees barricaded themselves into a wing of Derry Prison in December 1940 to draw public attention to their plight. Needless to say, this 'mutiny', as it subsequently became known, was ruthlessly and efficiently put down by the prison authorities amidst widespread allegations of police brutality and internee ill-treatment.[206] In the wake of this affair, the instance of republican prison agitation dropped appreciably, and few other incidents of confrontation were reported. The only high-profile escape attempt occurred in March 1943, when twenty-one prisoners broke out of Derry Prison using a tunnel that had taken over five months to construct. Ironically, these escapees were quickly captured by the Irish army in County Donegal and thereafter interned in the Curragh. In many ways this was a supreme illustration of the problems faced during this period by the IRA, which was now subject to intense repression on both sides of the border.[207]

In 1942, the IRA's northern command sought to kick-start its lapsed sabotage campaign and, on 3 April, a number of republicans killed an RUC constable in Dungannon and severely wounded his colleague. This was followed on Easter Sunday by the capture of six IRA volunteers amid a furious gun battle in Cawnpore Street, Belfast, after the shooting of another RUC constable earlier in the day. While all six men were quickly condemned to death for their involvement in this affair, the sentences of all but one were commuted: Tom Williams was executed on 2 September 1942. This spurred a renewed burst of IRA activity, and RUC barracks in Randalstown, County Antrim and Belleek, County Fermanagh were attacked. An RUC officer and a B-Special were also shot dead in Clady, County Tyrone, and there were reports of numerous shooting incidents throughout west Belfast. In any case, the IRA was effectively muzzled when the Northern Ireland government responded with a new round of internments. Throughout the remainder of September 1942 over 200 men were rounded up in border areas and another 120 suspects were arrested in Belfast. By the end of October there were over 400 republicans in detention.[208]

In contrast to de Valera, who had begun to sanction the release of internees in 1944, the Northern Ireland government did not feel sufficiently secure in its position to start the release of its own detainees until May 1945.[209] That Northern Ireland was entirely free of IRA activity by this stage was, as has been argued by Jonathon Bardon, 'mainly due to the unwavering repression administered by the Dublin government', rather than through the activities of its unionist counterpart.[210] On the strength of Gerald Boland's efforts, the IRA was now without a C/S and a functioning Army Council, and its much vaunted organizational continuity had been disrupted. What remained in Northern Ireland was simply the demoralized rump of an organization that had been effectively neutralized south of the border. Indeed, the term 'northern campaign' is a misnomer, as republican activity in Ulster was born more out of a 'generalized policy' of attacking the RUC than from any type of clear-cut strategy or organized plan.[211] Nevertheless, the intercession of the Northern Ireland government and the manner in which it applied its policy of internment was to compound what had been achieved by de Valera. Of the internees that had been detained during the war, over 80 per cent left the movement upon their release in 1945.[212] With the execution of Charles Kerins in November 1944, the Irish government could feel safe in the assertion that it had succeeded in its aim of finally eliminating the IRA from Irish politics.

3

'A Tireless, Ceaseless Effort':[1]
IRA Reorganization, 1948–1956

The cessation of hostilities in Europe in May 1945 heralded the inauguration of a more moderate approach from the government towards the IRA. While the ending of the European conflagration may have forced a fundamental re-evaluation of Irish internal security policy, a decline in IRA fortunes had been publicly apparent for some time. In 1944, Gerald Boland's triumphant announcement that the IRA was a dead organization was symptomatic of the prevailing mood within Fianna Fáil.[2] During the final months of the war the vast bulk of the internees were discharged, the military tribunal was discreetly wound up, and the Curragh camp was informally closed following the repeal of the EPA.[3] Although content to acknowledge the changed internal security situation, the government remained cautious and took the judicious step of maintaining some of its wartime counter-insurgency measures in reserve, lest the IRA regrouped. In July 1945 the internment provisions of the Offences Against the State (Amendment) Act were reactivated following de Valera's assertion that the IRA was again plotting the murder of members of the Gardaí.[4] Notably, there were no new internments and these powers were revoked by ministerial order in 1947.[5] As for the Special Criminal Court, which had fallen into abeyance following its last sitting in December 1946, the position was less clear-cut.[6]

By neglecting to issue the requisite proclamation abolishing the court, it appeared that the government was content to retain this body in existence, despite the fact that it was not in formal session.[7] In light of the IRA's wartime collapse, instances of politically inspired crime were now being prosecuted before the ordinary courts. Although this was broadly in agreement with the government's revised post-war internal security policy, it did throw up a number of unanticipated administrative difficulties. Following a review by the Department of Finance in June 1948, the renumeration received by the members of the Special Criminal Court was reduced from £450 per annum to £150, on the grounds that it 'had not functioned since 1946'.[8] The court's indeterminate status was further compounded by the early retirement of Colonel Bennet on medical grounds in September 1949 and Colonel Devlin's appointment as quartermaster-general of the defence forces in 1953.[9] Not wishing to draw attention to the continued existence of the court, the government, acting upon the advice of the Attorney-General, deferred filling these vacancies despite the fact that membership of the court was now below the required statutory minimum.[10] This was to leave the court in a continuous state of administrative limbo until its abrupt resuscitation in 1961 (see Chapter 7).

On a more general level, the ending of the war and Ireland's subsequent emergence from the self-imposed exile of neutrality was also to have a profound effect on a polity that had become characterized by an intense cultural and economic malaise. A series of agricultural crises loomed and the wet summer of 1946, followed by the coldest winter on record, created such a shortage of essential food supplies that further rationing was necessary.[11] Emigration continued at around 30,000 per year, unemployment increased and a series of lengthy and disruptive strikes by farm labourers, school teachers and industrial workers prompted the passage of the Industrial Relations Act of 1946 in order to promote more 'harmonious relations between workers and their employers'.[12] The cost of living index was also on the rise, increasing by almost two-thirds between 1939 and 1946. In tackling these matters the government showed little sense of urgency and attempted to offset these increases in inflation with the imposition of numerous wage standstill orders.[13] A series of scandals, including the controversy surrounding the sale of Locke's distillery in 1947, helped to further undermine public confidence in de Valera's government.[14]

Neutrality had insulated Irish society and a deep sense of isolation from the outside world was further compounded by the rigours of wartime censorship. The war also made it clear in Ireland that the concept of national sovereignty was no longer absolute. For a small neutral state, which was heavily dependent on others to help maintain the flow of essential supplies, the war proved to be a graphic illustration of the mutual dependence of nations, thereby vitiating previously held notions of self-sufficiency.[15] In response, de Valera sought to end Ireland's diplomatic isolation with an unsuccessful bid to join the United Nations (UN). Fortunately, this did not result in foreign policy stagnation as the Irish state was in a position to join a number of UN-sponsored bodies such as the World Health Organization (WHO) and the Education, Scientific and Cultural Organization (UNESCO). The diplomatic service was also expanded to include representatives in Sweden, Argentina and Australia, and in 1949 Ireland became a founding member of the Council of Europe.[16]

The divergence of the two Irish states was also becoming more manifest as the pursuit of neutrality served to further consolidate the division of the island. The shared experience of war had created a renewed bond between London and Belfast that was emphasized by Dublin's apparent refusal to stand by Britain during its hour of need. The successful execution of neutrality also proved to be an unequivocal demonstration of Irish autonomy, thereby removing any doubts as to the independence of the state.[17] Partition was now the final unresolved nationalist grievance, and the issue once again came to dominate the domestic political agenda. Public disillusionment with Fianna Fáil intensified. For an electorate seeking a more dynamic and proactive approach, de Valera's habitual rhetoric decrying the iniquities of partition was proving to be an insufficient panacea with which to mollify nationalist aspirations.[18] In November 1945 the first manifestation of this popular discontent found expression with the foundation of a parliamentary protest movement known as the All-Ireland Anti-Partition League (APL).[19] Although its existence was an implied criticism of de Valera's own anti-partition strategy, its failure to develop an effective constituency organization was to ensure that it posed little threat to Fianna Fáil's continued political hegemony. From de Valera's perspective, the emergence of a radical republican party named Clann na Poblachta, following the death of Seán McCaughey after a prolonged hunger strike, was a more menacing development.[20]

THE SEÁN MCCAUGHEY HUNGER STRIKE

In April 1946 republican prisoners began to step up their efforts to resist the Fianna Fáil government's attempt to depoliticize their actions, when Seán McCaughey embarked on a hunger strike aimed at securing his unconditional release.[21] Incarcerated for his part in the 'Hayes Affair', McCaughey, together with a number of other republicans including Tomás MacCurtain, were held in Portlaoise Prison, where they were classed as 'ordinary criminals'. Most republicans traditionally railed against this treatment and refused to obey the prison regime as part of a prolonged campaign orchestrated by MacCurtain aimed at securing prisoner of war status. Rather than wear a prison uniform, MacCurtain and his fellow inmates clothed themselves in smocks fashioned from blankets and refused letters because their prison numbers were written on the envelopes. Refusal to obey prison rules was punished by a withdrawal of privileges such as access to letters, visitors and newspapers. They were also held in solitary confinement, were not permitted to speak to one another and were forbidden to exercise in the open air.[22] McCaughey, who was singled out for particularly harsh treatment, spent over three years in continuous solitary confinement, where he had to be attended at one point for a nervous breakdown.[23] The arbitrary release from the Curragh, in 1945, of a number of his comrades who had been serving sentences for murder was the deciding factor in pushing McCaughey into making his protest.

Five days into his fast, when it became apparent that the prison authorities had no intention of conceding to his demands, McCaughey dramatically ratcheted up his action by also refusing water.[24] News coverage of the affair was initially sparse, possibly owing to the slow recovery of the newspaper industry after years of wartime censorship.[25] The first mention in the press did not actually occur until 29 April when the *Irish Independent* took note of the fact that McCaughey's protest had been inspired by a demand for 'political status'.[26] A week later the *Irish Press* reported on a public demonstration in Dublin seeking the transfer of the republican prisoners in Portlaoise to the Curragh, where they would be accorded 'political rights'. Invariably, as his condition began to deteriorate, updates on McCaughey's health began to appear with increasing regularity. On 9 May it was stated that he was unable to speak and that 'the end was expected at any time'. The Portlaoise prison doctor confirmed this, when he informed McCaughey's family that his death 'was imminent'.[27] In the intervening period, his protest had captured the public imagination and on 8 May a petition signed by 'several members of Dáil Éireann and Seanad Éireann' was presented to de Valera urging McCaughey's immediate release.[28] That evening the Gardaí baton-charged a group of protesters who were attempting to march on Leinster House and the following day over 300 turf cutters in the Phoenix Park went on strike in protest at McCaughey's continued detention.[29]

Unmoved by these displays of public solidarity, Boland reiterated the government's policy in respect of republican prisoners, claiming that the question of 'people on hunger strike' had been definitively settled in 1940. He was confirmed in this assertion by de Valera, when he stated that the government 'could not permit prisoners to secure their release by hunger strike'.[30] After enduring over twenty-three days of his protest, McCaughey eventually suffered cardiac failure and died on 11 May.[31] During the subsequent inquest, Seán MacBride's charged cross-examination of the Portlaoise prison doctor, D.J. Duane, was the source of much controversy when he asked the doctor if he would keep a dog in the same conditions in which McCaughey was incarcerated. Famously, Duane replied that he would not, prompting MacBride to dramatically withdraw from the inquest in protest.[32] With the release of McCaughey's remains for burial, a large funeral procession headed by 'a pipe band and an advance guard of ex-colleagues' left for his native Belfast following Requiem Mass in the Franciscan church on Merchant's Quay, Dublin.[33] Although a large number of RUC officers were deployed in Belfast the next day, the occasion of McCaughey's burial in the city did allow for a very public articulation of a culture of resistance intrinsic to republicanism and common to both sides of the border.[34] Moreover, the publicity afforded to the affair was to ensure that, for the first time, the conditions in which republicans were imprisoned was to emerge into the public domain.

The government was immediately inundated with calls for a public inquiry into Irish prison conditions, which were strongly resisted by Boland on the grounds that conditions in Ireland 'were well known to compare favourably with those in any other country'.[35] In fact, he went so far as to dismiss the hunger strike as a 'publicity stunt', claiming that, were it not for McCaughey and his fast, the IRA would have been 'a flop'. De Valera, in defence of his beleaguered Minister for Justice, added that 'If we gave way on the matter of the clothes then it was going to be on another matter and another matter until the prisoner got exactly what he wanted – immunity.'[36] Privately, the government felt justified in its position and had noted in a 1940 memorandum how the treatment of 'political prisoners' in Ireland was superior to that meted out to prisoners of a similar class in many other countries.[37] At the same time, de Valera's refusal to yield to McCaughey had further weakened the power of the hunger strike, paving the way for a more magnanimous approach to the question of the remaining republican prisoners. In December 1946 the sentences of twenty-four of these prisoners were remitted under section thirty-three of the OASA, to be followed over the coming weeks by the release of five more on health grounds.[38]

CLANN NA POBLACHTA AND RESURGENT REPUBLICANISM

In many ways, the death of McCaughey was to serve as a springboard for the various disparate political elements that would eventually coalesce around Seán MacBride and his call for the formation of a new constitutional republican political platform. Public disillusion with the pedestrian performance of a stale government had few viable outlets at this time as the formal parliamentary opposition found itself in considerable disarray. The previous general election in 1944 had proved to be an unmitigated disaster for both the Labour party, which had split over a bitter internal dispute, and a lethargic Fine Gael, which won just thirty seats – its worst electoral performance since its foundation in 1933.[39] Against this backdrop, the portents for the formation of what would become Clann na Poblachta were good, as the results of the 1945 presidential election indicated the presence of a marked anti-Fianna Fáil mentality among a jaded electorate. Vote transfers from the independent republican candidate, Dr Patrick MacCartan, went by a margin of over four to one to Seán MacEoin of Fine Gael, rather than to Fianna Fáil's Seán T. O'Kelly, who eventually won the election. A decade earlier such transfers would have been inconceivable.[40]

Encouraged by these developments, and outraged by the treatment of McCaughey, MacBride and several like-minded individuals, including Con Lehane, Noel Hartnett and Peadar Cowan, formally launched Clann na Poblachta at a press conference in Dublin in July 1946.[41] Espousing a mix of 'republicanism allied to social reform', this party boasted an executive that also included a number of other prominent republicans and ex-IRA men, including Michael Fitzpatrick and James Hannigan.[42] In deference to MacBride, his relative youth, boundless ambition, and undoubted administrative abilities and forensic legal skills were a central asset to the party, and it comes as no surprise to note that he was also unveiled as leader.[43] At any rate, his selection as leader also provided the final unifying bond around which an otherwise motley group of individuals could combine.[44] Propounding a policy that the party argued would achieve full employment, Clann promoted the concept of a comprehensive social insurance system and advocated the introduction of widespread reforms aimed at eliminating political patronage.[45] Needless to say, the party also held strong views on 'the national question' and preached a more traditional republican dispensation by declaring its ultimate aim to be 'the reintegration of the whole of Ireland as a Republic'.[46]

In many respects, Clann possessed an appeal similar to that of Fianna Fáil in 1932. This potential prompted the party to set about quickly establishing a nationwide network of branches and members. This paid immediate dividends, as Clann went on to stage one of the biggest political upsets in Irish electoral history when it secured two seats at the expense of Fianna Fáil in a series of by-elections in 1947.[47] The key to this remarkable success lay in the fact that after sixteen years of Fianna Fáil government contemporary circumstances within the economy and society were conducive to major political change. In particular, Clann's brand of vibrant republicanism threatened to poach much of Fianna Fáil's traditional constituency, while the party at large was able to act as a catalyst for various disaffected groups within Irish society.[48] According to the experienced TD James Dillon, Clann proved to be a 'very convenient landing ground for people who all their lives had been stalwart Fianna Fáil supporters, but who were now disillusioned and did not wish to commit the fearful treason of voting for Fine Gael'.[49]

In a blatant attempt to ward off this threat to his republican flank, de Valera responded by calling a snap general election in February 1948. Clann justifiably began to take itself seriously as a potential party of government but was somewhat optimistic in fielding ninety-three candidates. For an organization with limited resources a lengthy four week election campaign was to work to its disadvantage and, although the widely projected landslide did not take place, the party won a disappointing, if respectable, ten seats.[50] It can be suggested that Clann's major political legacy was to break Fianna Fáil's monopoly on power with its subsequent entry into government as part of an unlikely coalition with Fine Gael, Clann na Talmhan, a divided Labour party and an assortment of independents.[51] Based upon the negative consensus of excluding de Valera from office, this inter-party government, as it was widely known, was to remain in power until it collapsed in the aftermath of the 'mother and child scandal' of 1951.[52]

Internally, the party's decision to enter a coalition government headed by a Fine Gael Taoiseach, John A. Costello, was regarded with deep disdain by much of its hard-line republican rank and file. Although many on the party's national executive were trenchantly opposed to this move, only Seán McCool was prepared to resign over the issue. On the other hand, the position of a party in government that was broadly sympathetic to the aims of the IRA was to reap dividends for a resurgent republican movement throughout the early 1950s.[53] Intent on maintaining the unity of his nascent coalition,

Costello sought to placate the hard-line republican element within Clann by instructing the Minister for Justice, Seán MacEoin, to discuss the thorny issue of the remaining political prisoners with his new cabinet colleague and Minister for External Affairs, Seán MacBride. During the course of this conversation, which took place shortly after the election of the government, MacBride claimed that both Costello and MacEoin had indicated their willingness to release all the remaining prisoners and gave him a list of names to go through. According to MacBride, he spent several hours weeding out all the borderline cases that were not politically motivated, before returning it to MacEoin.[54] Costello moved quickly on MacBride's recommendations and in February 1948 the last remaining prisoners were released, bringing to an end the final instalment of the IRA's disastrous wartime interlude.[55]

In contrast with Clann na Poblachta, Sinn Féin was in the midst of a near terminal decline, precipitated by the IRA's decision in 1925 to sever its links with the party and by its continued reliance on a negative policy of parliamentary abstention. In 1941 Sinn Féin, which was in dire financial straits, was compelled to initiate legal proceedings aimed at securing the ownership of funds that had been lodged in the High Court in 1924 by the Sinn Féin treasurers in Ireland and the United States. The dispute over the ownership of this money had arisen in the wake of the Civil War split when the party divided into pro- and anti-Treaty factions. The assets of the party, which amounted to £8,610 at the time, quickly became a bone of contention between the two groups, as this not only represented a significant financial windfall but was also a matter of considerable symbolic importance. Ownership of the funds enabled the possessors to portray themselves as the true successors to the original Sinn Féin party, thereby legitimating their claim to inherit the Irish revolutionary tradition.[56] Ultimately, the Sinn Féin action was unsuccessful and, in his judgment, Justice Kingsmill Moore concluded that he 'could not substantiate any claim to the property of the members of the organization existing in 1922' as there was no legal continuity between these bodies.[57]

This proved to be a significant body blow to a largely moribund organization and in April 1945 the party leadership set about a process of reorganization with the establishment of a special coordinating committee for the purpose of raising funds.[58] This activity quickly came to the notice of the Special Branch, where it was noted that 'an attempt to reorganize the IRA under Sinn Féin *Cumainn* [sic] is at present under way'.⁵⁹ A number of newsletters were also in circulation, including *An Dé*, *The Sinn Féin Bulletin* and the Cork-based *An Claidheamh*, which declared in its inaugural issue that 'we ... are about to take up the struggle with renewed energy for the freedom of this country'.⁶⁰ Department of Justice officials closely monitored these developments for an appropriate opportunity to charge 'the Sinn Féin Committee' under the OASA.⁶¹ In respect of the party's offices, it was deemed 'inadvisable at this stage to make a closing order'. Therefore, apart from a series of minor incidents, including the display of a black flag during the presidential inauguration of Seán T. O'Kelly in June 1945, the continued quiescence of Sinn Féin seemed to justify this approach.⁶²

IRA REVIVAL

In the wake of the McCaughey hunger strike the activities of the militant republican movement remained largely subdued, as several abortive attempts were made to reorganize the IRA. The first of these was frustrated by the Gardaí in March 1947, with the arrest of ten prominent republican activists following a meeting held in the Ardee bar in Dublin. On this occasion, the suspicions of the authorities were raised when several notable members of the IRA, including Cathal Goulding and John J. McGirl, were observed entering the premises. After placing the bar under observation, it was decided to arrest the suspects as they left the meeting at 1.45 a.m. During the course of their raid, the Gardaí seized a document in the pocket of Patrick Fleming, which read:

> This meeting composed of representatives of Cork, Dublin, Leitrim and Mayo ... resolves that the surviving members of the 1938/39 executive be summoned to a meeting for the purpose of bringing the executive up to full strength.⁶³

This initial setback only served to delay the IRA reorganization and, following the expiation of relatively short prison sentences, those involved redoubled their efforts.⁶⁴ With the release of Anthony Magan and Michael Conway, a new IRA Army Council was elected, which in turn appointed Willie McGuinness as a new interim C/S. A full-time organizer was also appointed with instructions to contact republican sympathisers and appoint local O/Cs.⁶⁵

A certain amount of confusion seemed to attend these early efforts and in May 1947 the Special Branch received reports of a meeting called to consider the establishment of a new 'national newspaper to represent republican views'.[66] The impetus behind this move originated with a group of former internees including Tomas Ó Broin, James O'Kelly and James Doyle and the meeting itself was held under the auspices of the 'Seán McCaughey' *Cumann* of Sinn Féin.[67] Invariably, the 'pitiful plight' of the IRA was discussed, with one delegate, evidently unaware of the reconstitution of the IRA Army Council, requesting 'that some authority be given ... to reorganize or form a council as a number of young men were anxious to carry on'. As many present felt that the meeting was not sufficiently representative of the IRA, it was decided to shelve this proposal, as those in attendance proceeded with the more pressing business of appointing a committee tasked with organizing the launch of a new republican newspaper.[68] Subsequent meetings held to organize the publication of this organ inevitably reinvigorated the debate on the state of the contemporary IRA organization. Therefore, throughout 1947 and 1948 the reorganization of the IRA and the proposed launch of an independent republican newspaper went, in some respects, hand in hand.

In June 1947 the IRA made its public reappearance when Frank Driver gave the oration at the annual Wolfe Tone commemoration in Bodenstown, County Kildare.[69] In the background, preparations continued for the launch of a monthly newspaper, with the calling of a further meeting in an effort to make progress on the matter. However, Patrick McLogan sparked controversy when he suggested that the republican movement should start a civilian organization and

> give up the idea of forming fours, drilling etc ... [because] the first time they would parade or step over the line, the CID would get evidence and give the government the chance to put them out of existence.

Unsurprisingly, allegations of treachery abounded, with one delegate, Seán McCool, expounding the virtues of physical force. Although he received 'a great reception from the majority of those present', it was noted that the meeting broke up without any concrete proposals being put forward and that McCool and McLogan parted on bad terms.[70] In any event, *The United Irishman* was finally launched in May 1948 with the help of £60 provided by James Doyle. Notably, officials from the Department of Justice, anxious to examine it for seditious content, snapped up several copies of its inaugural issue.[71]

Confounding official predictions that it would not last long 'like many others of its kind in the past', the paper reached an estimated peak circulation of 139,000 copies per month in 1954.[72] While the government had the power to suppress the publication, it was felt that the journal had very little influence and that 'the best policy was to ignore its utterances, even when they are seditious'.[73] Initially, the paper was composed mainly of articles decrying Ireland's perceived economic subservience to the British empire. The right to the ownership of private property was jealously defended, but qualified by the belief that the state 'may deprive [an individual] of any property in excess'.[74] However, the paper was quickly appropriated as a mouthpiece by the IRA leadership, whereupon its tenor began to assume a more militant character.[75] Notices exhorting readers to join the IRA began to appear on a regular basis, as well as various pieces documenting the 'objects of *Oglaigh na hÉireann*'. In May 1949 the paper carried the full transcript of an IRA statement and in September the editors were feeling sufficiently confident in their position to state that 'force of arms' was one of the means by which the IRA was endeavouring to achieve its goals.[76]

In order to formalize the emerging new leadership cadre and draft a new set of viable policies for the organization, the conducting of a full army convention was a high priority for the IRA during this period. Owing to the continued vigilance of the Special Branch, which appeared to have had considerable success in infiltrating the IRA throughout this period, the organization of such a large-scale event without attracting any unwarranted attention was proving to be particularly difficult. The suspicions of the authorities had already been raised in May 1947 when a 'social evening' was held in the offices of the newly established Republican Prisoners Release Association (RPRA) in North Frederick Street, Dublin.[77] The site was kept under strict observation and several leading republicans, including Magan and Conway, were known to have attended the event. From their vantage point outside, Special Branch officers, who were understandably unwilling to enter the premises, were unable to determine if a convention had taken place.[78] In fact, the long-awaited convention, attended by a quorum of fifty delegates, did not actually take place until September 1948.[79] Magan emerged as C/S in place of McGuinness and a new Army Council, which included Patrick McLogan and Tomás MacCurtain, was elected.[80]

At this convention a number of crucial decisions were taken that were to have a profound effect on the future direction and conduct of the IRA. It was decided to end the IRA's political isolation and re-establish Sinn Féin as its ancillary. As the party had been reduced to 'a few ... *cumainn* in Dublin, one in Cork and one in Glasgow', the IRA's move to re-establish its link was broadly welcomed as several prominent IRA volunteers began to emerge as senior figures on its Ard Comhairle. This takeover was completed at the 1950 Ard Fheis, when Patrick McLogan replaced the long-serving Margaret Buckley as president and Charlie Murphy, the IRA's A/G, was elected as the party's general secretary.[81] The 1948 convention also recognized that continued militancy in the south was counter-productive and it was agreed that there should be no military operations within the borders of the Irish Republic. Instead, the IRA sought to focus its attention on the British presence in Ireland and a resolution was endorsed calling for the prosecution of a military campaign against British forces in Northern Ireland.[82]

This decision was of fundamental importance, as it essentially amounted to a more pragmatic recognition of the existence of prevailing political realities. The background that inspired such a fundamental shift in position was reflected by the growing trend within republicanism to differentiate between the two prevailing systems of government on the island of Ireland. While Britain was seen to be maintaining direct control over Northern Ireland, it was accepted that the south enjoyed a certain measure of autonomy which had been augmented by the constitutional reforms spearheaded by de Valera during the 1930s.[83] This position was to pose a significant dilemma for many republicans and was neatly summed up by Sinn Féin's *National Unity and Independence Programme*:

> The difference in the existing positions [between the northern and southern governments] ... makes the problem with which republicans are confronted more complicated and in many respects more difficult to solve. It presents them with the immediate problem of deciding whether a single line of policy can be formulated suitable to general application all over Ireland, or whether a different line will be necessary in respect of the two areas of existing government.[84]

The adoption of a northern campaign combined with the movement's renunciation of violence in the south, thereby effectively signalling the end of the IRA's struggle to overthrow the Treaty settlement in the south, was in many respects the logical resolution of this debate. Essentially, the movement had shifted from its primary aim of creating the 'real Republic', declared in 1916, to a straightforward emphasis on winning back 'the six counties' from the British.[85]

With control of *The United Irishman* and Sinn Féin firmly cemented, the IRA began to adopt a more visible public profile. At the 1949 Bodenstown commemoration, Cristoir O'Neill issued a call for recruits and announced the IRA's intention of prosecuting 'a successful military campaign ... in the six counties'.[86] In January 1950 Sinn Féin held a public meeting in Dublin that attracted over 200 people and, in March, proceeded to distribute republican literature at an international rugby match between Ireland and Wales in Belfast.[87] The widely held perception that the IRA had recommenced drilling with arms was also to become a contentious political matter when Fianna Fáil TD Frank Aiken raised the issue in the Dáil. During the course of a heated debate on the matter the Taoiseach refused to issue an appeal to the IRA to disband, on the grounds that the recent passage of the Republic of Ireland Act had effectively taken the gun out of Irish politics. Aiken pressed his case and asked the Minister for Justice, Seán MacEoin, if he was aware that arms had been publicly fired at a series of funerals in Dublin and Clare. MacEoin replied that, while he was aware of the incidents in question, he felt, given the 'present peaceful state of the county', that it was best to ignore them.[88] At this the matter rested but, despite its relatively trivial nature, the subject matter of this debate was indicative of the bearing that the increased emphasis on partition was having on Irish society.

THE REPUBLIC OF IRELAND ACT

The change of government occasioned by the rise of Clann na Poblachta in 1948 was perhaps the key factor in manoeuvring the partition issue into a more ascendant position. As part of its northern policy, Clann proposed the opening of the Oireachtas to northern representatives, claiming that it offered the basis for an anti-partitionist unanimity.[89] Furthermore, MacBride, in his capacity as the newly installed Minister for External Affairs, dramatically spurned the opportunity to join the North Atlantic Treaty Organization (NATO) on the grounds that the continuance of partition precluded Ireland from taking its 'rightful place in the affairs of Europe'.[90] In 1948, determined not to be outdone by the vociferous republicanism of Clann, de Valera undertook an extended anti-partition tour to the United States, Australia and New Zealand.[91] Nevertheless, it was to fall to the inter-party government in 1948 to repeal the External Relations Act with the enactment of the Republic of Ireland Act. This legislation, which involved Ireland leaving the Commmonwealth, formally came into force on 1 April

1949.⁹² In many ways, this was a particularly contentious move, not least because its critics claimed that it was announced by the Taoiseach on a visit to Canada, without prior cabinet approval. Although Costello defended this decision on the grounds that it was 'an instrument of domestic peace [and] national unity', the reality was to prove otherwise as the passage of this act evidently served to copper-fasten partition.⁹³

In London, these developments were regarded with unease as Lord Rugby, the British representative in Dublin, reported that:

> It is difficult to see much more in all this than a cheap score in party politics and personal antagonisms ... The true rivalry in Irish politics lay between a Commonwealth party and the Separatists. All now, willy-nilly, are Separatists. Henceforth the only rivalry in Irish politics is to outrival each other in the virulence of their anti-partition campaign.⁹⁴

On 20 November 1948 the British Prime Minister, Clement Attlee, invited his Northern Irish counterpart, Sir Basil Brooke, to stay at Chequers in order to discuss the situation. During the course of this meeting Brooke repeatedly impressed upon Attlee the need to focus on the Irish government's objectives in relation to partition, and called for an assurance that the constitutional position of Northern Ireland would not be affected by Ireland's decision to leave the Commonwealth.⁹⁵ After further consideration Brooke began to feel that a simple public assurance would not suffice and pressed Attlee to pass legislation that would 'provide more effectively for the proper functioning of the parliament and government of Northern Ireland'.⁹⁶ The Prime Minister relented and in January 1949 authorized a draft of the proposed Ireland Bill that contained a clause affirming that 'in no event would Northern Ireland cease to be part of the United Kingdom except with the consent of the parliament of Northern Ireland'.⁹⁷

In the face of this impending legislation, the Irish government reacted to the news of a snap general election in the north by convening an all-party conference with the aim of floating a fund to aid the election of anti-partition candidates. The government's perceived interference in northern affairs only served to further solidify the unionist camp and Brooke won a resounding victory.⁹⁸ In May the full text of the Ireland Bill was published, prompting the government to dispatch an *aide-méemoire* protesting the enactment of legislation 'purporting to confirm the unjust partition of Ireland'.⁹⁹ Despite Irish remonstrations, the passage of the act on 5 June 1949 served to highlight the government's continued inability to influence British policy on Northern Ireland. For many, the whole affair was a stark reminder of the limits of constitutional action and confirmed the widespread belief that the achievement of sovereignty took precedence over the aspiration to unity.[100] As a result, widespread dissatisfaction with the government's Northern Irish policy quickly became manifest in what appeared to be a growing trend that saw the use of force to end partition as a viable alternative to constitutional agitation.[101]

In early 1950 a former member of Clann na Poblachta, Captain Peadar Cowan, attempted to tap into this popular sentiment, when he started to organize his own private army to take back the north. In February he placed a number of advertisements in the morning papers stressing that 'Talk has never achieved anything, and will never achieve anything. Action, not talk, will end Partition.' At a meeting in Fairview in Dublin in May, Cowan reiterated that his aim was not the piecemeal occupations of territory or acts of sabotage: 'The force will be so organized that it will move across the border and take possession of the six counties within a day.' About 800 people attended this particular meeting, at which fifty men marched in military formation.[102] As ever, de Valera was particularly attuned to the subtleties of the situation and used the occasion of 'a long and friendly chat' with Lord Rugby, to 'express his anxiety at the tension developing on the question of the border'. Cowan's abortive and short-lived attempts to organize a volunteer force only served to confirm de Valera's view that it was simply a matter of time before 'a physical force group would enter the field'.[103]

ARMS RAIDS AND SPLITS

Actuated by 'anti-partition sentiments and influences', the reorganization of the IRA continued apace, with regular meetings of the Army Council taking place in various premises across Dublin, including the Castle Hotel in Gardiners Row, 62 Serpentine Avenue and 22 Nottingham Street.[104] With an estimated membership of approximately 200 in Dublin and 'not more than fifty' in Cork, the IRA also began to step up its recruiting campaign and initiated a drive for funds 'both through direct solicitation and through social events'.[105] Generally speaking, typical IRA recruits were young men in their late teens who were motivated by a desire to emulate the ongoing anti-colonial guerrilla struggles of the day, such as the National Liberation Front (FLN) uprising in Algeria, the *Enosis* movement in Cyprus and the Mau Mau insurgency in Kenya.[106] More often than not, these individuals were urban workers who came from stable family backgrounds with a strong republican tradition. In contrast to their northern counterparts, most southern recruits tended to have a lofty opinion of themselves as liberators, who identified with the notion of the British army as the enemy. On the other hand, northern aggression provoked by perceived Protestant discrimination generally tended to be directed towards the organs of government in Northern Ireland.[107]

Information received by the newly reinstalled Fianna Fáil government in 1952 indicated that 'a good bit of drilling had been going on in the northwest, particularly in the counties contiguous to the border' and that the IRA had been gradually accumulating a number of small arms. There was also 'abundant evidence' of widespread indoor training being carried out in the Dublin area, as well as the holding of a number of 'weekend camps and firing practices' in the Dublin mountains.[108] For an organization hoping to affect a large-scale military campaign, the shortcomings of its limited arsenal was proving to be of major concern. In an effort to counter this obvious shortage of heavy ordnance, the Army Council authorized the Derry unit to undertake an ambitious raid on the Territorial Army barracks in Ebrington in June 1951.[109] The raid, which took place in broad daylight, was small in scale: the party managed to escape with twenty Lee Enfield rifles, two Bren light machine guns, six BESA 7.92mm belt-fed machine guns and a quantity of ammunition.[110] Seeking to downplay this embarrassing incident, a statement released by British military headquarters in Northern Ireland declared that only 'a small number of arms and a small quantity of ammunition ... are missing from Ebrington Barracks'. Nevertheless, security was immediately stepped up along the border and 'all vehicular traffic in Derry was stopped and scrutinized'. When these measures failed to apprehend the raiders, the operation was fruitlessly extended to 'other areas in Northern Ireland'.[111] Enthused by this success, *The United Irishman* praised 'the men who carried out the operation for the foresight and efficiency displayed throughout' and declared that the weapons would be best used to 'drive the British army out of Ireland'.[112]

The proficiency of the raiders and the relative ease of their escape proved to be a much needed shot in the arm for an organization that had hitherto been lacking in morale and was instrumental in encouraging the Army Council to authorize a second raid in July 1953. The target, on this occasion, was the British army's officer training corps school in Felsted, Essex, which was successfully infiltrated by a three-man team of volunteers comprised of Cathal Goulding, Manus Canning and Seán Stephenson.[113] In effecting their escape, the raiders overloaded their van with a haul of over 'ninety-eight rifles, eight Bren guns, ten Sten guns, one PIAT, one Browning machine gun and six two-inch mortars'. Inevitably, the heavily laden vehicle attracted unwanted police attention, resulting in their arrest.[114] Charged with stealing the weapons 'with intent to enable other persons by means thereof to endanger life', they were returned for trial at the Hertfordshire assizes, where, in traditional republican style, they refused to enter a plea.[115] Goulding quickly accepted responsibility for his comrades and imprudently declared that the weapons were to be used by 'under-armed units in Ireland'. The three were found guilty and sentenced to eight years' imprisonment. The loss of Goulding was especially important, as he had been heavily involved in orchestrating the IRA's reorganization.[116] While the entire affair initially appeared to be an unmitigated disaster, it did occasion an unexpected amount of publicity for the IRA as Goulding's comments were widely reported in the media.[117]

Perhaps the most important development during this period was the IRA's reacquaintance with its overseas benefactors in the American Clan na nGael organization. This body, which had been effectively shut down by the Federal Bureau of Investigation (FBI) during the Second World War, was formally reorganized in March 1946 following a convention of its various branches.[118] Although Clan na nGael was numerically strong in New York, Chicago and Philadelphia, the FBI could confidently report that the IRA had not been engaged in any activity within the USA since 1947 and that there were no 'recent references' to the IRA in conjunction with Clan na nGael.[119] In fact, a lack of funding was proving to be a constant problem for the republican movement, as evidenced by the recurring appearance of notices in *The United Irishman* exhorting subscribers to settle their accounts on time.[120] Considering that this paper was retailing at only three pence a copy and that not more than three advertisements appeared in each issue, the authorities quickly began to suspect that it was in receipt of an external financial subsidy.[121] The sudden appearance in 1951 of a series of articles carrying details of various social events hosted by Clan na nGael heightened these suspicions and seemed to indicate that relations between the IRA and this organization had been amicably restored.[122] The subsequent disclosure of a series of peculiar visits to Ireland by a number of prominent Irish-Americans throughout late 1951 further served to confirm this viewpoint. The first of these visits occurred in September 1951, when Patrick O'Mahoney of New York and Thomas McMonagle of Philadelphia attended, on behalf of Clan na nGael, the unveiling of a Seán Russell memorial in Dublin. While McMonagle took a prominent part in the proceedings, it fell to O'Mahoney to deliver the oration, in which he assured onlookers that the IRA and Sinn Féin 'would never be alone in [the] fight [to free Ireland]'.[123] When reporting on the matter, G2 army intelligence also noted that the visit had been sponsored by the IRA Army Council and confidently surmised that O'Mahoney and McMonagle were 'undoubtedly the bearer of funds for that organization'.[124] Further incidents of this kind followed and in November G2 was alerted to the arrival of 'two Jews ... bearing introductions to the IRA from Clan na nGael'. During the course of a meeting with an IRA delegation, these individuals expressed the hope that they would be afforded an opportunity to discuss the subject of financial support for the IRA. Surprisingly, these overtures were rejected, leaving G2 to speculate that perhaps these individuals were members of 'some international organization from behind the Iron Curtain which might be interested in promoting trouble in this country'. This may well explain why the IRA refused to treat with them, given its avowed anti-communist stance.[125]

A number of weeks later this episode had a curious postscript with the arrival of Gerard O'Reilly from New York. Well known 'in labour circles' as a 'former member of Clan na nGael and the IRA', O'Reilly quickly made contact with the republican movement as well as with various 'communist and left wing leaders' in Dublin. While it ostensibly appeared that the purpose of his visit was to deliver an undisclosed sum of money to the Irish Workers League, G2 began to suspect financial dealings with the IRA but was unable to confirm if he had conducted business with that organization. Suitably baffled as to the purpose of this visit and the circumstances surrounding the visit of the 'Jewish delegation', G2 continued to monitor republican dealings abroad as contact with Clan na nGael was unquestionably stepped up.[126] In January 1951 copies of *The United Irishman* were distributed at the 'Annual Ball of the New York District Clubs of the Clan na nGael', while in April an invitation was issued to former IRA members resident in New York to join the Clan.[127] While the exact date upon which this contact was restored remains unclear, it was quite obvious that the nascent IRA reorganization was now being funded, in part, by financial contributions from the United States.[128]

Consequently, with a newspaper in circulation, its control over Sinn Féin cemented and the influx of regular financial aid from the USA, the IRA had managed to pull itself back from the precipice.

For some, however, this reorganization was not proceeding as rapidly as hoped for and high levels of secrecy, coupled with Magan's uncompromising style of leadership, prompted several volunteers to establish their own rival organizations. The first of these was formed in 1949 when Seamus Doyle established an organization initially knownm as An Rosc Catha, but later renamed Arm na Saoirse. Apparently dissatisfied with the direction of the IRA, the object of this exercise was to force the republican leadership to adopt 'a more virile and active policy ... particularly in regard to the border question'. Ironically, an internal power struggle resulted in Doyle's ousting from the leadership by a group comprised of Richard Timmons, Raymond Kenna and Jasper Hornibrook.[129] At the same time, another, lesser-known, organization styling itself the Irish Republican Brotherhood (IRB) surfaced when it claimed responsibility for an attempted bomb attack on the British embassy in January 1951.[130] Faced with these threats to its hegemony, the IRA responded robustly by kidnapping Hornibrook.[131] Unwilling to submit to this attempt at intimidation, Arm na Saoirse remained resolute, forcing the IRA to reach an accommodation with them, recognizing the legitimacy of their organization.[132] As for the IRB, this body was quickly subsumed into the IRA following a series of meetings between both organizations.

A far more damaging rupture was occasioned by the expulsion of the maverick Liam Kelly in 1951 for planning an operation without the consent of the Army Council. As 'a figure of some standing in East Tyrone and nationalist circles generally', Kelly simply reorganized his local power base and founded a military organization known as Saor Uladh. Influenced by the formation of Clann na Poblachta and particularly by Seán MacBride, Kelly also established a new political organization called Fianna Uladh, which argued for an end to abstentionism in the south and a concentration of republican effort against the state of Northern Ireland. Impressed by Kelly, MacBride pressed Costello, in return for Clann na Poblachta's parliamentary support, to ensure that the votes of several Fine Gael councillors would secure Kelly's election to the Seanad in 1954.[133] As a senator he addressed the chamber once, reiterating his recognition of the Constitution of the Republic of Ireland and his preparedness to work within its framework to extend its operation to the whole of Ireland.[134]

The public restatement of such views was to ensure that Saor

Uladh's relationship with the IRA rapidly soured, particularly as Kelly's organization began to engage in militant activity in Northern Ireland. In 1955 Saor Uladh was to become embroiled in major controversy following the death of Connie Green, a member of the organization, during an attack on an RUC barracks in Roslea, County Fermanagh.[135] In the days following the attack, local speculation had it that the coroner for north County Monaghan had made an order for the burial of Green following the convening of an inquest in a farmhouse. Under intense media pressure, the government confirmed these rumours by admitting that no attempt was made at this inquest to determine the exact circumstances of Green's death. Furthermore, the coroner concluded his proceedings without any adjournment or any effort being made to uncover the identity of the remains.[136] It also emerged that Kelly sought to have Green buried clandestinely, but the doctor who had been called to attend to his wounds insisted that this would not be possible. As a result, Kelly telephoned an unnamed member of Clann na Poblachta, who arranged for the inquest to take place.[137]

Unionist opinion in the north was outraged as Brooke accused the Irish government of being 'morally responsible' for the attack by reason of its failure 'to interfere in the activities of illegal organizations'.[138] In response, Costello delivered a strongly worded speech in the Dáil in which he attributed the attack to the IRA and placed the blame for the upsurge in violence firmly at the door of the British government. He also appealed to all unlawful organizations to end their activities and warned that if this appeal were not met the government would use 'all the powers and forces at [its] disposal to bring such activities effectively to an end'.[139] Fearing a substantive backlash from the authorities, the IRA immediately disclaimed all involvement in the affair as the Army Council wished to avoid a potentially disastrous confrontation with the Irish government, such as had occurred in the 1940s.[140] The situation was further compounded when another group of IRA volunteers, headed by Joseph Christle, 'revolted against the [Army Council]' and established their own 'splinter group' in late 1956. Some months later this organization was amalgamated with Saor Uladh and became involved in a series of armed robberies in Dublin and Kildare.[141] Such activity was regarded with alarm by the IRA leadership, as it was feared that it could provide the government with the pretence it needed to move against the republican movement.

In 1954, the loss of several by-elections persuaded the incumbent

Fianna Fáil government, which had been in power since the demise of the inter-party coalition in 1951, to call a general election in an attempt to reinforce its wavering majority in the Dáil.[142] Campaigning as an alternative government bloc, the former inter-party group, with the exception of Clann na Poblachta, which won a derisory two seats, performed well, predominately at the expense of Fianna Fáil. Reflecting on his party's poor performance, MacBride declined Costello's offer of the External Affairs portfolio and decided that, while Clann na Poblachta would not join the second inter-party administration, the new government would be assured of the Clann's continued parliamentary support.[143] As before, Costello continued to turn a blind eye to the activities of the IRA as it was deemed best not to afford the republican movement too much publicity, especially in the peculiar Irish circumstance where a disproportionately repressive response could win it a wide degree of sympathy. While this may have been a prudent course of action within the immediate post-war context, when faced with an emboldened subversive organization boasting an increasing public profile the pursuit of such a policy may not have been entirely appropriate. It not only served to further encourage a rejuvenated IRA to act with virtual impunity; it also prompted the Army Council to begin planning a series of more audacious and provocative initiatives.

In May 1953 the IRA issued an assured and poised statement reviewing the progress of the movement since 1945, in which it declared that

> a tireless, ceaseless effort has been in progress, to draw the threads of the organization together ... this was no easy task ... the difficulties met were legion ... [but] no longer is a struggle necessary to merely ensure the very existence of an army pledged to liberation. Such an army is now an accomplished fact – as yet maybe not quite as numerically strong or as well equipped as all would wish it to be, but still a highly effective well equipped unit.

By announcing the end of the IRA's 'period of retrenchment', this statement closed with a weighty pledge to 'engage the enemy at the earliest possible opportunity'.[144] Throughout the summer months the republican movement quickly moved to back up these assertions by undertaking a series of protests at the coronation of Queen Elizabeth II and her ensuing visit to Northern Ireland. In early June a bottle bomb was thrown at the window of the Northern Ireland government offices in London despite the fact that it had been damaged by a fire of 'doubtful origin' a few days previously.[145] Two weeks later the first in a series of bomb explosions along the border resulted in extensive damage to a cinema in Newry that had been showing a film of the coronation.[146] A further explosion in July also temporarily disrupted rail traffic conveying rail passengers from Dublin to Belfast in order to witness the visit of the new Queen.[147]

While these protests had served to make their point, it was obvious to the IRA leadership that a limited campaign of arson and petty vandalism could in the long run serve no useful purpose. Although the organization was working towards a more substantial armed offensive, it was also becoming increasingly apparent that the successful launch of such a campaign was dependent on the movement's ability to effect a dramatic enlargement of its armoury. In April 1954 a significant opportunity to address this issue was to present itself when an IRA volunteer reported that the gate to the Royal Irish Fusiliers barracks in Gough, County Armagh, was guarded by a sentry with an unloaded weapon. Buoyed by the success of the Ebrington raid and the positive publicity attached to the Felsted affair, the Army Council immediately authorized an incursion at Gough. To assist with the formulation of a highly detailed plan for the operation, Seán Garland was instructed to enlist in the British army with a view to infiltrating and reconnoitring the barracks. This bold move quickly paid off and within days of his enlistment the Army Council was awash with detailed intelligence relating to various sentry schedules, the layout of the base and, crucially, the location of the armoury.

Taking place on the afternoon of 12 June, the raid was intended to coincide with the visit of Lord Wakehurst, the Northern Ireland Governor, to Portadown, where most of the barracks' senior officers would be in attendance.[147] At approximately 3 p.m. a large cattle lorry approached the main gate of the barracks, whereupon a number of individuals alighted and made enquiries from the sentry on duty about joining the British army. When the sentry called a soldier from the guardroom, he was held up with an automatic pistol, while six to eight men dressed in full Territorial Army uniform emerged from the lorry and proceeded to disarm the astonished onlookers. One of the uniformed raiders then took the position of the captured sentry as the truck reversed into the barracks. After a brief search for the keys to the armoury the raiders managed to open the four-inch protective steel doors and quickly began to load the vehicle with weapons. Although this operation was widely observed throughout the barracks, activity continued as normal as the IRA party were assumed to be a group of Territorial Army recruits engaged in a training exercise. With the armoury stripped of all munitions, the lorry then drove out through the main gate, briefly stopping to collect the 'sentry' stationed outside, before proceeding at high speed towards the border.[149]

The alarm was not to be raised for another two hours and the raid proved to be a stunning success, as the raiders had effectively made good their escape with a substantial consignment of over 300 rifles, thirty-seven Sten guns, nine Bren guns and one Thompson submachine gun. Described as the biggest manhunt 'in Northern Ireland for years', the RUC immediately mounted an intensive operation in a vain attempt to keep watch on all roads leading to the Irish Republic. When it became apparent that the raiders had managed to evade the authorities by fleeing across the border, it was admitted that the chances of recovering the stolen weapons 'was slight'. Quick to capitalize on its success, the IRA swiftly issued a statement outlining how the raiders had cleared the barracks of all equipment.[150] To compound the embarrassment of the authorities, the circumstances of the incident were luridly reported in the media, where it was described as 'the most spectacular raid of arms from British forces ... for many years'.[151] In *The United Irishman* the 'split second timing' and 'amazing coolness' of the raiders was applauded and it was declared that the operation had 'quickened the spirit of freedom at home and abroad'.[152] In a more reasoned appraisal, the *Irish Times* also intuitively observed how

> it had been believed in political circles that the IRA now was a moribund force ... the latest exploit would appear to provide evidence of a well organized body ... [which will] particularly be a problem for the new Minister for Justice, Mr. Everett.[153]

As a corollary to the bold and daring manner in which the Gough raid was effected the IRA was to witness a marked increase in the number of recruits joining the organization.[154] Within weeks a large training camp was held in the Dublin mountains, where a technical film was produced for distribution among the republican network in Irish-America.[155] A number of county councils also moved to congratulate the IRA, and on one occasion a resolution was passed urging the government not to cooperate with the British authorities in investigating the matter.[156] On the other hand, the IRA was now faced with a lack of suitable ammunition for its new armoury. To counter this an additional raid was authorized on the Royal Inniskilling Fusiliers barracks in Omagh and, although it began propitiously, the raiders' failure to subdue one of the sentries was to result in the guard being alerted to their presence.[157] Following a brief gunfight in which two of the raiders and five soldiers were wounded, the attackers attempted to withdraw but there appeared 'to be some misunderstanding over transport arrangements'. As a result, a number of volunteers, including Philip Clarke and Thomas Mitchel, were left to make their own way to the border, where they were promptly arrested by the RUC.[158] These men were subsequently charged under the provisions of the archaic Treason Felony Act of 1848, receiving lengthy prison sentences as a result. Not only that, the weaponry captured during the Gough raid remained without suitable ammunition.

STATE REACTION

Coming just four months after the Gough affair, the abortive raid at Omagh was to signal for the government a disquieting escalation in the capacity and agency of the IRA. Both attacks attracted international attention, making headlines in the *New York Times* and the *Chicago Daily Tribune*, as well as inspiring an article attacking British imperial policy in the Spanish periodical *Arriba*.[159] In Ireland, the *Irish Times* noted that

> the raid last June upon the ... barracks at Armagh did no great harm to anybody. As anti-partition propaganda it served the purpose which it was intended to serve: it 'made news' throughout most of the world and showed the British authorities in a slightly ridiculous light ... Yesterday morning's raid [at Omagh] ... is another matter entirely. Men have been shot ... and neither the British War Office nor the northern government can afford to shut its eyes to what can only be regarded as a grave disturbance to the public peace.[160]

Inevitably, Costello issued the customary condemnation of the use of force as a means of ending partition and warned the IRA that the right to bear arms was solely vested in the Oireachtas.[161] This statement was endorsed by de Valera, who displayed an almost missionary zeal during this period in his lectures to the Dáil and the annual Fianna Fáil Ard Fheis, concerning the impracticality of force.[162]

On their own, however, these admonitions to the IRA, which were couched in vague and general terms, were not enough to quell the mounting concerns of the British government. In the wake of the arms raids a broad review of security precautions was instituted at various military and naval establishments in Britain and Northern Ireland, which concluded that

> there will be a continuing threat ... of attack by armed gangs of IRA agents on military establishments. The main object of these raids will be to gain prestige – and consequently recruits for the IRA, and at the same time to damage British military prestige.[163]

To counter this threat it was recommended that security be immediately stepped up, with the posting of additional sentries and the thorough inspection of all vehicles entering and leaving all military compounds. The army was also to be provided with the loan of a number of police dogs to assist them in this regard.[164] On the political level, however, the British government was far from satisfied by the apparent indifference shown by the Irish government and concluded that Costello was inclined to take 'a soft line' with the IRA.[165] While an approach to Dublin was considered, the Dominions Office stopped short of making a formal protest as it was decided that such a move would put the Irish authorities on the defensive 'and would not assist towards preventing further incidents'.[166]

Mindful of London's growing irritation with his apparent refusal to move against the IRA, Costello instructed the Irish Ambassador, Frederick Boland, to seek an urgent meeting with Percivale Liesching in the Commonwealth Relations Office in November 1954. During the course of this talk Boland admitted that the IRA 'was now resurgent and extremely well armed', but he was quick to assure Liesching that his government 'meant business' and was firm in its intention to take extremely strong action against the republican movement. To emphasize his point, Boland described how the police were being prepared with a view to the IRA's 'forcible suppression' and outlined how certain members of the Special Branch, who were flinching at the severity of the 'forthcoming exercise', were 'asking for a transfer to the uniformed branch'. He urged Liesching not to 'underestimate the drastic nature of the operation' and concluded the meeting by stressing that a formal protest from the British authorities could frustrate the Irish government by conveying the impression that they were acting under pressure from London.[167] Suitably mollified, Liesching gave the requisite assurances and retired to await the promised crackdown.

When it invariably failed to materialize, Liesching summoned Boland to a further meeting in December 1954 in which he was called to account. On this occasion Boland churlishly pointed out that he had not committed the Irish government to a particular timeframe and indicated that he was unsure as to the current position because of an unexpected difficulty in rallying public opinion. At a third meeting in January 1955, Boland attempted to justify the government's continuing inaction on the grounds that the IRA had gone underground owing to a growing incidence of division within its ranks.[168] Needless to say, this was dismissed by a skeptical Liesching, who was coming to the more likely conclusion that the Irish government was experiencing internal disagreement on the issue and, as such, was not strong enough to carry out its original intention.[169] Certainly, Costello was more than likely correct in his assessment of Irish public opinion, as the IRA, provided it maintained its focus outside the Irish Republic, seemed to court favourable public comment. On its own, however, this is an insufficient explanation for the lack of robust response on the government's behalf, particularly when faced with a direct challenge to its authority from a relatively well-trained and now well-armed subversive organization.

From as early as 1951, there is evidence to suggest that the first inter-party administration was reluctant to take firm action against the IRA. In September of that year the Department of Defence forwarded a memorandum to the Department of Justice, drawing attention to the particularly seditious content of the August edition of *The United Irishman*. After considering the matter, Justice officials decided that it was best not to take any action 'in respect of minor seditious utterances', as long-established ministerial policy '*was not to take any action in respect of drilling with arms* [my emphasis]' and seditious speeches in public. Informally referred to as 'the go-slow policy', this approach undoubtedly played a major role in allowing the IRA reorganization to gain sufficient momentum during these formative years.[170] Moreover, the British assessment of the position within the Irish cabinet may have been more accurate than originally thought. While there was some measure of resistance from the Labour party at the idea of suppressing the IRA, it must also be remembered that Clann na Poblachta occupied a key position in helping the government to maintain its majority in the Dáil. As already noted, the leadership of Clann was broadly sympathetic to the activities of the republican movement, and the threat of MacBride's withdrawal of parliamentary support may have persuaded Costello of the merits of a quiescent approach.[171] This assertion is further borne out when it is noted that MacBride precipitated a general election in 1957 because of

Costello's hostility to the outbreak of the IRA's border campaign and the government's overall handling of the economy (see Chapter 4).[172]

Whatever the reason, the continued prevarication of the government was a boon to the IRA leadership as brash moves like the arms raids began to pay dividends on the political front. In February 1952 Sinn Féin relaunched its *National Unity and Independence Programme*, in which it announced its intention of contesting all twelve Northern Irish constituencies in any future British general election.[173] In the Irish Republic, Sinn Féin also put itself forward as a single-issue party on an abstentionist basis when it unsuccessfully contested the 1954 Louth by-election. The party also nominated a number of candidates for the 1955 local elections, who pledged to take their seats on the grounds that active participation in county councils was not tantamount to recognizing the Irish state.[174] Some months later, Sinn Féin was finally presented with the opportunity to fulfil the pledge of its *National Unity and Independence Programme* when it ambitiously nominated a series of prisoner candidates to contest the upcoming Westminster elections. Faced with Sinn Féin's entry into this contest, the beleaguered Nationalist Party, which had been hitherto fighting a rearguard action to combat the ameliorative impact of the British welfare state, controversially announced its withdrawal for fear of splitting the nationalist vote.[175] In a report to the Department of External Affairs, Frederick Boland expressed his horror at this decision and impressed upon the Irish government the need to field moderate candidates in the traditional nationalist constituencies of Mid-Ulster and Fermanagh–South Tyrone. In his view, it was certain that Sinn Féin would fail to poll the full measure of nationalist opinion, thereby resulting in its loss of both constituencies.[176]

Despite these dire predictions, Sinn Féin managed to score considerable success with the election of IRA prisoner candidates Philip Clarke and Tom Mitchell in the Fermanagh–South Tyrone and Mid-Ulster constituencies.[177] While the party did poll an impressive 152,310 ballots in total, it must be remembered that the Sinn Féin vote was heavily inflated as the party had contested previously unchallenged seats in traditional unionist strongholds. It must also be pointed out that both Clarke and Mitchell were more than likely elected because many nationalists, faced with the lack of a viable alternative, cast their votes for Sinn Féin rather than see a unionist candidate take the seats. However, as both individuals were convicted felons under sentence, they were deemed to be ineligible to hold elective office. Following the application of his opponent, Col. R.G.

Grosvenor, Clarke was unseated by petition as the sitting MP for Fermanagh–South Tyrone.[178] In the case of Mitchell the position was less clear-cut as a by-election was required in Mid-Ulster to fill his seat following his formal disqualification by the British parliament. For Sinn Féin this was an unexpected propaganda coup as the party was able to make great play of how the nationalist voters of these constituencies had been effectively disenfranchised by the unionist administration.

In the ensuing by-election, held in August 1955, Mitchell again won the seat, this time with an increased majority, following a campaign characterized by allegations of widespread personation.[179] On this occasion, Mitchell's defeated opponent, Charles Beattie, wasted little time in lodging a petition under the Representation of the People Act, 1949, seeking a determination that Mitchell had not been duly elected owing to his conviction for Treason-Felony. In delivering his judgement on the matter, Justice J. Sheil held for Beattie on the grounds that Mitchell's disqualification was suitably warranted under the provisions of section two of the Forfeiture Act of 1870.[180] Some months later, Beattie was also disqualified for holding an office of profit under the crown. As a result, a second by-election was held in May 1956: Mitchell was finally defeated following the last-minute nomination of a Nationalist party candidate who served to split the vote.[181] Offset by the increased exposure and positive publicity generated by the affair, the incidental loss of the seat was significantly underplayed by a Sinn Féin party that had dramatically reasserted itself within the public domain. Moderate nationalist opinion was not so propitiate, being effectively deprived of adequate representation within the House of Commons.

For the IRA, the sizeable vote received by Sinn Féin was mistakenly interpreted as a straight licence for military action, rather than as a manifestation of broad Catholic discontent in Northern Ireland. Many contemporary republicans certainly felt justified in viewing the results of the 1955 general election as an endorsement of the IRA's upcoming military offensive, which was planned on this basis.[182] Against the backdrop of the ongoing Mid-Ulster débâcle there was another attempted arms raid in August 1955, this time on a British army depot in Arborfield, Berkshire. As with the previous incidents in Gough and Omagh, a bold and complex plan was devised that was to be effected by a seven-man team headed by Ruairí Ó Brádaigh. On the face of it the raid was a success, as the entire IRA party managed to escape with a substantial haul of weaponry, including fifty-five Sten guns and over 75,000 rounds of ammunition. The whole operation quickly disintegrated, however, when two of the raiders, Donal Murphy and Joseph Doyle, had the misfortune of being detained by the police after their lorry was stopped during the course of a routine traffic check. The discovery of a number of incriminating documents in their possession promptly led to the recovery of the stolen arms in an abandoned shop premises in London and the arrest of another of their comrades, James Murphy.[183] The decision to imprison these men for life provoked widespread criticism and led the Irish government to petition London for their release in the more tranquil political climate of 1962.[184]

On 2 June 1956, Anthony Magan was re-elected as IRA C/S following the holding of a general army convention at the Sinn Féin offices in Parnell Square, Dublin. In contrast to the previous convention held in 1948, the IRA had achieved a significant expansion of its membership, which now stood at over 900 individuals. Of these, over 360 were based in Dublin, its strongest centre, followed by Cork with a complement of ninety-three. In the main, many of these volunteers were reasonably well trained in the use of firearms, particularly after the holding of a series of camps and training events in Dublin, Wicklow, Louth, Clare, Limerick, Galway and Roscommon.[185] On these occasions instruction was usually offered in the use of Bren, Sten and Thompson machine guns, as against the .303 service rifle and the revolver, which the IRA was attempting to phase out. As a result of the arms raids, it was felt that, while the organization was now in possession of a significant arsenal, it was offset by an ongoing shortage of suitable ammunition.[186] Despite this shortage, however, it was felt within the organization that circumstances were now conducive to a successful assault on Northern Ireland, leading the Army Council to begin formal planning for its long-awaited campaign.

Former army officer Seán Cronin was recruited as director of operations in late 1955 and tasked with developing a new training programme for the organization as well as devising a plan for the proposed offensive in the north.[187] In April 1956 Cronin tabled a document for the Army Council's consideration entitled 'Operation Harvest: General directives for a guerrilla campaign'. Ambitious in scope, Operation Harvest envisaged a sustained guerrilla assault on various military installations, communications infrastructure and the road and rail network, in an attempt to 'liberate' large areas of Northern Ireland by breaking down 'the enemy's administration'. Backed up by local IRA units in the north, this onerous task was to fall to a series of specially trained 'flying columns' based primarily in the Irish Republic. In the interim, the republican movement would consolidate its hold on these so-called 'liberated areas', which would be linked up over time with other similar areas across the province. Through the use of unspecified 'propaganda' it was also hoped to win over the local population, before moving to intensify the campaign.[188]

The IRA leadership, divided along lines of seniority, remained to be convinced. For the older members of the Army Council, Operation Harvest was marred by a number of flaws, while its overall success was dependent on the ability of the IRA to mount such an ambitious operation. While the republican movement undoubtedly experienced an unprecedented turn of fortune in the early 1950s, a core group of 500 with basic military training and a limited supply of arms and ammunition was not an adequate force with which to implement such a strategy. In relying heavily on the support of the public, the plan also ignored the fundamental realities of the Irish siuation, as the majority Protestant population in the north was unlikely to foster the necessary conditions needed to prosecute a guerrilla campaign. Traditional support among the Catholic population was also on the wane and qualified by the IRA's ability to deliver some measure of success. For the junior members of the Army Council, youthful exuberance was to win the day, and they were successful in persuading Magan and MacCurtain to dispense with their private reservations and adopt the plan as IRA policy.

Although the requisite preparations were subsequently set in motion, the Army Council was forced to bring forward its preferred timetable for a campaign launch in the autumn of 1958, following Christle's defection to the Saor Uladh organization. This move served to encourage further departures, particularly from Christle's former unit in Dublin, with the promise of more to follow. Mindful of a growing impatience among the rank and file, the Army Council deemed it prudent to dispense with its original intention of preceding the launch of Operation Harvest with a campaign of organized passive resistance.[189] In Ruairí Ó Brádaigh's view this was a mistake, as a campaign of organized civil disobedience would have 'prepared the ground' for the IRA campaign by highlighting Catholic grievances in Northern Ireland.[190] Nevertheless, the Army Council pressed ahead, and in December 1956 all training officers in Northern Ireland were called to Dublin for a briefing, where they were ordered to select targets of opportunity within the capacity of the units under their supervision. During this briefing it emerged that a target date for the launch of operations had been set and that all arms dumps had been transferred to the border. Ultimately, the original date of 10 December 1956 had to be abandoned due to 'logistical problems', and the Army Council ordered the commencement of operations on the following day, thereby initiating the IRA's first full-scale military campaign since 1939.[191]

4

'The National Revolutionary Resurgence':[1] Campaign and Reaction, December 1956

On 12 December 1956, the IRA's long envisaged campaign of 'organized resistance' in Northern Ireland began with a series of coordinated attacks on various infrastructural and military targets across the province.[2] Under the cover of seasonally intemperate weather, these raids were carried out by a force of up to 150 volunteers, mainly from the Irish Republic, who had successfully evaded the authorities and crossed the border without being detected.[3] To curtail the movements of the security forces, the first major operation of the evening was preceded by a concerted attempt to disrupt the northern transport network with a series of assaults on several strategically located bridges.[4] Although a number of these bridges in Derry were successfully collapsed, both the Carry Bridge outside Enniskillen and the Lady Brooke Bridge near Newtownbutler remained intact.[5] In many cases, the attackers were simply hampered by the poor quality of their makeshift ordnances, as the requisite explosions were not 'sufficiently powerful to do any permanent damage'.[6] Undeterred by these relatively minor setbacks, the IRA's makeshift volunteer force pressed ahead and continued with the opening series of operations largely as planned.

By 2 a.m. it was reported that 'sirens whined all over border areas' as the authorities were called out in response to a series of 'heavy explosions' across 'the six counties'.[7] In Enniskillen, a Territorial Army barracks was partially destroyed by a bomb blast, while a group of nine men under the command of Seamus Costello seized the caretaker of the Magherafelt quarter-sessions court house before setting the building alight.[8] Meanwhile, following a series of explosions in Armagh, locals observed a car leaving the scene of a foiled attack on the city's telephone exchange. While attempting to intercept this vehicle, RUC Constable Malcolm McKeown was wounded in the arm and the shoulder when his patrol exchanged gunfire with the occupants.[9] A B-Special training hut was destroyed in Newry, while Derry was the scene of a major incident when a homemade bomb 'wrecked' the interior of a BBC transmitter. A number of shots were also fired at an RUC barracks in Ballycastle, County Antrim, and a large quantity of gelignite was stolen from a quarry in Goraghwood 'just inside the border beside the Dublin–Belfast railway line'.[10]

Several IRA parties also became involved in a number of open engagements with the authorities, including an incident at Newtownbutler when the RUC returned the fire of a group of individuals 'fleeing towards the border'. Further north, 'a bleak stretch of coast road' was the scene of an intensive gun battle between a small RUC patrol and an IRA column under the command of Anthony Cooney. On this occasion, Cooney and his colleagues were surprised by a small police patrol while attempting to make their way to the RAF radar station at Torr Head, County Antrim.[11] According to Sergeant William Bacon, 'the men jumped from their van, their Sten guns blazing' and

> for fully five minutes a rapid volley of shots was exchanged. Bullets shattered the police car window, as the policemen, ducking behind, kept up their fire. The raiders ... hid behind a ditch. Then a shout was heard and the raiders made off across the open fields still blazing away with Sten guns and revolvers.[12]

Remarkably, there were no fatalities and the RUC, reinforced by 'thirty police cars from Belfast, Ballymena and Ballymoney', quickly instituted an 'exhaustive manhunt' in an attempt to apprehend the attackers.[13] Although Cooney and two of his colleagues were later arrested and charged with the attempted murder of Sergeant Bacon, the search for the remainder of the column continued for several days without success.[14]

While these incidents in themselves constituted 'the most serious show of force yet made by illegal groups in Northern Ireland', by far the most significant action of the night was an aborted raid on Gough military barracks.[15] Patrolling sentries within the barracks were alerted to the presence of the IRA attackers when Seán Garland and his men attempted to place a homemade mine at the front gate of the installation.[16] With the aid of a new watchtower, constructed in the aftermath of the IRA's previous foray at the barracks, the attackers were repulsed following a brief exchange of gunfire. A series of explosions was then heard in the vicinity of Barrack Hill as a number of mistimed bombs detonated before they could be used in the attack. Under heavy fire, Garland and his men proceeded to throw petrol bombs at the outer wall of the installation, while an assault group attempted to place a large canister of explosives beneath the watchtower. When this device failed to explode, the column withdrew and the attackers were then observed retreating towards the border.[17] Two of the fleeing raiders were arrested following a brief altercation with a B-Special patrol on the outskirts of Armagh. During their arraignment before a special court sitting the following day, both men notably refused to recognize the court and made no application for bail.[18]

The following day the circulation of a detailed IRA statement, drawn up by Seán Cronin and couched in the usual rhetoric of militant republicanism, confirmed that these attacks were not to be a one-off event:

> Spearheaded by Ireland's freedom fighters, our people in the six counties have carried the fight to the enemy. They are the direct victims of British Imperialism and they are also the backbone of the national revolutionary resurgence.

Calling on all Irishmen and women to 'cease being tools of ... Imperialism', this statement counselled against British attempts to fan 'the fires of bigotry', and warned the RUC that if they rejected 'this plea' they would be judged as renegades and 'treated accordingly'. As if to emphasize the singular and independent nature of the republican struggle, all offers of foreign aid were suitably disclaimed and the statement closed by asserting that 'out of this national liberation struggle a new Ireland will emerge, upright and free'.[19] The release of this statement was immediately followed by a series of flyers specifically warning the RUC that if they continued to assist the British army in their operations, they would, after a brief 'grace period', also be open to attack.[20] Two days later the republican propaganda machine issued a 'special bulletin' of *The United Irishman*, in which it was declared that attacking forces 'penetrated the enemy's defences system despite the oft-repeated boasts ... that they were safe from attack'.[21] Indeed, despite several minor setbacks, the IRA leadership had reason to be upbeat, as the first night of operations had caused thousands of pounds' worth of damage, while much of the attacking force had escaped back to the sanctuary of the Irish Republic.[22]

The relative success of these operations is all the more remarkable given that the British government had warned of a major attack on Northern Ireland as early as April 1955.[23] In the main, however, the northern authorities were caught largely unawares by the opening salvoes of the IRA's offensive, as the receipt of 'garbled' information and faulty intelligence was to throw the normally ubiquitous RUC off the scent.[24] In their defence, the northern Premier, Lord Basil Brookeborough, was quick to affix the blame for the RUC's lack of forewarning on a complicit Irish government, which was lambasted in the unionist media for its failure to negotiate an extradition treaty between the two jurisdictions.[25] Fearful of reprisal attacks, Brookeborough counselled the unionist population against any attempts to 'go off the deep end' and warned that it would be of 'no service to Northern Ireland' if any action 'was taken outside of official action'.[26] Security was immediately stepped up across the province with the extraordinary mobilization of the entire B-Special reserve of 11,600 men, equipped with a vast array of Bren guns, Sten guns, rifles, pistols, grenades and two-inch mortars.[27] On 15 December, the northern government, following a 'six minute conference in the Belfast Law Courts', also re-invoked the SPA and empowered the authorities 'to take all such steps ... as may be necessary for preserving peace and maintaining order'.[28]

This decision was primarily motivated by a desire to implement the provisions of regulation twenty-three of the SPA, which allowed for the detention of suspects without trial. Under this regime the civil authority could order the arrest of any person without warrant upon suspicion of having acted, or of being about to act, in a manner 'prejudicial to the preservation of the peace'. Such persons could then be detained at the discretion of the Minister for Home Affairs.[29] Individuals held in these circumstances could not be admitted to bail unless directed by the civil authority and, while it was possible to proffer criminal charges, such decision was entirely dependent upon the Minister for Home Affairs. Although the Offences Against the State (Amendment) Act did endow the Irish government with similar powers of arbitrary imprisonment, it differed in the respect that it also established a limited supervisory role for the Oireachtas.[30] There were no such safeguards embodied within the SPA, as the commencement and duration of detention under regulation twenty-three was entirely dependent upon the discretion of the civil authority. If needed, the SPA also contained provisions for the outright use of internment with even more far-reaching encroachments on the liberty of the subject. Not only was the minister entitled to intern any person by order for any period, access to legal assistance could be obtained only with the goodwill of the relevant authorities. These draconian provisions were not activated on this occasion, as the northern authorities were content to detain republican suspects under the provisions of regulation twenty-three.[31]

Despite the implementation of such repressive measures, the IRA continued with its operations and on 13 December engaged in a sustained gun attack on a police barracks in Lisnaskea, County Fermanagh. During the course of this incident a bomb planted at the entrance of the barracks was detonated and a volley of hand grenades was thrown at the outer wall. According to police sources a moan was heard during the resultant gun battle, which was taken to be that of a wounded raider, but no trace of blood was found afterwards.[32] A similar attack on Derrylin RUC barracks was also repulsed, while it was reported that a bridge in Maguiresbridge had been blown up and that telegraph poles in many areas had been cut down.[33] In justifying these raids, the IRA leadership was quick to inform the Inspector-General of the RUC that, contrary to the demands of their campaign proclamation, the police and B-Specials 'had participated in attacks on freedom fighters, co-operated in searches and acted as guides for the military'.[34] Having failed to 'stand aside from the conflict' the RUC were now considered to be legitimate military targets. Remarkably, members of the B-Specials were exempted from attack provided they were not part of a mixed army or police patrol, on the basis that they were a 'sectarian paramilitary force'.[35]

DETENTION: CRUMLIN ROAD

With mounting arrests arising from a crackdown on the IRA, the northern authorities were quickly forced to confront the problem of finding adequate accommodation for the growing number of republican prisoners detained under the SPA. By the end of January 1957, there were 145 such individuals in custody, prompting the Minister for Home Affairs to make provision for their detention in Crumlin Road Prison, Belfast.[36] Described as a 'typical nineteenth century jail', this prison was built upon the principle of the 'spokes of a wheel plan', where the various wings branched out from a large central hall. Such a configuration was particularly well suited to the intentions of the prison authorities as the republican prisoners could be housed in 'D wing' of this facility, where they would be effectively segregated from the rest of the prison population. Classed as 'political internees', they were accommodated one to a cell and were largely left to their own devices as they were given the run of the wing throughout the day. In general, the regime was relaxed; the detainees were not required to do any work and were allowed to wear their own clothing. They were also permitted to exchange two letters a week with their families and receive one visit of twenty minutes' duration every fortnight.[37]

As was standard republican practice, the prisoners began to organize themselves along military lines and elected a prison staff with responsibility for the morale and welfare of those under their control. The detainees observed their own discipline and took it upon themselves to clean their common areas and cells. Despite this, it was noted that the standard of hygiene varied from person to person, with the majority of detainees showing little inclination 'to live in comfort consistent with cleanliness'. While official intervention was not needed to enforce the cleaning of the wing, the general unwillingness to partake in this exercise was taken by the prison authorities as an indication of the detainees' 'state of mind' and their 'lack of self-pride'.[38] In order to pass the time the detainees were more proactive in organizing a series of regular classes and lectures and on several occasions they were permitted to hold a series of plays, concerts and pageants. Opportunity for physical exercise was more limited, owing to the inadequacy of the small prison yard. Described as 'a bare square surrounded by high walls', it contained a 'grassless surface', which was cut up and much marked owing to its overuse from football and 'hurley'. During wet weather this area was reputed to turn into a 'quagmire', with the ground becoming a thick mixture of mud and cinders. On such occasions the only shelter provided was a 'barn-like lean to', which was equipped with a limited number of tables where internees made rudimentary attempts to conduct courses in Irish.[39]

In March 1958 officials in the Department of Home Affairs authorized the visit of a Red Cross delegation to Crumlin Road in order to dispel allegations of the ill treatment of detainees within the prison. The report of the committee was generally favourable and commended the prison warders for the 'friendly co-operation' that was accorded to the delegation during the course of their inspection. Noting how the detainees were adequately accommodated in their own individual cells, the report criticized the authorities for the deficiencies of the ablution and canteen facilities and were 'unfavourably impressed' by the conditions under which the detainees passed their time. In particular, the delegates condemned the prohibition on work as an aspect of the prison regime that 'cannot but be conducive to relatively rapid moral and physical deterioration'. In support of this contention, it cited the contrast of the industrious and cheerful nature of the regular convicts with the 'sullen looks, grumbling and apathetic behaviour' of the detainees. Significantly, the detainees themselves, in a series of private meetings with the delegation, expressed their satisfaction with the conditions within Crumlin Road and admitted that the rules and regulations laid down for the treatment of prisoners were correctly, though severely, applied.[40]

Unsurprisingly, relations with the prison warders appeared to have been strained and blighted by mutual suspicion. While it was reported that the warders regarded their charges with a 'cold and severe attitude', the administration of prison discipline, although strict and harsh, was not unduly severe. Similar to the established practice in the Irish Republic, the detainees were provided with the opportunity to secure their release from detention by swearing an undertaking to refrain from subversive activities. According to Joe Cahill, few of his colleagues availed themselves of this option for fear of being stigmatised as a sell-out.[41] As the campaign wore on, however, it was noted by officials at the Department of Home Affairs that the prisoners' initial unity of ideals appeared to be on the wane, giving the impression that many were prepared to renounce their detainee status except for 'the loss of face which this would entail'. This was subsequently attributed to the presence of a 'few diehards', whose influence in organizing the 'hard core' of resistance within the prison effectively restrained the others 'from returning to their families and surrendering their ideals as republican martyrs'.[42]

THE POLITICAL REPERCUSSIONS

For the Irish government, inhibited by its reliance on the parliamentary support of Clann na Poblachta, the 'recrudescence of armed violence in the north' was to represent a thorny political dilemma. Any undue haste in moving against the IRA had the potential to swing previously ambivalent popular opinion in its favour, while at the same time failure to take sufficient action would represent an abdication of authority, thereby creating a dangerous political vacuum.[43] By contrast, the position for the northern government could not have been any clearer. Costello's continued prevarication was to render his government complicit in the IRA attacks and all appropriate measures were to be applied in order to produce the desired result – the complete suppression of the militant republican movement. In light of the unfolding Suez débâcle in the Middle East, the beleaguered government of Sir Anthony Eden was heavily dependent on the votes of the

Ulster Unionist Party (UUP) at Westminster, which now exhibited few qualms in exploiting its unique position of influence.⁴⁴ Eden, who was proving himself to be sufficiently malleable to unionist demands, was extensively lobbied to exert diplomatic pressure on the Irish government, despite a recent marked improvement in Anglo-Irish relations.⁴⁵

Allied to these efforts, the Ulster Unionist MP William Orr pressed John Hare, the British Secretary of State for War, for a statement, claiming that 'the main cause of the trouble was the scandal that ... Éire ... continued to afford sanctuary and succour to terrorists'. Although this was immediately rejected by Hare on the grounds that there was no evidence to suggest that the Irish government approved of the attacks, the lack of official comment from Dublin did little to invalidate this assertion.⁴⁶ In fact, the only definitive statement issued from Leinster House was that of Fianna Uladh Senator Liam Kelly, who expressed his regret that some members of the raiding parties had been captured by the authorities. As if to compound the situation, Garda headquarters also confirmed that 'there was no special civic guard activity along the border', as the matter had, in their opinion, 'begun and ended in the north'.⁴⁷ Unionist opinion was suitably incensed and during the course of a 'heated meeting' with the British Home Secretary a UUP delegation demanded that 'the strongest possible pressure [be put] on the government of the Republic to prevent further raids'. The leader of the Northern Irish senate added his voice to the clamour when he called on Costello to suppress the IRA, while Brookeborough, for his part, demanded British defensive measures consonant with an attack 'on Surrey, Yorkshire or Devonshire'.⁴⁸

Faced with such a provocative use of language, the Irish government was finally prompted to issue a statement on the matter after holding a marathon six-hour cabinet meeting on 14 December – a full two days after the campaign had begun. In affirming the government's determination to take positive steps against the republican movement, it recalled the Taoiseach's appeal to the IRA to cease 'all unlawful activities' in November 1955, by noting that:

> For some time it appeared that [this] ... warning had been heeded by the organizations concerned. Since however, that is evidently no longer the position, and since those organizations have again arrogated to themselves powers and functions that belong to the duly elected representatives of the people ... the government have now determined to take, in conjunction with the

Garda Síochána and the Defence Forces, such steps as ... necessary ... to prevent activities which ... would inevitably cause loss of life and would involve the danger that Civil War might ensue.[49]

Suitably militant in an effort to placate some of the more nationalist-minded members of the Dáil, the statement was also conspicuously ambiguous as to what type of action the government proposed to take. In Belfast it received only a lukewarm response from Brookeborough, who stated: 'I will await the outcome of this action and will believe the results when I see them.'[50] It was more warmly endorsed in Westminster, as the House of Lords moved to convey its delight at the fact that 'the Republican government' had chosen to express its views.[51]

Privately, Costello and his colleagues were quickly coming to the conclusion that the need for swift preventative action against the IRA was the most desirable course of action in order to 'obviate the necessity of a full scale clash'. While it was recognized that the IRA was by no means anxious to engage the Irish military or civil forces, it was felt that the government's attitude should be 'intelligently intensified', but that overtly aggressive action should be avoided. To this end, it was suggested that the Special Branch should be reorganized so that Garda border stations could be augmented with selected members of this force, who would operate a localized intelligence system.[52] Several units of the Irish army, together with a number of Special Branch detectives, were also deployed along the border as the government prepared to make its first definitive move against the IRA.[53]

Two days later, in an obvious show of intent, a combined force of Gardaí and military arrested thirteen men during the course of a 'lightning swoop' on a disused farmhouse in Scotstown, County Monaghan. Just one and a half miles from the Fermanagh border, the raid on the house, which had been occupied for over a week, began just after 2 a.m. with the arrival of a convoy of six police cars and two army jeeps from Monaghan Garda station. The two-storey premises was then encircled, while leading members of the party knocked on the door and demanded admittance. When the door was opened the Gardaí were admitted without any opposition and proceeded to arrest the suspects, who offered no physical resistance.[54] After questioning at Monaghan Garda station the suspects were released without charge, prompting the *Irish Times* to speculate that

> [With] the swift action in Monaghan ... the government is in earnest in its determination to stamp out illegal armed activities in the Republic. By this quick show of force the government may hope to put a curb to such activities without having to use more stringent powers under the Offences Against the State Act.[55]

It subsequently emerged that the Gardaí failed to uncover any arms or incriminating documents in the farmhouse, and that the men were released after giving an undertaking to return to their homes.[56]

By authorizing this raid the government hoped to appease Brookeborough by effecting the type of 'swift preventative action' that it was hoped would discourage the IRA from continuing with its campaign. Conversely, the leniency of this operation also suggests that Costello was attempting to maintain his coalition's internal balancing act, by not giving his parliamentary colleagues in Clann na Poblachta any cause for offence.[57] However, as participation in government had failed to deliver on any of Clann's republican aspirations, the party had recently begun to adopt a more militant nationalist tone. At its 1955 Ard Fheis a motion was passed maintaining that:

> Dáil Éireann shall claim and exercise the authority of government, so far as practicable over the thirty-two counties of Ireland. Dáil Éireann will order and direct such resistance – passive or otherwise – in the six occupied counties as will make government by any other body impossible in that area. All the resources of the government shall be utilized to support such resistance.[58]

Such views were not limited to the rank and file, as evidenced by the release of a series of statements from the front bench congratulating all those who had taken part in the IRA arms raids. This was further compounded by Fionan Breathnach, a member of Clann's Ard Comhairle, who accused the major political parties of 'going back into their shells as regard partition'. In his opinion the only way the issue could be kept alive 'was by [involving] young people who were prepared to fight and suffer'.[59]

The government's gambit failed to have the desired effect in any quarter, as the IRA continued its campaign with an ambush on an RUC patrol car near Lisnaskea. During the attack several volleys of shots were fired at the car, wounding Constable William John Ferguson in the leg and shoulder. Although his colleagues immediately returned fire, the attackers 'made off in the darkness' and were successful in effecting their escape.⁶⁰ It later emerged that the patrol car had been sent to investigate reports that a lorry containing a large number of men had been observed in the area. Following the ambush, a security cordon was immediately established as troops of the Royal Warwickshire regiment were deployed to aid in the search for the IRA party, reputed to contain up to thirty men.⁶¹ In London, Brookeborough added to the sense of political crisis when he made reference to the attack during the course of an interview on the BBC television programme *Panorama*.⁶² His Minister for Home Affairs, Col. W.W.B. Topping, also maligned the Taoiseach when he expressed his disappointment that the 'Dublin government's decision to call on the troops and the civic guard had not been accompanied by decisive action'. The situation threatened to escalate further when unionist MPs at Westminster began to lobby the British government to consider the introduction of economic sanctions 'if the disturbances in the north did [not] cease'.⁶³

In eventually succumbing to unionist pressure, Eden determined to press Costello into taking a more robust stance with the IRA through extraordinary diplomatic means. On 18 December, Eden instructed his ambassador, Sir Alexander Clutterbuck, to deliver an *aide-mémoire* to the Taoiseach's office outlining his government's 'great concern at the recent border incidents'.⁶⁴ Considering that both governments had previously exchanged a series of *aides-mémoire* in relation to IRA activity, in itself this was not an unusual move.⁶⁵ What was significant, however, was the very public circumstances in which this approach was made. Clutterbuck's visit to the Taoiseach was widely reported in the press, as Eden was clearly hoping to use the weight of international opprobrium to coerce Costello into taking the desired course of action.⁶⁶ In Stormont, news of the British representations was greeted with cheers from crowded government benches, particularly when Brookeborough informed the house that he had been assured of Eden's priority in maintaining the defence of the province.⁶⁷ This was followed by a speech in Westminster on 19 December 1956, in which Eden reaffirmed his government's policy in respect of Northern Ireland:

> In the Ireland Act 1949 the Parliament of Westminster declared Northern Ireland to be an integral part of the United Kingdom. This is a declaration which all parties in this house are pledged to support. The safety of Northern Ireland and its inhabitants is therefore a direct responsibility of Her Majesty's government, which, they will, of course, discharge.⁶⁸

In the meantime, a second high-profile Garda raid resulted in the arrest of eight men in a disused cottage four miles north of Dundalk, where they were held under section thirty of the OASA.[69] In Derry, Canice O'Kane also gained the unwelcome distinction of being the first person to be held under regulation twenty-three of the SPA.[70] Politically, the difficult position of the government was further compounded when Seán MacBride demanded that the Taoiseach make public any replies that he had made to Eden's recent representations about the border raids.[71] Costello duly obliged with the dissemination of the government's response, which was framed in stark and uncompromising terms. In condemning the activities of the IRA as a challenge to the democratic institutions of the state, the government resolved to use all such means as it deemed appropriate to bring such unlawful military activity to an end. Such measures, however, were for the sole determination of the Irish government in light of their experience and judgement in the 'discharge of their duties to Dáil Éireann'. Pugnaciously, Costello left Eden in no doubt as to whom the Irish government held ultimately responsible for the raids, as the root cause of these attacks was blamed on Britain's continued partition of Ireland. Eden's claim that Northern Ireland was 'an integral part of the United Kingdom' was also summarily dismissed and the statement closed with a pointed reminder that 'the six counties are of course a part of the national territory of Ireland'.[72]

As on previous occasions, the government had unsuccessfully attempted to appease all quarters by issuing the requisite denunciation of the republican attacks, tempered by reference to the rhetoric of Irish national irredentism. Invariably, the northern authorities began to look to their own resources in an effort to check the unrestricted movement of IRA volunteers across the border. Starting on 21 December, a battalion of the Royal Northumberland Fusiliers was tasked with blowing craters in a number of roads on the border between Counties Armagh and Monaghan, in order to render them impassable. Similarly, a number of bridges in County Fermanagh were also demolished.[73] After a brief Christmas respite, these efforts were resumed when local Gardaí in County Cavan discovered a party of British soldiers at work demolishing the main road between Ballyconnell and Derrylin in County Fermanagh. In addition, the Garda sergeant in Kiltyclogher, County Leitrim, was informed by his RUC counterpart of the impending demolition of roads between Manorhamilton and the villages of Aughavanney, Cashel, Kilcoo, Dooard and Askill, all situated in County Fermanagh. Such measures were not effected without some degree of resistance, however, as the crater in one road near Cashel, used extensively 'by foot and cycle traffic', was filled in by locals, prompting the RUC to return and reopen it.[74]

In all over 200 roads were closed, leaving only sixteen points of entry between the two Irish jurisdictions. As most of the roads in question were 'unapproved roads', they were exempt from customs and excise controls on household merchandise and were heavily used by locals in the course of their daily lives. This course of action was to have profound consequences for economic activity throughout the border region, as well as occasioning much inconvenience for individuals in these areas. In one instance, the closure of the main road between Omeath, County Louth and Newry, County Armagh, not only involved taking a thirty-mile detour; residents in Omeath also faced an impeded emergency service, owing to a heavy reliance on doctors across the border. The lucrative tourist industry in the region, which is situated on the scenic Carlingford peninsula, was also heavily curtailed by the closure of this road. The closure of another road, which linked two points in County Fermanagh by running across a small salient of County Cavan, almost completed isolated Drumully village from the Irish Republic, precipitating lengthy detours for anyone wishing to visit the area.[75]

As well as taking this action, the northern authorities also began to promulgate a series of emergency regulations under the SPA, allowing for the imposition of curfews in specified areas 'should the necessity arise'. Other such regulations prohibited the publication of information relating to the movements of the police and made it an offence to be in possession of 'ciphers or codes for secretly communicating information'.[76] It also became an offence to interfere or tamper with any 'apparatus for transmitting telephonic or telegraphic messages', to inflict damage to railways or to be 'near any bridge with intent to do injury thereto'.[77] Backed up by these measures, the Department of Home Affairs also authorized a series of pre-dawn raids on the homes of known republicans throughout Belfast, Derry, Tyrone and Armagh, resulting in the detention of thirty-two individuals under regulation twenty-three of the SPA. Up to fifty other men whom the RUC wished to interview in connection with their alleged republican activities went missing from their homes when news of the police raids became known. In particular, it was noted that several prominent members of the Gaelic League and the Gaelic Athletic Association (GAA) were staying away from their homes for fear that they might be mistaken for militant republicans.[78]

With Christmas approaching, the IRA leadership felt it prudent to withdraw their forces across the border in order to affect a brief suspension of operations. While many volunteers, who felt that any withdrawal would rob them of the element of surprise, greeted this decision with incredulity, the IRA leadership maintained that their recently acquired combat experience and their increasing confidence would offset any such loss.[79] Also, a second 'special bulletin' of *The United Irishman* was published on 22 December as a counter to a perceived negative bias within the mainstream media. Self-assured in its belief that the campaign 'is supported and backed by the nationalist population of the six counties', it reported that an unnamed 'freedom fighter', who was recovering from a leg injury, received a 'tremendous ovation' when he addressed a Sinn Féin meeting in Dublin. During the course of this gathering he claimed that 'people in the south were not getting a true picture of events in the north' and stated 'you did not hear about the people leaving their beds to cheer us as we left Lisnaskea barracks'.[80] Certainly, the Army Council had much to be confident about, as the opening weeks of the campaign had been attended by a certain measure of success. However, given the importance of Belfast as the republican heartland of the north, the lack of activity in this city perplexed many contemporary observers.[81]

The initial and widely held belief that Belfast was deliberately excluded so as to avoid the possibility of sectarian conflict has recently been called into question by several leading republicans.[82] The most important of these has been Ruairí Ó Brádaigh, who claimed that the disorganization occasioned by the arrest of the Belfast O/C, Paddy Doyle, forced the Army Council to abandon its plans for the city.[83] This is disputed by the testimony of the late Joe Cahill, who provided compelling evidence that the Belfast brigade had been compromised by informers, necessitating its exclusion from the campaign. In pointing out that this unit had received its share of weapons from the arms raids of the early 1950s, Cahill recalled how his suspicions were aroused with the failure of a number of unspecified operations within the city.[84] Taking it upon himself to investigate the matter, Cahill alleged that the supposed informer, judging by the quality of the information being leaked, had to be either 'a member of the Battalion staff or someone close to the Battalion staff'. In outlining his concerns to Anthony Magan, the IRA C/S, Cahill revealed how he was instructed to remove all arms from their dumps in Belfast and secure them in new dumps under his own control. According to Cahill, it appears that Magan, in light of this information, took the decision to keep the details of the campaign secret from prominent republicans in the city.[85]

From the RUC's perspective, the discovery of an unexploded bomb in Belfast docks on 14 December was taken as evidence of an impending escalation of the IRA's campaign with a series of proposed attacks within the city. Although the responsibility for planting this device was later attributed to Kelly's Saor Uladh organization, it prompted the RUC to make a number of enquiries, leading them to conclude that the relative immunity afforded Belfast thus far was about to end. According to intelligence received by the Crime Special Branch, the Army Council had set preparations in motion for the commencement of operations within the city, and an attack would certainly follow within 'the next two weeks'. Symbolic sites listed for attack included the parliament building at Stormont, the Courts of Justice, Belfast Custom House and the Inland Revenue offices, as well as a number of strategic targets, including Belfast Airport, the Harland and Wolff shipyard and Belfast gasworks. It was also reported that the 'IRA set-up in Belfast was to be changed', as known members were ordered to leave their jobs and 'go on active service'. Volunteers from Dublin were then to take over operations within the city and begin liaising with other units throughout Northern Ireland.[86] When these attacks failed to materialize, security preparations across Belfast were gradually scaled down, as it became apparent that the republican organization within the city was not being prepared for combat operations.

Elsewhere, the number of reported incidents across the province continued to rise, despite the IRA's temporary suspension of operations over the Christmas period. On 23 December a number of RUC stations in County Derry were attacked by small arms fire, occasioning minor damage.[87] Sinn Féin was also formally proscribed by the northern authorities and its office in Belfast was raided.[88] RUC headquarters received a letter purporting to be from the IRA warning that police stations would not be immune from attack because they contained married quarters. This prompted a bemused response from the Department of Home Affairs, when it was pointed out that in previous attacks on RUC stations the IRA had shown scant regard for the presence of women and children.[89] While police searches continued for those involved in the raids, the B-Specials were themselves to become embroiled in controversy following the accidental shooting of a County Fermanagh farmer.[90] South of the border, charges were proffered against the eight republicans arrested in Dundalk when they were arraigned before the Dublin District Court. During the course of the hearing, the accused refused to recognize the court, as was standard republican practice, and were granted bail pending trial for offences under the Firearms Act, 1925. They were subsequently convicted of these charges and sentenced to six months' imprisonment.[91]

After its brief Christmas recess the IRA signalled the resumption of its campaign with a more ambitious attack on the RUC barracks in Derrylin, County Fermanagh. On this occasion the column involved in the original assault on 13 December was augmented with the addition of a number of men under the command of Ruairí Ó Brádaigh. On New Year's Eve the column O/C, Noel Kavanagh, arranged for a local IRA unit to block the roads into Derrylin in order to slow down the arrival of RUC reinforcements. The column itself then entered the village on foot and proceeded to split into two groups – a cover party and an assault team. At 10.20 p.m. the assault party proceeded to detonate 'a heavy bomb' at the front door of the barracks, while Kavanagh directed the cover party to concentrate their fire on the opening caused by the explosion. An intensive gun battle ensued, during which the attackers were successful in tossing a grenade through a second-storey window, effectively destroying the radio room. When a second mine failed to detonate, Kavanagh ordered the party to withdraw, leaving 'a wrecked police station' in its wake. RUC Constable John Scally was mortally wounded during the course of the raid and was pronounced dead on arrival at Fermanagh County Hospital.[94] It subsequently emerged that Scally, who was a Roman Catholic, had joined the RUC in August 1953 and had been commended for 'good police duty' for his part in the last IRA raid on Derrylin barracks.[93]

Within thirty minutes of the attack the alarm went out over 'the whole of Northern Ireland' as armed police endeavoured to carry out an extensive search of the area. Although numerous roadblocks were set up it quickly became apparent that the IRA party had been successful in making their escape across the border. However, during the course of their trek over the foothills of Slieve Rusheen the raiders lost their bearings and missed their base in the Irish Republic, ending up in the Ballyconnell district of County Cavan. Alerted to the attack and the possible presence of the raiders in their vicinity, local Gardaí began an intensive comb-out of the area, resulting in the arrest of Ó Brádaigh and several of his colleagues. Although they were unarmed, having dumped their weapons in Northern Ireland, Ó Brádaigh was in possession of a haversack, which contained ammunition and a copy of the Operation Harvest document.[94] Dressed in green boiler suits and 'a mixture of British, US and Irish army fatigues', the men were quickly escorted to Dublin for questioning in relation to the Derrylin attack.[95] In Belfast, unionist opinion indicted the Irish government for permitting the IRA to organize within their jurisdiction and placed the blame for Scally's death firmly at Costello's door.[96] For the IRA, the relative success of the Derrylin attack acted as a morale-boosting catalyst among the rank and file, prompting Seán Garland, the O/C of a second IRA column on patrol in County Fermanagh, to undertake an ambitious attack on the nearby Brookeborough RUC station.[97]

THE BROOKEBOROUGH ATTACK

The column that attacked Brookeborough, best described as a group of 'amateur soldiers of very mixed training', assembled for active duty on 26 December 1956. After several days on patrol in the border regions of south County Fermanagh and an attempted ambush on an RUC roadblock, the column returned to their local safe house, or 'billet', in order to plan the proposed Brookeborough attack.[98] With the use of a 'tipper truck' that had been stolen from a resident in the nearby town of Lisnaskea, Garland and his deputy, Daithí Ó Conaill, devised an elaborate plan that 'hinged on speed, mobility and surprise'. Intending to enter the village just after dark, Garland divided his column into a separate assault and cover group for the operation. Using the lorry for protection, the cover party, grouped around a Bren gun manned by Seán South and Patrick O'Regan, were to lay down machine gun fire while their comrades in the assault party were to detonate a pre-prepared mine at the front of the station. In order to ensure a quick withdrawal, one of the volunteers was tasked with clearing civilians from the area, while Vincent Conlon was to remain in the cab of the truck in order to keep the engine running.[99]

Following hasty last-minute preparations, the column entered the town of Brookeborough just after dark on the evening of 1 January 1957. Owing to the presence of children on the street, Conlon failed to stop the lorry in the correct position, leaving the cover party dangerously exposed to RUC fire.[100] Once the lorry had halted, all the volunteers began implementing their allotted tasks, not realizing that this major error had been made.[101] A number of hand grenades were then thrown at the station, as the assault party made their way forward to place the rudimentary gelignite mine at the front door of the barracks. Unbeknown to the raiders, however, this mine had been rendered ineffective after being accidentally dropped into a drain of water three nights previously.¹⁰² When the mine failed to explode, RUC fire from a Bren gun inflicted significant casualties on the exposed cover party in the lorry, prompting the column's hasty withdrawal with police reinforcements in pursuit. With six wounded men, including the 'badly hurt' Fergal O'Hanlon and the unconscious Seán South, the group began to make its way towards the border, but owing to the damage to their truck the raiders were forced to abandon their transportation at Altawark Cross and continue their journey on foot. By this stage it was apparent that both South and O'Hanlon were mortally wounded and it was decided to leave the unconscious volunteers in a disused cattle shed, where locals were instructed to summon a doctor.¹⁰³

Within minutes, the RUC had converged on the scene and began to open fire with machine guns in an attempt to attract return fire and thereby locate the retreating column. Following a brief silence, another 'long burst of fire' was heard by the fleeing raiders, which they assumed 'was a *coup de grace* to Seán and Fergal'.¹⁰⁴ In the hours following the raid, Garland and the remainder of his party successfully managed to evade the RUC manhunt and crossed the border near Knockatallen, County Monaghan. While the four remaining casualties were placed in a safe house outside Scotstown, several members of the column returned to the border in order to dump their weapons, only to be arrested by the Gardaí the following morning. In the interim, Ó Conaill became concerned for the well-being of his injured comrades, who were still 'losing a lot of blood', and proceeded to contact the local Garda station in order to get medical assistance.¹⁰⁵ The wounded men were then escorted to Monaghan County Hospital, where they were detained by the authorities. In the days following the raid, it was widely reported that if O'Hanlon had received adequate medical attention 'in reasonable time' his life could have been saved. Needless to say this was angrily rejected by his comrades, who claimed he had been murdered in cold blood. This was disputed by the findings of the inquest, which concluded that none of his wounds had been caused at close range.¹⁰⁶

Although the raid was a military failure, the circumstances in which both South and O'Hanlon met their deaths were to ensure that the events at Brookeborough were quickly appropriated as a relative moral victory. Both individuals were immediately added to the canon of republican martyrs, as O'Hanlon, a young clerical officer from Monaghan, was praised for expounding the virtue of sacrifice in the attainment of freedom, while South was singled out as a striking exemplar of fundamental Gaelic virtue.[107] Motivated by a political philosophy aimed at the establishment of a corporatist state that would implement papal social encyclicals, South was retrospectively described as 'one of the most literate and articulate republicans in Limerick'.[108] A passionate and fluent Irish speaker, he began his political career as a member of Clann na Poblachta, leaving the party in 1948 following its decision to enter into government with Fine Gael.[109] Writing extensively for numerous Irish language publications, South also published a republican magazine called *An Gath* and in 1949 founded a group called *Seadairí na Saoirse*, which aimed 'to unite all Irish speakers of Ireland in one great army'.[110] He was also an active member of An Realt, the Irish-speaking section of the Legion of Mary, and in 1949 was the founder of the Limerick branch of Maria Duce, a Catholic lay organization campaigning for the constitutional recognition of the Roman Catholic Church as 'the one true Church'.[111] South had also achieved a degree of notoriety in Limerick, owing to his vociferous opposition to the Hollywood movie industry, which he saw as a 'Judaeo-Masonic' front for the dissemination of 'insidious' communist propaganda.[112] He joined the IRA in April 1954.[113]

News of his death was greeted with shock in Limerick, where he was eulogized in the press as an:

> unselfishly sincere and ardent lover of Ireland as ever breathed. Deeply religious, he was widely read and cultured and was in every action of his life motivated by the highest ideals and motives. A genius in many respects, his talents were both marked and many sided. Ireland and everything Irish had in him an ardent and practical supporter. He was intimately and actively associated with the Irish Ireland cause in its several phases and was never sparing in his efforts for its advancement.[114]

With the release of his remains for burial, the occasion of his funeral organized by Sinn Féin on 4 and 5 January 1957 was the scene of a massive public demonstration of attachment to romantic republicanism.[115] It was intended that the remains would be conveyed to Limerick through Dublin in order to provide the population with an opportunity to pay their last respects. Departing from Monaghan after Mass at St Macartan's Cathedral, the cortege, consisting of 'about 700 people', arrived in Dundalk, where 'considerable numbers lined the footpath'.[116] However, prior to its arrival in Drogheda, members of Sinn Féin had to approach shopkeepers in the town in order to ask them to close their shops and draw their blinds as a mark of respect. While most complied with this request, 'blinds were not drawn in all instances' and it was reported that 'the response in Drogheda fell short of expectations'.[117]

This minor display of public indifference was not to be repeated, as a large 'lunchtime crowd' lined the principal streets and thoroughfares of Dublin in order to greet the arrival of the cortege.[118] At the junction of the Drumcondra and Clonliffe roads it was met by 'men wearing black arm bands and members of the Fianna Éireann boy scouts movement', while it was reported that women wearing 'green uniforms' were in the crowd. The procession then made its way to Parnell Square, where the hearse was surrounded by a nine-man 'guard of honour', while a decade of the rosary was recited. After a two-hour wait the procession, accompanied by 'a large crowd', resumed its journey towards Limerick, where it arrived after a nine and a half hour journey at around 10.15 p.m.[119] 'A scene quite without parallel' was to ensue when the cortege was greeted by 'a large concourse of the general public which had waited in heavy rain'.[120] Also in attendance was the mayor of the city, members of the Corporation, as well as representatives of the County and Borough Councils, the Limerick Harbour Board, the County Vocational Committee and the local GAA.[121]

A twelve-man guard of honour consisting of known local republicans moved to escort the hearse, which was followed by approximately 4,000 people to St Michael's Church, where the remains were laid overnight. A guard of honour maintained a vigil at the church until 1 a.m., to be resumed at 8 a.m. the following morning.[122] After Requiem Mass at 10.30 a.m. the funeral procession, led by 'twenty priests of various religious orders', left for the republican plot in Mount St Laurence cemetery. Again it was noted by the Gardaí in attendance that 'all business premises along the route were closed and several thousand people lined the footpaths on both sides'. Reprising their respective roles from the night before, the mayor as well as representatives from 'almost all organizations and shade of public opinion' marched in the procession, which was estimated to contain up to 11,000 mourners. Local republican Dermot O'Donoghue delivered a brief oration at the graveside before South was finally laid to rest. 'A large amount of wreaths' were then placed on the grave before 'those present then dispersed'. The detailed Garda report of the event closed with the terse observation that 'there [was] no untoward incident to record in relation to the assemblage on 4 and 5 January 1957'.[123]

BROOKEBOROUGH: THE POLITICAL FALLOUT

The immediate political fallout from the Brookeborough raid was immense, as the IRA's campaign, now impelled by three fatalities, posited grave implications for the security of the Irish state and its relationship with Britain. Emotions in the Irish Republic were certainly running high, as many people, while notionally opposed to the IRA's use of violence, remained broadly sympathetic to the aims and ideals of these 'misguided youths' – who were more often than not the product of the contemporary political culture.[124] Indeed, the resonances with the aftermath of the 1916 executions were not lost on the Irish government as several county councils and Dublin City Council immediately passed resolutions of sympathy with the families of South and O'Hanlon. In fact, Tipperary County Council went so far as to urge the government to 'desist from all operations along the border and release the prisoners now in custody'.[125] Criticized by Fianna Fáil for its failure to take 'firm and prompt action to quell [the IRA]', de Valera also accused the government of 'gravely setting back' the cause of Irish unity. It was within this context that Costello, who was also under intense diplomatic pressure from the British government, decided to address the nation in a 'widely publicized broadcast' on Radio Éireann on 6 January 1957.[126]

Contrasting with the bellicose and truculent tenor of his previous statements, Costello struck a surprisingly judicious note when he pointed out that 'three young Irishmen' had been killed within the space of a week. Although he reiterated the government's 'ardent desire' to see the reunion of Ireland, he admonished republicans for 'seeking to embroil our country in war' and condemned the use of force to end partition. He continued:

> There would be a hardening of resolve among Irishmen in the north-east to remain divided from us, to rely on support from another country and to give to that other country the loyalty that is Ireland's due. Many more lives would be lost. Peace and order would vanish. Our democratic institutions would be undermined and the hope of a United Ireland would be defeated.

Pointing out that there could be only 'one government, one parliament and one army in the country,' he decried the existence of 'a second body assuming to itself the prerogatives of government ... [while] maintaining an armed force to carry out its dictates'. Most importantly, Costello also committed his government to taking more decisive action against the IRA when he declared that the consequences that would follow a continuance of these attacks must now be clear to the whole nation. So far as they are directed from within the territory under our jurisdiction, it is the duty of the government of this state to prevent their continuance. That duty we are resolved to perform.[127]

Hailed as a 'courageous statement' by Brian Maginess, the Attorney-General of Northern Ireland, it was also welcomed by W.W.B. Topping, the Minister for Home Affairs, who expressed the hope that 'it would be accompanied by real actions'. For his part, de Valera was 'in entire agreement' with the thrust of the Taoiseach's speech and endorsed the government's belief that 'the problem of partition cannot be solved by force'.[128] However, in implementing its newfound resolve to tackle the IRA, the government was to encounter a number of significant problems. Having embraced a policy of non-aggression within the Irish Republic, most IRA volunteers were unarmed when intercepted in border areas by Gardaí. As the act of simply crossing the border was not in itself illegal, there was technically no suggestion that these individuals had broken any law within the Irish jurisdiction, despite being actively engaged in trying to subvert a neighbouring state.[129] From a strictly legal standpoint there was very little the government could do when faced with this *fait accompli*, except, where appropriate, charge these men under the OASA.[130] In most cases, conviction in these circumstances entailed the imposition of light custodial sentences, earning unionist opprobrium for the perceived leniency with which IRA suspects were being treated.

On the other hand, the government was also hampered by the unreliability demonstrated by certain members of the judiciary when it came to dealing with the first raft of political cases arising from the recent desultory crackdown. When confronted with republican prisoners who insisted on not recognizing the legitimacy of the courts, most district justices, while sympathetic, discharged their duty and held strictly to the letter of the law. In one instance, District Justice Michael Lennon created a public sensation by appearing to openly favour the case of Ruairí Ó Brádaigh and his colleagues, who had been arrested in the wake of the Derrylin attack a number of weeks previously. Appearing in the Dublin District Court on 22 January 1957, the accused were charged with failing to account for their movements in accordance with section fifty-two of the OASA. As this section was included in part five of the act, it was operative on the basis of a governmental proclamation made in 1939. During the course of the hearing, the prosecuting solicitor handed a copy of this proclamation to District Justice Lennon, who sensationally declared that it did not end with the words 'God Save the King'. When the prosecuting solicitor asked if he was supposed to make any comment on this assertion, the district justice replied by saying:

> Yes. I remember proclamations of this kind made in regard to myself and they always ended up with the words God Save the King. This Proclamation was made in the time of the Monarchy.[131]

Lennon then moved to dismiss the charges against Ó Brádaigh and his colleagues. Needless to say they were hastily re-arraigned before District Justice Kenneth Reddin, where they were eventually convicted of the charges and sentenced to six months' imprisonment.[132] Horrified, the government moved to order an investigation into the conduct of Lennon pursuant to section twenty-one of the Courts of Justice (District Court) Act, 1946. Under the provisions of this act, the Minister for Justice was empowered to ask the chief justice to appoint a member of the Supreme Court to make the relevant enquiries.[133] On 24 February 1957, Justice Thomas Teevan delivered his report on the matter to the government: he found the behaviour of the district justice to be objectionable, meriting disapproval, but 'not misconduct justifying motion for removal from office'. Lennon was duly informed of the findings of this report, whereupon he expressed regret for his actions and voiced his disapproval of the continuing IRA raids. Although allowed to continue in office, his very public display, coupled with the government's growing rift with Clann na Poblachta, served from a political standpoint to undermine Costello's increasingly precarious position as Taoiseach.[134]

For a government elected on a platform of controlling inflation, the rising prices of bacon, tea, stout and tobacco throughout 1954 were the signal of worse to come. A severe balance of payments deficit in 1955 prompted the Minister for Finance, Gerard Sweetman, to impose import levies on sixty-eight 'non-essential' goods in March 1956, while his budget two months later brought further increases in the prices of petrol and cigarettes. The loss of several by-elections, as well as Fianna Fáil's retention of its Cork seat in August of that year, was another setback for the government, which was further shaken in September when the Labour TD James Larkin criticized Sweetman's economic measures and called for greater capital investment to resolve the country's economic problems. MacBride responded by calling for a ten-year national plan, as Fianna Fáil's victory in two further by-elections in mid-November 1956 handed Clann na Poblachta the balance of power in the Dáil. Coupled with its indecisiveness in dealing with the IRA, the portents for the survival of Costello's government were not good.[135]

Against this backdrop, the arrest of Seán Cronin, Noel Kavanagh, Robert Russell and Patrick Duffy in Belturbet, County Cavan, was the occasion of another highly unusual episode within the Irish courts, with the discovery of a copy of the Operation Harvest during a follow-up raid in Cronin's home.[136] With two copies of this document now in the government's possession, its relative importance in terms of the IRA's campaign was slowly becoming apparent. In a confidential letter to the Taoiseach, the Minister for Education, Richard Mulcahy, urged that immediate action be taken in respect of the document, otherwise, if kept in 'police or government pigeon holes', it would become 'a tormenting source of indecision and awkwardness'. In his opinion, Operation Harvest demonstrated a 'fully informed intent' on the part of the IRA, which was demonstrating a 'Dundrum asylum mentality' in pursuit of its objectives. He advised its immediate publication, whereby its obvious implications for the security of the country would 'end all sentimental nonsense' and 'constitute a growing challenge to anybody continuing to associate themselves' with the IRA. In this respect, its production in open court together with the simultaneous circulation of a complete transcript to the press would best serve the government's purpose.[137]

The first available opportunity came on 17 January, when Cronin and his colleagues were returned for trial before the Dublin District Court. During the course of the proceedings, the prosecuting solicitor sought permission to lay a copy of the document before the court, despite Cronin's protestations that this would 'put the lives of men operating against the occupying forces in the six counties into jeopardy'. When District Justice Reddin intimated that it was hardly necessary to proceed with this proposed course of action, as it was not material to the case, the prosecuting solicitor replied that 'my instructions are to read the document [as] it is an exhibit'. A verbatim report of the contents of Operation Harvest was then delivered and it was widely reported in the press.[138] This was maligned by republicans as an 'act of sabotage', and the Taoiseach's office was immediately inundated with representations from various republican organizations throughout Australia and the USA, outraged by this perceived 'betrayal of [the] resistance movement' with the publication of its plans in the press.[139] Many republicans certainly felt that this was a convenient way of alerting the northern authorities to proposed attacks on specific targets, without having to engage directly with the government in Stormont.[140] However, the IRA was still successful in causing severe damage to a newly constructed Territorial Army barracks in Dungannon, despite the fact that it was one of the key targets listed for attack.[141]

This embarrassing episode served to highlight the continued inadequacy of cross-border policing arrangements, given the 'cursory and truculent' nature of official contact between Dublin and Belfast.[142] In some instances, however, it appeared that cooperation between the Gardaí and the RUC may have been established, without direction from, but with the apparent acquiescence of, their respective political masters.[143] In light of the close physical proximity within which both forces operated, it was not unusual to note that daily local meetings along the border were a normal part of the police relationship. In 1954 relations were put on a more formal footing, when the Irish government responded to British requests for greater action against the IRA by establishing 'secret and effective contact and interchange of information' between the heads of both police forces.[144] There was no question of agreeing to the British suggestion that the Irish cabinet permit the extradition of IRA suspects, as it 'would be entirely contrary to international practice' and was something that 'no Irish government could contemplate in principle'.[145] However, with the outbreak of the border campaign, the limited liaisons between the Gardaí and the RUC were immediately stepped up as the exchange of 'sound intelligence' between forces was given tacit approval by Dublin and London.[146] As it was sanctioned only on a local and discreet basis this overt cooperation did not extend to the opening of a more direct dialogue between the Irish and Northern Irish administrations.

With the Irish government now beginning to follow through with the commitments made in Costello's Radio Éireann address, mounting opposition within Clann na Poblachta found dramatic expression in a party motion condemning the Taoiseach for embarking on 'a policy of repression against republicans'.[147] On 10 January it was reported that extra Gardaí had been posted to border stations and that there was intensive police activity in County Tipperary following the theft of a 'huge quantity of gelignite' from a board of works store in Nenagh.[148] This was quickly followed by a coordinated raid in Dublin by Special Branch detectives, who arrested a number of prominent republicans, including Tomás MacCurtain and Anthony Magan, who were transferred to the Bridewell, where they were kept in solitary confinement.[149] Three days later another Special Branch operation netted thirty-one men in pre-dawn swoops in Cork, Dublin, Limerick and Waterford. Seven of them were released after questioning, while the remainder were charged under the OASA for being members of an illegal organization, for which they all received prison sentences ranging from three to six months.[150] As hoped, centralized control at the top of the IRA had been temporarily disrupted as the republican movement struggled to co-opt new members on to a makeshift Army Council, while at the same time endeavouring to maintain the momentum of the campaign.[151]

Speaking at the Portadown Chamber of Commerce annual dinner on 22 January, Topping gave a qualified welcome to the actions taken by the Irish government 'to stamp out armed raids'.[152] Needless to say, prominent Irish-American opinion was not proving to be quite so quiescent, as several organizations, including the American League for an Undivided Ireland, the United Ireland Committee and the Knights of the Red Branch, began to openly censure the government.[153] Fearful of alienating moderate Irish-American support, Costello sanctioned the drafting of a detailed rebuttal, to be sent in response to hostile correspondence. Outlining the government's position in respect of the IRA and the use of force to end partition, it posited a robust defence of the decision to publicize the contents of Operation Harvest.[154] While failing for the most part to mollify its target constituency, it provoked a rejoinder from the MacSwiney chapter of the American League for an Undivided Ireland, calling for 'a little leniency [to be] extended to the boys'.[155]

In February, the anxieties of the Irish government were further excited with the receipt of a telegram from the consulate in New York stating that it had been in contact with informants who claimed that there was to be an arms shipment to the IRA within the coming days. Suspicions were immediately aroused, however, when a payment of $15,000 was demanded for the particulars of the scheme and the full details of the 'republican army apparatus' in the United States.[156] The consulate was immediately ordered not to pay any money as the US State Department and the FBI were fully apprised of the situation.[157] Several days later, two men in their 'late twenties' called to the consulate and spoke to officials Eamonn Gallagher and James Kirwan. Identifying themselves as 'Lyjohn' and 'Bellucci', they informed the consulate officials that they knew the IRA to be involved in trying to obtain weapons in the United States and alleged that quantities of arms were being shipped to Ireland 'all the time'. They also intimated that 'four trunk loads' containing Thompson sub-machine guns and hand grenades were due for immediate shipment to Ireland, but declined to proffer any more information until they had received payment from the consulate. When informed that the consulate did not have money at its disposal for the purchase of information the two men left the office, declining to leave contact addresses. The following day a representative of the US Customs Services arrived at the consulate; he dismissed the matter on the grounds that 'if any extensive gun running was taking place ... his office would know about it'. When the consulate failed to receive any further communication from Lyjohn and Bellucci they were categorized as 'confidence tricksters' and the affair was closed.[158]

GENERAL ELECTION

In the wake of Costello's Radio Éireann address the republican constituency within Clann na Poblachta became mobilized in its opposition to the government's new-found hostility towards the IRA. Speaking at a party meeting on 18 January, MacBride was scathing when he indicted the Taoiseach for his lack of leadership on the question of partition, thereby allowing the IRA to take centre stage.[159] Coming during a period of intense economic crisis characterized by a severe balance of payments deficit and a sharp rise in the rate of unemployment, this rupture with Clann could not have occurred at a worse time.[160] Already censured by the public for its ineptitude in managing the economy by the loss of three by-elections to a rejuvenated Fianna Fáil, MacBride decided to use the issue as a stick with which to beat the government. He wrote to the Taoiseach urging him to take immediate action to deal with the economic situation. When he received no reply, he warned that 'the Clann cannot continue indefinitely to be a party to a policy of inertia and drift or to the continued recourse to uneconomic and inadequate expedients ... the situation is too grave'. It was in this context that a meeting of Clann's Ard Comhairle was held on 26 January, in order to consider the propriety of the party's continued support for the government.

Dominated by a republican majority led by Con Lehane and Fionan Breathnach, the meeting of the Ard Comhairle urged a hesitant MacBride to withdraw support from Costello on the grounds that they were not prepared to sustain a government that was actively engaged in rounding up republicans. MacBride, mindful of the consequences involved in pursuing such a course of action, protested by pointing out the inherent dangers entailed for republicans with the return of a Fianna Fáil administration. While this was accepted by both Lehane and Breathnach, both felt that in all conscience they could no longer support the government and, against MacBride's advice, instructed him to put down a motion of no-confidence in the government. Although MacBride relented, he insisted that if Clann were to bring the government down it would not be on the northern issue alone.[161] Two days later, the party publicly announced its intention of withdrawing its support from the government and proposed a motion of no-confidence that regretted the administration's failure to adopt a comprehensive economic development programme and to formulate a positive policy on partition.[162] This was accompanied by the release of a strongly worded statement, which confirmed the party's primary motivation:

> The government is embarking on the pursuit of unnecessary and provocative measures of coercion which we must emphatically decry. We have repeatedly pointed out that the failure to formulate and implement a positive policy [on partition] was bound to create a dangerous internal situation in which the government would assume responsibility for maintaining the *status quo* and would undertake the role of acting as Britain's policeman against a section of the Irish people.[163]

With the loss of Clann's support, the mathematical permutations in the Dáil did not inspire confidence in the government's ability to defeat the motion. Rather than face the humiliation of losing the vote, Costello took the step of dissolving the Dáil, thereby precipitating a general election on 5 March.[164] In the view of the Minister for Agriculture, James Dillon, Costello, 'weary of the business of governing' following the recent death of his wife, gave in too easily as the government collapsed, primarily because parts of it had suffered an erosion of will.[165] As a result, it was now up to all parties to gear up for an election 'which nobody really wanted'. At the Fine Gael Ard Fheis Costello proceeded to launch a broadside against his erstwhile partners in Clann by outlining how:

> The real reason why people are burdened with expense and turmoil of a general election is that the government has done its national and international duty and discharged the unpleasant task of accepting in the name of the people the challenge to

democracy and peace which have been made by lawless forces who refuse to accept principles either of democracy or morality and decline to acknowledge the lawful Constitution of the state.[166]

In launching its own campaign, the Fianna Fáil party astutely emphasised how the IRA's resort to force was understandable but counterproductive, believing that the 'young men of the IRA needed "friendly sympathy and advice" to desist from violence'. In outlining its republican credentials, the party was also at pains to stress that it was working for 'the ideals of 1916', while at the same time explaining that 'it had the unity, capacity and will to curb the IRA'.[167]

Perhaps the most remarkable aspect of what was an exceptionally insipid election campaign was the participation of Sinn Féin following its years in the political wilderness. Mindful of its previous achievements in the Mid-Ulster and Fermanagh–South Tyrone elections of 1955, the party endeavoured to capitalize on its success with the nomination of nineteen candidates, seven of whom were prisoners.[168] Campaigning on an abstentionist basis, it boldly committed itself to a radical social policy in a period of intense economic crisis. Purporting to 'accomplish the task of freeing Ireland from the yoke of foreign occupation', its election manifesto advocated the maintenance of 'a national economy consonant with the Nation's requirements'. It also sought to promote 'private enterprise' and encouraged 'the agricultural community to make the utmost of their holdings ... to meet the full home needs'. In campaigning against the backdrop of the IRA's continuing offensive in Northern Ireland, the party vigorously promoted its message, stressing to canvassers the need to avoid 'political arguments of a heated nature'.[169]

For its part, the IRA made an effort to regroup following the setbacks inflicted by the government crackdown, with an unsuccessful attempt to blow up a bridge in Ballygawley, County Tyrone and an attack on an electricity transformer outside Moneymore, County Derry. An assault on a Territorial Army camp at Duncreggan, County Derry, on 15 February led the authorities to suspect that the attacking party had sustained casualties, when sentries reported hearing a scream after a brief exchange of gunfire. The following night, a raid on the headquarters of the Ulster Light Anti-Aircraft Regiment in Coleraine was narrowly averted when an alert guard challenged a number of men attempting to take up attacking positions in a field close to the outer fence. A day later, road and rail services between

Dungannon and Omagh were seriously curtailed when another IRA party achieved more success in blowing up a number of bridges in that area.[170] Despite this, the increasing number of arrests on both sides of the border were beginning to inhibit the IRA's capacity to mount a higher intensity offensive.[171] With most of the leadership in Mountjoy Prison, control of the organization fell to a temporary Army Council headed by Tomás Ó Dubhghaill, who endeavoured to establish a more efficient underground courier, supply and service system in order to minimize arrests. At the same time, Ó Dubhghaill attempted to ratchet up the campaign by directing a number of units to carry out a series of ambushes on police patrols and British troop convoys.[172]

In the meantime, the election campaign intensified, as Fianna Fáil continued to press its obvious advantage in regard to the IRA question. Gerald Boland was at pains to stress the government's culpability in providing 'illegal organizations' with a *'carte blanche'* to 'arm, drill, openly recruit, hold public collections ... and publish a newspaper'. This was followed up by Seán MacEntee, when he accused Costello of 'evading his responsibilities in regard to illegal organizations' on the grounds that he 'knew the men behind these subversive organizations held the life of his coalition in their hands'.[173] Within this context, the government's position was further undermined when the IRA managed to pull off a spectacular operation in which a group of three masked men halted a train, ordered the crew to leave at gun point and sent it crashing into Derry railway station.[174] Estimated to have caused over £20,000 of damage, the contrast between Fianna Fáil's robust wartime response and Costello's vacillation in regard to the IRA could not have been move vivid.

As was widely expected, the election resulted in Fianna Fáil's return to power. However, the resounding manner in which this was effected proved to be a surprise to many contemporary observers. In spite of a 'dull campaign', *The Times* noted that it was a heavy poll which attracted a substantial turnout. As counting began it quickly became apparent that Fianna Fáil was well placed and had increased its first preference vote in many areas, mainly at the expense of Fine Gael.[175] In eventually securing seventy-eight seats in total, de Valera's triumph was heralded as 'the greatest victory in any Irish general election', with the coalition parties suffering heavy losses. Notably, Fine Gael lost ten seats, Labour lost eight and Clann na Poblachta lost two: MacBride was sensationally ousted by his constituents in County Dublin. Perhaps the most startling performance, however, was that of Sinn Féin, garnering 65,640 first preference votes, primarily at the expense of the coalition parties. In doing so it secured the election of four TDs: Éighneachán O'Hanlon in Monaghan, John Joe Rice in South Kerry, John Joe McGirl in Sligo–Leitrim and Ruairí Ó Brádaigh in Longford–Westmeath. Remarkably, McGirl topped the poll in Sligo–Leitrim, where he displaced the independent candidate Ben Maguire, while Ó Brádaigh finished a close second to Fine Gael's Seán MacEoin, at the expense of Fianna Fáil's Frank Carter.[176]

Joe Lee attributes Sinn Féin's success to its commitment to radical social policies rather than to its support of the IRA.[177] However, given the public displays of solidarity and empathy that had been occasioned by the deaths of South and O'Hanlon, the evidence would also seem to suggest that there was a degree of admiration for what the IRA was trying to achieve. In many ways, Sinn Féin's limited electoral success was an amazing result for a party that had endorsed a paramilitary campaign and rejected participation in parliament.[178] Although disappointed that it had not secured more seats, given the basis of its victory Sinn Féin confidently surmised that, if it had contested all constituencies,

> the overall average secured in the nineteen contested constituencies would also have been secured in all of the forty constituencies. This would have given a result of approximately 140,000 which coupled with the vote of over 152,000 obtained by candidates of the republican movement within the six counties in the last general election to Westminster indicated a very practical and satisfactory demonstration of a national resurgence that gives hope for the ultimate cause of Ireland's liberation from British aggression.

In viewing the election of a new Fianna Fáil administration as an 'anti-government vote', the party also naively believed that the public had given their support to de Valera 'in the firm belief and hope that coercion and imprisonment of republicans would cease'.[179]

Needless to say, this interpretation of events proved to be a grave miscalculation, which was to have adverse long-term effects on the IRA's capacity to prosecute its campaign in Northern Ireland. Governed by its self-image as the vanguard of Irish nationalism, Sinn Féin also took its large vote as a mandate for the continuation of violence, rather than regarding it as a manifestation of broad public discontent that could be developed and fashioned towards specific republican goals.[180] More importantly, the IRA had heavily misjudged de Valera's position on the use of violence, believing that their continued assurance of remaining quiescent in the Republic of Ireland would be sufficient surety for the southern authorities to ignore their presence.[181] In a clandestine meeting in 1956 an IRA group met de Valera and asked him

> to assist in their attacks, or at least connive at them. De Valera gave them not the slightest encouragement. He was indeed extremely forthright with them and impressed upon them his belief, often stated publicly, that partition could not be solved by force of arms. Their movement, he said, was bound to fail; it would cause great suffering without any visible weakening of partition.[182]

While consistently insisting that no task was 'more hateful' to an Irish government than 'having to deal severely with any section of the Irish people', de Valera was often the leading advocate in the Dáil of strong legal measures to suppress the campaign.[183] Following the election, de Valera immediately took steps to reiterate his position when asked at a press conference 'if measures similar to those adopted by the government during World War Two would be used to combat illegal military forces?' The terse reply that followed left many in no doubt as to his intentions: '… private armies cannot be tolerated. That would lead to anarchy.'[184] As a result, with his formal election as Taoiseach on 20 March 1957 there was an immediate and very marked shift in policy.[185] While anti-partitionist rhetoric continued unabated, practical steps were quickly taken to deal with the IRA. Garda–RUC liaison was stepped up, and extra police and soldiers were deployed in border areas.[186] Moreover, the signs were ominous for the IRA and did not augur well for a successful conclusion to its campaign. In keeping with his previous track record, de Valera was to waste little time in coming to grips with the republican movement, in what was to be his final tenure of office.

5

'The Nettle Had At Last Been Gripped':[1] Forkhill and the Reintroduction of Internment, July 1957

The inauguration of a new Fianna Fáil government in March 1957 was greeted with a muted response in Belfast and London as de Valera's remark about private armies failed to elicit a reply from either quarter. While his return to power was broadly welcomed by the unionist press, as he was certain to be 'master of his own house', de Valera was quick to signal his intention of adopting a cautious and low-key approach to the live wire issue of 'illegal organizations'.[2] Reluctant to criticize the actions of his predecessor in office, de Valera instead fell back on his favoured position of stressing the futility of force as a means of ending partition.[3] In many ways he was content, for the moment, to remain imprecise as to the government's intentions, even when the thorny matter of republican prisoners came before the Dáil. As a gesture of goodwill, the independent Deputy Jack McQuillan sought the release of all persons imprisoned under the OASA and sparked heated debate when he asserted that it was as a direct result of British pressure that the 'full machinery of the law' had been employed. Needless to say, this provoked the angry intervention of several Fine Gael deputies before the new Minister for Justice, Oscar Traynor, had an opportunity to confirm that the government would only be prepared to release republicans who agreed to sign a written undertaking guaranteeing their future conduct.[4]

Initially, the government was vindicated in its mellifluent approach, particularly as the institution of a raft of new security arrangements in Northern Ireland seemed to be having the desired effect. Specifically, a new planning committee was established by the RUC to coordinate all operations against the IRA, while the number of B-Specials who were mobilized for full-time duty was reduced to 910 men.[5] This reduction, however, was more than offset by the creation of two reserve platoons of the RUC, equipped with 'armoured, long wheel-base land rovers'. Stationed at Fivemiletown, County Tyrone, and Moneymore, County Derry, these platoons proved adept at keeping many IRA volunteers on the run through the establishment of random roadblocks and the execution of numerous foot patrols along the border.[6] While these provisions posed a considerable impediment to the IRA, they were not entirely insurmountable, as demonstrated by a series of operations on 7 March 1957. Successful in evading the authorities on both sides of the border, two parties of IRA volunteers managed to mount coordinated attacks on an army recruiting office in Newry, which was partially destroyed by a mine, and the beleaguered RUC barracks in Derrylin, County Fermanagh. The raid on the barracks, although interrupted by an RUC patrol, resulted in 'a fierce gun battle', during which a police constable was wounded by splintered glass.[7] Although a failure, this incident incited Brookeborough to draw an emotive parallel with 'the critical times in the early 1920s' when he was 'a commandant of the Fermanagh B-Specials'.[8]

Faced with a reduced capacity to prosecute its campaign, the IRA quickly resorted to incidents of low-level sabotage in an effort to maintain the momentum of its offensive. In many cases this involved the cutting of telegraph wires and the demolition of telephone kiosks, at considerable inconvenience to the civilian populace.[9] Attempts to disrupt the north's transportation network were also incorporated and on 11 March the main road between Roslea and Fivemiletown was severed when an explosion, 'which was heard over a wide area', completely destroyed a small stone bridge over the Derryneece river.[10] Two days later, three armed men engaged in a brazen attempt to rescue 'political internee' Thomas Lennon from police custody in Belfast City Hospital, where he was recovering from an operation for appendicitis. Foiled by the actions of a plain-clothes police officer who was on duty beside Lennon's bed, the men immediately decamped in a taxi before being detained at an RUC roadblock a number of hours later.[11] Arrests were also on the increase: seven men were held by the RUC after firing a number of shots at the Territorial Army barracks in Dungannon, County Tyrone. Two weeks later, the authorities also struck a paralyzing blow to the republican organization in Derry with the arrest of twenty-three suspects and the discovery of a huge arsenal in a number of concealed arms dumps throughout the city.[12]

Needless to say, the continuation of the IRA's campaign, which had now entered its fourth month, was proving to be a heavy drain on the limited resources of the Northern Ireland exchequer. To begin with, increased security costs ensured that the 1956–57 estimates for the B-Specials had to be increased almost threefold, from £480,004 to £1,287,522. In an effort to check this surge in expenditure, the Department of Home Affairs authorized the implementation of a series of new regulations governing the payment of expenses arising from the emergency mobilization of the B-Specials.[13] With control of the security budget now established, the authorities were faced with another unanticipated outlay, as the Department of Home Affairs was inundated with claims for compensation for damage to private property. To address this problem, Brookeborough recommended the passage of a Criminal Injuries Bill, which would allow the Northern Ireland government to make a 50 per cent grant towards malicious injury claims against local authorities, provided that the damage was caused by people residing outside its jurisdiction. The remaining burden of the claim would then to be shared by ratepayers throughout Northern Ireland.[14] As the number of incidents increased, however, it was felt that the government should bear the full burden, with the proviso that, if the costs involved appeared to be prohibitive, then the British government would be lobbied to provide a subvention.

In agreeing to proceed on this basis, Topping publicly announced his government's intention of giving immediate legislative affect to these proposals.[15] Needless to say, mounting unionist outrage was not allayed by this measure, as it was underpinned by a growing consensus that the Irish government was complicit in the raids and should, therefore, foot the bill. Matters came to a head following the Derry train incident in February, when Robin Chichester-Clarke, the leader of the UUP in Westminster, signalled his intention of raising the question of compensation in parliament, as the incident, in his view, 'could be pinned on the Republic'.[16] Having already made private representations on the matter to the Irish Department of External Affairs, the Dominions Office was anxious to discourage Chichester-Clarke from this course of action and persuaded him to hold off until de Valera had 'some time to get into the saddle'.[17] They were supported in this view by Sir Alexander Clutterbuck, who felt that de Valera should be given 'a clear run' as 'anything which might be interpreted as prodding from Britain' would be likely to do more harm than good.[18] When Chichester-Clarke eventually insisted on tabling the question anyway, the British government was put in the embarrassing position of having to admit that, while a formal approach had been made to Dublin, 'no subsequent communication had been held with the government of the Irish Republic'.[19]

The matter was not pursued further, despite the fact that the northern administration was also coming under increased pressure to settle claims for damage to property outside its jurisdiction. On one occasion, James Sealy, a farmer residing on the Leitrim side of the border, discovered that the force of an explosion set off by an RUC service party who were demolishing local roads had cracked the front wall of his house. When he complained of the incident he was told to send his claim for compensation to the local RUC sergeant stationed in Garrison, County Fermanagh.[20] Although it was felt that Sealy's claim was 'obviously inflated', his was not an isolated case and after much deliberation it was decided that the Northern Ireland government would negotiate and settle 'the claims on account of damage caused by service demolition parties in southern Ireland'.[21] A number of difficulties arose, however, when, as was often the case in rural areas, the exact delimitation of the border was not known. With the awkward spectre of a minor territorial dispute between the two Irish jurisdictions looming on the horizon, the matter was discreetly shelved amidst the bureaucratic intricacies of the British civil service, where it was safely diffused. This issue was not followed up by the Irish government, which was becoming ever more preoccupied with the increasing instances of unauthorized British military excursions into its jurisdiction.

Although forays of this kind were rare, they were usually overlooked as inappropriate and over-zealous, but nonetheless innocent, transgressions on behalf of the perpetrators. Unfortunately, a spate of such incidents by the northern and British authorities throughout January and February, including a volatile confrontation in Pettigo, County Donegal, received substantial coverage in the local press and prompted fears of an escalation. The first of these incidents occurred on 10 January 1957, when an RUC constable accompanied by two British soldiers crossed the border at Scotstown, County Monaghan, to examine a parked car and van. Although the local Gardaí reported that there was not much in the affair, they felt it prudent to immediately apprise their superiors as it was widely observed by a number of civilians.[22] At this the matter rested until 3 February, when a detachment of twenty British soldiers, under the command of an officer, entered the Donegal portion of Pettigo village. Dismounting from a truck, the troops remained for about ten minutes before returning across the border. Immediately, a number of local residents assembled to protest at this 'invasion', but the troops had decamped before any incident could occur.[23]

Two days later, the troops staged a repeat performance, when two trucks deposited them in the main street, where they were seen openly carrying arms. Again remaining for ten minutes, they departed back across the border but not before a large number of local residents congregated outside 'the Garda station where they demanded the immediate ejectment of the troops'. Serious trouble was threatened and it was reported that several individuals 'expressed the intention of taking the law into their own hands'. While the situation was diffused, an 'alarming account' of the incident appeared in the *Donegal Democrat*, prompting fears that it might be carried in some of the daily or cross-channel newspapers. To prevent a recurrence, the local Garda superintendent paid an informal visit to his RUC counterpart in Kesh, County Fermanagh, where he was assured that the troops had inadvertently crossed the border, being unfamiliar with the surroundings. In order to prevent a repeat, the RUC officer took it upon himself to provide for a local guide for all military patrols in his area. Satisfied with these arrangements, the government did not pursue the subject with the British government and instead organized to have joint Garda and military patrols 'performed thrice weekly in this area … as the public would seem to appreciate the presence of force, on occasions, on our side'.[24]

In 1961 a series of more significant border incursions finally prompted the Irish government to make formal representations to London. The first of these incidents occurred on 31 August 1961, when Gardaí stationed in Manorhamilton, County Leitrim, received reports that an RUC patrol had been fired upon 'from the Éire side of the border'. Arriving at the scene, the Gardaí were confronted with an RUC party in uniform, led by a head constable, who admitted that he had crossed the border and penetrated to a depth of up to 600 yards in order to carry out a search for the IRA perpetrators. When informed that they had to return to their own jurisdiction they did so, 'but with very bad grace', as their manner was aggressive and truculent.[25] The following day, Detective Garda Patrick Barrett encountered a similar situation during the course of his regular rounds, when he discovered four men lying in 'ambush positions' in a field outside Kiltyclogher, County Leitrim. Garda Barrett immediately approached the men, who were clad in civilian attire, where he satisfied himself that they were RUC officers. He promptly escorted these individuals to the border, which they reluctantly crossed, and they remained in a field 'for some time'.[26]

In reviewing the situation the Minister for External Affairs, Frank

Aiken, agreed that these incidents 'could lead to a very serious situation' and instructed Hugh McGann, the Irish Ambassador in London, 'to inform the British authorities of our serious concern ... and to request that a stop be put to such practices'.[27] During the course of his ensuing interview with Sir Henry Lintott of the Commonwealth Relations Office, McGann outlined the position as instructed and received assurances that the subject matter of the government's complaint would be looked into immediately. Following a brief investigation by the British authorities, the Commonwealth Relations Office contacted McGann in December and admitted to the encroachments by the RUC. Although there was no apology, Aiken was encouraged and felt that, as a result of the Irish government's representations, 'the RUC are likely to be more careful in the matter of border infringements in the future'.[28] At the same time, the local Garda chief superintendent in Sligo contacted his RUC counterpart in Enniskillen, where he was informed that there would be no repetition of these transgressions.[29]

THE CAMPAIGN AND THE UNITED NATIONS

While the simmering diplomatic wrangles over the IRA's campaign throughout this period did result in several urbane, but nonetheless firm, exchanges between the Irish and British governments, the matter clearly remained within the ambit of friendly discord between neighbours.[30] On the other hand, the opportunities afforded by Ireland's recent entry into the United Nations in 1955 to bring about an escalation of this situation was not lost on the more 'nationally minded' members of Dáil Éireann in 1957.[31] Tending towards Western positions on most international issues, Ireland was initially characterized by a fairly unremarkable performance within this international forum. Fortunately, however, Ireland's one advance in the sphere of international organizations, such as the Council of Europe, was the abandonment of Seán MacBride's incessant rehearsal of the irredentist claim to Northern Ireland, which was known colloquially as the policy of 'the sore thumb'. Justified on the grounds that '[we] should not be merely anti-British, or else we will be completely discounted', the then Taoiseach, John A. Costello, was forced to defend this position by asserting that:

> Anybody who has experience of international affairs and of attendance at international organizations must have seen how

particular countries and particular individuals who are constantly putting forward their own interests and their particular grievances to the exclusion of all other interests lost all influence and came to be regarded as nothing but a mere nuisance.[32]

The return to power of Fianna Fáil in 1957 changed fundamentally Ireland's policy and image at the UN, as Frank Aiken embarked on a campaign of activism that placed Ireland firmly among the diplomatically forward-looking 'middle powers' of the period. The outbreak of the IRA's campaign threatened the Irish government's new-found diplomatic moderation, particularly when Jack McQuillan and Patrick Finucane proposed a motion in the Dáil calling on the government to demand the immediate despatch of UN observers to the 'occupied part of the national territory'.[33] By exploiting the publicity occasioned by the ongoing IRA offensive, this motion, which could not be countenanced by the government, was a blatant attempt to embarrass Britain in the eyes of the international community. Such a move not only threatened to reignite the nationalist fervour previously exhibited by the populace, it would place the Irish state's cordial relationship with the British government on a more hostile and confrontational footing, thereby damaging the government's more reasoned anti-partition efforts. As expected, the government voted to resoundingly defeat the motion on the grounds that it was for them 'to decide content and timing of any motions to be put before the UN'.[34]

Surprisingly, there is evidence to suggest that the arguments for McQuillan's motion were not immediately discounted, as an official in the Department of External Affairs was instructed to prepare a memorandum detailing the merits of such a move. The document noted that the motion as advanced by deputies McQuillan and Finucane did not state what the UN observers were expected to observe and it was pointed out that the motion failed to 'indicate what use, if any, is to be made of the results of their observation'. Yet, in surmising the various avenues through which the government could conceivably pursue this course of action, the tenor of the memo seemed to intimate a brief flirtation with the idea. Ultimately casting doubt on Ireland's ability to secure the necessary majority in either the Security Council or the General Assembly in favour of such an intervention, this proposal was eventually dismissed on the grounds that 'any discussion of our possible action in the UN in the context of the present motion would not only be a concession to the deputies concerned but also to the IRA'.³⁵ In spite of these recommendations, however, the suggestion that the government might seek to raise the issue of partition at the UN was not entirely dismissed by certain members of the diplomatic corps.

In April 1957 Frederick Boland, the government's permanent representative at the UN, wrote to Conor Cruise O'Brien back in headquarters in Dublin to propose a new departure in the government's ongoing international campaign against partition. The fact that there was such contact between these two individuals was in itself significant, as both were key figures within the Irish diplomatic service. Boland, who had served as Secretary of the Department of External Affairs during the tenure of Seán MacBride, had been instrumental in securing O'Brien's recruitment to that department in 1944. By 1957, O'Brien himself was a particularly experienced diplomat and an influential member of Irish delegations to the UN in 1957 and 1958.³⁶ In his letter to O'Brien, Boland felt that instead of raising the issue of partition as a whole it would be better to concentrate on 'some particular aspect of six county discrimination on which we could make an effective showing'.³⁷ While O'Brien advised him that the best tactic would be to concentrate 'on some concrete aspect of discrimination' such as the allocation of local authority housing, he seized the opportunity to submit a new approach of his own. In his view it was best to 'abandon anti-partition propaganda in all its forms', and he enclosed a detailed memorandum in defence of his views. Although accepting that it was unlikely that these views would gain acceptance, he resigned himself to the present situation by surmising that 'if partition propaganda is still to be carried on', then the government should not ignore the 'opportunities afforded by the United Nations'.³⁸

Forthright in his opinions, O'Brien's brief but compelling memorandum was to foreshadow the future evolution of official policy in respect of Northern Ireland. In pointing out that the government had ruled out 'the use of force for the unification of the country', it was argued that any attempt by Britain to coerce the unionist population to live in a united Ireland must also be denied. It therefore followed that any attempt to persuade the British government of the merits of Irish unity should be abandoned and switched to an all-out effort designed to win a majority in favour of unity 'inside the six counties itself'. As a necessary first step, it would naturally fall to the government to do all it could to diminish the tensions which would make it 'impossible at present even to launch … any campaign of persuasion' by crushing 'completely the organizations responsible for the futile and irritating border raids'. All 'anti-Stormont' campaigning must cease and the government must then state 'frankly and plainly' that 'we hope and believe that the six counties will one day rejoin us but we accept that they are free to sit out as long as a majority so desires'. Such a declaration would, in his mind, 'lay the basis of possible friendship between the two great sections of Ireland and therefore the basis of eventual union'.[39]

In replying to O'Brien's suggestions, Boland felt that 'any abrupt or sudden change of policy ... would imply a confession of failure'. Instead of launching a direct attack on the injustice of partition in Ireland, Boland recommended that the government 'use the question of Cyprus as a peg on which to hang a criticism of territorial partition as a political expedient'. In doing so, the Irish government would be making a proactive contribution to the counsels of the UN, while at the same time remaining consistent with its own irredentist grievances. Rather than taking a 'negative line in describing the evils of partition', Boland favoured the formulation of a more positive policy designed to 'define the kind of conditions which it is in everybody's interests to bring about in order to enable historic units, now divided, to be reunited'.[40] In such circumstances, he advocated that the Irish delegation intervene in the ongoing discussions of the special committee on the Report of the United Nations for the Unification and Rehabilitation of Korea. Although the cabinet vetoed these proposals, the discourse initiated by the consideration given to McQuillan's initial motion seems to have provided the impetus for an eventual restatement of Irish policy, in favour of a more consensual accommodation with the unionist population.

THE FORKHILL AMBUSH

Throughout April and May 1957, the number of serious violent incidents in Northern Ireland began to decline, as the security efforts of both Irish governments were enjoying an increasing measure of success. While this was openly acknowledged by Topping, he also recognised that the longer hours of daylight 'might bring a slowing up of ... the campaign' and stated that his government did not intend to relax its security measures 'until there is no doubt ... that normal conditions have been completely restored'.[41] Whereas de Valera may have been in full agreement with these sentiments, the near simultaneous discharge of a number of prominent republicans on the expiry of brief prison sentences threatened to tarnish his government as it was mistaken as an act of leniency on his part.[42] Not only that, the release of these men threatened to reanimate the campaign, as they began to make high-profile appearances at republican rallies and events throughout the country. In Dublin, Michael Traynor thanked 'a packed meeting' in College Green for their support in the recent general election, while Seán Cronin outlined that the IRA's campaign was directed solely against 'the British occupation and not against any portion or any section of the Irish people'.[43] In Limerick, Seán Edmonds used the occasion of his release from Mountjoy to address a large and enthusiastic crowd and explain the rationale for the IRA's refusal to recognize the Irish courts:

> We refused to recognize the courts because we held that the proceedings against us were fraudulent. They were instigated by Britain and arose out of a colossal fraud, the fraud perpetrated by Britain on Ireland in the so-called peace settlement of 1921, when Ireland was partitioned in defiance of the will of the Irish people.[44]

The practical consequence of all this was that the IRA Army Council once again found itself back up to full strength with a commensurate increase in activity.[45] On 4 April a bomb was hurled at the RUC barracks in Coalisland, County Tyrone, where it exploded outside the married quarters of Sergeant Arthur Ovens. While no one was injured, the force of the blast shattered several windows and created a small crater in the garden.[46] Several days later, a small explosion at the RAF radar station at Torr Head, County Antrim, resulted in the loss of running water at the facility after causing severe damage to a water pump.[47] A number of powerful explosions also caused extensive damage to two transformer stations near Derry, disrupting the local electricity supply.[48] Predictably, this spate of incidents was quickly cited as evidence that the extensive security measures instituted by the northern authorities were inadequate protection against continuing raids. Indeed, accusations abounded in the Northern Ireland senate that there had been 'leakages of information': the unionist representative, H. Quin, informed his fellow members that 'the raiders had plans of every government building'. This provoked an indignant response from the nationalist members of the house, who expressed the hope that these remarks were 'not intended to foreshadow more discrimination against the minority'.[49]

Perhaps one of the most spectacular operations of this period was to take place in the early hours of 13 May 1957, when an armed group successfully managed to blow the locks on the Newry canal, causing immense damage at a minimal cost in stolen gelignite.[50] This was not the work of the IRA, but a joint operation between Joe Christle's splinter grouping and Liam Kelly's Saor Uladh. At 4.50 a.m. a group of three armed and masked raiders called at the home of the lockmaster of the main sea-going lock in Newry and, at gun point, ordered him and his family out of the house.[51] With the help of a professional demolitions expert, two heavy charges of explosives were planted at the lock gates, which were detonated when the lockmaster and his family had been escorted to a safe distance.[52] Causing damage in excess of £50,000, the Newry canal was put out of operation and the port was temporarily closed.[53] In the immediate aftermath, members of the Newry Port and Harbour Trust sat in emergency session and passed a resolution 'condemning this dastardly action', calling on the governments of Northern Ireland and the Irish Republic 'to take strong measures to control these "unlawful elements"'.[54]

This was not to be the last high-profile incident during this period, as on 4 July the IRA was successful in carrying out an ambush of an RUC patrol that had been surprised by an armed party concealed behind a high wall near the border.[55] While reports differ as to the number of men involved in the operation, the party managed to open fire on the unsuspecting patrol, offloading over one hundred rounds of ammunition into the wooden sides of the military tender in which they were travelling.[56] Receiving wounds to the head and chest, Constable Cecil Gregg was killed instantly, while his colleague, Constable Robert Halligan, who 'was hit by several bullets', was seriously injured.[57] During the course of the attack a mine consisting of over one hundred sticks of gelignite was placed on the road in front of the lorry, but it failed to explode. Returning fire, the RUC patrol managed to use a radio transmitter in the lorry to call for reinforcements before the IRA party effected their escape. In claiming responsibility for the attack, the IRA alleged that Constable Halligan, who 'had toppled from the lorry on to the roadway', had been abandoned by his colleagues, who fled the scene.[58]

Predictably, unionist opinion was outraged and within hours of the incident Brookeborough had made fresh representations in London in an attempt to have the British impress upon the Dublin government the need to act.[59] Speaking in Belfast, Topping severely admonished the Irish authorities and said that steps may have to be taken, whether they be 'pleasant for the ordinary people or not', to bring the campaign to an end.⁶⁰ From de Valera's perspective the incident, although detestable, was particularly embarrassing given the proximity of the ambush site to the border and the fact that the tracks of the raiders were clearly visible, leading back towards the Irish Republic.⁶¹ All hope that the campaign was fading out had been dashed, and 'the Forkhill incident' ensured that once again the activities of the IRA came to dominate the Irish political agenda. In London, fears of retaliatory attacks from militant unionist elements and an escalation in the border situation prompted the British government to exert mounting diplomatic pressure on de Valera to take decisive action against the IRA.⁶² He needed little persuasion and, when confronted with this disturbing upsurge in violence, de Valera and his cabinet colleagues unanimously elected to end the temporary rapprochement with the IRA by taking the dramatic step of reintroducing internment.⁶³

The speed with which this punitive measure was introduced surprised most, if not all, contemporary observers. Beginning on Saturday 6 July, a number of plain-clothes detectives detained most of the Sinn Féin leadership at a meeting of its Ard Comhairle in Dublin, thereby signalling the start of a coordinated countrywide operation that was to result in the arrest of sixty-three known republicans. Following this raid, Special Branch detectives proceeded to the offices of *The United Irishman*, while their uniformed colleagues effected arrests in Ennis, Westport, Claremorris, Dundalk, Athlone, Portlaoise, Drogheda, Nenagh, Navan and Belturbet.⁶⁴ By Sunday evening, most of the key members of the IRA leadership, including Patrick McLogan, Tomás MacCurtain, Thomas Doyle, Michael Traynor and Anthony Magan, were in custody.⁶⁵ While there was no immediate official comment forthcoming, the scale of the Garda operation and the intensive media speculation that it occasioned encouraged the government to issue a curt statement on 8 July.⁶⁶ Disseminated through the Government Information Bureau, it confirmed that the internment provisions of the Offences Against the State (Amendment) Act had been reactivated, and announced that 'a commission to inquire into the grounds of detention of any persons detained under the Act' would be established forthwith.⁶⁷

This move was understandably welcomed by the British government, who felt that the IRA was preparing to perpetrate 'further outrages on the traditional Orange holiday in Ulster'.⁶⁸ In *The Times* de Valera was applauded as 'the most formidable leader of his country', whose 'bold stroke' was 'prompted by a fundamental necessity which is well understood in Belfast and in London as well as Dublin'. In observing how he had cast his net wide, it went on to congratulate him for his resolve in attempting to seize the gun 'from the hands of the militants'.[69] Speaking in County Fermanagh, Brookeborough was more restrained in his welcome and simply expressed the hope that 'the nettle had at last been gripped'. In his opinion the accolades were premature as it was too early to see what the ultimate effect of internment would be.[70] In marked contrast to the situation in 1939, the actions of the Irish government were also the subject of negative comment and criticism from abroad, owing to the extensive media coverage occasioned by the reintroduction of internment.

The Taoiseach's office was inundated in particular with numerous correspondence and motions from various Irish-American organizations expressing outrage at the introduction of the 'evil methods of Communist, Fascist and other tyrannies in dealing with political opponents'.[71] Vilified by practically all shades of Irish-American opinion, the government attempted to avert a potential public relations crisis with an all-out charm offensive. The first step was the authorization of a blanket reply to be sent to correspondents 'conveying unfavourable comments on the government's action[s]', which would then be supplemented by the release of an 'exclusive statement' by de Valera to the *Herald Tribune*.[72] Reiterating the government's official line that the use of force to end partition was a counter-productive exercise, this statement justified the reintroduction of internment on the grounds that the IRA was able to defeat the ordinary law processes 'by secret conspiracy' and 'intimidation of the private citizen'.[73] When these efforts failed to stem the flow of hostile correspondence, a more robust defence of the government's position was drawn up and circulated to the Irish embassy in Washington and the various consulates in New York, Boston, Chicago and San Francisco.[74]

Perhaps the most damaging criticism was to come from Sinn Féin, who skilfully exploited the arrest of its Ard Comhairle members to fullest advantage. Portraying itself solely as a 'constitutional movement', the party attempted to depict these arrests in terms of a cynical Fianna Fáil attempt to destroy and disrupt a legitimate political opponent. In claiming to hold a broad electoral mandate, Sinn Féin challenged de Valera to 'put the issues of coercion and support for England before the Irish people', and accused his government of using the arrests as a ploy to detract from its 'inadequacy to deal with the present economic crisis'.[75] By describing de Valera's actions as 'totalitarian', the party also sought to draw emotive parallels with the methods of Nazi Germany and insisted on describing the reopened internment facility at the Curragh as a 'concentration camp'.[76] To counteract these claims, the government was forced to release a succinct statement on 8 July intimating that 'no one had been arrested because of membership of the Sinn Féin organization'.[77] However, as the Sinn Féin propaganda position continued to gain currency in the mainstream media, de Valera himself was forced to issue a more substantive statement decrying these allegations.

Embarking on a counter-offensive, de Valera opened by refuting Sinn Féin's claims as 'utterly false and a mere pretence', adding that 'whatever may be the true character of the present Sinn Féin organization, no one has been arrested because of membership of it'. In mounting a robust defence of the government's position, he was bellicose and unapologetic. The recent arrests had been effected 'because of the armed activities causing loss of life' of the IRA, who persisted in acting in contravention of the constitution. He continued:

> The twelve men arrested on the 6 July ... were arrested because they were believed to belong to an unlawful organizsation ... The men detained include the so-called 'Chief of Staff', 'Adjutant-General', and members of the 'Army Council' of one of the unlawful organizations.[78]

Two days later, in a supplementary statement, the use of internment was validated on the grounds that the activities of the IRA could not be allowed to continue without embroiling 'our people not only in war with another country but in a hateful Civil War as well'.[79] Nevertheless, in spite of its bullish façade, and its attempts to put a positive spin on the situation, the republican movement could not escape the fact that the raids of 6 July were to represent a significant and potentially lethal blow to its campaign ambitions. Within the space of six months most of the IRA leadership were again in government custody, this time facing an indefinite period of detention.

THE OPERATION OF INTERNMENT – 1957

In activating part two of the Offences Against the State (Amendment) Act, the government was required to fulfil a number of statutory obligations. Specifically, the cabinet had to issue a proclamation declaring that the use of internment was necessary 'to secure the preservation of the public peace and order', before moving to establish the Detention Commission envisaged under section eight of the act.[80] To consider these issues, a conference attended by Aindrias Ó Caoimh

(Attorney-General), Peter Berry (Secretary of the Department of Justice) and Maurice Moynihan (Secretary of the Department of An Taoiseach) was held in government buildings on 6 July. Among the issues discussed was the preparation of the government's proclamation, which was to be published in the *Iris Oifigiúil* and the daily newspapers, and the proposed composition of the Detention Commission. On this occasion, a decision on the commission was deferred as the Attorney-General pointed out that the act did not make express provision for its immediate institution; rather, it was to be established 'as soon as conveniently may be'.[81] In fact, the Detention Commission was not actually set up until 16 July, when the government appointed Barra Ó Briaín, who was a judge of the Circuit Court, District Justice Edward Ryan and Col. John Vincent Joyce to be its members.[82]

As on previous occasions, it was widely anticipated that the old Tintown camp in the Curragh would be used to house the internees. While the records fail to indicate if any other options were considered, it is apparent that recourse to this measure had been exercising the collective mind of the government for some time. In October 1950, the Department of Justice wrote to the Department of Defence to ascertain what arrangements had been made in the case of 'an emergency' necessitating the internment of those involved in 'subversive activities'. This was immediately met with a certain degree of resistance by officials within the Department of Defence, who felt that it would be inappropriate to house such persons in military custody as it would be likely to create the impression abroad 'that there are serious internal security problems necessitating military aid'. In their opinion, the detention of civilian internees within the Curragh during the Second World War caused a number of significant problems for the army, 'arising from certain activities such as conspiracies to escape'. A future recurrence of this situation, taking place as it did within 'the centre of the largest military establishment in the country', was a wholly unappealing prospect that could not be accepted by the minister or the military authorities.[83] Flying in the face of these vociferous objections, officials in the Department of Justice overruled their colleagues, whom it was felt could be persuaded to undertake 'all internment work' should the need arise.[84]

Once all of these issues had been satisfactorily resolved, the transfer of prisoners to the Curragh began on 9 July 1957. Owing to the disrepair of the Tintown site and the haste with which internment was reintroduced, it was decided that the internees would be temporarily detained in the Glasshouse until more adequate accommodation could be prepared.[85] Throughout the day, bedding and blankets were delivered to the Curragh, while a number of civilians from the army corps of engineers were observed erecting barbed wire barriers and sentry towers in the compound that had been used to house German internees during the Second World War.[86] An *Irish Times* reporter also ascertained that several electricians had been instructed to report to the area in order to install floodlighting. In the midst of this activity, the first consignment of thirty internees departed the Bridewell for the Curragh in a convoy of 'three covered police lorries and four patrol cars'. A small crowd assembled outside to witness the procession, whose members 'responded haphazardly with a few words of "A Nation Once Again"'. Although the remainder of the journey through Kildare was described as 'uneventful', it was reported that the new internees defiantly sang national songs and could be heard shouting 'up the Republic' on approach to the sentry post outside the Curragh.[87] They were to be followed by another convoy containing twenty-six of their colleagues later that evening.[88]

By the end of this first day there were a total of fifty-six internees in detention, although it was broadly anticipated that this number would substantially increase with the impending release of a number of republicans who had been serving short custodial sentences in Mountjoy.[89] The prisoners themselves were particularly conscious of this and were not surprised by their re-arrest outside the gates of the prison on the morning of their release. A member of the Gardaí then read out a brief proclamation, before they were loaded into a lorry and accompanied by a number of 'Special Branch men' on their journey to the Curragh.[90] A similar scene ensued on 15 July, with the release of fifteen more republicans.[91] By September, 109 individuals were interned in the Curragh – eventually reaching a peak of 152 the following June. By November 1958, the number of internees had dropped to 121 before a steady trickle of releases eventually culminated in the closure of the camp in March 1959.[92] While substantially fewer republicans were interned on this occasion than during the Second World War, these figures were significant in so far as they were representative of the government's resolve 'to carry through the most firm measures so far devised to take the gun out of Irish politics'.[93]

On 10 July 1957, the Minister for Justice signed the Offences Against the State (Amendment) Act, 1940, (Detention) Regulations Order, to provide for the day-to-day administration of 'a camp for the internment of civilians'.[94] As was the case in 1939, the running of the camp was entrusted to an officer of the defence forces, who was appointed by the adjutant-general as 'camp commandant'. In this instance it was Commandant Carl O'Sullivan who was selected to fill this role, assisted by a camp staff and a medical officer. To maintain discipline, Commandant O'Sullivan was empowered to administer a select series of punishments, including the imposition of solitary confinement, for a period not exceeding three days, a restricted diet and the removal of mattresses. In the case of a severe breach of discipline the use of irons 'for the purpose of restraint' was also authorized. These regulations also provided that internees would be permitted to wear their own clothing, be granted the right to associate freely and, where practicable, to take regular exercise. Visits from relatives were to be permitted once a month and internees were allowed to write one letter per week, with no limitation on the number of letters they could receive. Packages from outside the camp containing clothing, books, newspapers and stationery were also sanctioned, subject to the commandant's approval.[95] In order to cater for the religious welfare of the internees, a chaplain, provided he had the written authority of his bishop, was allowed to officiate in the camp.[96]

Following their temporary sojourn in the Glasshouse, the internees were transferred to their hastily improvised accommodation at the Tintown site. Containing a number of huts that were best described by former internee Tony Hayde as 'the big nissen type', just like the kind 'you'd see in the films of the last world war', this compound was surrounded by six fences of barbed wire. A seventh fence was placed another fifty yards out in the Curragh plain, to prevent 'over inquisitive local people' from coming too close.[97] Within the compound itself, the internees were housed in three of four dormitory style huts that had a rotating occupancy to facilitate frequent searches of the vacated huts. Next to the entrance was the dining hall, followed by a recreation hut that had been partitioned at one end in order to house a sub-branch of the Kildare county library. Across a rough roadway from the line of the dormitory huts stood the ablutions building and a new chapel, leaving a long open strip for recreation, with an incinerator at the bottom. Over time a separate sports field was provided, which was accessible from the main compound via a wooden footbridge surrounded by 'a barbed wire tunnel'. Initially, the camp was supervised by four main sentry towers on the perimeter, although this was later increased to seven, complete with a number of searchlights. At the principal sentry tower beside the main gate, a guard armed with a Gustor sub-machine gun overlooked the inner compound, the camp inner guardroom and the visitors' boxes. Towers at the northeast and northwest corners were also staffed with sentries armed with .303 rifles.

Upon arrival from Mountjoy it appears that many internees were immediately struck by the superior quality of the food served in the Curragh, as the recollection of their first meal seems to be a common and recurring theme. According to Noel Kavanagh, his arrival in the Curragh was the occasion of his 'first decent breakfast' since his incarceration in Mountjoy.[98] Patrick O'Regan was particularly struck by the smell of fried onions on his approach to the camp, and described how he was presented with 'a small meal' of steak, potatoes and onions on his arrival. For him, the food in Mountjoy was adequate in that it would 'put weight on you', but was very poor in quality when compared with that served in the Curragh.[99] This was not a view shared by all of his comrades, as Tony Hayde described how many internees from rural areas, who were often better fed than their compatriots from Dublin, complained incessantly in this regard.[100] The other immediate and notable feature of life in the camp was the sudden and complete loss of privacy that this type of detention entailed. Unlike Mountjoy, where each prisoner had his own cell, internees in the Curragh were housed forty-four to a hut, giving an average space per person of 815 cubic feet. On the other hand, this was more than offset by the increased prospect for recreation in the open spaces of the compound and the opportunity to spend more time out of their 'cell environment'.[101]

Daily routine within the camp was somewhat unstructured and varied depending on the inclination of the individual involved. Rising at 7.30 a.m. the internees, under the direction of the camp O/C, Tomás MacCurtain, would form up and march to the dining hall to receive breakfast at 8.00 a.m. Apart from observing a similar discipline at lunchtime and suppertime, an internee's time was his own, to do with as he pleased.[102] While the military authorities provided a range of hobbies and handicrafts in order to pass the time, it appears that many preferred to attend the wide variety of instructional and educational classes organized by their own camp leadership. In drawing on their various professions, several school teachers, including Ruairí Ó Brádaigh, Thomas Gill and James Hughes, taught classes in Irish, French and German, while Gerard McCarthy provided instruction in electrical engineering. For his part, MacCurtain taught several of the internees his own 'very colourful interpretations' of all 1,200 lines of Brian Merriman's 'The Midnight Court'.[103] Apart from that, everyone had their own particular way of 'putting down the day' and many would spend the remaining time sleeping, reading or 'kicking football'.[104] On various occasions chess tournaments and sports days were organized and from time to time there was 'seasonal theatrical carry-on'.[105]

In spite of the close quarters and difficult personal conditions in which the internees were held, it appears that life within the camp was pervaded by a strong sense of camaraderie. The typical internee was young and unencumbered by the personal family commitments of some of their older comrades. In fact, many of these men were already firm friends at the time of their internment, having spent lengthy periods on the run with one another. Needless to say there was an element of 'horseplay' among the younger men, which was not extended to the more senior volunteers who had been interned during the 1940s. It was generally understood that 'you didn't mess' with the older men, who were held in high esteem by their colleagues. On several occasions both Tony Hayde and Noel Kavanagh recall being enthralled by the stories of these individuals, some of whom had been out during 'the Tan war'.[106] MacCurtain was particularly revered as an imposing military man, who was deeply committed to republicanism and regarded as an outstanding chess player. As was typical of the IRA in such situations, the internees immediately organized themselves along military lines and elected a set of hut O/Cs who reported directly to a camp council headed by MacCurtain.[107] Owing to the substantial cross-over in membership with Sinn Féin, meetings of this organization's Ard Comhairle were also a regular occurrence within the camp.[108]

In relative terms, some of the internees adjudged the environment within the Curragh to be fairly satisfactory given the circumstances. A stir was created, however, following the release on 13 August 1957 of a Sinn Féin statement that was strongly critical of the conditions within the camp. Alleging that the huts were dirty and ramshackle, often allowing the wind and rain to penetrate, it claimed that internees were locked up from sundown to sunset, entailing over sixteen hours of close confinement during the winter. The footwear and clothing provided was decried as highly 'unsuitable' for the camp conditions, given that the military authorities were only prepared to supply the men with boots when they became barefoot. The soap allowance was lamented as inadequate and it was also charged that there were no appropriate facilities provided for the conduct of educational classes. The statement also criticized the opportunities for parole, contending that since the camp had opened only 'one prisoner was allowed [out] for twenty-four hours'.[109]

For a government that was attempting to portray an image of reasoned restraint and benevolence in its administration of internment, the publication of these allegations in the mainstream media was of major concern. De Valera was particularly upset by the recurring usage of the term 'concentration camp', implying as it did that 'conditions in the detention camp are similar to those associated in the public mind with concentration camps in certain other countries'. From his perspective, a brief perusal of the detention regulations would be enough to 'convince any fair minded person that they provide for the humane and reasonable treatment of detained persons'. In response, he ordered a brief enquiry into the conditions at the camp so that a point-by-point rebuttal of the Sinn Féin statement could be prepared. On 18 August a special conference was convened in the Curragh, chaired by O.M. Clarke, the Assistant Secretary of the Department of Defence. It was attended by Lieutenant-Colonel O'Hanlon, the executive officer of the Curragh command, Commandant P. McGann, who was representing the adjutant-general, and Commandant O'Sullivan and his staff.[110]

After a lengthy consultation with Commandant O'Sullivan a report was compiled and presented to the government outlining the actual conditions in which the internees were detained. In refuting allegations that the huts were dirty, it was found that they had been thoroughly cleaned prior to use and that, as was the custom observed during the 1940s, the sanitary arrangements within the camp were primarily the responsibility of the internees. To facilitate this, the necessary brushes and materials were supplied and it was remarked that the detained men had been maintaining a very high standard of cleanliness. However, as the huts had been neglected since 1946 it was accepted that they were in a severe state of disrepair. According to Patrick O'Regan they were initially 'very draughty' and on some occasions the roofs were known to leak. It was noted that the necessary roof repairs were being carried out as a matter of urgency and that the insides of the huts were being lined to prevent the draughts.[111] While work on this project was slow to make progress, it was generally agreed that once the lining had been installed the huts were 'comfortable enough'.[112] Heating stoves had also been installed as a short-term expedient and it was noted that work on equipping the huts with flush toilets had recently been completed.

Sleeping arrangements within the camp were rudimentary, with the provision of board and trestle type beds arranged in open dormitory fashion.[113] While acknowledging that such a situation was not entirely conducive to fostering a sense of privacy among the internees, it was pointed out that individual cubicles could not be erected within the huts for obvious security reasons.[114] Although the diet of the internees was adjudged to be 'plentiful but unvaried', provision was made for the daily visit of a mobile canteen, from which they could purchase 'an assortment of foods'. A supper ration consisting of bread, butter, tea, sugar and milk had also been introduced, together with the installation of a plug point for the use of an electric kettle in each of the three dormitory huts. An initial soap allowance, in line with standard army issue, of one and a third ounces per week was originally provided before being increased to two ounces when it was learned that the detained men were expected to wash their own clothes. In addressing the sensitive issue of familial visits, the report also noted that, while there was no accommodation available for relatives, a hut was being prepared as a waiting room and that the necessary work would be completed without delay.[115]

To highlight their predicament the internees began a campaign aimed at securing the intervention of the International Red Cross, prompting an inspection of the camp by a deputation headed by Tom Barry's wife, Mrs Leslie Barry, in February 1958. According to Ruairí Ó Brádaigh, news of the impending inspection provoked an immediate improvement in the facilities within the camp, as the stalled roof repairs were completed, new toilets provided and new beds distributed.[116] Needless to say, the Red Cross delegates were favourably impressed by what they found and commented on the lack of 'undue overcrowding' within the camp. The ample facilities for recreation afforded to the internees were commended, the medical facilities were deemed to be adequate and MacCurtain was quoted as saying that the men had 'no complaints with regards to treatment, discipline and food'. The only area of potential concern was the relative lack of personal privacy allowed to the men.[117] Therefore, absolved of any suggestion of ill-treatment or impropriety in respect of its dealings with the internees, the government felt secure enough in its position to refuse a similar request to inspect the camp from the Irish Association for Civil Liberties in August 1958.

By far the most notable aspect of life in the camp was the relative absence of any kind of discord between the internees and the military authorities. In fact, the relative harmony that characterized this relationship was in marked contrast to the situation in the 1940s, when the atmosphere was belligerent and at times openly confrontational. Evidence of this new regime quickly manifested itself when the military police made their own recreational facilities available to the internees while the Tintown compound was being prepared.[118] In general, it appears that the various sentries and camp guards kept to themselves and performed their duties in a benign and even-handed manner. A few exceptions were known to occur, particularly in the case of one army sergeant nicknamed 'Scaldy', who was renowned for being cantankerous and aggressive.[119] The intense media interest surrounding the reintroduction of internment undoubtedly contributed to the more genial attitude of the military authorities, as did the diffusion of the so-called 'Civil War mentality' of the 1940s. During this time both the IRA and the army still included many long-serving individuals who had participated in this divisive conflict, and in such circumstances it was inevitable that these cleavages would again become manifest within the enclosed environment of the Curragh. On the other hand, the inauguration of a more professional and impartial ethos in the army goes some way towards explaining the more emollient character of internment in 1957.[120]

For its part, the IRA played a role by extending its policy of non-aggression to cover relations with the Curragh military authorities. The personal antagonisms of the 1940s had been disastrous for the movement and a more passive approach was needed in order to avoid a recurrence.[121] A 'soft-policy' was introduced by MacCurtain and the camp leadership, as the internees were ordered to set about 'cooperating in making camp life as tolerable as can be both for ... themselves and for the military personnel in immediate control of the camp'.[122] For a select group of hard-liners, however, this was a bitter pill to swallow, as the considered proper course for republicans 'was to make life difficult for their jailers in the time honoured fashion'.[123] This group was particularly aggrieved by the leadership's conservative escape policy, which discouraged any attempts that could precipitate the use of force or provoke confrontation. At the same time, both MacCurtain and Anthony Magan had been rebuffed by the Army Council when attempting to dictate the course of campaign policy and resented the intervention of Charlie Murphy instructing them to limit their concerns solely to the internment camp.[124] This situation was further compounded with the arrest and internment of Murphy in late 1957, as opposition to MacCurtain's escape policy began to coalesce under his leadership.

In the face of this simmering confrontation MacCurtain sanctioned the formation of an escape committee, and in August 1957 authorized the construction of a tunnel under the perimeter fence of the camp. When the military authorities detected this operation 'in the initial stages', those involved were 'deprived of certain privileges' in line with detention regulations.[125] Instead of satisfying the escape enthusiasts, as MacCurtain had hoped, this simply whetted their appetites and in May 1958 Vincent Conlan, John Kelly and Seán O'Toole managed to effect an opportunistic break for freedom, after sawing through an iron grille outside a bathroom window in the camp hospital.[126] A thorough search of the surrounding countryside was quickly initiated by the authorities, which included the establishment of several roadblocks between Kildare town and Newbridge, resulting in severe traffic congestion.[127] Two days later, both Conlan's and O'Toole's short-lived escape was ended after their discovery in a ditch on the outskirts of Kilcullen, County Kildare. Kelly, on the other hand, managed to achieve slightly more success in evading the authorities by remaining at large for ten days.[128]

In attempting to mollify Murphy and the malcontents, MacCurtain was pressed into giving his reluctant assent to a more considered escape scheme presented to him in September 1958 by Daithí Ó Conaill and Ruairí Ó Brádaigh. In doing so, MacCurtain also hoped to reassert his authority over the IRA Army Council, by sending word to the incumbent C/S, Seán Cronin, suggesting that one of the senior internees be selected as a member of the escape party. Facing a severe manpower shortage, Cronin overruled MacCurtain on this point and instructed that only young volunteers with operational experience were to be involved.[129] Both Magan and MacCurtain took umbrage at this perceived slight, but determined on this occasion to press ahead with the escape.[130] The plan, as put forward by Ó Conaill, had its origins in a sports day held by the internees a few weeks previously. In preparing for this event, the long grass on the sports pitch had been cut and brushed up to the inner fence, where it lay for some time. Taking notice of this, Ó Conaill conceived the idea that if this grass was thrown over the fence it could be used as cover for a volunteer to hide until nightfall before cutting the remaining fences and making his escape. By bringing Ó Brádaigh and Kavanagh into his confidence, it was suggested that a canvas with hay glued to it could be used to construct a camouflage, which could be effectively used to conceal two men.

With MacCurtain's approval, both Ó Brádaigh and Ó Conaill were selected as the candidates for escape, while Kavanagh's role was limited to crawling through the first fence to make sure that the other two had been adequately disguised. With the construction of the camouflage cover using two British army groundsheets, a number of practices were conducted on the stage in the recreation hut where the internees could conceal their activities. Then, during the course of 'a spirited football match' on the evening of 24 September 1958, Kavanagh used the distraction to cut open the bottom of the inner fence before ushering Ó Brádaigh and Ó Conaill through, where they assumed their assigned position amidst the grass. When the match ended, the internees took the opportunity of a heavy shower of rain to rush *en masse* back to the main compound in order to confuse the count of the sentries on duty. The ruse was completed with the creation of two 'dummy beds', thereby ensuring that their absence was not discovered by 'Scaldy' until the following morning.[131] A brief but fruitless search for the escapees ensued. In the interim, both Ó Conaill and Ó Brádaigh hoped to rejoin the IRA's ailing campaign, which had just suffered another setback with the arrest and internment of Cronin and three other members of the Army Council. The conclusion to this episode came several weeks later when Cronin, who had been attempting to maintain a neutral line in the escalating dispute between the Murphy faction and the camp leadership, relented and gave his unqualified support to MacCurtain and Magan.[132]

Eventually taking matters entirely into their own hands, Murphy's group decided to concentrate their resources on a large-scale 'unofficial' escape, in a blatant attempt to embarrass MacCurtain and Magan. In a carefully prepared plan, fourteen men managed to break out of the camp in a high-profile skirmish with the military authorities. Beginning at 3.50 p.m. on 3 December 1958, while most of the internees were playing hurling in the recreation field, several groups of men, at a signal, started to rush the perimeter fence. A number of improvised smoke bombs were ignited, while pincers that had been smuggled into the camp were used to cut open the wire. Thirty men then fled through the gap, and by the time the alarm was raised many of them were already openly running across the Curragh plains. After ignoring repeated orders to halt, the sentries began to open fire and launched a number of tear gas grenades at the fleeing men. As a result, two of the internees received wounds to the legs, as it appeared that the sentries were deliberately aiming low in order to avoid fatalities. In spite of their best efforts, however, reduced visibility resulting from the tear gas and the smoke bombs ensured that fourteen of the internees were successful in their escape.[133]

A massive manhunt immediately ensued as up to 500 troops were deployed across the Curragh plains in an effort to detain the men. This operation yielded little apart from the discovery of a blood-stained shirt on the grounds of Sheshoon Stud and was eventually called off on 4 December.[134] In the internment camp itself, a number of emergency and punitive measures were immediately invoked but, remarkably, it was noted that the internees 'were not treated harshly and there was no change in the attitude of the [camp] guards'.[135] According to Sinn Féin, a news blackout was temporarily imposed on the internees, with heavy restrictions placed on the receipt of newspapers and mail. All visits were temporarily cancelled and the use of the playing field and the camp recreation facilities was withheld as security inspections were stepped up.[136] For MacCurtain and Magan the rupture with Murphy and his faction was now irreconcilable. Murphy had wilfully disobeyed established camp policy and in doing so had irreparably undermined their authority. In addition, this controversy also threatened to engulf the members of the Army Council, who were still at large as the escapees presented themselves for 'active duty'. Confronted with the prospect of having to reinstate these individuals, they pragmatically resolved to overlook their alleged insubordination in the face of an ongoing manpower shortage. In the face of bitter opposition from Magan and MacCurtain, they were formally re-admitted to the IRA organization, resulting in a very damaging rupture across the republican movement (see Chapter 7).[137]

The growing discord among the detainees was a timely and propitious development for the government, as the use of internment was fast becoming a political liability. Not only had the virtual evaporation of the IRA's campaign removed all domestic justification for continued recourse to this measure, it had begun to attract negative comment abroad.[138] Moreover, the acceptance of the petition of former internee Gerard Lawless by the European Commission of Human Rights in August 1958 was perhaps the most significant factor in persuading the government of the merits of closing the camp.[139] Within this context, the declining number of internees prompted rumours of the Curragh's imminent closure. By January 1959 the cabinet was already discussing the possibility of re-admitting some of the detained men to their former employment in the civil service.[140] Provided that there was no escalation in the number of border incidents, it was also felt that the OASA gave adequate provision to prosecute IRA suspects under section fifty-two for failing to account for their movements.[141] In February therefore, it was formally decided at a meeting of the cabinet to begin the release of the remaining internees in batches.[142]

Alarmed by these developments, the British ambassador, Sir Alexander Clutterbuck, requested a meeting at the Department of External Affairs where he expressed his government's unease at the release of the internees. These overtures were rebuffed and he was tersely informed by the Minister for External Affairs, Frank Aiken, that contemporary circumstances were conducive to their release and that, while the government intended to maintain the powers of internment, 'resort to them is not now justified'.[143] The implications were clear – while the government intended to close the internment camp forthwith, it did not propose to rescind its proclamation deactivating the Offences Against the State (Amendment) Act until such time as it was felt prudent to do so. By March, the camp was empty, and in a breach of diplomatic etiquette the British Prime Minister, Harold MacMillan, used the occasion of a speech in Belfast to express his 'concern' at the government's decision to release this 'hard core of the IRA'.[144] As ever, de Valera was forthright in pointing out that the government's actions were 'based on their knowledge of the needs of the situation and their judgement of what is best calculated to serve the interests of peace and order'.[145] Fortunately, further diplomatic confrontation was avoided and the use of internment was not again resorted to. Significantly, the government did not formally divest itself of these powers until March 1962, when it issued a proclamation deactivating the Offences Against the State (Amendment) Act.[146]

6

'The Powers of Detention Should not Again be Exercised':[1] the Lawless Case, 1957–1961

The decision to close the Curragh internment camp in March 1959, prompted by the declining number of violent incidents along the border, was taken in light of a significant legal challenge to the government's powers of internment. This was the first such action to be faced since the decision in the Burke case of 1939 provoked 'a major constitutional crisis' and necessitated the release of over fifty internees. Although the judgement of the Supreme Court, upholding the constitutionality of the Offences Against the State (Amendment) Act, was to fully resolve these issues, it also ensured that the executive's statutory powers of detention were immune from further judicial review.[2] The problem from the government's perspective arose when the Irish state found itself in the unfamiliar position of being forced to justify the use of internment before an international legal tribunal. With the signature of the European Convention for the Protection of Human Rights (ECHR) in 1949, the government, together with a number of other European states, had acquiesced in the creation of a supranational authority to guarantee fundamental rights by taking precedence over national law. Pressed upon the government by the then Minister for External Affairs, Seán MacBride, as means of pursuing a more active foreign policy, the exercise of the domestic law was, for the first time, subject to a fully enforceable international writ that could run against the state.[3] As such, given the contemporary political circumstances, it was inevitable that this machinery would be used to mount a challenge to the government's right to detain republicans without trial.

The case in question was initiated in 1957 when twenty-one-year-old Gerard Lawless began legal proceedings aimed at securing his unconditional release from internment in the Curragh camp. Represented by MacBride, Lawless unsuccessfully petitioned the Irish courts before litigating his case the whole way to the European Court of Human Rights in 1961. Though ultimately unsuccessful, the case determined important legal precedents that were to restrict the executive's right to re-employ internment in the future. A preliminary action before the Detention Commission was also to highlight a number of unanticipated difficulties with the operation of this body, thereby representing a further dilution of the government's powers.[4] The significance of the Lawless case was not solely limited to the domestic sphere, as it was the first time that the European Court of Human Rights was called to adjudicate between a state and a private individual. In doing so, it ensured the full operability of the ECHR and guaranteed that the assertion of the individual rights enshrined therein could not be denied by any of the signatory states.[5] The intense publicity occasioned by such a celebrated case also exposed the Irish government to a significant degree of international media censure for its conduct in dealing with subversive organizations within its jurisdiction.

In its aftermath, it was noted by Charles Haughey, the incumbent Minister for Justice, how a feeling now prevailed among his cabinet colleagues that

> the powers of detention *should not again be exercised* [my emphasis] except as a last resort and only where any other effective means of a less repugnant kind were not available.[6]

A root and branch re-evaluation of established counter-insurgency policy followed, as the decision in the case was to have a direct bearing on how succeeding Irish governments chose to deal with armed subversive organizations. Certainly, the progression of the case was a decisive factor in the government's hurried decision in 1959 to close the Curragh internment camp, while the decision in itself undoubtedly led to the wholesale abandonment of internment as an acceptable defence against the IRA. This position became manifest in 1961 when the government opted instead to reconstitute the Special Criminal Court to deal with an IRA attempt to resuscitate its floundering campaign.[7] Designed to frustrate the tampering of juries through armed conspiracies, the Special Criminal Court was given an expansive jurisdiction to deal with a wide range of politically motivated offences.[8] It quickly proved to be an effective weapon in the state's arsenal as custodial sentences for relatively minor offences under the OASA could now be imposed in terms of years instead of months.[9] Its overall success in prompting the collapse of the IRA border campaign was underlined by the decision to establish a new Special Criminal Court in 1972, in response to the spill-over effects of the civil conflict in Northern Ireland. Notably, internment in the Irish Republic was not used on this occasion, despite the fact that contemporary circumstances may have arguably warranted its reintroduction.

BACKGROUND

Gerard Lawless was born in August 1936 into a working class family in Dublin's north inner city where his father found regular employment in the docks.[10] Described as a 'van driver by occupation', he began to exhibit marked republican sympathies from an early stage, when at the age of seventeen he was convicted in the Children's Court of malicious damage to a plate glass window bearing an image of Queen Elizabeth II.[11] Discharged under the Probation of Offenders Act, 1907, he was ordered to pay a sum of £5 17s. as compensation for the damage caused. An erstwhile member of Na Fianna Éireann, the republican boy-scout organization, he joined An Fórsa Cosanta Áitiúil (FCA), the Irish army reserve, in March 1954 and was posted to the 11th cavalry regiment at McKee barracks, Dublin.[12] It was during this period that he began his association with the IRA, joining at an unspecified date in 1955, and he quickly earned a reputation as 'a tough violent and undisciplined agitator', who was skilled in the use of firearms and explosives. In June 1956, Lawless severed his links with the IRA and joined Joe Christle's rival splinter group, which was amalgamated with Liam Kelly's Saor Uladh in 1957.[13]

It was during this period that his subversive activities were to come to the attention of the authorities, leading to his formal discharge from the FCA. This was prompted by the discovery, in September 1956, of Lawless and a number of his comrades in a disused shed near Keshcarrigan, County Leitrim, together with one machine gun, six rifles and over 400 rounds of ammunition. Many of these firearms, he subsequently admitted, had been stolen from a retired British army officer living in County Donegal.[14] The group were returned for trial before the Dublin Circuit Criminal Court in November 1956, where they were charged with the unlawful possession of the arms contrary to section thirteen of the Criminal Justice Act, 1951. Headed by Seán Geraghty, they refused to recognize the authority of the court and were acquitted on a point of law. Specifically, adequate proof had not been advanced that the accused did not possess the requisite firearms certificate for the weapons in their possession.[15] Upon his discharge, Lawless resumed his subversive activities and in January 1957 was suspected of being involved in a burglary at the explosives depot of the Imperial Chemical Industries in Moorestown, County Dublin. He was also involved in a similar operation in May, when a group of armed men raided the explosives magazine of the Fleming Fireclay Company in Athy, County Kildare, before absconding with an amount of Amonel powder and fuse wire.[16]

Prompted by the evidence of witnesses at the scene, together with information garnered from a Garda informant, Lawless and eight other members of Christle's splinter group were arrested for their part in this burglary.[17] When searched by the Gardaí, Lawless was found to be in possession of incriminating documents, one of which was a sketch map of the border showing the position of British customs posts and barracks marked with the words 'infiltrate', 'annihilate' and 'destroy'. A follow-up search of his home also uncovered a number of other seditious documents, including a copy of the Operation Harvest handbook. Although Lawless accepted full responsibility for these documents, he denied being a member of the IRA with the statement: 'I am in nothing now.' According to the arresting Gardaí, Lawless used this specific formula of words to frustrate the authorities by attempting to convey the impression that he was technically not a member of that organization, despite his continued engagement with Christle's dissident grouping.[18] Lawless was duly returned for trial before the Dublin District Court on 16 May 1957 on charges of being in possession of incriminating documents and for being a member of an illegal organization.

'Lively scenes' ensued during this trial as Lawless and his co-defendants, Seán Geraghty and Joseph Christle, refused to recognize the authority of the court, which they sensationally claimed was 'being used to safeguard the last remnants of the British Empire'. A middle-aged man from the public gallery then interrupted proceedings by verbally abusing the head of the Special Branch, Detective-Inspector Philip McMahon, who had been called to give evidence. Tensions were further increased when Lawless alleged during his testimony that he had been beaten while in Garda custody on the specific authority of Detective-Inspector McMahon. Needless to say, McMahon vigorously denied these accusations and attributed the incident to Lawless's refusal to have his fingerprints taken.[19] Lawless subsequently refuted McMahon's account of this incident in an affidavit sworn several months later, claiming that his refusal stemmed from the fact that his hands had been bandaged after receiving minor injuries at work. He continued:

> When the police tried to tear the bandages off my hands I resisted but they caught me by the arm around my back and twisted

> it up to my shoulder-blade causing extreme pain. While one arm was like that the fingerprints of the other hand were taken but I am certain that I lost consciousness for a short period with the severity of the pain ... When this was over ... I was left standing alone with all of the police officers behind me. They were evidently waiting for me to turn around and I suspected they wanted to take my photograph. I did not turn around so one detective struck me with his fist and knocked me down and when I was getting up again my photograph was apparently taken ... When I got to my feet I heard Detective-Inspector Philip McMahon say to the other detectives present 'give him a punch'. Immediately all five detectives attacked me and seized me under the armpits and under the knees ... While I was in this position I was punched in the eye, on the nose, on the mouth, on the cheek and was hit in the stomach with someone's knee and kicked in the stomach with someone's foot and also kicked in the leg. My nose and mouth were bleeding ... After the beating stopped I was taken to a disused cell.[20]

Although he was acquitted on this occasion of being a member of the IRA, Lawless was convicted for being in possession of incriminating documents, for which he received a term of one month's imprisonment. Geraghty and Christle were remanded in custody, however, as the Gardaí attempted to build a case for their involvement in the raid at Flemings.[21] During the course of this investigation Geraghty was positively identified as one of the raiders, but the case, which was heard before the Dublin Circuit Criminal Court in July 1957, collapsed owing to the intimidation of witnesses. Ironically, this episode further served to strengthen the government's hand in asserting that internment was a necessary expedient to deal with the IRA.[22] As for Lawless, he was released from prison upon the expiration of his sentence in June 1957 and was placed under observation by the Special Branch. Acting on the suspicion that he was attempting to flee the country to avoid internment, the Gardaí intercepted Lawless in Dun Laoghaire on 11 July as he was about to board a mail boat bound for Britain. Detained under section thirty of the OASA, he claimed that during the course of his interrogation in the Bridewell Detective-Inspector McMahon offered him money if he agreed to become an informant. He declined this offer and was informed that his detention was being extended for another twenty-four hours pursuant to the provisions of the OASA.[23] On 13 July he was transferred to the

Curragh camp, where he was presented with a warrant signed by the Minister for Justice, Oscar Traynor, ordering his arrest and indefinite detention under section four of the Offences Against the State (Amendment) Act. Arising from his association with Christle, Lawless was actively ostracized by the other internees and was housed in a separate hut, where he served out his detention until his release in December 1957.

THE DETENTION COMMISSION

As an internee there were a number of possible routes open to Gerard Lawless if he wished to be released. The first and most effective way of securing his liberty was to give an undertaking to respect the constitution, as required by the government. He refused to compromise his republican principles in this manner and instead applied to have his case reviewed by the Detention Commission. In making this application, Lawless's solicitor, P.C. Moore, made it clear to the government that he expected to be 'accorded the usual rights' enjoyed by legal representatives in a court of law, including the right to cross-examine and sub-poena witnesses.[24] These were important contentions to make, as the legislation governing the creation of this body was conspicuously silent as to the mechanics of its operation.[25] This appears to have been a deliberate omission as the government did not intend for the Commission to act in a formal judicial manner. Moore was informed of this when it was noted that the terms of his submission were 'based on a mistaken view of the statutory position'. In fact, the Offences Against the State (Amendment) Act did not make provision for entertaining applications subject to the conditions that Lawless and his solicitor were attempting to impose on the government.[26]

It appears that the uncertainty as to the exact legal standing of the Detention Commission was an issue that was also exercising the mind of its chairman, Judge Barra Ó Briain. He was particularly concerned with the question of whether or not it had the power to administer an oath to witnesses. Writing *en route* to Westport in July 1957, Ó Briain outlined his concerns to a colleague: 'The point that you mention about taking evidence on oath occurred to myself going down on the train on Friday night.' As he did not have access to a law library in his holiday accommodation Ó Briain requested that his correspondent 'drop me a line ... setting out the general position as to administering oaths'. When this matter was not resolved to his satisfaction he wrote to the government, in advance of the commission's first ever sitting, intimating that he would be seeking the assistance of counsel in this regard.

In making their own preparations for the impending hearing, Moore's office briefed Seán MacBride and his colleagues, Seamus Sorahan and Thomas J. Connolly, to represent Lawless, while the government approved the presence of its counsel only for the purpose of assisting 'the Commission on questions of procedure'. As justification for Lawless's continued internment, it was also proposed that the Department of Justice would supply the commission with a dossier containing:

1. A Garda list, in chronological order, showing IRA outrages committed in 1957.
2. Copy of a Garda report dated 12 September, 1957 as to Ó Laighleis's [Lawless's] IRA history.
3. Copy of Garda reports in relation to Ó 'Laighleis's conviction for possession of incriminating documents in May, 1957.
4. Copy of Garda reports in relation to charges proferred against Ó Laighleis for illegal possession of firearms in September, 1956.
5. A note stating –
   (a) that Ó Laighleis was told after arrest on 11 July 1957, and before a request was made by the Gardaí for a detention warrant, that he would be released on giving an undertaking that henceforth he would not be a member of any unlawful organization, and
   (b) that Ó Laighleis was informed in writing on 16 August, 1957 that he would be released on signing an undertaking in the following terms:

I _____, undertake to respect the Constitution of Ireland and the laws, and I declare that I will not be a member of or assist any organization which is an unlawful organization under the Offences Against the State Act 1939.[27]

Occasioning much media interest, the Detention Commission sat for the first time in the history of the Irish state on 17 September 1957 in the courts martial room of Connolly barracks in the Curragh. As was expected, legal argument relating to the 'jurisdiction and proper procedure of the commission' was to comprise most of the first day, as the opinion of counsel was sought on three separate but interlinked issues. The first of these concerned its right to hold the proceedings in public or *in camera*, depending on the exigencies of the situation. According to MacBride, the commission was, in his opinion, 'a judicial court' which did not have any discretion to sit in private, being able to appropriately discharge its function only if it sat in open court. After a brief adjournment, the commission decided that it did not agree with this assessment of the situation and concluded that it had the right to hear submissions in private, as it saw fit.[28] The next issue to be resolved concerned the commission's right to administer an oath to witnesses. In determining that they did not in fact have this power, Ó Briain was to add a pointed rider: 'If we had the power I have very little doubt that we should avail of it.'

Perhaps the most vexatious matter facing the commission was the question of ascertaining where the onus for establishing the grounds for Lawless's continued detention lay. Having regard to the sensitive nature of this enquiry, Judge Ó Briain ordered that the remainder of the hearing be held in private, before he went on to reveal how he had received a file from the Department of Justice marked 'secret and confidential'.[29] Openly critical of its contents, he noted how it contained a number of reports that had been prepared 'by police officers who were anonymous and whose standing in the force was not apparent'. He admonished the government for not providing the original documents and felt that it would have been more appropriate if they had been furnished by 'a responsible officer of the Minister for Justice', who would be in a position to inform the commission of 'the implications thereof'. In doing so, he also ruled that the commission was not bound by the rules of evidence and 'reserved the right to hear and receive evidence and documents' without disclosing their contents to the applicant. Although MacBride argued that Lawless's interests had been gravely prejudiced by these rulings, the commission indicated that in all probability it would read the file and agreed that the onus for justifying Lawless's detention rested with the Minister for Justice. This duty could only be discharged through an officer of the Gardaí, who would have to be present in order to supply the commission with the requisite documents.[30] The commission then adjourned its sitting until 20 September.

The next day, 18 September, MacBride proceeded to lodge an application in the High Court seeking a writ of *habeas corpus* on the grounds that the Detention Commission had misdirected itself, making it impossible for him and his team to discharge their duty.[31] This was not an assessment shared by Peter Berry, the Secretary of the

Department of Justice, who noted how the government 'had won the first round'. In light of these developments, the commission proceeded to temporarily suspend its inquiry, as the matter was now *sub judice*.[32] In the interim, the High Court granted MacBride's application and a writ of *habeas corpus ad subjiciendum* was served on the commandant of the internment camp, Carl O'Sullivan, for the production of Lawless in court 'unless cause be shown to the contrary'.[33] A number of affidavits were duly filed by the government on 24 September, including one by Commandant O'Sullivan, where he averred that he had received Lawless into his custody, together with a warrant authorizing his detention under the Offences Against the State (Amendment) Act.[34] Notwithstanding cause shown, MacBride moved to have this conditional order of *habeas corpus* made absolute and a full hearing was opened in the High Court on 8 October 1957.

During these proceedings, MacBride gave an early indication of his intended future approach when he invoked the ECHR. As a signatory state, he asserted that it was no longer open to the Irish government to rely on powers that were in contravention of this agreement and contended that Lawless's detention was therefore illegal.[35] The High Court did not agree and in a reserved judgement dismissed the application on the grounds that the provisions of the ECHR had no standing in Irish domestic law. In fact, it was found that, according to the constitution:

> while the state [may] be a party to [the ECHR], [it] cannot of itself in any way qualify or affect our domestic legislation. Where there is an irreconcilable conflict between a domestic statute and the principles of international law or the provisions of an international Convention, the courts administering the domestic law must give effect to the statute.[36]

Despite an appeal to the Supreme Court, this decision was upheld, as the Chief Justice, C.J. Maguire, noted that the insuperable obstacle to importing the ECHR into the domestic law was that the Oireachtas had not determined that it was part of the domestic law. Therefore, no rights were granted or obligations imposed on the executive in addition to those of the domestic law and no argument could prevail against the express command of the constitution. In his opinion:

> The court ... cannot accept the idea that the primacy of domestic legislation is displaced by the state becoming a party to the Convention for the Protection of Human Rights and

Fundamental Freedoms. Nor can the Court accede to the view that in the domestic forum the executive is in any way estopped from relying on the domestic law. It may be that such estoppal might operate as between the High Contracting Parties to the Convention ... but it cannot operate in a domestic court administering domestic law. Nor can the court accept the contention that the Act of 1940 is to be construed in light of, and so as to produce conformity with, a convention entered into ten years afterwards. The intention of the Oireachtas must be sought in the conditions which existed when it became law.[37]

Two days after the release of this decision, Lawless lodged a formal complaint with the European Commission of Human Rights, contending that his continued internment was a breach of his rights under article five of the ECHR.[38] The Irish government had agreed upon its ratification of the ECHR in 1953, to recognize the right of the European Commission of Human Rights, which was established as an adjunct to the Council of Europe, to receive petitions from any persons or non-governmental organizations claiming a violation of their human rights. It had also agreed to recognize the jurisdiction of the as yet unestablished European Court of Human Rights, in matters pertaining to the interpretation and application of the ECHR.[39] Before he could pursue his case through this mechanism, however, Lawless was first obligated to exhaust all domestic legal remedies. As such, the attention of all parties reverted back to the Detention Commission on 6 December 1957, as it moved to resume its *in camera* sitting, which had been adjourned the previous September. On this occasion, the presence of the Chief State Solicitor as a representative of the Attorney-General was an indication of how seriously the government was beginning to take the case. He read briefly from the Supreme Court decision before withdrawing to his office, where he advised the commission that he would be available to assist it in any way as to procedure.

Remaining to represent the government was Garda Chief Superintendent P. Carroll, who was prevailed upon by the commission to elaborate on the grounds for Lawless's continued detention. In this capacity, he tendered a dossier to its members detailing 'various allegations' against Lawless and his involvement with the IRA, before protesting against MacBride's request to be furnished with a copy, on the grounds that it would endanger police informants and compromise the security of the state. As a necessary compromise, the commission agreed to read the document into the record, except for two key paragraphs which the chief superintendent had indicated should not be disclosed to Lawless or his legal advisors. Once complete, MacBride encountered surprisingly little opposition from the commission as he moved to cross-examine Carroll, despite the fact that express provision for the use of this procedure had not been made by the legislation governing the operation of the Detention Commission. In the ensuing interrogation, the chief superintendent refused to divulge the authorship of the Garda document, except to say that he had made personal investigations into the allegations contained therein and was fully satisfied that they were true. He also outlined how he had received a number of reports from various Garda officers confirming that Lawless had taken part in the robbery at Flemings the previous May. The proceedings were then adjourned when MacBride requested that these reports be made available to the commission at its next sitting.[40]

These unexpected developments were proving to be a matter of deep unease for the government, as the operation of the Offences Against the State (Amendment) Act, as originally envisaged, was now being fundamentally threatened. Essentially, the proceedings before the Detention Commission were beginning to resemble those of a formal court sitting, which was at variance with the government's view of this body as a purely administrative organ. To forestall this, Aindrias Ó Caoimh, the Attorney-General, made a personal appearance before the commission on 10 December and outlined the grave concern of the government 'at the report of the line of cross-examination allowed on the last hearing'. In his submission, he explained how an examination of the 'relevant legislation' revealed that cross-examination was never contemplated as it could result in 'imperiling third parties or the security of the state'. A more appropriate procedure for the commission would be to hear the representative of the government in private, where he could supply them with the documents relative to the case at hand. Then, 'with due regard for the security of the state', the commission could indicate to the applicant the nature of the allegations made against him. In his view:

> The Commission was not a court and could *act judicially* [my emphasis] without adhering to the form and procedure of Courts. *It could itself* [my emphasis] test by cross-examination testimony tendered but in the interest of state security and that of third parties it should conduct such examination in private ...

[because of] the dangers implicit in conclusions which might be drawn by an applicant from answers to a cross-examination conducted in his presence.[41]

In making this assertion, the Attorney-General placed the Detention Commission in a difficult position, as it could not ascertain how it was expected to act in a judicial manner if it was not a court. While conceding the government's point about supplying the applicant with information that could endanger the security of the Irish state, the commission was unable to see how it could be in a position to test evidence by cross-examination if its members were required to do this by themselves. Specifically, they would not be in a position to know which parts of the testimony the applicant would contradict and would therefore be incapable of conducting an effective cross-examination from his point of view. MacBride concurred and repeatedly contended for his right to continue with his cross-examination of Chief Superintendent Carroll, forcing the commission to retire in order to consider its position. For the Attorney-General, it was becoming increasingly apparent that Judge Ó Briain was 'constitutionally incapable' of conducting the inquiry 'divorced from the trappings of court procedure' and that the commission would return with an adverse decision. When proved correct, he immediately requested an overnight adjournment to enable him to consult with the government. As the commission indicated that it would not be able to reconvene for several days, MacBride, who was reported to be 'very elated at his success', offered to defer his cross-examination until a later date to allow the proceedings to continue.

After a break for lunch, MacBride read out an affidavit sworn by Lawless in which he denied his participation in the robbery at Flemings and averred that at no time in 1957 was he a member of an illegal organization.[42] At this point the Attorney-General, 'seeing an opportunity of avoiding collision with the Commission on the question of cross-examination', informed those present that if Lawless was prepared to give an undertaking as to his future conduct he would recommend his release to the government. After a 'deal of fencing by Mr. MacBride', it was agreed by all parties that Lawless would give an amended form of the official government undertaking, provided the Gardaí reopened their investigation into the allegations made against him. Lawless then came forward to the witness chair, where he declared that 'I will not at any time in the future engage in any activities which are illegal under the Offences Against the State Acts

1939–1940.'⁴³ He later defended his decision to take this particular form of the government undertaking on the grounds that he was not swearing to uphold the constitution, parts of which he found objectionable, but was simply agreeing to refrain from further unlawful activity. The commission then adjourned *sine die*, and on 12 December 1957 Lawless was released from the Curragh on the instruction of the Minister for Justice.[44]

Upon his release, Lawless immediately amended the terms of his original application to the European Commission of Human Rights to seek damages and costs for the period of his detention.[45] Although his decision to give the undertaking was understandable, this move had fundamentally prejudiced his application, as the immediacy of the alleged injustice against him was now considerably diminished. Had he refused freedom, it is likely that his application would have merited a higher priority, prompting a more detailed investigation by the European Commission.[46] While the government was glad to have discharged Lawless from its custody once he had invoked the ECHR, the sequence of events, which had transpired before the Detention Commission, offered some food for thought. In providing the government with the power of internment, the architects of the Offences Against the State (Amendment) Act sought to incorporate some provision to protect the ordinary citizen from the abuse of these powers, while at the same time maintaining the security of the Irish state. In establishing the Detention Commission as an administrative body, it was felt that this balance had been successfully struck. The experience in the Lawless case was to indicate otherwise, as the commission sought to hold proceedings like 'those of a court and permitted the cross-examination of a Garda Chief Superintendent who attended to produce documents'.[47]

According to the Minister for Justice, such an interpretation of the role of the Detention Commission was to 'threaten the efficacy of the power of internment' by diluting the government's ability to detain IRA suspects on suspicion alone. Indeed, the very basis of this power rested on the premise that the government could hold suspected IRA members when it was not in a position to proffer criminal charges. The rulings of the Detention Commission now meant that the suspicions of the Gardaí would have to be sufficiently established by cross-examination and investigation, raising the possibility that police informants would have to be produced before it. This was to create a certain amount of apprehension in government circles as it was felt that any future sittings of the commission may result in a clash between that body and the Gardaí if they refused to disclose the sources of their information. On the other hand, it was also recognized that the Detention Commission might be deemed to be lacking in efficiency if it did not endeavour to test the validity of information laid before it. In the view of the Attorney-General, if the commission did not attempt to do this in some manner there could be no rationalization for its existence, as the internment of an applicant could be simply justified by an unsupported Garda statement.[48]

Needless to say, this prompted immediate calls for the reform of the Detention Commission in order to bring its operation in line with the original conception of its duties as envisaged by the Offences Against the State (Amendment) Act. Specifically, the Department of Justice advocated the removal of Justice Ó Briain as chairman, followed by a public presentation of the predicament in which the Irish government would find itself if this so-called 'legal formalism' were to prevail.[49] This was resisted by the Attorney-General, who offered a more reasoned appraisal of the situation by suggesting that the passage of amending legislation could empower the Minister for Justice to make regulations governing the procedure of the commission. Regulations could then be introduced 'providing that the "evidence" of those appearing on behalf of the government should be heard in the absence of the applicant and should not be disclosed to him or to any other person'. In any case, this debate proved to be academic as Lawless's application turned out to be the only one to be heard by the Detention Commission. While it fell into abeyance with the release of all remaining internees in 1959, it was not formally wound up until 1962, when the government finally released a proclamation rescinding the activation of part two of the Offences Against the State (Amendment) Act.[50]

EUROPEAN COMMISSION OF HUMAN RIGHTS

With the formal conclusion of these proceedings, Lawless began the protracted process of pursuing his case through the machinery of the European Commission of Human Rights. With the tenth formal ratification, by Luxembourg, in September 1953, the provisions of the ECHR came into official operation across the member states of the Council of Europe, which had been established as a non-communist intergovernmental forum in 1949. In addition to laying down a catalogue of civil and political rights and freedoms, the ECHR also provided for the establishment of three interlinked institutions tasked with ensuring its enforcement – the Committee of Ministers of the Council of Europe, the European Commission of Human Rights and the European Court of Human Rights. Although the Committee of Ministers had been formally instituted with the foundation of the Council of Europe, the Commission of Human Rights had not been set up until 1954, when it was initially empowered to hear and receive petitions from the various signatory states in connection with the operation of the ECHR. With the lodgement of six requisite declarations, including one from Ireland in July 1955, an optional clause contained within the ECHR was activated, giving the European Commission of Human Rights the jurisdiction also to hear petitions from private citizens.[51] Elected by the Committee of Ministers, the commission was composed of individuals of high moral character with a recognized competence in either national or international law, who would serve a term of office tenable for up to six years.[52]

On the other hand, the European Court of Human Rights could not come into existence until its jurisdiction had been accepted by eight member states, delaying its formal inauguration until January 1959. Consisting of a number of judges equal to that of the members of the Council of Europe, membership of the court was renewed one-third at a time, with each member state nominating three candidates for election.[53] As part of its many duties, the court was predominantly tasked with settling cases concerning the interpretation and application of the ECHR, provided that these cases were referred to it by either the European Commission or the Council of Ministers.[54] The same right of referral was not allowed to individual petitioners, as only delegates from the commission and the representatives of the state which was a party to the case were permitted any standing before the court. While this was to present certain problems in providing for the contentions of the applicant before the court, the establishment of this body, which could affect the rights of an individual against his own or a foreign state, was of considerable innovational significance.[55] Intent on prosecuting his application through this complex system, the fundamental import of Lawless's application in terms of international jurisprudence lay in the fact that it was the first case to be heard by the court in 1961.

Before such a stage could be reached, this application would be subject to an involved and detailed examination by the European Commission, which would first consider the admissibility or otherwise of the case at hand. Designed as a filter in order to sift out vexatious and unsuitable petitions, this initial stage of the proceedings was concerned with a number of issues, including whether or not the petitioner had exhausted all domestic legal remedies.[56] If the application was deemed to be admissible, the next stage involved the European Commission placing itself at the disposal of the parties involved, in an attempt to broker a friendly settlement. If no such settlement was forthcoming it would then conduct a full investigation before drawing up a report establishing the facts and expressing an opinion on the merits of the case. This report was then to be transmitted to the Council of Ministers, who could either make a formal and binding decision in the case, or refer it to the European Court of Human Rights for further adjudication.[57] Once the court received the case, a series of written memorials and other documents were to be filed with the court's registry prior to an oral hearing. Upon the conclusion of this hearing, the court would then retire to consider its decision, which, when delivered, was final and binding on all parties.[58]

On 8 November 1957 Lawless formally embarked on this lengthy process with the lodgement, on his behalf, of an official 'Statement of Complaint and Claim' with the Secretary-General of the Council of Europe. In drawing up this document, MacBride argued that Lawless's internment was a flagrant breach of the rights to liberty, security of person and the proper administration of justice enshrined in articles five and six of the ECHR and claimed that the government's limited right of derogation from these obligations was inapplicable.[59] In this regard, the ECHR was not wholly inflexible in its guarantees of liberty and trial, and provided signatory governments with an exemption from the execution of these provisions during times of military crisis. Under article fifteen, signatory states were permitted to take measures that were in conflict with the ECHR during a period of 'public emergency threatening the life of the nation', provided that they were to the 'extent strictly required by the exigencies of the situation'. Any government availing itself of this right of derogation was obliged to inform the Secretary-General of the reasons thereof, prompting a letter from the Minister for External Affairs in July 1957 notifying him of the activation of the Offences Against the State (Amendment) Act.[60] In doing so, he also made it clear that, insofar as the activation of the government's special powers of arrest and detention *might be* termed to be in breach of the ECHR, then, and only then, should his letter be regarded as a notice of derogation.[61]

In making the complaint, MacBride argued that the wording of this letter rendered it invalid as it was drafted in such a manner so as not to admit derogation, unless the European Commission decided that the measures taken by the government constituted a breach of the ECHR. Notwithstanding the continuation of the IRA's campaign, he also sought to deny that that there was a public emergency in Ireland that could justify derogation and proposed that the use of internment against the republican movement was not strictly required by the exigencies of the situation.[62] To resolve these issues, the European Commission invited both parties to make a number of written submissions on the admissibility of the application at hand, leading to the exchange of a number of voluminous and repetitive pleadings between Lawless and the government.[63] At this juncture, the facts of the case were deemed to be irrelevant, as the European Commission sought a determination on *prima facie* admissibility based on a number of key issues, including the validity of the government's supposed derogation. It was also to be ascertained whether Lawless had exhausted all domestic remedies prior to making his application and whether or not he was debarred from taking a case under article seventeen of the ECHR. This provision explicitly prohibited anyone who was involved in an organization that was trying to supplant the freedoms contained therein from invoking it in their favour. In this respect, Lawless's alleged membership or otherwise of Christle's splinter group was a crucial factor.

At the onset, the government appeared to be adopting a relatively cavalier attitude to the proceedings when it filed an unsigned and undated memorandum by way of justifying the inadmissibility of Lawless's complaint. Contained in it was a succinct history of the struggle between the Irish state and the republican movement in order to justify the use of internment, and two other documents dealing separately with the application of Lawless and a similar legal action taken by Ruairí Ó Brádaigh.[64] Contending that Lawless's application was politically inspired and made for the purposes of propaganda, the government sought to deny its admissibility under article seventeen, alleging that he was a member of an illegal organization at the time of his arrest in July 1957.[65] The manner in which this memorandum was tendered merited a rebuke from MacBride, who dismissed its contents as having no bearing on the case, being principally composed of 'political arguments and suggestions'.[36] In his ensuing reply, Lawless consistently refuted the allegation that he was a member of the IRA, maintaining that he had disassociated himself from Christle's splinter group 'sometime towards the end of 1956'.[67] When a second round of written exchanges failed to resolve these issues, the European Commission moved to convene an oral admissibility hearing on 19 and 20 June 1958.

In taking the view that the government should be strongly represented at this hearing, the Attorney-General, Aindrias Ó Caoimh, assembled an experienced legal team including the Chief State Solicitor Donogh O'Donovan, Senior Counsel Brian Walsh and Anthony Hederman, Thomas Coyne of the Department of Justice and Seán Morrissey of the Department of External Affairs. As was the case before the Detention Commission, Lawless was again represented by MacBride, Sorahan and Connolly. Lasting one and a half days, this hearing was dominated by staid and tendentious legal argument, the highlight of which revolved around MacBride's failed effort to introduce an affidavit sworn by the Lord Mayor of Dublin, James Carroll. By averring that there was a complete absence of civil disorder in the Republic of Ireland, the introduction of this affidavit would have represented a setback for the government's efforts to contend that the continuation of the IRA's campaign justified derogation from the provisions of the ECHR. Once this document was eventually rejected on procedural grounds, the President of the European Commission, C.H.M. Waldock, thanked both parties for their contribution and retired to consider its reserved decision, leaving informed contemporary opinion divided as to the likely outcome of the hearing.[68]

At a conference in the Department of Justice on 17 July 1958, it was felt that, while the government's case had 'none of the law but all of the merits', it was 'anybody's bet which way the cat would jump'. If the first leg of the proceedings was lost, the overall feeling was that the second 'might easily' follow, thereby serving the government right for having signed and ratified the ECHR in the first place.[69] In any case, the decision was not long coming, as the European Commission released its judgement on 30 August 1958. In shelving the derogation issue, the European Commission sensationally decided to permit the application. Specifically, it felt that it was not in a position to make a determination on the basis of article seventeen, as Lawless's membership of the IRA was a point of conflict between the parties, and one on which it was not possessed of sufficient evidence to make a pronouncement. It deemed it more appropriate to open a full investigation into the matter, thereby leading to a consideration of the merits of the case. In pursuit of this undertaking, it was incumbent upon the European Commission to establish a sub-commission of its members tasked with ascertaining the facts before compiling a secret report of its findings. In ordinary circumstances this report would then be transmitted to the Committee of Ministers, where the case would be finally decided.[70]

In line with established conventions, this sub-commission was to comprise seven members, five of whom were chosen by lot and one each appointed by the parties involved. As to be expected, the Irish government appointed James Crosbie, the Irish member of the commission, to represent its interests in the case. MacBride, however, gambled on selecting the British representative and President of the Commission, C.H.M. Waldock. Having regard to Waldock's nationality, this was a strategy fraught with danger. While the complaint was made against the Irish government, it did concern actions within Northern Ireland, which was a *de facto* part of the United Kingdom. In grappling with the same IRA threat, both Irish governments had responded by introducing internment. In MacBride's mind, it was reasonable to assume that Waldock would be loath to condemn the actions of the Irish government as this could also be construed as an implied criticism of the actions of a subordinate political entity to the Westminster parliament. However, Waldock, like Crosbie, did have a detailed knowledge of the Irish situation and had already proven himself sympathetic to the Irish government's position when he initially opposed admitting Lawless's application in the first place. He was also in a unique position of influence in his capacity as president of the commission. The continental members of the commission would have been aware of the commonality of language and legal systems between Britain and Ireland, which sprang from a common political, constitutional and legal history. They would therefore have a natural inclination to rely on the opinions of Waldock on these issues. In deference to MacBride, then, this was a clever attempt to neutralize one of the most potent members of the commission, as Waldock, who was required to act in an impartial manner, was now presented with a clear conflict of interest. MacBride hoped that he would attempt to resolve this conflict by putting his impartiality to the commission above his loyalty to his country. This turned out not to be the case, as Waldock consistently argued against Lawless during the deliberations of the sub-commission.[71]

BRITISH INTEREST

While Lawless made his complaint solely against the Irish government, it was recognized by the British authorities that a decision in this case could have a subsidiary effect on Northern Ireland, especially if Dublin were required to release all internees in its custody. Such an eventuality would invariably give 'a tremendous boost' to the IRA, which was something to be 'avoided at all costs'.[72] Wedded to this, internment had not only been used in Northern Ireland; it had also been employed in several other 'dependent territories', including Cyprus and Kenya, where it had been implemented to overcome the Mau Mau insurgency. Any adverse decision could therefore go some way towards casting contemporary imperial policy in a particularly unfavourable light. Britain, like Ireland, was also obliged to derogate from the ECHR in order to institute such measures, lodging the requisite notice of derogation in respect of Northern Ireland on 27 June 1957.[73] Although satisfied that most of the provisions of the ECHR presented 'no difficulty to this country', the Foreign Office was concerned with the phraseology of article fifteen and as to what exactly constituted a public emergency threatening the life of the nation. It was hoped that a decision in the Lawless case could help to clarify this issue with a more rigid definition of the exact circumstance in which derogation was allowed.[74]

With Britain already holding a substantive interest in the case, the decision as to its admissibility prompted Gurth Kimber, an embassy official in Dublin, to make an approach to the Department of External Affairs in order to discuss the matter of the Irish notice of derogation. As this notice did not make explicit mention of a public emergency, Kimber intended to propose that an amendment be made in such terms, but stopped short on this occasion, deciding that 'it would be better to leave them ... to make up their own minds'.[75] He counselled against any attempt to raise the issue by making formal political representations, pointing out that if the Irish government was prepared to invoke a state of emergency

> [they] risk rebuff in the Human Rights Commission where MacBride and others would use all legal means to frustrate them, and have to face, as they did in the past, severe criticism of the practice of imprisonment without trial from highly respectable local persons and organizations.

In his mind, if such representations became public they would make action 'more and not less difficult' as the 'general mass of people whilst probably not sympathetic to [the] IRA, are likely to react instinctively to any suggestion of pressure from [the] Northern Irish or British governments'.[76]

It was some months later, during the course of a private interview with de Valera, in which it was considered more appropriate to raise the matter, that Kimber suggested that the Irish government's difficulty with the European Commission would 'be overdone by declaring a state of emergency'. While expressing his own private concerns about the implications of the admissibility decision, de Valera was loath to take this step, on the grounds that he would encounter 'great political difficulty in this course'.[77] As it was becoming more apparent that the Irish government would not be persuaded in this matter, London responded by making a number of discreet enquiries in order to ascertain if there were any possibility of lobbying the European Commission. Specifically, the British government sought some mechanism through which they could place before it the 'political implications' of a decision requiring the closure of the Curragh. However, as the European Commission was deemed to be an independent 'quasi-judicial body', any hope of a positive intervention on Ireland's behalf was dismissed until the application was passed to the Committee of Ministers.[78] Stung by its inability to exert any influence over the proceedings, British diplomats withdrew from further discussion with Dublin until a formal request was made for their assistance, which would then be supplied behind the scenes in order to ensure that Lawless's application was unsuccessful.

REFERRAL

With the inauguration of a European Commission of Human Rights sub-commission tasked with considering the merits of the case, the next phase of the proceedings was signalled by the exchange of another round of written submissions. Following the receipt of the European Commission's admissibility decision, Lawless was given until November 1958 to file a memorial outlining the central thrust of his case before the government was given a chance to respond.[79] Although the substance of these pleadings was substantially the same as that covered by the admissibility hearing, it must be noted that, while the material facts of the case remained the same, the legal issues had changed. Attention had now turned to the central issues of whether internment breached the ECHR, and if the Irish government had been entitled to derogate from its obligations owing to the circumstances that pertained in Ireland at the time.[80] Naturally, Lawless persisted with his assertion that his internment in the Curragh without charge or the intervention of the due processes of law constituted a violation of the freedoms enshrined in the ECHR, and sought to deny the validity of the government's derogation on a number of grounds.

By formally lodging James Carroll's affidavit with the sub-commission, MacBride hoped to undermine the government's assertion that the continuation of the IRA's campaign in Northern Ireland constituted an emergency threatening the life of the state. Relying on the fact that the government tendered no proof of the existence of such a situation, he pointed out that the parliament and courts in Ireland were functioning normally. As the constitution had already made express provision for the operation of 'various special courts' during such a situation, surely the threat of the IRA's campaign would have initially merited recourse to these measures? In fact, he questioned whether or not the government was actually pleading derogation in the first place, by arguing that the onus for establishing if the provisions of article fifteen applied lay solely with the government. By referring to the language employed in the notice of derogation, MacBride demonstrated that the government had reneged on this responsibility by asking the Secretary-General to consider if the use of internment was a violation of the ECHR. The phraseology of this letter was constructed in such a manner as to admit derogation only if the Secretary-General deemed the use of internment to be in breach of the ECHR. In his view, 'this is not a plea of derogation; it is merely an indication that in the event of an adverse finding ... the respondent government may then plead derogation'.[81]

In filing its rebuttal on 12 January 1959, the government chose to counter MacBride on the derogation issue, asserting that

> in so far as any actions taken by the government in relation to the applicant may have been contrary to the provisions of article five of the Convention (and it is not admitted that it was) the government submit that their actions were taken in exercise of their right of derogation under article fifteen of the Convention.

As to the form of the derogation, it was argued that the terms of the ECHR did not lay down any specific framework within which it must be drafted. The only stipulation was that it must keep the Secretary-General fully informed as to measures taken and the reasons thereof – an obligation it was felt had been fully complied with. The government also submitted that the activities of the IRA in Northern Ireland not only had the potential to 'involve the state in a war', it also represented a grave threat to the internal civil order. As it appeared that the 'ordinary methods of enforcing the law ... had not proved effective to prevent the violent activities of [the IRA]', it was therefore the government's duty to take immediate remedial action with the introduction of internment.[82]

To tease out these contentious issues the sub-commission scheduled an oral hearing for 17 April 1959, in which it was to hear Gerard Lawless and the head of the Special Branch, Detective-Inspector Philip McMahon, on the question of his alleged membership or otherwise of the IRA. For the government's part, the sub-commission was also anxious to determine the full circumstances of the Irish state's supposed derogation and sought to ascertain the considerations that merited recourse to internment.[83] In preparation for this hearing, the Department of Justice briefed Detective-Inspector McMahon as to the evidence he was called on to give, taking specific note of an interview he conducted with Lawless while he was in Garda custody in July 1957. Departmental officials also concluded that Garda enquiries into Lawless's alleged involvement in the raid on Flemings depot had been thorough and exhaustive, declaring that

> under no circumstances could ... the source of the information against Lawless ... in which very experienced police officers had the fullest confidence [be disclosed]. It would be fatal to further work against unlawful organizations ... to take any step which might enable persons in such organizations to deduce the identity of the source against Lawless. It would shake the confidence of such persons in the police and their help is vital.[84]

Although Lawless was to consistently deny involvement with any militant republican organizations throughout this period, the authorities were not inclined to take his assurances at face value and continued to maintain a watching brief on his movements. In a Garda report prepared in December 1958, it was noted that Lawless continued his association with the 'activities of the splinter group IRA', despite the advice of his senior counsel, and maintained contact with several former comrades, including Seán Geraghty. In fact, he had been observed on numerous occasions attending meetings at 39 Mary Street, Dublin, where the Special Branch had it on good account that 'the furtherance of the re-organization of the splinter group' had been discussed. Moreover, when the Saor Uladh leader, Liam Kelly, came to Dublin on a 're-organizing campaign', both 'were the first volunteers of the splinter group to place themselves at Kelly's disposal'. In April 1958, Lawless was also involved in a 'skirmish' between members of Na Fianna Éireann and members of the splinter group and in October he participated, together with his barrister, Seamus Sorahan, in a picket of the Fianna Fáil Ard Fheis.[85] It was on the presumption that Lawless continued to be an active member of the splinter group that the government decided to re-present its case to the sub-commission hearing.

In his testimony, Lawless, who offered a collected and erudite façade in the face of sustained cross-examination, consistently maintained that at no time in 1957 was he a member of any illegal organization. During the initial portion of the questioning, led by members of the sub-commission, both Waldock and Crosbie pressed heavily on this matter but Lawless refused to be drawn into giving any more precise details. When asked what steps he actually took to sever his connection with the IRA, Lawless replied that he had simply ceased to attend parades and had discontinued all activities in furtherance of illegal organizations. Crosbie in particular expressed severe reservations on this point and put it to Lawless that his 'resignation from the IRA is purely fictitious'. Again he denied this allegation and explained that, as the IRA was not getting the support of the 'mass of the people', he had come to the conclusion that the ending of partition was a matter solely for the government. Under severe cross-examination by the Attorney-General, Lawless denied that he had continued his association with the splinter group upon his release from detention, maintaining that the meetings he had attended in Mary Street were for the benefit of the Republican Prisoners' Committee.[86]

Upon the completion of Lawless's lengthy testimony, Detective-Inspector McMahon was called to the stand, where he summarized the government's belief that on all occasions in 1957 Lawless was an active member of the IRA. The sub-commission specifically examined McMahon as to what had transpired during his interview with Lawless prior to internment and asked if he had enquired of Lawless whether he was a member of the IRA or not. Stating that he had not, McMahon informed the sub-commission that his conversation with Lawless proceeded on the basis that he was a member, feeling that this was a reasonable assumption to make, as Lawless neither denied nor confirmed membership during the interview. As to Lawless's post-internment activities, McMahon outlined his conviction, based on continued Special Branch observations, that he was still a member of the splinter group. Detective-Inspector McMahon was then asked to step down, as the sub-commission returned to its consideration of the substantive legal issues surrounding the case, on which it heard sustained argument from both sides. With the termination of these proceedings, the sub-commission retired to consider its report, which was finally released after a lengthy period of deliberation in December 1959.[87]

In considering the case at length, this substantial document made a number of important findings. Firstly, though no special form was prescribed, the character and terms of the letter sent by the government to the Secretary-General of the Council of Europe was ruled to be a valid notice of derogation. Leaving the Secretary-General in no doubt as to the government's intentions, it was drafted with the purpose of complying with article fifteen of the ECHR, though the vagueness of the language employed did leave it open to a certain amount of criticism. Secondly, in finding that a sufficient state of emergency was in existence in Ireland at the time, the sub-commission ruled that each government had certain discretion in determining the measures it could take in order to protect the civil order. Relatively speaking, the IRA attacks in Northern Ireland had the possibility of igniting inter-communal strife and, in light of the circumstances in which the political division of Ireland came about, the sub-commission appreciated that the Irish government would bear a certain responsibility in this regard. As the attacks of the IRA were being orchestrated in the territory of the Irish Republic, it was incumbent on the government to take such steps as necessary to prevent further republican activity. Based on these findings, the sub-commission found in favour of the Irish government and duly transmitted its report to the European Commission for final adjudication. However, owing to the sensitive nature of the case thus far, the European Commission took the landmark decision to have the matter referred to the newly established European Court of Human Rights for a final and binding decision.[88]

DECISION

Following this momentous decision, the Lawless application, much to the discomfiture of the Irish government, began to attract significant international media attention. Although the regional and national papers had only previously devoted sporadic attention to the case, the public announcement of the commission's decision served to rekindle intensive press interest.[89] Indeed, a press conference given by A.B. McNulty, the Secretary of the Commission, at which he explained the general procedures to be followed by the European Court, received almost blanket coverage in Ireland and the United Kingdom.[90] In one instance it was also reported that daily updates in the case were being 'pumped out' by Radio Free Europe to 'listeners behind the Iron Curtain'.[91] In describing how the court would establish a chamber of seven judges, under the chairmanship of the British peer Lord McNair, in order to hear the case, *The Times* even noted that there was a possibility of the hearing taking place in public.[92] Much attention was also focused on Lawless himself, as the *Daily Express* managed to scoop an interview with 'this shy fellow' who had devoted himself to full-time study so he could take a BA degree in history and economics. Explaining how he had spent some time working in London, Lawless expressed the hope that the case would be successful, as the compensation awarded would be used to pay his university fees. The image of scholarly dedication was completed when Lawless defended his decision not to travel to Strasbourg for the hearing, as 'he could not afford the time' away from his books.[93]

Having defeated Lawless's claim before the European Commission the government was understandably wary of now suffering a reversal in the full glare of the media and insisted on raising a number of procedural objections in order to frustrate the application.[94] During a protracted hearing that took place between October 1960 and July 1961, the European Court was called upon to issue three separate judgements, thereby establishing much of its early case law. Two of these judgements were concerned with Lawless's personal role in the proceedings, as the European Commission, appearing in its appointed capacity as a defender of the public interest, attempted to afford him some standing before the court. Under article thirty-one of the ECHR, the commission's report was to be transmitted only to the Council of Europe and the government of Ireland, who were not at liberty to publish it. The commission, however, had also sent a copy to Lawless to obtain the observations of his counsel on the issues raised by this document. In considering this matter, the court ruled that the commission had not exceeded its powers in transmitting the report to Lawless as it was deemed to be in the interests of the proper administration of justice that the court should have knowledge of and, if need be, take into consideration the applicant's point of view. In its second judgement, handed down on 7 April 1961, the court also ruled that the commission, when it considered it desirable to do so, had the right to invite the applicant to place some person at the disposal of the delegates of the European Commission, usually the senior counsel of the applicant, as is the practice today.[95]

Once these procedural matters had been addressed, the court then moved to examine the merits of the case, releasing its final judgment on 1 July 1961.[96] The fundamental principles involved related to whether or not a person could be imprisoned by ministerial order without charge or trial and under what circumstances a state could suspend the operation of the ECHR.[97] Throughout the course of the hearings, the Irish government persisted with its assertion that Lawless was deprived of the protections of the ECHR under article seventeen, owing to his alleged membership of the IRA. It also argued that, because of the continuation of the IRA's campaign, the government was entitled to avail itself of the right of derogation enshrined in article fifteen. In considering these arguments, the court ruled that several of the government's contentions were flawed, particularly in respect of article seventeen. Essentially, article seventeen was solely designed to prevent anyone justifying, by implication from the language of the ECHR, the right to engage in certain activities. Specifically,

> this provision ... cannot be construed *a contrario* as depriving a physical person of the fundamental individual rights guaranteed by articles five and six of the Convention; whereas in the present instance G. R. Lawless has not relied on the Convention in order to justify or perform acts contrary to the rights and freedoms recognized therein.

The court also ruled that internment conflicted with the government's obligations under article five, as Lawless was not charged with any crime, nor brought before a judge for the purpose of trial. It added: 'If the construction placed by the court on the aforementioned articles is not correct, anyone suspected of harbouring intent to commit an offence could be arrested and detained for an unlimited period on the strength merely of an executive decision.'[98]

In spite of these findings, the decision in the case turned on the court's ruling in respect of the government's right of derogation as laid down by article fifteen. By accepting that the government's letter of July 1957 did in fact amount to a notice of derogation, the court then set about determining if there was actually a public emergency threatening the life of the nation in existence in Ireland at the time internment was introduced. The court, setting a precedent by inquiring into this matter, firmly laid the burden of responsibility to prove that such an emergency did exist at the feet of the respondent government. The Irish government's defence in this matter was based on three premises. Firstly, there was in existence in the Republic of Ireland 'a secret army, engaged in unconstitutional activities and using violence to attain its purposes'; secondly, the fact that 'this army was ... operating outside the territory of the state', jeopardizing the relations of the Republic of Ireland with Northern Ireland; thirdly, that there was 'a steady and alarming increase in terrorist activities from the autumn of 1956 and throughout the first half of 1957'. In reaching its final decision the court crucially agreed with these assertions, stating that:

> the application of the ordinary law had proved unable to check the growing danger ... whereas the sealing of the border would have had extremely serious repercussions ... beyond the extent strictly required by the exigencies of the situation ... therefore the administrative detention instituted under the act ... of 1940 ... appeared, despite its gravity, to be a measure required by the circumstances.[98]

This was a crucially important finding to make, as the court established on this basis that the government had been entitled to derogate from the ECHR under article fifteen. It therefore ruled in the government's favour and held that it had not breached the ECHR when it had interned Gerard Lawless in July 1957.[100]

POSTSCRIPT

The release of this judgement was of little practical consequence in the immediate short term, owing to the closure of the Curragh internment camp in March 1959. However, the case had proved to be a groundbreaking lawsuit that had implications, not only for the future development of Irish counter-insurgency policy, but also for the application of the ECHR. From a domestic point of view, it is reasonable to assume that the government's decision to close the internment camp, taken against the backdrop of declining IRA activity, was partly facilitated by the progression of the Lawless case. In particular, the unexpected manner in which the Detention Commission sought to discharge its statutory obligations gave the government pause for thought. The government felt that the Detention Commission, by seeking to act as a judicial body before which witnesses could be called for cross-examination, had brought about a dilution of its power to detain republican suspects. The relative success experienced by Lawless in having his case admitted by the European Commission of Human Rights was also to ensure a large degree of international media attention – a source of significant embarrassment for the government. Despite the Irish government's success in defeating the application, the judgement laid down by the European Court was in itself to have implications for the future use of internment within its jurisdiction.

The strength of the application lay in the fact that it graphically demonstrated that the use of measures that may be deemed to contravene the ECHR were reviewable by an international legal tribunal, despite the bar placed by the constitution. The government could now no longer rely on the use of internment with impunity, because to do so could expose the Irish state to another claim before the European Commission – one which it might not necessarily defeat. The decision by the European court also placed a number of limitations on the executive's right of recourse to article fifteen. By determining for itself that conditions existed to justify derogation from the ECHR, the court could decide if circumstances within a state warranted such action, taking this contention out of the hands of a signatory government. It was no longer open to the government to decide arbitrarily that the activities of the IRA posed sufficient threat to the Irish state as to justify the use of internment; this was a decision that now had to be validated by the European Commission. Within the broader realm of international human rights law, the ECHR was the first international treaty to bestow fully enforceable rights on individuals. With the receipt of the Lawless application, the full mechanism designed to protect these rights came into effect with the operation of the European Court of Human Rights. Evolving together with supranational judicial entities such as the European Court of Justice, this body has today become indispensable in the application and construction of international law.

Despite these notable achievements, several observers, including Brian Doolan, have criticized the decision of the European Court by questioning whether the factual conclusions it reached were correct. Doolan is particularly critical of the sub-commission for not conducting a fact-finding visit to Ireland during its investigation of the merits of the case. By not doing so, he believed that the sub-commission failed in its duty to adequately investigate the case because, in his view, Lawless would have won the case 'if such an investigatory visit had occurred'.[101] Certainly, from a strict legal standpoint this could be argued, as there was little evidence to suggest a state of emergency in Ireland analogous to the spirit of article fifteen of the ECHR. In making this assertion, however, Doolan has adopted a somewhat ahistorical perspective by fundamentally underestimating the serious nature of the IRA campaign in Northern Ireland. This offensive had not only brought Ireland to the brink of a severe diplomatic confrontation with the United Kingdom, it also had, for a brief period, the potential to ignite serious sectarian strife across Northern Ireland. The difficulties experienced by the Irish authorities in obtaining convictions and securing appropriate custodial sentences has also been overlooked. Therefore, in moving to reintroduce internment in July 1957, de Valera was simply pursuing an established policy designed to deal with subversives that had proven highly effective in the past.

As for Lawless himself, given his conduct throughout 1955 and 1956, together with subsequent Garda accounts of his behaviour, it would seem reasonable to suggest that on the balance of probabilities he remained a fully engaged member of Christle's splinter group throughout the period in question. Following the conclusion of his case, he migrated to London, where he became involved in a number of controversies when attempting to join the Islington branch of the British Labour party. Described by his Labour colleagues as being 'very left wing', Lawless began to indulge in 'socialist propaganda of a type not approved of by the Labour Party authorities'.[102] Holding sway 'over many Irish members', a split was occasioned in the constituency when local party authorities refused to expel him from the party in spite of his republican past.[103] Little was then heard from Lawless until 1965, when the Department of External Affairs became aware of attempts to establish a branch of the Communist Party in Dublin under his direction.[104] In October 1968, Lawless's attendance at a civil rights march in Derry was noted, together with the renowned radical agitator Éamonn McCann. By the early 1970s he had became an established journalist at the *Sunday World* newspaper, where he regularly contributed articles on the Northern Irish conflict.[105] Once his career as a journalist ended, Lawless fell into relative obscurity. He continues to make his home in London.

7

'This is not an Abandonment of the Campaign, but a Strategic Retreat':[1] Closing Stages, 1957–1962

As Gerard Lawless attempted to prosecute his case before the European Court of Human Rights, the IRA, although maintaining a marginal interest in the affair, remained steadfastly committed to its campaign in Northern Ireland. With the introduction of internment, however, republican hopes of pursuing this offensive to a successful conclusion were severely curtailed. For an organization with a membership of up to 900 individuals, the detention of over 150 of its most active and senior volunteers was to represent a significant blow to its limited military capacity. A corresponding decline in the number of recorded incidents throughout the second part of 1957 can be directly attributed to these arrests.[2] As a result, it fell to an extemporized Army Council, headed by Seán Cronin as C/S and Charlie Murphy as A/G, to decide how best to revive the campaign's flagging fortunes.[3] Given the disruption occasioned by the July internments it was decided to prioritize planning for an upcoming winter offensive while simultaneously attempting to maintain a degree of short-term low-level activity.[4]

In furtherance of these aims, a number of training camps were held in County Tipperary, where experiments were carried out as to how to produce a more effective mine for use against fixed, defended positions. The IRA also attempted to update its limited communications, intelligence and supply networks in Northern Ireland, while at the same time organizing a series of debates, concerts and meetings, culminating with the annual republican Wolfe Tone commemoration in Bodenstown. This event, which took place on 23 June 1957, attracted over 8,000 people. The assemblage was addressed in particularly trenchant terms by Seán Duggan, who gave the traditional oration, where he declared himself to be 'a representative of a generation now engaged in the struggle to end ... British tyranny'. Although this commemoration served as a platform through which the IRA hoped to rally waning public loyalty to its cause, the address of Tom

McMonagle from Philadelphia hinted at widespread disaffection among the IRA's Irish-American backers. His pledge of support from 'the few of us left in the United States who still believe in the principles enunciated by Wolfe Tone' was hardly a convincing expression of overwhelming American endorsement.[5]

The ongoing activities of Joe Christle's splinter group were also proving to be a source of continuing irritation for the IRA, particularly following the destruction of a war memorial in Pery Square, Limerick.[6] Undertaken as part of an ongoing campaign to divest public spaces of the perceived symbols of British imperialism, this was simply the latest in a string of attacks on various monuments, including the Lord Gough statue in the Phoenix Park. In Limerick, the force of the explosion was reported to have caused extensive damage to several properties in the area, including the nearby Carnegie Library, which had several windows blown in. Needless to say, these acts of sabotage quickly merited a rebuke from the *Irish Times*, which accused those involved of engaging in acts of 'adolescent vandalism' aimed at the wilful destruction of public property. Since the splinter group had engaged in overt displays of militarism 'contrary to republican policy within the twenty-six counties', the IRA were particularly concerned that the Irish government would seek to use these incidents to cement its case for the continued use of internment. This prompted a veiled warning from *The United Irishman* demanding that Christle desist from his activities.[7]

These admonitions did little to dampen Christle's enthusiasm for such stunts and in August 1958 his organization was involved in another explosion in St Stephen's Green, Dublin, which destroyed a statue of Archibald William, the Earl of Eglinton, and almost resulted in three unintended fatalities. On this occasion, the perpetrators set a charge containing 50 lbs of explosives and two yards of safety fuse wire at the base of the statue before lighting the detonator and quitting the scene. The park night watchman, Michael Kavanagh, who was alerted to the presence of the raiders during the course of his rounds, immediately raised the alarm by placing a call to the park superintendent. Upon his arrival at the scene, the superintendent together with two Garda officers proceeded towards the statue before beating a hasty retreat when they observed smoke issuing from its base. The resultant blast scattered jagged bronze shrapnel over the vicinity and damaged over 100 windows in the salubrious surroundings, thereby occasioning much negative publicity.[8]

The IRA's campaign eventually reassumed its prominence in the public mind in August 1957, with a series of synchronized attacks. In Newry, the offices of the Northern Ireland Electricity Board were targeted: a powerful explosion blew the roof off the building, littering the surrounding streets with broken glass and office records of various descriptions. A fire was also set at a Post Office garage elsewhere in the town, causing an estimated £50,000 worth of damage, despite the best efforts of the local fire brigade. A machine gun attack on an RUC barracks in Swatragh, County Fermanagh, was beaten back by sustained police fire and a customs post in nearby Mullan was destroyed by a bomb blast. A new IRA campaign manifesto was extensively promulgated across the province the day after these attacks. Referring to previous proclamations, it called upon members of the RUC 'to remember that they are Irishmen' who had since been put on 'a war footing' to be 'used in conjunction with British forces'. In such circumstances, 'the resistance can hardly be expected to differentiate between men, trained, organized and equipped along military lines (although clad in police uniforms) and British troops'. The implications of this proclamation were immediately clear – the RUC must cease all hostile activity, or continue to suffer the consequences of being considered legitimate targets.[9]

The Department of Home Affairs reacted strongly to these developments by imposing a curfew from 11 p.m. to 5.30 a.m. throughout Newry and its environs.[10] With breaches punishable on summary jurisdiction with up to two years' imprisonment, recourse to this measure served to provoke the local nationalist populace, resulting in a tense standoff between the RUC and 'a crowd of youths'.[11] In the ensuing riot, these youths were baton charged by the police before the crowd was dispersed and the streets cleared.[12] In this highly charged atmosphere, Topping served to further inflame the situation when he admonished locals for their support for the republican movement and declared that the duration of the curfew 'would depend on themselves'.[13] Encouraged by local members of the IRA, a large crowd intent on defying the authorities assembled in the town square for the second evening in succession, where they proceeded to sing 'party songs'.[14] In anticipation of a night of violence a cordon of police officers in riot gear together with a number of Crossley-Tenders and land rovers were stationed on the main road leading out of the square. It was only after the local head constable addressed the crowd, advising them to 'have sense' and go home, that the situation was peaceably diffused.[15]

In Dublin, an already taut political situation was further compounded when an anonymous telephone call sparked a bomb scare at the British embassy. After a thorough search of the building by the Gardaí revealed nothing untoward, embassy officials were readmitted and normal business resumed. The simmering situation in Newry also threatened to reignite when the Belfast general branch of the Irish Labour party issued a strongly worded statement condemning the Stormont government for resorting to the use of a curfew. Calling it 'a provocative act' that could have a detrimental effect on public opinion, the statement criticized the curfew's imposition as a sop to 'the lunatic fringe on the government flank that has been urging retaliation on the minority'. Seeking the curfew's immediate removal, the statement unequivocally drew attention to the possibility of increasing 'civil strife' as a result of the government's actions. While this appeal was ignored, local tensions were further ratcheted up when a group of jittery B-Specials accidentally shot dead an innocent civilian while out on patrol in County Down. During the subsequent inquest it emerged that the victim and his wife had failed to heed calls to stop as they approached a mobile checkpoint, prompting the patrol to open fire. A verdict of accidental death was returned.[16]

Despite the widespread distribution of posters calling on people to defy the curfew, the situation in Newry remained remarkably calm, eventually prompting its removal on 10 September 1957.[17] In making the announcement, Topping expressed the hope that the peace in the area would be maintained, an assertion backed up by local nationalist MPs.[18] In the end, the net effect of republican agitation in the area, which it was hoped would trigger an 'uprising' against the Stormont authorities, was a marked increase in the number of RUC patrols around Newry and east Tyrone. This was not without its attendant long-term benefits for the IRA, however, as an increased army and police presence in the area offered more opportunity to engage these units in an ambush. The IRA also unveiled a deadly new tactic in its arsenal, when an anonymous telephone call was used to lure a combined British Army/RUC service party to a disused house in Brackaville, outside of Coalisland, County Tyrone, in the early hours of 19 August 1957. Upon arrival, this party, consisting of two soldiers and three police constables, observed that the main door to the house had been left 'partly open' and that there was 'a light showing behind it'. Unbeknown to them, the house had been rigged with a booby trap bomb that was activated when RUC Sergeant Arthur Ovens pushed against the door.

The blast, which demolished the house, killed him instantly and blew the remainder of the party out on to the street, where they all sustained injuries of varying severity.[19] A general alarm was immediately sounded and the entire area was cordoned off by police under the command of RUC County Inspector R.T. Hamilton. Tracker dogs were brought to the scene as a number of explosives and forensic experts conducted an examination of the debris.[20] Several individuals were quickly detained for questioning, as the local RUC, 'enraged by the death of a colleague', began a vigorous investigation aimed at bringing the perpetrators to justice.[21] It was widely speculated that Topping would respond with the re-imposition of a curfew in the area, but it quickly became apparent that no such action was contemplated when he released a statement condemning the killing of Sergeant Ovens as 'deliberate and callous'. South of the border, the *Irish Times* vilified those who were involved in this 'operation', which was 'marked by a mean stealthiness' that had few parallels 'even at the worst periods of our country's history'. The death of Sergeant Ovens was also reviled at a number of Masses throughout County Tyrone.[22]

Despite the wholesale revulsion engendered by the manner in which Ovens met his death, the republican movement persisted in its assertions that members of the RUC were legitimate targets. In September 1957, *The United Irishman* attempted to justify the actions of the IRA, claiming that:

> No one reading the RUC account of the incident could doubt for a moment the war-like and death-dealing nature of that expedition [the RUC service party]: machine guns at the ready, grenades primed and held in the hands, co-ordinated movements and so forth. When they set out to kill should they be surprised if death meets them on the way?[23]

In the face of intensive police enquiries and the detention of a number of local men for questioning, progress in the case was slow, notwithstanding numerous appeals for information in exchange for financial reward. Significant headway was not made until November, with the arrest of several individuals who were believed to have been involved in, or complicit in, the death of Ovens.[24] Of those in custody, two were particularly singled out as suspects, and on 8 January 1958 Kevin Mallon and Francis Patrick Talbot were formally charged with capital murder.

THE MALLON AND TALBOT AFFAIR

The circumstances surrounding the arrest of Mallon and Talbot were to occasion much controversy when it was alleged that signed confessions by these men had been extracted under duress while in police custody. In detailing how they were the individuals responsible for placing the telephone call that lured Ovens to his death, it was these confessions that provided the basis upon which both men were charged with capital murder. Faced with the gravity of this indictment, the IRA leadership, acting on the advice of Seán MacBride, arranged to have them represented at their trial by Mr Elwyn Jones as senior counsel.[25] The republican movement also mounted a vigorous publicity campaign to highlight the supposed ill-treatment of these men at the hands of the RUC. Claims of torture and systematic beatings were quickly taken up by the mainstream media, inflamed by the circulation of a pamphlet by the 'Irish Republican Publicity Bureau' (IRPB), which was emotively entitled: *British Torture in Ireland*. The southern press pursued this campaign with vigour, as *The Leader* laid down the gauntlet to the Stormont government to establish the truth or otherwise of these allegations.[26] The initial indictment and subsequent trial of Mallon and Talbot were also prominently detailed in the *Irish Times* and the *Irish Press*, while further copies of the IRPB pamphlet were distributed with the January 1958 edition of *The United Irishman*.[27]

In their version of events, both Mallon and Talbot asserted that they were subjected to intensive bouts of interrogation at Dungannon RUC station, during which they were 'beaten with fists, punched in the stomach and face, caught by the hair and their heads banged against the wall'.[28] After their interrogation they were handcuffed and taken in a car to a deserted by-road, where they were beaten on the roadside and prodded with rifles.[29] When transferred to Belfast they were again faced with 'relays of interrogators' who made various threats against their homes and families. Throughout, it was stated that their interrogators consistently implied that 'it made no difference who was got but that "someone was going to be got for the Brackaville job and it might as well be them"'.[30] Mallon claimed to have been particularly singled out and recalled being in a 'bad condition' after enduring a harsh beating during which he was stripped naked and had the lighted end of a cigarette pressed against his lips.[31] Continuing into the next day and night, their ordeal's climax came:

> [when] one of the youths returned to his cell in the dark ... lay on the bunk [and] discovered the pillow was covered in blood.

A detective followed and said: 'This is the sheet that covered Ovens.' And he added: 'It will cover another body soon.'[32]

These allegations aroused much indignation among the southern political establishment, as the Clann na Talmhan deputy, Michael Donnellan, signalled his intention of asking the Taoiseach if he was aware that 'a torture mill [had] been established in occupied Ireland by the Stormont junta'. In light of its emotive and provocative nature the ceann comhairle requested that Donnellan resubmit the question in less inflammatory terms.[33] In addressing this query, Maurice Moynihan, the secretary of the government, wrote to the Department of Justice requesting a copy of the IRPB pamphlet.[34] In an effort to determine the veracity of the allegations detailed therein, the Secretary of the Department of Justice, Thomas Coyne, wrote to the Garda Commissioner asking 'if any of your people [can] throw light on the matter?'[35] When informed that the government had no information relative to the case, save for what had been published in the newspapers, a reply was drafted on this basis, which was delivered in the Dáil by the Taoiseach's parliamentary secretary, Donnachadh Ó Briain. It stated:

> I am aware that allegations of the nature mentioned by the Deputy have been made. I have, of course, no official information on the matter and no means of securing evidence that would enable me to come to a judgment on the facts.[36]

Legal proceedings in the case were formally initiated on 8 and 9 January 1958, when both men appeared before a specially convened sitting of the Belfast City Commission. During this hearing, RUC County Inspector J.G. Nelson testified to taking the statements of the accused, which detailed how both men had been summoned to a meeting with two unidentified IRA men in a disused house near Brackaville, a week prior to the death of Sergeant Ovens. At this meeting, they were asked about potential targets for attack in the district before being instructed 'to keep an eye out for anything that could be done'. Before this gathering broke up, they were told that there would be 'a bit of an operation' on the following Saturday night and that they were to meet the IRA men at Patterson's Corner, situated about half a mile from the house. Meeting as arranged, they were directed to go to the nearby village of Edendork and make a telephone call to the police in Coalisland at 11 p.m. to say that they had seen a number of people acting suspiciously outside the disused house. Placing the call as requested, Mallon and Talbot then parted company and made their ways home separately. Mallon later reported hearing a loud explosion coming from 'the direction of Brackaville', which he claimed he did not know about, but had a 'fair idea' of what it was.[37]

After being remanded in custody, they were returned for trial before the Belfast City Commission on 15 January. These proceedings had to be postponed, however, when junior counsel for the defence fell ill at short notice.[38] At the resumed sitting in April, the coincident illness of one of the jurors necessitated a further postponement until 28 July. Eventually, at the third attempt, the trial proceeded to a successful conclusion before Lord Justice Black in the Crown Court of the Belfast City Commission.[39] In making his case, Elwyn Jones argued the inadmissibility of the confessions on the grounds that they had been extracted by 'undue terror and menace on the part of the police'. During his testimony, Mallon expanded on his allegations of ill-treatment, producing as evidence a grey shirt that was torn down the front.[40] The RUC vigorously denied these charges and prosecuting counsel successfully persuaded Lord Justice Black to admit the confessions into evidence.[41] Following two more days of legal argument, Jones, in his closing statement, urged the jurors to return a verdict of not guilty, reminding them that the prosecution case rested solely on the contested statements of Mallon and Talbot. Bar these confessions, the prosecution had not brought forward any other compelling evidence, leaving the jury to retire with the reminder that they could not convict on suspicion alone.[42]

In a final remarkable twist, both men were acquitted of the charges during a tense sitting of the Belfast City Commission on 6 August. Following loud applause from the public gallery, Mallon and Talbot then made their way out of the dock while shaking hands with their solicitors, before being confronted by a detective who barred their way. They were immediately re-arrested and within 'forty-five minutes of leaving the dock [they] were back in the police office attached to the Belfast courthouse'.[43] Although detained under the SPA, it was decided by the Department of Home Affairs that a variety of new arms and explosives charges should be proffered against them in order to give the RUC, who had come out of the trial 'rather badly', a chance to 'redeem themselves'.[44] On 8 August, both Mallon and Talbot were duly charged, leaving *The United Irishman* to denounce what it saw as an attempt 'to cover up this gross action which put "British justice"... in a most embarrassing position'. It denied the accusations made against Mallon and Talbot and criticized the Irish government for its failure to comment 'on the torture revelations'. In the end, both men were convicted of these charges and sentenced to a total of twenty-two years in prison.[45] The Stormont authorities resisted subsequent calls for an independent enquiry into 'police methods in Northern Ireland', thereby exposing the RUC to further charges of bias in respect of its dealings with the minority Catholic population.[46]

DECLINING FORTUNES

Throughout September and October 1957 the IRA began to engage in a number of small-scale sabotage operations in preparation for a more sustained winter offensive. In September an explosion damaged an electricity transformer in Newcastle, County Down, and a number of telegraph poles were cut down. An RUC training hall in Tullintrain, County Derry, was also badly damaged by an explosion and a customs hut was blown up at Clontivrin, County Fermanagh. In October, a number of bridges were targeted, there was an attempt to set fire to the Coalisland labour exchange, a post office garage in Enniskillen was damaged by an explosion and another electrical transformer, at Creagh, County Fermanagh, was demolished.[47] More importantly, the IRA also sought to modify its tactics with a move away from attacks on fixed police and army positions in favour of ambushing British armoured patrols. The planned ambushes did not prove to be all that effective, as the authorities, who were wary and well armed, consistently refused to be drawn into exposed positions by staged republican enticements. In fact, IRA units had very limited success in this regard, as the only attack of note resulted in minor wounds to a B-Special Constable who had been on patrol near the Tyrone/Monaghan border.[48]

On 27 September, there was a failed attempt to assassinate the Deputy Inspector of the RUC, Albert Kennedy, when a small bomb exploded under his car as he was driving to Belfast.[49] This was followed two weeks later by yet another attack on Roslea RUC station, during which an IRA assault party opened fire on the barracks after detonating a gelignite bomb outside the front door. There were no injuries on this occasion and the party quickly retreated when the RUC returned fire.[50] In acknowledging this as the first in a new series of anticipated winter attacks, the northern authorities took immediate remedial action. Police and military patrols in Fermanagh were stepped up and proposals were accepted concerning the use of air raid sirens for police purposes. In the Irish Republic, de Valera moved to augment border patrols with the arrival of 150 Gardaí, while cooperation between the Special Branch and the RUC was dramatically expanded. This was to yield immediate results, with the detention of over forty-five republican suspects, as well as the discovery of another substantial arms dump in Derry city.[51] Under intense pressure from the authorities on both sides of the border, the IRA was also obligated to hold its first Army Convention since 1955 in order to regularize the temporary leadership of Seán Cronin and his deputy, Charlie Murphy.[52]

It was during this period that the IRA was to experience its single greatest loss of life since the inception of the campaign, when an explosion in a farmhouse at Edentubber, County Louth, resulted in the deaths of five individuals. From the onset, it was apparent that the house was being used by an IRA party to prepare for a raid in Newry as a number of guns and fuses were discovered among the debris.[53] These suspicions were later confirmed when an IRA statement was circulated in Dublin identifying the deceased. Four of the dead, Paul Smith, Oliver Craven, George Keegan and Patrick Parle, were named as members of the IRA, while the fifth, Michael Watters, was the owner of the cottage. It subsequently emerged that a mine, which the group had been preparing for an unspecified operation on Armistice Day, had detonated prematurely, razing the cottage to the ground. Upon arrival, Gardaí were greeted by 'a gruesome scene', with debris scattered over a radius of two hundred yards. It was later reported that the authorities spent some time collecting the scattered remains of the deceased, before transporting them to Dundalk morgue, where they were reassembled.[54] After formal identification the remains were released to relatives and on 14 November, Smith, Craven and Watters were buried in the republican plot in Dundalk, following 'the largest funeral the town has seen'. Keegan and Parle were interred the next day in Enniscorthy and Wexford.

In his graveside oration in Dundalk, John Joe McGirl attempted to rally flagging republican spirits when he enjoined his comrades to build a 'fitting memorial' to the memory of the deceased with the establishment of the 'Republic proclaimed by the men of 1916'.[55] Needless to say, the Edentubber incident was a significant blow to fading republican morale, as it was becoming ever more apparent that the IRA was limited in its ability to pursue anything more than a campaign of low-level sabotage.[56] A series of coordinated attacks centred upon an assault on Swatragh RUC barracks in January 1958 was to signal a brief return to more intensive campaign operations. Prior to this raid, a number of bridges throughout County Derry were destroyed together with an electricity transformer at Rashaskin, County Antrim. At 10.15 p.m. an IRA party opened fire on the barracks from the front and rear. In an exchange of gunfire that lasted over twenty minutes, one B-Special officer, Constable James Murray, was wounded before his colleagues were successful in sending up a number of flares calling for reinforcements. The IRA party then broke off and successfully managed to evade capture, despite an intensive search of the locality.[57]

This spirited showing quickly proved to be a one-off, and was not, as many feared, the start of a long-term escalation in republican activity along the border. In fact, it was by now patently obvious to many contemporary observers that the campaign was foundering as the implementation of internment in both Irish jurisdictions seemed to be having the desired effect. The frequency and efficiency of RUC operations against the IRA not only paid dividends in the form of arrests and arms seizures, the constant pressure exerted by the police forced many volunteers to concentrate their efforts solely on evading capture rather than on the campaign itself. For their part, the efforts of the Gardaí were also beginning to tell, as their growing proficiency in detaining republicans fleeing across the border was to deny the IRA much of the sanctuary it had previously enjoyed in the Irish Republic.[58] According to *The United Irishman*, there were over 400 republicans incarcerated throughout Ireland and Great Britain and, while it is reasonable to assume that not all of these were militarily involved in the campaign, this still represented a significant drain on limited manpower resources.[59] A rudimentary examination of the number of violent incidents in Northern Ireland between December 1956 and January 1958 seems to bear out this assertion.

According to contemporary government sources, a cursory inspection of press reports for the first seven months of the campaign, up to July 1957, revealed that the total number of violent and abortive incidents across Northern Ireland stood at approximately 121. In employing a similar methodology for the next seven-month period up to January 1958, this figure was seen to have dropped dramatically to sixty-seven. Upon closer examination, it was also evident that there was a gradual shift away from coordinated, high-profile attacks in favour of low-level sabotage operations, such as the burning of customs huts, the cutting down of telegraph poles and the demolition of bridges. Therefore, on the anecdotal evidence alone, it would seem that the number of violent incidents in Northern Ireland had dropped by 45 per cent in the seven months since the introduction of internment in the Irish Republic. However, as the government did not appear to make a more systematic effort to compile more verifiable campaign data, these figures must be treated with caution. Garnered from contemporary press reports, this list of figures was compiled as part of the government's submissions in the ongoing Lawless application and it is possible then that these figures may have been slightly inflated in order to strengthen the Irish state's case. Moreover, an examination of contemporary print media is not the surest way of assembling a definitive list of this kind, as not all incidents would have been reported given the vagaries of more newsworthy items.[60] In spite of its shortcomings, however, this list was indicative of an overall decrease in the IRA's military capacity and its ongoing difficulties in prosecuting its campaign.

In identifying this trend, the IRA leadership attempted to ramp up its campaign: Seán Cronin proposed a hazardous incursion in to Blandford Army Camp in Dorset in order to secure some mobile artillery. This scheme was formally approved by the Army Council in January 1958 and a team of six volunteers was selected for the operation.[61] Taking place in the early hours of 16 February, the raid began when an unmarked car containing the IRA party entered the camp through the front entrance and proceeded towards the magazine armoury.[62] At 1.15 a.m. a man emerged from this car dressed in a British army uniform and approached the adjacent guardroom, where several off-duty sentries were resting. Gaining entry with a knock on the door, three other armed men were reported to have burst into the room, where they identified themselves as members of the IRA before moving to subdue and restrain the sentries.[63] At the same time two other soldiers, who were on duty behind the armoury, were confronted by a separate group of raiders and ordered into the guardroom. When they resisted, their captors opened fire, wounding one of them in the stomach.

The noise of this struggle quickly alerted a nearby civilian telephone operator, who immediately placed a call to the headquarters of the camp, which was located several hundred yards away. Sergeant W. Robinson was dispatched by the duty officer to investigate, before being quickly intercepted by two of the raiders, who thrust him into the guardroom. Comically, two other corporals, who happened to be returning from a night out, were also apprehended and held with their colleagues. In all, ten soldiers were now bound and gagged inside the guardroom, including the aforementioned Sergeant Robinson. Realizing that the alarm would be raised as soon as Robinson was missed from his post, the raiders decided it would be more prudent to withdraw rather than face the possibility of detection.[64] Soon after, the imprisoned soldiers managed to raise the alarm, whereupon local police converged on the camp and established a series of roadblocks 'over a wide area'. Despite best efforts, the discovery of the raiders' car indicated that they had been successful in making their escape. This was later confirmed by the release of an IRPB statement claiming that all those involved 'have now been safely accounted for'.[65]

Although the raid was a failure, the fact that several IRA volunteers had infiltrated a British army barracks with a garrison of over 5,000 troops was to provide weakening republican morale with a welcome shot in the arm. In the ensuing investigation, the British authorities were able to identify only one of the raiders, an army corporal named Frank Skuse, who had also been serving as an active member of the IRA.[66] When it emerged that he had been convicted on separate charges in Dublin under the pseudonym 'Paul Murphy', the Chief Constable of the Dorset police force wrote to the Irish Department of External Affairs seeking his extradition. In the absence of such an agreement, however, the Irish government deemed it inappropriate to hand him over on the basis of a British warrant, as he was being charged with 'a crime of a political nature'.[67] At the same time, the audacity of the raid was seen by officials within the British Air Ministry as the first stage in an IRA plot to extend its campaign to the United Kingdom, and it was noted in an internal memo how:

> The present [IRA] leadership are now known to favour less dangerous operations in this country as there is no fear of internment, besides which their exploits in Britain carry a high propaganda value abroad, particularly so as some striking parties have entered the country and returned to Éire with apparent ease.[68]

Although it was recognized that Northern Ireland would remain the central focus of the IRA's campaign, the need for continued vigilance was stressed as it was felt that 'it is not improbable attacks will occur in the United Kingdom'.[69] Security was immediately increased across all British military establishments, as it was anticipated that the forthcoming anniversary of the 1916 Rising would be the spur to further raids of this kind.

The British government were not alone in being preoccupied with the subversive dangers posed by the IRA, as Scott McLeod, the US Ambassador in Dublin, was reported to be in receipt of constant updates on the activities of the Irish republican movement in the USA.[70] Of particular concern to the authorities were the ongoing efforts of several Irish republican organizations to solicit funds from sympathetic Irish-American benefactors. Thus, the State Department began to pay close attention to the activities of the IRA Dependants' Fund Committee of Pittsburgh, the Prisoners' Aid Society and the Irish Freedom Committee, and sought their registration under the Foreign Agents Registration Act.[71] Passed in 1938 as a means of controlling the large number of Nazi propaganda agents within the USA at the time, this piece of legislation required the registration of any persons or organizations actively engaged in lobbying American opinion. The fact that the State Department was monitoring these Irish republican organizations was, therefore, indicative of an increased desire to keep a tighter rein on their fundraising activities throughout the USA.

PRISON AGITATION

With nearly all of the Army Council and Sinn Féin Executive either interned or in jail, the IRA's campaign, hindered by the loss of the limited sanctuary previously enjoyed in the Irish Republic, continued to misfire throughout the spring and early summer of 1958.[72] Against this backdrop, republican prison agitation began to reassume its position centre stage. Belfast was the scene of particular controversy, as the discovery of a tunnel in Crumlin Road triggered a protracted riot between detainees and the prison authorities. Work on this tunnel had been ongoing for some time following the discovery by the detainees of an air-shaft which ran behind the wall of an occupied cell into the basement boiler room. A hole was knocked in the wall in order to provide access to this shaft, that later formed the basis of the tunnel. Despite the fact that the hole in the cell wall had been concealed with pictures and postcards, the disposal of waste clay was proving to be problematic.[73] On 11 March 1958, the tunnel was uncovered by prison officers, just before the detainees were due to return to their cells after 'evening association'. The two officers involved then proceeded to lock the cell door in order to prevent the escape of any detainees working in this tunnel, before going to get reinforcements. When the detainees discovered the locked door they attempted to gain entry into the cell using an array of 'improvised weapons'. After battering down the door, the general body of the prisoners then staged 'a short demonstration', during which they brandished their weapons and shouted threats at the prison officers present.[74]

The purpose of this confrontation was to deflect the attention of the prison authorities while two men who had been in the tunnel at the time were surreptitiously retrieved.[75] A brief stand-off ensued as the prison warders ordered a total lock-up and a systematic search for the improvised equipment that had been used in the excavation of the tunnel. Although routine searches of the internees' accommodation had previously been carried out on a regular basis, the prison authorities had not yet had occasion to carry out a personal search of the men themselves. In anticipation of this, the detainees armed themselves with 'formidable pieces of wood' in order to resist this search, which was to be carried out the following evening. Owing to the tense situation within the prison, it was felt that it would be best not to involve the prison warders in this search as they were in constant daily contact with the internees. Instead, a contingent of the RUC Special Reserve was called in order to 'ensure that the rigorous search that was necessary should be carried out'. A twenty-minute running battle was to result, however, as a number of internees violently resisted the search and 'had to be subdued'. According to the Ministry of Home Affairs, 'only such force was used as was necessary', with no hint of 'strong-arm methods' being employed on this occasion.[76]

This version of events was hotly contested by the detainees, claiming that they had made 'no organized attempt at resistance', and were the victims of an unprovoked 'orgy of brutality' at the hands of the RUC.[77] As Joe Cahill recalled, the prison authorities had no real intention of searching the detainees, as they proceeded to smash 'personal items, handicrafts, family pictures and religious pictures'. During the ensuing mêlée, it was reported that several of the men were subjected to harsh beatings whereby they sustained serious injuries.[78] These allegations were immediately denied by the Ministry of Home Affairs, which noted that only three men had asked to see the prison doctor on the morning after the search in order to treat injuries of a 'very minor character'. Seven men requested to see the doctor on 14 March and there were no visits on 15 March, which was a fact that was felt to speak for itself.[79] On the other hand, several of the detainees quickly began an unsuccessful civil action for damages against the prison authorities, which served to publicize their version of events.[80] Stung by allegations of ill-treatment, the Ministry of Home Affairs jumped upon this action as a clear indication that the civil rights of the detainees had been preserved, as they had not been deprived of 'the legal remedies to which as citizens they may be entitled'.[81]

As punishment for the disturbances, all privileges enjoyed by the detainees were withdrawn from 13 March, together with a ban on visits and on the receipt of letters and parcels. These restrictions immediately served to arouse republican indignation, and three days after the riots a small crowd, composed mostly of women, assembled outside Crumlin Road Prison demanding to see their husbands and relatives. Gaining access to the complex after they stormed the outer gate, the protesters vociferously continued with their demands to see the detainees. Following a lengthy operation by prison staff to forcibly eject the intruders, the remaining protesters sang verses of 'A Soldier's Song', 'Kevin Barry' and 'The Belfast Brigade' as they symbolically hoisted a tricolour on the railings of Belfast Courthouse, before dispersing peaceably.[82] Following this emotive demonstration, tensions within the prison gradually began to diffuse and on 29 March all restrictions concerning the receipt of visits and letters were lifted.[83] With a complete return to normality, the regime previously enjoyed by the internees was gradually reintroduced. It was not until January 1960, however, that the northern authorities felt sufficiently secure in their position to begin ordering the release of detainees. By Christmas of that year, all but eleven remained in custody, as two of whom, drunk on contraband alcohol, made a derisory escape attempt by trying to scale the outer wall of the prison during a sleet storm. Notwithstanding this minor incident, these detainees were released shortly thereafter, before the northern government formally dispensed with the use of its powers of detention, in March 1961.[84]

In Dublin, the Irish government was to become embroiled in its own confrontations with convicted republican prisoners in Mountjoy, despite the institution of a relatively permissive regime for those convicted of 'political offences'. On 8 May 1958, eighteen prisoners announced their intention of going on hunger strike in protest over the withdrawal of privileges following a failed attempt at escape by scaling the outer wall of the prison. On this occasion, a number of warders immediately rushed to the scene, where they became involved in 'a fierce struggle' with the prisoners before eventually forcing them back into their cells. While many of the prisoners were reported to be 'cut and bleeding', it also emerged that eight of the warders had to receive medical attention as a result of injuries sustained during this disturbance.[85] As a disciplinary measure, those involved were locked into empty cells without any beds or mattresses and all meals were handed in without any spoons, knives or forks. In protest, the prisoners announced their intention of going on hunger strike until this new punitive regime was lifted.[86] Wary of courting negative publicity, the government immediately announced that the new regime within the prison was a temporary disciplinary measure that would be revoked after two weeks.[87] Despite these assurances and apparently without the sanction of the IRA leadership, the prisoners elected to continue with their protest until they received a guarantee that they would not be interned upon completion of their sentences.[88] The situation was diffused, on 23 May, only when the IRPB released a statement ordering the men to cease their hunger strike as it was not necessary to 'permanently injure themselves' in order 'to establish their right to unconditional release'.[89]

STAGNATION

The continuing long-term decline in the number of serious incidents along the border was certainly a key motivating factor in the government's swift move to reinstate privileges to republicans held in Mountjoy. Under constant and increasing pressure from the authorities on both sides of the border, the IRA's capacity to prosecute anything more than even a campaign of low-level sabotage was now beginning to come into question. Apart from a few high-profile incidents, the campaign did not now extend much beyond nuisance level. Faced with a largely indifferent population in the Irish Republic, the government was also mindful of a certain amount of empathy for what the IRA was trying to achieve. Partition remained a live issue in Irish politics and, although the use of force was widely regarded as foolhardy and misguided, the fact that the IRA was trying to be proactive in this regard was something to be applauded. According to Tom Mitchell, while the people may not have approved of the campaign, they would have discussed partition in a rational manner.[90] In recognising this, the government still felt it necessary to tread warily in respect of their dealings with the republican movement, but was particularly shocked to uncover evidence of illicit contact between certain members of the defence forces and the IRA.[91]

In the summer of 1958 the activities of Lieutenant Patrick Dolan, who was stationed in Collins barracks, Dublin, gave particular cause for alarm when it emerged that he had been involved in giving ammunition for a Vickers machine gun to senior members of the IRA. Kept under surveillance for several weeks, he was eventually arrested together with his IRA contact, Charlie Murphy, at a clandestine meeting on 31 May 1958.[92] Formally charged with 'scandalous conduct unbecoming an officer' for stealing the ammunition and improperly giving it to Murphy, he was returned for court martial on 26 June. When convicted and sentenced to two years' imprisonment, Dolan was unapologetic, claiming that he had been victimized by the government because of his 'republican sympathies'. He also denigrated the army's role in helping to maintain the border and claimed that 'I, in common with other members of the Defence Forces today resent the attempts of politicians to turn this force into John Bull's other army.'[93] While the extent of these allegations remains difficult to substantiate, the fact that there were no further incidents of this kind gives rise to the belief that these assertions were either exaggerated or wholly fabricated.

As this episode was swiftly brought to an end, the republican movement was to experience further setbacks, with a series of three fatalities following in quick succession. The first of these occurred on 2 July 1958, when a group of Saor Uladh volunteers were surprised by an RUC patrol when they crossed the border near Newtownbutler, County Fermanagh. An exchange of gunfire ensued in which one of the raiders, twenty-year-old Aloysius Hand, was killed, while an unnamed colleague was reported to have sustained serious gunshot wounds.[94] In commenting on Hand's death, Topping said that he did not regard it 'as case for satisfaction' and expressed the hope that 'it might prove to be a turning point'. In marked contrast to the deaths of South and O'Hanlon, Hand's funeral in Clones, County Monaghan, where the coffin was carried by local members of Saor Uladh, was a relatively low-key affair. Liam Kelly was expected to attend but was arrested at his home and detained for questioning by the Gardaí before being released without charge the following day.[95] In many ways, the shooting of Hand was to signal the end of Saor Uladh as a force in militant Irish republicanism. Some months later, Kelly departed for the USA for a number of unspecified reasons, before formally winding up the organization in 1960.[96] Several days after Hand's death, Patrick McManus, a member of the mainstream IRA, was killed in an accidental explosion in Derryrelt, County Cavan. Again the funeral failed to invite significant public attention, despite him being eulogized as a 'brave man and a born guerrilla leader'.[97]

Although neither of these incidents impinged significantly on the public consciousness, it was to be the death of James Crossan, in

August 1958, amid allegations that he had been shot by the RUC on the Irish side of the border, that threatened to stir up significant political controversy. In fact, Crossan, who was an organizer for the local Sinn Féin party, was not even a member of the IRA. On the night in question, he was seen drinking in Swanlinbar, County Cavan, in the eclectic company of a local IRA volunteer named McHugh, a B-Special sergeant and the secretary of the local Fianna Fáil *cumann*. As the night drew to a close, Crossan proceeded to the border in order to see off some of his associates who resided in Northern Ireland.[98] As they approached the customs hut at Mullan, County Fermanagh, the RUC reported that the police on duty challenged Crossan and McHugh, who began to flee back towards the border. Although McHugh was quickly apprehended, Crossan was chased into a field, where he ignored repeated requests to halt, before a member of the patrol opened fire. He was killed instantly.

During the ensuing inquest, the local RUC head constable, W.J. Liggett, described how he discovered Crossan's body lying face down in a field, 'about one hundred yards from the border' with the Irish Republic.[99] The republican movement, however, was incensed at what it saw as the callous shooting of an unarmed man. In a statement released by the IRPB it was claimed that Crossan had, in fact, been pursued across the border, where he had been shot – an assertion repeated in the graveside oration given during his funeral.[100] Concerned at these allegations, the Department of Justice dispatched the local Garda superintendent to the scene to make enquiries as to the circumstances of the shooting. The spot in which Crossan's body was found was pointed out and careful measurements in relation to its proximity to the border were taken. It was noted that, while there was no blood at the scene, there was blood on the grass at a point that was 'twenty-nine yards on the County Fermanagh side of the border'. It was later established that this blood was from a heifer that had been slaughtered by a local farmer the day before the shooting, thereby giving the Gardaí no basis to believe that Crossan had been shot within their jurisdiction.[101]

These politically damaging allegations refused to fade away and in October the Clann na Poblachta deputy, John Tully, sought to raise the matter in the Dáil.[102] In preparing the government's reply, officials at the Department of Justice informed the Taoiseach's office that the 'Gardaí have no doubt that Crossan was shot by the RUC at the spot in County Fermanagh indicated by them'.[103] Heated scenes were to ensue in the Dáil chamber, however, when Tully pressed the government to establish the precise circumstances in which Crossan was shot. In response, de Valera's parliamentary secretary, Donnchadh Ó Briain, read out a statement in which it was pointed out that the government would not be in a position to conduct a full investigation into the circumstances surrounding Crossan's death without the cooperation of the RUC. Hoping that the controversy would dissipate, the government was content to let sleeping dogs lie and did not press the issue with London. Crossan's case, despite the best efforts of republicans, quickly fell into relative obscurity.

Throughout the summer of 1958 the IRA leadership began to make use of a house in Serpentine Avenue, in Ballsbridge, Dublin, as a safe haven in which to formulate a substantive plan for a proposed autumn/winter offensive.[104] As a prelude to this, it was decided that the campaign would continue in the meantime at a sufficient level to warrant the continuation of an expensive security operation on both sides of the border. Numerous bridges were damaged by explosives, telephone lines were cut in many areas and attempts continued to ambush British army patrols. In September 1958, a series of incidents gave both Irish governments cause for alarm, as it appeared that the IRA was in a position to once again intensify its campaign. On 31 August, a group of gunmen with automatic weapons staged a series of coordinated attacks on two RUC stations in Bellaghy and Maghera, County Derry.[105] This was followed by a similar attack on 2 September, the discovery of an unexploded bomb outside Gough barracks on 5 September and the demolition of an Orange hall at Kinawley, County Fermanagh.[106] Speaking in Lisburn, Topping harangued the Irish government and declared that 'there is little hope of friendly co-operation between north and south while murderous gunmen are permitted to come across the border.' Although acknowledging that de Valera had taken some action, he called in particular for the suppression of *The United Irishman* and the internment of Liam Kelly.[107]

In late September, an opportunity to demonstrate its earnestness in dealing with the campaign, without having recourse to further repressive measures, finally presented itself to the Irish government when the Special Branch happened upon the IRA Army Council safe house in Serpentine Avenue. After keeping the house under surveillance for a number of days, the Gardaí moved to interrupt a meeting of the Army Council, resulting in the arrest of several key figures, including the IRA C/S, Seán Cronin.[108] Together with the detention of Michael McCarthy and the internment of Magan, MacCurtain and Grogan, this proved to be a crippling blow to the IRA, which was again deprived of a substantial proportion of its leadership cadre. To counter this, Ruairí Ó Brádaigh, recently escaped from the Curragh, was elected as the new C/S at an IRA meeting in October 1958, on the basis that he was the only remaining member of the 1956 Army Council who was still at large.[109] Coupled with the growing controversy involving the Curragh escapees, the chances of formulating a coherent strategy for the coming months had been effectively scotched by the arrests in Serpentine Avenue.

In December 1958 the Curragh controversy came to a head when fourteen of the escapees presented themselves for active duty. As members of the Charlie Murphy faction within the camp, the reinstatement of these individuals quickly became a bone of contention among those who felt that their actions had significantly undermined the official leadership of MacCurtain and Magan. On the other hand, the escapees felt that it was vital for their actions to be accepted as proper before guaranteeing their participation in any future IRA operations. Between December 1958 and June 1959 the issue came to dominate the IRA agenda as an effective formula for their reinstatement was sought. Eventually, the Army Council agreed to readmit these individuals if they agreed to sign a form entailing a limited recognition of wrongdoing on their part.[110] Moreover, with the closure of the Curragh in March 1958, both Magan and MacCurtain were infuriated by the presence of Murphy at a joint meeting held to amalgamate the former camp leadership with the incumbent Army Council. When several of Murphy's supporters proposed a resolution exonerating his faction of all misconduct, a protracted and heated argument was to follow, as MacCurtain refused to endorse this position. In the end the meeting was wound up without agreement and it was decided to hold a General Army Convention in order to decide the matter.[111]

Although this convention, which was held in May 1959, formalized the reinstated leadership of Magan and MacCurtain, Murphy continued to press his resolution. After several hours of heated discussion, interspersed with pleas to the middle ground by Seán Cronin, a majority of delegates voted in favour of a motion to shelve the issue. Magan and MacCurtain could not accept this, and refused to allow the convention to ratify their positions on the IRA Army Executive until a motion was passed formally reprimanding Murphy. The convention was steadfast in its refusal even to consider such a proposal and pressed ahead with the election of Magan and MacCurtain, in the face of their continued protestations, to a new twelve-member executive. Both individuals immediately responded by resigning from this body, thereby triggering the election of another executive with responsibility for appointing a new Army Council. Seán Cronin was subsequently selected to fill the vacated post of C/S, while Ó Brádaigh and Cathal Goulding were appointed as A/G and QMG respectively.[112] Although the Curragh dispute had finally been resolved, the issue had irreparably damaged the IRA. There had been a widespread loss of centralized control during this infighting, with an injurious effect on the organization's limited military infrastructure. Consequently, apart from an aborted machine-gun attack on Roslea RUC barracks in November 1958 and the ambush of an RUC patrol at Crockada Bridge in August 1959, the republican movement continued to maintain a relatively low profile throughout this period.[113]

In June 1959 Seán Lemass succeeded de Valera as Taoiseach, following the latter's election as President, bringing with him a fresh approach to the partition question by abandoning 'the overt irredentism of previous governments'. On the whole, Lemass preferred to say nothing about Northern Ireland and his simplistic view was that the best way to end partition was to raise living standards in the south so markedly that northern Protestants would be eager to reunite the country.[114] During his tenure, Lemass was to preside over the dismantling of the self-imposed tariff walls that had been the mainstay of Fianna Fáil's economic policy since its foundation. This was to signal an orderly retreat from the orthodoxy of economic protectionism, which was to be offset by a new dynamic drive to draw foreign firms into the Irish Republic and a commitment to join the European Common Market. Remarkably, a number of overtures to the Northern Irish government, particularly on social and economic issues, were also made. Although initially unsuccessful, these advances, coupled with Lemass's historic meeting with the Northern Irish Premier, Terence O'Neill, in 1965, was to usher in a brief but compelling optimism about the future of north–south relations.[115]

According to Henry Patterson, the origins of these policies predated Lemass's premiership, having been shaped by the abject failure of the anti-partition campaign of the early 1950s and the ongoing economic and demographic crisis faced by the Irish state.[116] The timely departure of de Valera simply allowed for the maturation of this new approach under the stewardship of Lemass, who upon his accession as Taoiseach quickly asserted his government's commitment 'to prevent the maintenance of illegal armed forces for any purposes'. For the unionist administration, however, this statement was simply the reiteration of a 'familiar formula of words, with no hint of any concrete measures against terrorists'. Coming after a period of relative quiet, the incident at Crockada prompted an exasperated Brookeborough to make renewed representations to London on the issue of ongoing cross-border raids. The Irish government was particularly alarmed when several unionist politicians called upon the British government to postpone upcoming discussions on a new Anglo-Irish trade agreement in order to induce Dublin to take a tougher stand against the IRA.[117] To the British government, this seemed like an overreaction, as they felt that the suspension of these talks could not be justified on the basis of a single incident, followed as it was by 'a vigorous denunciation of terrorism by Mr. Lemass'. In considering the matter, both the Home Office and the Commonwealth Relations Office agreed that 'some action should be taken' and instructed Gurth Kimber 'to make vigorous representations to the Éire government'.[118] Calling on Lemass on 5 September, Kimber was suitably mollified when informed that, while the Gardaí were taking 'all possible steps', the continuation of such incidents was to be expected as 'illegal organizations had to stage some to maintain public interest'.[119] A week later, the Home Secretary dispatched a letter to Brookeborough notifying him of his government's decision not to 'seek to influence the Republican government by postponing the trade talks'.[20] In his reply, Brookeborough stated that he was glad to hear that 'strong representations have been made to Dublin', but was disappointed to learn that the suspension of the trade talks 'could not be used as a lever' to impress on the Irish government the need for positive action.[121] Two days later, the anxieties of Lemass were assuaged when Lord Brocket formally notified the Irish Ambassador that his government had no plans to institute proposals respecting economic sanctions 'for the purpose of achieving objectives of a non-economic character'.[122]

Undaunted, the UUP continued to press this agenda, and in November a delegation led by Lt Col. Grosvenor called on David Campbell, of the Commonwealth Relations Office, in order to seek assurances that 'there would be no more concessions in the trade field' until Lemass 'put his house in order'. Campbell rejected these overtures as he explained that the British government could not countenance such a policy given the difficult economic position of the Irish Republic.[123] Of course Campbell's assertions were quickly overtaken by events, when an IRA ambush on an RUC land rover in County Antrim prompted the Home Secretary, Richard Butler, to announce his intention of travelling to Belfast to discuss the situation with Brookeborough.[124] Controversy immediately ensued, however, when it appeared that Butler, during a press conference in Belfast, refused to rule out the use of trade sanctions.[125] Faced with rampant media speculation, he was forced to clarify his stance on the matter and claimed that he did not use the word 'sanction' at all, 'except in reply to a question that had been put to him by one of the interviewers'.[126] In the wake of this diplomatic gaffe the issue was not mentioned again and in February 1960 Lemass confirmed that a series of upcoming discussions with the British government would be confined 'purely to matters of trade'.[127]

SPECIAL CRIMINAL COURT

By early 1960, it seemed that the continuation of the IRA's campaign had become a politically worthless exercise as it had been effectively reduced to a series of low-level attacks aimed at the RUC.[128] In such circumstances it was obvious that the IRA could not succeed in its stated aims and on several occasions the movement was forced to deflect criticism that it was simply glorifying a tradition of violence. Speaking at the Sinn Féin Ard Fheis in November 1958, Patrick McLogan maintained that IRA volunteers were not facing 'death or imprisonment and hardships just to maintain a tradition of militarism or self-sacrifice. The struggle today is striving to achieve the task of full freedom.'[129] In light of the ineffectual nature of the IRA, however, the use of such rhetoric simply added to the widespread perception that the campaign had become an irrelevant self-indulgence, a fact reflected by Sinn Féin's desultory performance in the 1959 British general election.[130] As the party had been banned, it was unable to participate legally and was reduced to nominating a number of 'shadow candidates' in an elaborate protest scheme, where people were asked to spoil their vote by writing in the name of the Sinn Féin candidate on the ballot paper.[131]

The results were derisory, as the election was to witness a collapse of the Sinn Féin vote of 1955. In West Tyrone, out of 153 spoiled votes, only three were for the designated republican candidate, J. Doherty. There was slightly more success in the traditional nationalist strongholds of Mid-Ulster and Derry, where Tom Mitchell won 30 per cent of the total vote, while his colleague, Manus Canning, received 27 per cent. In any event, this was still a significant drop as Mitchell's poll was down by over 15,000.[132] Overall, the Sinn Féin vote fell from 152,000 to 64,000, with a unionist candidate elected in every constituency. The Nationalist Party, which did not put up any candidates, blamed Sinn Féin's 'disastrous intervention' for the unionist victory.[133] In Belfast, Sinn Féin's decreased vote was taken as further evidence of 'a rejection of violence by the minority'. This precipitous decline in Sinn Féin's electoral performance was to become even more apparent in the 1961 general election in the Irish Republic: the party lost all four of its seats when it garnered just 3 per cent of the vote.[134]

Official figures compiled by the British authorities provide a striking confirmation of the commensurate decline in the fortunes of the IRA. From the start of the campaign in December 1956 to December 1959, there had been a total of 518 incidents, 'of which half were major incidents and the rest minor'. While 25 of these took place in December 1956, 341 in 1957 and 126 in 1958, there were only 26 violent incidents recorded throughout the entirety of 1959.[135] In 1960, the number of incidents remained static, all of them classed as low-level sabotage operations.[136] In spite of this, the authorities still remained concerned at the possibility of an upsurge in republican activity, as the relative absence of violence was regarded as a temporary lull during which the IRA was attempting to regroup. Moreover, given the apparent decline in the ongoing security threat, it was pessimistically noted that 'there is no chance of persuading Mr. Lemass into more drastic action', such as the further strengthening of Garda measures along the border. In fact, Lemass was extremely loath to take such steps, as he felt that they would not be enough 'in themselves to bring terrorism wholly to an end'. From London's perspective, the only action that might achieve these objectives would be the reimposition of internment within the Irish Republic – a prospect that was discounted owing to Ireland's ongoing difficulties with the Lawless case in Europe.[137]

In January 1961 the assassination of RUC Constable Andersen, just a few yards from the border near Roslea, County Fermanagh, seemed to bear out the assertions of the British government.[138] What set this death apart from the others was the fact that Andersen was deliberately targeted because he was believed to be collecting intelligence in the locality. The premeditated nature of this attack, which appeared in retrospect to be a harbinger of later tactics employed by the IRA, shocked contemporary public opinion and was condemned by Lemass as 'a brutal murder'.[139] This prompted the immediate release of a statement by the IRPB, in which it was asserted that the widely held description of Constable Andersen as 'a village constable' was misleading. It alleged that Andersen was heavily involved in 'espionage activities in the twenty-six counties' and detailed how he had frequently threatened 'a twenty-six county resident who had business interests in County Fermanagh'.[140] While these contentions were roundly disparaged, the political fallout from this killing was outlined in an insightful editorial in the *Irish Times*, when it was observed how

> the assassination of Constable Andersen has given the government the most serious setback ... the government now will be faced inevitably with the choice of an even more rigorous use of its emergency measures or the danger that new incidents may recur.[141]

These observations were proved correct as the IRA hoped to use this incident as a springboard from which to reinvigorate its campaign. This perception was given further currency when the March edition of *The United Irishman* carried a banner headline proudly proclaiming a renewal of 'guerrilla attacks' in the north, following an assault on Glassdrummond Bridge in south Derry.[142] In April, two more bridges in west Fermanagh were targeted and the main railway line between Dublin and Belfast was cut.[143] In the Dáil, Oscar Traynor used the occasion of the debate on the annual estimates for the Department of Justice to reassure deputies that the government was 'taking determined measures' to bring the IRA's 'futile campaign of violence to an end'.[144] An extensive security operation was subsequently mounted along the border, precipitating a sharp decline in the number of violent incidents as this flurry of republican activity abruptly came to a halt.[145] At the same time, perturbed by the IRA's perceived dogged determination to continue with its struggle, the government began to consider recourse to more serious legislative provisions aimed at suppressing the campaign once and for all.

Although the decision in the Lawless case seriously constrained the government if it wished to resort to the use of internment, the revival of the Special Criminal Court was an option that had yet to be fully explored. Certainly there was a degree of trepidation about considering this course of action, as it was thought necessary to issue a proclamation declaring that the ordinary courts were unable to maintain law and order. The Irish government had already been suitably embarrassed by the proceedings in the Lawless case and did not wish to draw undue attention to the fact that provision for the use of special non-jury courts remained on the statute books. In September 1961, officials at the Department of Defence presented the cabinet with an elegant solution to this problem. In a confidential memorandum it was observed that the Special Criminal Court, which had been established in August 1939, had not been formally abolished in 1946 owing to the government's failure to issue the requisite proclamation under section thirty-five of the OASA.[146] The retirement of Colonel Bennett in 1949 and Colonel Devlin in 1953 did not alter this position, despite the fact that membership of the court was now below the required statutory minimum. While the Defence officials did not wish to make any official recommendations at this stage, they did urge the cabinet to give some consideration to the desirability or otherwise of recalling part five of the OASA. If it was felt that this was not a prudent course of action, the government was advised to bring the membership of the Special Criminal Court 'back up to the statutory minimum', with the proviso that 'no publicity need be given to changes in ... personnel'.[147]

On 12 November 1961, an IRA ambush outside Jonesborough, County Armagh, precipitated the need to reach a decision in this regard, as it had resulted in the death of another RUC constable, William Hunter. On this occasion, Hunter and his colleagues had been surprised while on patrol and were 'raked with machine-gun fire' from behind the wall of a local Protestant churchyard.[148] This incident was immediately and roundly condemned on both sides of the border. Lemass issued a particularly stinging rebuke to the IRA. In his opinion, these 'murderous activities', which were directed by 'some sinister influence', had been emphatically repudiated by the Irish people and could not but serve to harm the national interest.[149] For its part, the British government instructed the Commonwealth Secretary to make further representations to the Irish government 'about the activities of the border raiders'.[150] Such measures were to be premature, however, as the government, with little public forewarning, simply declared a reconstituted Special Criminal Court to be in operation, with the appointment of three new members: Col. James H. Byrne, Lieut.-Col. Joseph Adams and Lieut.-Col. William Rea.[151] Lemass was again forthright in defence of the government's position:

> The Government regard the step of bringing persons for trial by a special Criminal Court instead of by the ordinary courts as justified only in grave circumstances. It is their judgment however that these circumstances now exist. The bringing of offenders of

this character for trial before the District Court does not permit of sentences being imposed appropriate to the gravity of the offences and may have occasioned some misunderstanding amongst those concerned with them as to the seriousness with which the government view the position and their determination to deal with it. Because the persons concerned have constantly displayed their contempt for the fundamental principles of democracy, it would be undesirable to rely on trial by jury which might expose jurymen and witnesses to the danger of intimidation.[152]

Remarkably, domestic criticism of the government's policy was muted as the court quickly proved itself to be an invaluable tool in the Irish state's ongoing struggle with subversives. In the first month of sittings alone, twenty-five republicans had been sentenced to a combined total of forty-three years' imprisonment, as the appeal in the Special Criminal Court lay in its discretionary sentencing policy.[153] As those appearing before the court were engaged in violent activities outside its jurisdiction, in Northern Ireland, the type of charges that could be brought to bear were limited. More often than not, they were technically guilty of only minor infractions of the law, which carried nominal custodial sentences if tried before the District Court. The Special Criminal Court was not constrained in the length of sentence it could impose upon conviction for a scheduled offence under the OASA. As a result, IRA members appearing on the relatively minor charge of failing to account for their movements were now receiving lengthy prison sentences. The case of Michael McEldowney is a prime example: he had previously served six months on arms charges in 1959 but received an eight-year prison sentence when convicted on similar charges by the Special Criminal Court in 1961.[154]

According to Ruairí Ó Brádaigh, while the introduction of such 'repression' was not enough in itself to stop the IRA, it certainly contributed to the organizational difficulties experienced at the time.[155] Given the ongoing decline in public support for the campaign, the republican movement was now faced with an unsustainable loss in manpower. These problems were accentuated in December 1961, when Clan na nGael sent word from the USA that it was no longer in a position to fund the IRA's offensive. Within this context, Seán Garland felt that the introduction of a severe sentencing policy in the Irish Republic was the last critical factor in persuading the IRA to abandon its campaign.[156] As the incumbent C/S, Ó Brádaigh certainly urged this course of action, feeling that there was no point in continuing if the IRA was limited to simply blowing up bridges and burning down customs huts. On 18 January 1962, the Army Council met to consider its position before adjourning without a decision. A second meeting in February was more fruitful, and after a 'careful examination of the situation' it was unanimously agreed to end the campaign.[157] A special directive was then issued to all units ordering them to dump arms, and on 26 February, in a statement drafted by Ó Brádaigh, the IRA formally announced the end of its offensive.[158]

Taking this decision 'in view of the general situation', the statement identified 'the attitude of the general public', whose minds had been deliberately 'distracted' from the 'supreme issue facing the Irish people', as the foremost factor in motivating the IRA's decision. While this has since been construed by several authors as an implied criticism of northern nationalists for their perceived failure to support the campaign, Ó Brádaigh has recently claimed that these comments have been misinterpreted.[159] In fact, the 'distracted public' was an oblique reference to Ireland's recent application to join the European Common Market and 'the belief of some that it would create a shortcut to the ending of British rule in Ireland'.[160] In this vein the statement continued:

> Other and lesser issues have been urged successfully upon them and the sacrifices which could win freedom in the political, cultural, social and economic spheres are now stated to be necessary to bolster up the partition system forced on the Irish people by Britain forty years ago.
>
> This calculated emphasis on secondary issues by those whose political future is bound up in the status quo and who control all the mass media of propaganda, is now leading towards the possible commitment of the twenty-six counties in future wars.
>
> The resistance movement stands firmly against any such course of action while Ireland is unfree and will use all its resources towards restoring in full to the Irish people their sense of national values.[161]

Concluding by renewing the IRA's pledge of 'eternal hostility to the British Forces of occupation', it also called on the Irish public to show greater support in its preparations for 'the final and victorious phase of the struggle for the full freedom of Ireland'. Beneath the rhetoric of this rallying call, however, far from drawing up the battle lines for the next confrontation, the collapse of the border campaign had caused the IRA to slip into a mood of deep despondency.[162]

8

Conclusion

In many ways the termination of the border campaign in February 1962, despite the pugnacious nature of the rhetoric employed, was to represent a significant setback for the Irish republican movement. In welcoming the news of the cessation, the Fianna Fáil Minister for Justice, Charles Haughey, condemned this 'foolish resort to violence' and warned that the Irish government would no longer be prepared to tolerate the existence of 'unofficial organizations'.[1] For its part, the *Irish Times* was particularly critical of the IRA, as it felt that its decision to abandon 'terrorist attacks' stemmed not from an altruistic motive, but reflected 'the success of the strong measures taken by the government to suppress the physical force movement'.[2] Reaction in Northern Ireland was more muted, as the release of the statement by the IRPB gave rise to much speculation that disaffected volunteers would form 'militant splinter groups' to carry on the struggle. Such fears were given added currency when Brian Faulkner, the Minister of Home Affairs, observed that Tom Mitchell had organized a meeting in Dublin to sound out the extent of the support he could expect in this regard. He was eventually dissuaded in this course of action by Seán MacBride, who advised that the Irish government would probably clamp down on such a group 'as severely as had latterly been the case with the IRA'.[3]

Yet, the apprehensions of the Northern Ireland authorities remained to be dispelled. In 1963, the Secretary of the Irish Department of Justice, Peter Berry, met with William Craig, the Minister for Home Affairs, to discount rumours of an upsurge in IRA training activities along the border.[4] The Irish government was more inclined to take the IRA's statement at face value, and within weeks of its circulation recalled a number of Garda 'wireless cars' from border patrol duty and began the process of rescinding some of its more provocative counter-insurgency measures.[5] On 6 March 1962, without much discussion at cabinet level, the government finally issued a proclamation under section three of the Offences Against the State (Amendment) Act, formally divesting itself of the power of internment.[6] Such a move was hardly unexpected, particularly in light of the difficulties experienced in the Lawless case and the fact that the Curragh internment camp had already been closed for some time. By contrast, the propriety in maintaining the operation of the Special Criminal Court continued to be a matter for some debate within the cabinet, especially as the Minister for Justice felt that 'the ordinary courts are now adequate' to perform their allotted functions.[7]

In receiving these recommendations, Lemass authorized the circulation of a memorandum proposing the dissolution of the Special Criminal Court and invited submissions on this issue from all 'interested' departments.[8] Officials in the Department of External Affairs did offer a dissenting voice, feeling that it might be prudent to defer this decision 'having regard to possible reaction in Belfast'.[9] Such objections were not enough to dissuade the cabinet, however, and on 2 October 1962 the government issued a proclamation deactivating part five of the OASA and formally dissolved the Special Criminal Court.[10] Universally lauded in the domestic press as a return to normality, the *Irish Times* expressed the hope that 'the drastic and undemocratic provisions of the Offences Against the State Acts can [now] be happily forgotten'.[11] In some respects, this was not a wholly inaccurate observation to make, as this proved to be the final occasion on which internment was employed within the jurisdiction of the Republic of Ireland. It was not re-introduced, despite the significant threat posed to the stability of the Irish state by the outbreak of the civil conflict in Northern Ireland in 1969. The effectiveness of the Special Criminal Court as a means of suppressing the IRA in 1961 ensured that it now became the central plank on which the government's revised counter-insurgency policy rested. Re-established in May 1972, this judicature remains operative to the present day and is still used to prosecute ongoing instances of politically motivated crime.[12]

REPUBLICAN INTROSPECTION

Within the republican movement, the decision to terminate the border campaign was greeted with a general air of despondency, despite the exhortations of Tomás Mac Giolla to view it as an opportunity to 'gird ourselves to move forward' to the 'next phase in the struggle for freedom'.[13] Enlivened by the Curragh disputes, the atmosphere within the IRA throughout the summer of 1962 became ever more recriminatory, especially when Magan and MacCurtain renewed their efforts to have their conduct in the internment camp vindicated. With Magan's resignation from the organization and the appointment of Cathal Goulding as the IRA's new C/S, the issue became a dead letter, as the republican movement embarked on a protracted period of introspection and self-examination.[14] Of particular concern to many republican ideologues was the marked indifference shown by much of the general public to the IRA's campaign. For a movement which claimed that its mandate for the use of violence came from the Irish people, this was an unwelcome and disquieting development.[15] Under the direction of Goulding, the IRA instituted an extensive reappraisal of the republican position to discover why the movement had been unable to succeed, in spite of the fact that the people engaged in its revolutionary activities were willing to make any sacrifice for it.

The conclusion reached by this internal debate was that the people had no real knowledge of the objectives of the IRA, largely because the movement did not really have any. In Goulding's own words:

> The fight for freedom had become an end in itself to us. Instead of a means it became an end. We hadn't planned to achieve the freedom of Ireland. We simply planned *to fight* [my emphasis] for the freedom of Ireland. We could never hope to succeed because we never planned to succeed.[16]

In these circumstances, the most fundamental challenge faced by the IRA was to devise a policy that could win popular support by promising social and political emancipation to the ordinary citizens of Ireland. Needless to say, this immediately rekindled many of the old tensions between those who advocated a traditional policy of physical force nationalism and those who argued that partition could only be ended through a revolution that also embraced radical economic and social change.[17] The proponents of a decisive widening of the IRA's agenda argued that what was needed was a war of national liberation that could only be won by a movement which had mobilized the people for revolutionary change. In effect, this led to a recrudescence of a vaguely Marxist ideology, similar to the one originally advocated by the likes of Peadar O'Donnell in the 1930s, which had as it goal the aim of a socialist republic.[18]

By 1962 the portents for such a shift were good, as Goulding, together with his valuable socialist allies Anthony Coughlan and Roy Johnston, declared himself amenable to considering the possibility of endowing the republican movement with a full-blown radical programme. Johnston, in particular, felt that the timing was right for such a venture, as the IRA now seemed to him to be more receptive to new ideas and influences than at any time since the split with O'Donnell's Republican Congress organization in 1934. In their new approach both Coughlan and Johnston sought to emphasize the intellectual bankruptcy of the modern republican movement and highlighted the need for the formulation of political theory. In their view, republicanism had proven itself incapable of developing the substantial body of theoretical writing associated with their forebears and applying it to contemporary circumstances. For example, where was the searing critique of the reasons for the failure of the Irish cultural and language movement and the ruthless analysis of the failure of the Irish republican movement to significantly influence government policy in the south? There was neither, and as a result the IRA had little to no meaningful engagement with some of the most crucial questions of contemporary politics – and no avenues through which it could mobilize its target constituency.[19]

To address these issues, Johnston, with the blessing of Goulding, in 1963 formed a republican socialist study group called the Wolfe Tone Society. Significantly, Peadar O'Donnell and several other Saor Éire veterans were invited to address this organization and to lead the discussions on how contemporary republicanism might incorporate a radical political perspective.[20] The resonances with the 1930s did not end there, as O'Donnell was quick to make the link between the themes that had divided Republican Congress in 1934 and contemporary issues now facing republicans. In the debate that had split Republican Congress, O'Donnell claimed that the adoption of the slogan the 'Worker's Republic' would have allowed de Valera to hegemonize workers and small farmers by powerfully identifying Fianna Fáil with the concept of the 'Republic'. In O'Donnell's mind, the primary aim of congress was not to demonstrate to the masses that Fianna Fáil were not socialist, but rather that they were not real republicans. The difficulty in doing this, however, arose when the start of the Economic War in 1933 and the embrace of protectionism allowed de Valera to claim continuity with traditional republican objectives. According to O'Donnell, this was still to be the main concern for the republican movement, as contemporary conditions in 1963 were now more favourable to the successful achievement of this goal.[21]

Lemass, in particular, had begun to change the direction of Irish economic policy by breaking with the protectionist measures of the

1930s. The gradual phasing out of these, the vigorous attempt to attract foreign capital and the preparation for Ireland's membership of the European Common Market simply signalled the final capitulation of Fianna Fáil. Whereas de Valera had taken some steps to weaken the link with Britain, Lemass had given up this effort entirely. Consequently, the way was now paved for the republican movement, through the adoption of a wider radical agenda, to become the trailblazer for a new united front that would bring an end to Ireland's economic subservience to Britain and its 'neo-imperialist' policies. Encouraged by this interpretation of contemporary political circumstances, a new nine-point statement was circulated within the IRA calling for economic and social agitation, the creation of a national liberation front composed of republicans, trade unions and small farmer organizations and, most controversial of all, the end of parliamentary abstention. The IRA rank and file enthusiastically endorsed all except the last point: it seemed that the movement was now on the cusp of embracing this new socialist direction.[22] A new handbook was also issued, making it clear that the IRA leadership wanted republicans generally to become more socially active, through infiltrating civil rights organizations and trade unions, so that the movement could be accepted 'in leading positions in the mass organizations of the people'.[23]

The net effect of this was to draw much of the republican constituency into the burgeoning campaign for civil rights in Northern Ireland. Although such involvement was not antithetical to the movement's traditional concerns, in the eyes of some individuals it did tend to blur the issues at hand, leading to an increase in the simmering tensions between the traditional militarists and the radicals. For some, including Joe Cahill, this was simply the first step in a creeping parliamentarianism that would end with Sinn Féin in Leinster House. He resigned from the republican movement in 1963 in protest at what he saw as an insidious attempt to transform the IRA 'from a revolutionary guerrilla organization into a far-left political party'.[24] He was not alone in his views, as Ruairí Ó Brádaigh felt that the ending of abstentionism and the embrace of constitutional politics would lead to a compromise of republican principles. At an IRA army convention in 1965 his public articulation of these views exposed, for the first time, the growing fissures within the organization over the issue of its future direction. Thereafter, organized opposition to the radical republican platform of Goulding and his supporters began to coalesce under Ó Brádaigh's leadership.[25]

In January 1970, under the growing pressure of events in Northern Ireland the movement eventually split, as a group styling itself the 'Provisional IRA' rejected what it saw as the socialism and the incipient parliamentarianism of Goulding and his ilk. In moving to represent the resurgence of the Catholic nationalist militarist tradition, the 'Provisionals' set about developing a strategy that embraced the use of less discriminate tactics within the hotbed of the emerging northern conflagration. At the same time, their erstwhile comrades, in what was known as the 'Official IRA', attempted to become the vanguard of a broader-based struggle.[26] In marked contrast to the 1950s, however, the Provisionals enjoyed considerable support, particularly in Belfast, where they proved themselves adept at identifying the aspirations of the constituency whose backing they sought. Crucially, the organizational abilities of Seán Mac Stiofáin proved to be a boon in obtaining large quantities of arms, as his aptitude for guerrilla warfare was to manifest itself in the Provisional IRA's increased technical sophistication in what was predominantly an urban conflict.[27]

Unlike the Officials, who emerged from the split in a materially better position in terms of arms, facilities and money, the Provisionals, shorn of any pretence of republican socialism, now possessed a priceless asset in the form of credibility and legitimacy in the United States. There the organization happily purveyed an unreconstructed, visceral anti-British rhetoric calculated to warm the heart of even the most fervent anti-communist. This quickly translated into a growing command of republican opinion both in the USA and in Ireland, which was to ensure the Provisionals' initial weakness in terms of funding and weaponry was quickly overcome.[28] It was overtaking its rivals, and the response of the British authorities that was to ensure that the Provisional movement would be the long-term victors in the struggle for custody of the republican flame. The ineptitude of the Northern Irish Prime Minister, Brian Faulkner, in reintroducing internment in 1971, in the utterly inappropriate context of inter-communal civil strife, proved to be a pivotal turning point in the history of the Provisional IRA.

By casting its net recklessly wide, the Northern Ireland government made a fatal error. Of the total of 342 people rounded up by the British army in 1971, fewer than 100 were actually members of either the Provisional or Official IRA. In acknowledging its mistake, the Northern Irish government released 116 of these people within forty-eight hours. By then, however, the damage was done. Of the remainder who were actually interned, over half were sent to Crumlin Road

Prison, with the balance accommodated on the hulk of the *Maidstone* moored in Belfast docks. Not a single loyalist was interned, a fact bitterly noted by an increasingly politicized Catholic constituency.[29] The manner in which internment was effected generated massive support and sympathy for the Provisional IRA in the Republic of Ireland and constrained the efforts of Jack Lynch's Fianna Fáil government to contain it. Internment also increased support for the Provisionals abroad, particularly among Irish-Americans, thus increasing republican financial resources. Most significant of all, it brought a hitherto inconceivable surge of recruits to the Provisionals, as the incompetence of the British army in implementing this measure starkly exposed the shortcomings of internment as a political weapon when incorrectly applied in unsuitable circumstances.[30]

As the civil conflict in Northern Ireland intensified throughout the early 1970s and the coincident danger to the stability of the Republic of Ireland became more manifest, the Irish government elected not to reintroduce internment. Instead, the Special Criminal Court was re-established in May 1972 and, significantly, it was composed solely of judges and former judges.[31] Although the fallout from the Northern Ireland government's recent inept recourse to internment had politically constrained the Irish government in this regard, the influence of the Lawless case was ever present. Even if the political will existed to pursue such a course of action, the difficulties experienced with the operation of the Offences Against the State (Amendment) Act and the judgement of the European Court of Human Rights together constituted a significant impediment. For the Irish political establishment this was of fundamental import, as it necessitated a radical re-conception of what had previously been a central tenet of Ireland's counter-insurgency policy. The utilization of internment during the 1950s IRA border campaign was a graphic illustration of its success, when employed in appropriate circumstances, in frustrating the ambitions of a militant subversive organization.

Shaped in many ways by the experience of internment and its effectiveness in Ireland during the Second World War, the success of this policy in defeating the IRA in the late 1950s is beyond dispute. In one fell swoop, the detention of a large number of militant republicans not only disrupted the momentum of the IRA's campaign; it was also a convenient means of circumventing the difficulties that had pertained in obtaining appropriate convictions for IRA men before the ordinary courts in 1957. Moreover, the dynamics of division and disagreement that had been such an integral part of life within the

Conclusion 209

Curragh internment camp during the 1940s again manifested themselves to such an extent that the IRA's campaign was effectively stymied by the severe organizational infighting that occurred in 1959. Hindered by the developments in the Lawless case, the Irish government was understandably wary of reinstating internment in the wake of a brief resurgence in the border campaign in 1961. In response, the Special Criminal Court was reconstituted and its surprising effectiveness in bringing the IRA to heel did not go unnoticed. In light of the current domestic circumstances inaugurated by the signing of the Good Friday Agreement, the fact that the Committee to Review the Offences Against the State Acts has recently recommended its retention is indicative of its continued import.[32]

Notes

CHAPTER 1

1. National Archives of Ireland [hereafter NAI], Department of Justice [hereafter DJ] JUS8/1061, Copy of 'Operation harvest, general directive for a guerrilla campaign', undated.
2. IRA campaign manifesto, 12 December 1956 (private collection); Charles Townshend, *Ireland: The 20th century* (London: Arnold Publications, 1999), p. 176.
3. J. McGarrity (pseudonym), *Resistance: The Story of the Struggle in British Occupied Ireland* (Dublin: Irish Freedom Press, 1957), p. 27; *Irish Times*, 19 December 1956; Joseph Bowyer Bell. *The Secret Army: The IRA* (Dublin: Poolbeg, 1990), p. 293.
4. For more on the split within the IRA see: M.L.R. Smith, *Fighting for Ireland? The military strategy of the Irish Republican Movement* (London: Routledge, 1997), pp. 72–80 and Richard English, *Armed Struggle: A history of the IRA* (London: Macmillan, 2003), pp. 81–147.
5. Seosamh Ó Longaigh, *Emergency Law in Independent Ireland, 1922–1948* (Dublin: Four Courts Press, 2006), pp. 35–7, 46–7, 75; Eunan O'Halpin, *Defending Ireland: The Irish State and its Enemies since 1922* (Oxford: Oxford University Press, 2000), p. 42.
6. Diarmaid Ferriter, *The Transformation of Ireland, 1900–2000* (London: Profile Books, 2004), p. 419; Caoilfhionn Ní Bheachain, 'The lost republicans: Seán McCaughey and the disruption of the Free State narrative' (MA thesis, National University of Ireland, Galway, 1997), p. 37; O'Halpin, *Defending Ireland*, p. 201; Michael Farrell, *The Apparatus of Repression* (Derry: Field Day, 1986), p. 11.
7. The Offences Against the State Act, 1939 (1939 no. 13) (14 June 1939) s. 54.
8. Ó Longaigh, *Emergency Law*, p. 230.
9. Michael S. O'Neill, 'In time of "war": Irish domestic security legislation, 1939–45', *Irish History: A Research Yearbook*, vol. 2, 2003, p. 81; Joe Lee, *Ireland, 1912–1985: Politics and Society* (Cambridge: Cambridge University Press, 1989), p. 221.
10. English, *Armed Struggle*, p. 53; Jane Cole Woods, '"To blow and burn England from her moorings": The Irish republican army and the English bombing campaign of 1939' (PhD Thesis, University of Kentucky, 1995), p. 34.
11. Lee, *Ireland*, p. 221.
12. Gary McGladdery, *The Provisional IRA in England: The Bombing Campaign, 1973–1997* (Dublin: Irish Academic Press, 2006), pp. 43–4.
13. Ó Longaigh, *Emergency Law*, p. 284.
14. NAI, DJ JUS8/1056, Report of discussion re: allegations by Sinn Féin, published in *Sunday Independent*, 5 September 1957; NAI, Department of An Taoiseach [hereafter DT], S 13785 B, Returns under section 9 of the Offences Against the State (Amendment) Act, 1940, period from 8 July 1957 to 21 December 1957, undated, period from 8 July 1957 to 1 June 1958, undated, period from 1 June 1958 to 1 November 1958, undated, period from 1 November 1958 to 1 March 1959, undated.
15. Patrick O'Regan, a former internee, is a particular exponent of this view, pointing out how the detention of his comrades prevented them from engaging in the IRA raids in Northern Ireland. With limited manpower resources available to this organization, this proved to be a heavy blow for a group struggling to maintain the flow of regular attacks in Northern Ireland. See: Interview with Patrick O'Regan, 31 August 2006.

16. *Irish Times*, 23 November 1961. In their works, both O'Halpin and Bowyer Bell incorrectly refer to the reintroduction of 'Military Tribunals' in November 1961 (O'Halpin, *Defending Ireland*, p. 300 and Bowyer Bell, p. 333). In fact, the tribunal that was set up was clearly provided for under part V of the Offences Against the State Act, where it was described as 'A Special Criminal Court'. See The Offences Against the State Act, s. 38 (1). While this legislation clearly envisaged the establishment of a court where serving military officers could act in a judicial manner, the Special Criminal Court differs from the military tribunals that were created under the Public Safety Act of 1931, and the military tribunal that was established by the Emergency Powers Act of 1939. See The Constitution Amendment (No. 17) Act, 1931 (1931 no. 37) (17 October 1931) s. 4; The Emergency Powers Act, 1939 (1939 no. 28) (3 September 1939) s. 10; The Emergency Powers (No. 41) Order, 1940 and Ó Longaigh, *Emergency Law*, pp. 230–60.
17. Bowyer Bell, *The Secret Army*, p. 333. As an indication of the new-found status of the Special Criminal Court as the state's main defence against subversives, it was re-established in May 1972 as a direct response to the growing northern conflagration. See *The Report of the Committee to Review the Offences Against the State Acts, 1939 to 1998 and Related matters* [R.I.], (Dublin, 2002), p. 215.
18. Brian Doolan, *Lawless V Ireland: The First Case before the European Court of Human Rights. An International Miscarriage of Justice?* (Dartmouth: Ashgate, 2001), p. 10.
19. NAI, Attorney General's Office [hereafter AGO] Gerard Lawless Papers [hereafter GLP] Box No. 2, Folder entitled 'Offences Against the State Commission Papers' – Justice to unknown recipient, 31 January 1958.
20. Anthony J. Jordan, *Seán MacBride: A Biography* (Dublin: Blackwater Press, 1993), p. 157.
21. Fearghal McGarry, 'Introduction', in Fearghal McGarry (ed.), *Republicanism in Modern Ireland* (Dublin: University College Dublin Press, 2003), p. 1.
22. In common law the writ of *habeas corpus* is a judicial mandate to a prison official ordering that an inmate be brought to a court so it can be determined whether or not that person is imprisoned lawfully and whether or not he should be released from custody. In 1679 an act of the English parliament confirmed this procedure's status as a defence against imprisonment without trial. The absence of comparable legislation in Ireland was first raised as a grievance during the sole right controversy of 1692 and became a central patriot demand until remedied by Sir Samuel Bradstreet's Liberty of the Subject Act, 1782. With the coming of independence the Irish state inherited the procedure of *habeas corpus*, which was guaranteed by article 6 of the Constitution of the Irish Free State. In 1937 this was superseded with the enactment of Bunreacht na hÉireann, which set out a detailed *habeas corpus* procedure without actually mentioning the Latin term. See: Bunreacht na hÉireann, article forty; Kevin Costello, *The Law of Habeas Corpus in Ireland: The History, Scope of Review and Practice under Article 40.4.2 of the Irish Constitution* (Dublin: Four Courts Press, 2006).
23. As a result of this 'oversight' several prisoners who were being detained without charge were successful in obtaining a writ of *habeas corpus* because the authorities had not taken the precaution of seeking a warrant for their arrest under the *Habeas Corpus* Suspension Act. See Costello, *The Law of Habeas Corpus in Ireland*, pp. 17–18.
24. David Dickson, *New Foundations: Ireland, 1660–1800* (Dublin: Irish Academic Press, 2000), p. 209.
25. Gerard Hogan and Clive Walker, *Political Violence and the Law in Ireland* (Manchester: Manchester University Press, 1989), p. 12.
26. Costello, *The Law of Habeas Corpus in Ireland*, p. 20.
27. R. V. Comerford, *The Fenians in Context: Irish Politics and Society 1848–82* (Dublin: Wolfhound, 1998), pp. 12, 16–17; Robert Kee, *The Green Flag: A History of Irish Nationalism* (London: Penguin, 2000), pp. 270–89, 335–8; F. S. Lyons, *Charles Stewart Parnell* (London: Fontana, 1978), p. 35.
28. Ó Longaigh, *Emergency Law*, p. 7; Colm Campbell, *Emergency Law in Ireland, 1918–1925* (Oxford: Clarendon Press, 1994), p. 8.
29. The Defence of the Realm Act, 1914, 4 & 5 Geo. V, c. 29 [U.K.] (8 August 1914) s. 1.
30. In the immediate aftermath of the Rising, the Irish Lord Lieutenant proclaimed a state of martial law in Dublin. Hours later, the government took steps to allow courts martial instead of the ordinary courts to try persons on charges of breaching the Defence of the Realm Regulations. This was compounded on the Friday of Easter Week when General Sir John

Maxwell arrived in Ireland as 'military governor' with 'plenary powers under martial law over the whole country, the Irish government having placed themselves at his disposal to carry out his instructions'. By these actions the government brought into simultaneous existence two inconsistent legal regimes. For his part, Maxwell, compelled to work under the Defence of the Realm Regulations, did so in such a way as to approximate martial law. By doing so it appears that he may have acted unlawfully, in particular by conducting the trials of the insurgents in secret. Effectively, these courts martial, which were established under DORA, were subject to law – rather than operating under martial law. While DORA made provision for the use of courts martial to try breaches of the various Defence of the Realm Regulations, the procedures for these courts martial were governed by the 1881 Army Act which provided that 'proceedings shall be held in open court in the presence of the accused, except on any deliberation amongst its members, when the court may be closed'. Furthermore, by trying the insurgents before field general courts martial, the authorities deprive the plaintiffs of the right to have defence counsel present, as the procedures governing the operation of these judicatures did not require the presence of a judge advocate or any other legally qualified member of the court. For more on this see Adrian Hardiman, '"Shot in cold blood": Military law and Irish perceptions in the suppression of the 1916 rebellion', in Gabriel Doherty and Dermot Keogh, *1916: The Long Revolution* (Cork: Mercier Press, 2007), pp. 225–49.

31. D. George Boyce, *Nationalism in Ireland* (London: Croom Helm, 1982), p. 309; Kee, *The Green Flag*, p. 570; Ferriter, *Transformation of Ireland*, p. 153; Hogan and Walker, *Political Violence and the Law in Ireland*, p. 13; Campbell, *Emergency Law in Ireland*, p. 12. For differing interpretations of the aftermath of the Rising see: Lee, *Ireland*, pp. 29–36; Feeney, *Sinn Féin*, pp. 58–9; Bowyer Bell, *The Secret Army*, pp. 12–13.
32. National Library of Ireland [hereafter NLI], 1A 2167, M. Bean Ui Bhuachalla, *Sinn Féin 1905–1956: A Proud History Gives Confidence of Victory* (Dublin: Beatha Éireann as Phoblacht, 1956), p. 3; Feeney, *Sinn Féin*, pp. 38–9; Lee, *Ireland*, p. 38.
33. The National Archives, UK [hereafter, NAUK], War Office [hereafter WO] 32/9571, Memorandum by Irish Law Officers, 9 May 1916, quoted in Townshend, *Easter 1916*, p. 277.
34. Michael F. Noone and Yonah Alexander (eds), *Cases and Materials on Terrorism: Three Nations' Response* (London: Martinus Nijhoff, 1997), p. 305; Townshend, *Easter 1916*, p. 277.
35. It was proposed that such a link could be derived from the landing of Roger Casement, the attempted landing of arms from the German ship *The Aud* and by the passage in the 1916 proclamation referring to 'gallant allies in Europe'.
36. Townshend, *Easter 1916*, pp. 275–8; Seán McConville, *Irish Political Prisoners, 1848–1922: Theatres of War* (London: Routledge, 2005), pp. 452–5; Joost Augusteijn, *From Public Defiance to Guerrilla Warfare: The Experience of Ordinary Volunteers in the Irish War of Independence 1916–1921* (Dublin: Irish Academic Press, 1996), p. 57.
37. McConville, *Irish Political Prisoners*, p. 466.
38. Campbell, *Emergency Law in Ireland*, p. 12.
39. English, *Armed Struggle*, p. 15.
40. Augusteijn, *From Public Defiance to Guerrilla Warfare*, p. 55.
41. Hogan and Walker, *Political Violence and the Law in Ireland*, p. 13.
42. Smith, *Fighting for Ireland*, pp. 35–9.
43. Harkness, *Ireland in the Twentieth Century: Divided Island* (Basingstoke: Macmillan, 1995), pp. 39–41.
44. Smith, *Fighting for Ireland*, p. 38.
45. Keogh, *Twentieth Century Ireland*, p. 2; Smith, *Fighting for Ireland*, p. 66.
46. Kee, *The Green Flag*, pp. 732–3; Tim Pat Coogan, *The IRA* (London: Harper Collins, 2000) p. 38.
47. Charles Townshend, *Political Violence in Ireland: Government and Resistance in Ireland since 1848* (Oxford: Clarendon Press, 1983), p. 362.
48. Keogh, *Twentieth Century Ireland*, pp. 2–3.
49. O'Halpin, *Defending Ireland*, p. 2.
50. O'Halpin, *Defending Ireland*, p. 11; John M. Regan, *The Irish Counter-Revolution 1921–1936* (Dublin: Gill & MacMillan, 1999), pp. 124–5.
51. Francis Costello, *Years of Revolt: The Irish Revolution and its Aftermath, 1916–1923* (Dublin: Irish Academic Press, 2003), p. 291.

Notes

52. O'Halpin, *Defending Ireland*, pp. 15–17.
53. English, *Armed Struggle*, p. 35.
54. Ó Longaigh, *Emergency Law*, pp. 20–8.
55. O'Halpin, *Defending Ireland*, p. 30; English, *Armed Struggle*, p. 37; Ó Longaigh, *Emergency law*, p. 29.
56. Townshend, *Political Violence in Ireland*, p. 375.
57. Ó Longaigh, *Emergency Law*, pp. 39–40.
58. Ó Longaigh, *Emergency Law*, pp. 36–8; The Public Safety (Emergency Powers) Act, 1923 (1923 no. 28) (1 August 1923) s. 1, 2, 3 & 8.
59. O'Halpin, *Defending Ireland*, p. 43.
60. See The Public Safety (Powers of Arrest and Detention) Temporary Act, 1924 (1924 no. 1) (31 January 1924).
61. The Public Safety (Emergency Powers) Act, 1926 (1926 no. 42) (19 November 1926) s.1; *Parliamentary Debates, Dáil Éireann*, 16 November 1926, vol. 17, cols 39–40.
62. Civil Authorities (Special Powers) Act (Northern Ireland), 1922 (1922 no. 4) (7 April, 1922), s. 1 (1).
63. Laura K. Donohue, 'Civil liberties, terrorism and liberal democracy: Lessons from the United Kingdom', Belfer Centre for Science and International Affairs Discussion Paper, John F. Kennedy School of Government, Harvard University, 2000, p. 4.
64. Brian Hanley, *The IRA 1926–1936* (Dublin: Four Courts Press, 2002), p. 49.
65. Lee, *Ireland*, p. 154; Ó Longaigh, *Emergency Law*, pp. 80–3; The Public Safety Act, 1927 (1927 no. 31) (11 August 1927) s. 4 & 22. Under the act an organization was deemed to be unlawful if it: '(a) has among its professed objects, or advocates or encourages, or professes to encourage the overthrow by force of the Government of Saorstát Éireann or the alteration by force of the constitution of the law, (b) without lawful authority organizes or maintains or endeavours or purports to organize or maintain an armed force, (c) promotes or encourages the unlawful possession of firearms by its members, (d) engages in, promotes, encourages, or advocates any act, enterprise, or course of action of a treasonable or seditious character, or promotes, encourages or advocates the attainment of any object of a treasonable or seditious character, (e) promotes, encourages, or advocates the commission of crimes or interference or the obstruction or interference with the administration of justice or the enforcement of the law, (f) promotes, encourages or advocates the non payment of monies payable to the Central Fund or any other public fund whether by way of taxation or otherwise or the non payment of local taxation.' Section 4.
66. This confirming authority was to be an army officer nominated by the government, who was not below the rank of colonel. Section 24 (2).
67. Ó Longaigh, *Emergency Law*, p. 85.
68. *Parliamentary Debates Dáil Éireann*, 10 November 1927, vol. 21, col. 1,208.
69. Ó Longaigh, *Emergency Law*, p. 85.
70. Smith, *Fighting for Ireland*, p. 61.
71. Hanley, *The IRA 1926–1936*, p. 177.
72. The land annuities were the mechanism through which Irish farmers repaid the British state, through the Land Commission, for advances given to them to purchase their farms under the 1891 and 1909 Land Acts. Donal Ó Drisceoil, *Peadar O'Donnell* (Cork: Cork University Press, 2001), pp. 44–50, Henry Patterson, *The Politics of Illusion: Republicanism and Socialism in Modern Ireland* (London: Radius, 1989), pp. 1, 31.
73. Hanley, *The IRA 1926–1936*, p. 179.
74. Ronan Fanning, *Independent Ireland* (Dublin: Helicon, 1983), p. 103; Ferriter, *Transformation of Ireland*, p. 414.
75. Ó Drisceoil, *Peadar O'Donnell*, p. 68.
76. Hanley, *The IRA 1926–1936*, p. 179; Lee, *Ireland*, p. 157; Ó Longaigh, *Emergency Law*, p. 279.
77. Farrell, *The Apparatus of Repression*, p. 8; Ó Longaigh, *Emergency Law*, p. 126; The Constitution (Amendment No. 17) Act, s. 2.
78. Ó Longaigh, *Emergency Law*, pp. 117–18, 280; The Constitution (Amendment No. 17) Act, schedule, s. 4.
79. Bowyer Bell, *The Secret Army*, p. 100.
80. Hanley, *The IRA 1926–1936*, p. 126.
81. Maurice Manning, *The Blueshirts* (Dublin: Gill & Macmillan, 1988), p. 60.

82. Hanley, *The IRA 1926–1936*, pp. 126–8.
83. O'Halpin, *Defending Ireland*, pp. 116–17, 120.
84. John Bowman, *De Valera and the Ulster Question, 1917–1973* (Oxford: Oxford University Press, 2000), p. 125; Hanley, *The IRA 1926–1936*, p. 127.
85. Seán Cronin, *The McGarrity Papers: Revelations of the Irish Revolutionary Movement in Ireland and America 1900–1940* (Tralee: Anvil Books, 1972), p. 166; Hanley, *The IRA 1926–1936*, pp. 15–18.
86. Ó Longaigh, *Emergency Law*, p. 140. For more on the IRA's conflict with the Blueshirts and the ACA generally see Hanley, *The IRA 1926–1936*, pp. 84–92 and Manning, *The Blueshirts*.
87. Ferriter, *Transformation of Ireland*, p. 414; O'Halpin, *Defending Ireland*, p. 121.
88. Lee, *Ireland*, p. 180; Bowman, *De Valera and the Ulster Question*, p. 125.
89. Ó Longaigh, *Emergency Law*, pp. 147–8; Hanley, *The IRA 1926–1936*, p. 60.
90. Fanning, *Independent Ireland*, p. 103; Tim Pat Coogan, *Ireland in the Twentieth Century* (London: Random House, 2003), p. 213; Hanley, *The IRA 1926–1936*, pp. 104–9.
91. Patterson, *Politics of Illusion*, p. 58.
92. Ferriter, *Transformation of Ireland*, pp. 414–15.
93. Ó Drisceoil, *Peadar O'Donnell*, p. 83.
94. Hanley, *The IRA*, p. 109; Patterson, *Politics of Illusion*, p. 58.
95. Patterson, *Politics of Illusion*, p. 31.
96. Coogan, *Ireland in the Twentieth Century*, p. 214.
97. Hanley, *The IRA 1926–1936*, p. 106; Smith, *Fighting for Ireland*, p. 62.
98. *Parliamentary Debates, Dáil Éireann*, 29 May 1935, vol. 56, col. 2,089.
99. Coogan, *Ireland in the Twentieth Century*, p. 215; Keogh, *Twentieth Century Ireland*, p. 79; Ó Longaigh, *Emergency Law*, p. 172; Robert W. White, *Ruairí Ó Brádaigh: The Life and Politics of an Irish Revolutionary* (Bloomington: Indiana University Press), pp. 21–2.
100. *Irish Independent*, 9 May 1935.
101. *Irish Times*, 25 and 26 March 1936; *Irish Press*, 25 March 1936; Bowyer Bell, *The Secret Army*, p. 126; Coogan, *Ireland in the Twentieth Century*, pp. 215–16; Keogh, *Twentieth Century Ireland*, pp. 78–9.
102. *Irish Times*, 27 April 1936; Keogh, *Twentieth Century Ireland*, p. 79.
103. Hanley, *The IRA 1926–1936*, p. 144.
104. *Parliamentary Debates, Dáil Éireann*, 26 March 1936, vol. 61, col. 357.
105. *Irish Press*, 30 April 1936; Townshend, *Political Violence in Ireland*, p. 378.
106. Bowyer Bell, *The Secret Army*, pp. 126–7; Lee, *Ireland*, p. 180; Fanning, *Independent Ireland*, p. 133. For the relevant legislation conferring this power on the government see The Constitution (Amendment No. 17) Act, schedule, s.19.
107. Seán MacBride [Caitriona Lawlor (ed.)], *That Day's Struggle: A Memoir, 1904–1951* (Dublin: Currach Press, 2005), pp. 122–3; Bowyer Bell, *The Secret Army*, p. 138; Fanning, *Independent Ireland*, p. 134.
108. Bunreacht na hÉireann, article 39.
109. Bunreacht na hÉireann, article 38 (3).
110. Bunreacht na hÉireann, article 38 (4.1°).
111. O'Neill, 'In time of "war"', p. 82.
112. The Offences Against the State Act, s. 29 (1) & s. 30 (3). Any Garda officer not below the rank of chief superintendent, who was satisfied that 'evidence of or relating to the commission or intended commission of an offence under any section or sub-section of [the OASA]' could be found in a particular location, was authorized to issue a search warrant to any Garda of the rank of inspector or above.
113. The Offences Against the State Act, s. 52.
114. The Offences Against the State Act, s. 19 & 21.
115. The Offences Against the State Act, s. 38.
116. The Offences Against the State Act, s. 39, 40, 41 & 44; O'Neill, 'In time of "war"', pp. 82–4.
117. The Offences Against the State Act, s. 55.
118. O'Neill, 'In time of "war"', p. 84.
119. Ó Longaigh, *Emergency Law*, pp. 227–8; *Irish Press*, 26 August 1939; NAI, DT S 11837 B, Department of Defence memorandum, 3 November 1951.
120. O'Halpin, *Defending Ireland*, p. 200; Bowman, *De Valera and the Ulster Question*, p. 210.

Notes

CHAPTER 2

1. *United Irishman*, August 1951.
2. Cronin, *The McGarrity Papers*, p. 158.
3. MacEoin, *The IRA in the Twilight Years*, p. 18.
4. Ó Longaigh, *Emergency Law*, p. 210.
5. McGladdery, *The Provisional IRA in England*, pp. 29–32.
6. MacBride, *That Day's Struggle*, p. 121–2; Bowyer Bell, *The Secret Army*, p. 130.
7. Woods, '"To blow and burn England"', p. 19; Cronin, *The McGarrity Papers*, p. 162.
8. Cronin, *The McGarrity Papers*, p. 162; McGladdery, *The Provisional IRA in England*, p. 31; O'Halpin, *Defending Ireland*, p. 128.
9. NAI, DJ JUS8/802, Copy of report from *Daily Mirror*, 15 August 1936 and Special branch, re: Seán Russell QMG IRA, 9 November 1937.
10. Noel Browne, *Against the Tide* (Dublin: Gill & MacMillan, 1987), p. 89.
11. O'Halpin, *Defending Ireland*, p. 126; MacBride, *That Day's Struggle*, p. 124; Bowyer Bell, *The Secret Army*, p. 133; Meda Ryan, *Tom Barry: IRA Freedom Fighter* (Cork: Mercier Press, 2003), p. 219.
12. McGladdery, *The Provisional IRA in England*, p. 32.
13. Ryan, *Tom Barry*, p. 219–26; Cronin, *The McGarrity Papers*, pp. 163–5; O'Halpin, *Defending Ireland*, p. 127; MacBride, *That Day's Struggle*, p. 124; O'Halpin, *Defending Ireland*, p. 127; Bowyer Bell, *The Secret Army*, pp. 134–5; Ryan, *Tom Barry*, pp. 225–6.
14. Woods, '"To blow and burn England"', p. 23; McGladdery, *The Provisional IRA in England*, p. 34; Richard English, *Radicals and the Republic: Socialist Republicanism in the Irish Free State, 1925–1937* (Oxford: Clarendon Press, 1994), p. 257.
15. English, *Armed Struggle*, p. 61; Woods, '"To blow and burn England"', pp. 24–9.
16. Cronin, *The McGarrity Papers*, p. 166.
17. 'Oglaigh na hÉireann general headquarters to his Excellency the Rt. Hon Viscount Halifax', 12 January 1939 quoted in Bowyer Bell, *The Secret Army*, p. 166.
18. Smith, *Fighting for Ireland*, p. 63.
19. *Irish Press*, 17 January 1939; Coogan, *The IRA*, p. 126.
20. *Irish Times*, 18 January 1939; *Irish Press*, 19 January 1939.
21. *Irish Times*, 5 and 6 February 1939.
22. Bowyer Bell, *The Secret Army*, p. 156; English, *Armed Struggle*, p. 61 *Irish Press*, 25 July 1939; Woods, '"To blow and burn England"', p. 333.
23. *Irish Press*, 26 August 1939.
24. *Irish Times*, 26 August 1939.
25. Bowyer Bell, *The Secret Army*, p. 162.
26. Brian O'Higgins, *Martyrs for Ireland: The Story of McCormick and Barnes* (Dublin: Irish Book Bureau, 1940), pp. 4–5.
27. NAI, Department of External Affairs [hereafter DEA] S 113(a), de Valera to Dulanty, 19 December 1939.
28. Smith, *Fighting for Ireland*, pp. 63–4.
29. Bowyer Bell, *The Secret Army*, p. 159.
30. English, *Armed Struggle*, p. 63; Brian Hanley, '"Oh here's to Adolph Hitler"? The IRA and the Nazis', *History Ireland*, vol. 13 no. 3, p. 32; *United Irishman*, October 1951.
31. NAI, DJ JUS8/802, Report of Frederick Boland, 6 June 1946; *United Irishman*, October 1951; English, *Armed Struggle*, p. 63; Robert Fisk, *In Time of War: Ireland, Ulster and the Price of Neutrality, 1939–45* (Dublin: Gill & MacMillan, 1983), pp. 342–3. In fact it appears that Russell died of a perforated duodenal ulcer. He was buried at sea with full German military honours.
32. English, *Armed Struggle*, p. 64.
33. Brian Girvin, *The Emergency: Neutral Ireland, 1939–45* (London: Macmillan, 2006), pp. 179–80. It has been argued that Görtz was deliberately allowed to remain at liberty so that the Irish authorities could keep a check on all those he came in contact with, including the German Minister in Ireland, Dr Eduard Hempel. See Hull, *Irish Secrets*, for a more in-depth study of German espionage in Ireland during the Second World War.
34. Woods, '"To blow and burn England"', pp. 371–2.
35. Ó Longaigh, *Emergency Law*, p. 230.
36. Seosamh Ó Longaigh, 'Preparing law for an emergency: 1938–1939', in Dermot Keogh

and Mervyn O'Driscoll (eds), *Ireland in World War Two: Neutrality and Survival* (Cork: Mercier Press, 2004), pp. 36–7; O'Neill, '"In time of war"', p. 81.
37. *Parliamentary Debates, Dáil Éireann*, 2 September 1939, vol. 77, col. 5.
38. O'Neill, '"In time of war"', p. 85; Doolan, *Lawless V Ireland*, p. 17.
39. The Emergency Powers Act, 1939, (1939 no. 28) (3 September 1939), s. 2.
40. Ó Longaigh, 'Preparing law for an emergency', p. 47; Ronan Fanning, '"The rule of order": Eamon de Valera and the IRA, 1923–40', in John P. O'Carroll and John A. Murphy (eds), *De Valera and his Times* (Cork: Cork University Press, 1983), pp. 167–8.
41. Lee, *Ireland*, p. 222.
42. Ó Longaigh, *Emergency Law*, p. 233.
43. *Parliamentary Debates, Dáil Éireann*, 27 September 1939, vol. 77, col. 247.
44. Donal Ó Drisceoil, *Censorship in Ireland, 1939–1945: Neutrality, Politics and Society* (Cork: Cork University Press, 1996), pp. 234–5.
45. NAI, DT S 11436, Government statement, 15 September 1939. About seventy warrants were issued in total. See Ó Longaigh, *Emergency Law*, p. 233.
46. The Offences Against the State Act, s. 59.
47. NAI, DT S 11436, Government statement, 17 September 1939.
48. Ó Longaigh, *Emergency Law*, p. 236.
49. Woods, '"To blow and burn England,"' p. 395.
50. Seosamh Ó Longaigh, 'Emergency law in action, 1939–45', in Dermot Keogh and Mervyn O'Driscoll (eds), *Ireland in World War II: Neutrality and Survival* (Cork: Mercier Press, 2004), p. 64.
51. English, *Armed Struggle*, p. 55.
52. Coogan, *Ireland in the Twentieth Century*, p. 329. See also: NAI, DT S 11515, Tobin to de Valera, 8 November 1939.
53. Ó Longaigh, *Emergency Law*, pp. 236–7; Lee, *Ireland*, p. 222.
54. The State (Burke) V Lennon and the Attorney General [1940] IR, pp. 136–8.
55. [1940] IR, p. 152; Doolan, *Lawless V Ireland*, p. 18; Ó Longaigh, *Emergency Law*, pp. 239–41.
56. [1940] IR, pp. 157–9.
57. Coogan, *The IRA*, pp. 135–6; English, *Armed struggle*, p. 54; Fanning, '"The rule of order,"' p. 167.
58. *Parliamentary Debates, Dáil Éireann*, 3 January 1940, vol. 78 col. 1,310.
59. Ó Longaigh, *Emergency Law*, p. 243; The Emergency Powers (Amendment) Act, 1940, (1940 no. 1) (5 January 1940), s. 2.
60. *Parliamentary Debates, Dáil Éireann*, 3 January 1940, vol. 78, col. 1,311.
61. For the appropriate wording see The Offences Against the State Act, s. 55 (1) and The Offences Against the State (Amendment) Act, 1940, (1940 no. 2) (9 February 1940), s. 4 (1).
62. The Offences Against the State (Amendment) Act, s. 8 & 9.
63. *Parliamentary Debates, Seanad Éireann*, 5 January 1940, vol. 24, col. 563.
64. In re Article 26 of the Constitution and the Offences Against the State (Amendment) Bill, 1940 [1940] IR, p. 479.
65. NAI, DT S 11515, Hunger strike – calendar of principal events, undated.
66. NAI, DT S 11515, de Valera to Mrs Dillon, 2 April 1940.
67. NAI, DT S 11515, Hunger strike – calendar of principal events, undated.
68. Military Archives, Irish Defence Forces [hereafter MA], CP204, Grogan, O'Flaherty, White, Byrne, McGuinness, Adams to Arbour Hill Governor, 18 April 1940; and Governor, Arbour Hill to Provost Marshall, 20 April 1940.
69. NAI, DT S 11515, Plunkett to McRory, 14 March 1940.
70. NAI, DT S 11515, de Valera to McRory, 20 March 1940.
71. NAI, DT S 11515, Hunger strike – calendar of principal events, undated.
72. Coogan, *Ireland in the Twentieth Century*, p. 330.
73. NAI, DT S 11515, de Valera to Clarke, 20 April 1940.
74. NAI, DT S11515, Hunger strike – calendar of principal events and de Valera to Clarke, 20 April 1940.
75. NAI, DT S11515, Hunger strike – calendar of principal events and copy of record made of telephone conversation between Minister for Justice and Father O'Hare, 19 April 1940.
76. NAI, DT S 11515, Seán Ó Caomhánaigh, Governor, Mountjoy prison to Secretary, Department of Justice, 19 April, 1940.

77. NAI, DT S 11515, Hunger strike – calendar of principal events.
78. Coogan, *Ireland in the Twentieth Century*, p. 330; MacBride, *That Day's Struggle*, p. 133, NAI, DT S 11515, Hunger strike – calendar of principal events.
79. Girvin, *The Emergency*, p. 79.
80. George Sweeney, 'Self-immolation in Ireland: Hungerstrikes and political confrontation', in *Anthropology Today*, vol. 9, no. 5 (1993), p. 13. During the Civil War over 8,000 prisoners and internees went on a hunger strike which lasted from October until November 1923. The government responded by offering the prisoners release conditional on a pledge of loyalty to the Free State. Within a month all but 200 had taken up the offer of freedom.
81. In this instance, thirteen internees held in No. 1 Internment camp went on strike in relays, demanding their unconditional release. Although most of them abandoned their protest after thirty days or so, Seán McCool remained on hunger strike for fifty days in total before the protest collapsed in the face of governmental intransigence. See NAI, DT S 13277.
82. Ferriter, *Transformation of Ireland*, p. 419.
83. Ó Longaigh, *Emergency Law*, p. 246; Fanning, '"The rule of order"', p. 170.
84. Ó Longaigh, 'Emergency law in action', pp. 66–7
85. Ó Longaigh, *Emergency Law*, p. 254.
86. O'Halpin, *Defending Ireland*, p. 202; Doolan, *Lawless V Ireland*, p. 20.
87. Ó Longaigh, *Emergency Law*, pp. 251, 255; Bowyer Bell, *The Secret Army*, p. 187; Keogh, *Twentieth Century Ireland*, p. 110.
88. Ó Drisceoil, *Censorship in Ireland*, p. 239.
89. O'Halpin, *Defending Ireland*, p. 202; Coogan, *Ireland in the Twentieth Century*, pp. 331–3; Ó Drisceoil, *Censorship in Ireland*, p. 239.
90. MA, 2/69123, Director of Engineering memo, 21 September 1939.
91. MA, 2/69123, Defence, to Finance, 21 & 22 September 1939.
92. MA, 2/69123, Department of Finance memo, 25 September 1939.
93. MA, 2/69123, Director of Engineering to Corps of Engineering, 11 January 1940.
94. *United Irishman*, May 1951.
95. MA [Unnumbered file], List of sentenced prisoners in military custody.
96. MA [Unnumbered file], List of sentenced prisoners in military custody; MA [Unnumbered file], Division of internees and prisoners in No. 1 internment camp; Ó Longaigh, *Emergency Law*, p. 284 and 'Emergency law in action,' p. 68; Lee, *Ireland*, p. 223.
97. In fact Pearse Kelly managed to bring this fact to the attention of a local bishop, who intervened to have Goold-Verschoyle transferred to Mountjoy prison. See Uinseann MacEoin, *The IRA in the Twilight years, 1923–1948* (Dublin: Argenta Publications, 1997), p. 919.
98. O'Halpin, *Defending Ireland*, p. 202.
99. *United Irishman*, August 1951.
100. John McGuffin, *Internment* (Tralee: Anvil Books, 1973), p. 53; Seán Edmonds, *The Gun, the Law and the Irish People: From 1912 to the Aftermath of the Arms Trial 1970* (Tralee: Anvil Books, 1971), p. 169.
101. Transcript of interview with Tomás Ó Broin, 5 March 2003 (MA, courtesy of Akajava Ltd.); Edmonds, *The Gun*, p. 169; *United Irishman*, August 1951.
102. *United Irishman*, August 1951.
103. Edmonds, *The Gun*, p. 169.
104. *United Irishman*, May 1951.
105. Quoted in MacEoin, *The IRA in the Twilight Years*, p. 508.
106. Ó Broin, 5 March 2003.
107. Quoted in MacEoin, *The IRA in the Twilight Years*, p. 448. According to Burke: 'I was always hungry; I can recall fellows hanging around outside the cookhouse kitchen ready to grab bones being thrown out. Peadar McAndrew ... was on a special diet of frequent bread eggs and milk. Some of us would hang close to him ready to grab anything he might leave.'
108. McGuffin, *Internment*, p. 53; Edmonds, *The Gun*, p. 169.
109. Transcript of interview with John L. McCormack, 21 March 2003, (MA, Courtesy of Akajava Ltd).
110. Quoted in MacEoin, *The IRA in the Twilight Years*, p. 508.
111. McCormack, 21 March 2003. According to McCormack, the sinks in the wash house were so large that some of his fellow inmates often availed of the facility to have a bath.

112. Transcript of interview with Eddie Keenan, 13 March, 2003 (MA, courtesy of Akajava Ltd.)
113. MA, CP/108, Governor, military detention barracks, Arbour Hill to Provost Marshal, Department of Defence, 26 February 1940.
114. *United Irishman*, May 1951.
115. Keenan, 13 March 2003.
116. McCormack, 21 March 2003; MA, PM335, Commandant No. 1 internment camp to Provost Marshal, 3 December 1941.
117. McCormack, 21 March 2003.
118. McCormack, 21 March 2003.
119. Ó Broin, 5 March 2003.
120. McCormack, 21 March 2003.
121. *United Irishman*, August 1951.
122. *United Irishman*, May 1951.
123. O'Halpin, *Defending Ireland*, p. 43.
124. Brendan Anderson, *Joe Cahill: A Life in the IRA* (Dublin: O'Brien Press, 2002), p. 144; MacEoin, *The IRA in the Twilight Years*, p. 919. Significantly, Goold-Verschoyle and his comrades were avowedly in favour of signing-out in order to assist 'Russia's revolutionary war'. Inevitably, this generated further tension among the IRA leadership within the camp, who remained stoic in their determination 'never to yield'.
125. Transcript of camera interview with Eddie Keenan, 13 March 2003, (MA, courtesy of Akajava Ltd.).
126. Quoted in MacEoin, *The IRA in the Twilight Years*, p. 448.
127. MA, CP 97, Standing orders no 1. internment camp and Arbour Hill detention barracks, 23 March 1943.
128. NAI, DT S 11925 A, Department of Defence memorandum, 12 June 1940. According to defence force regulations, military police were authorized to fire live ammunition only in defence of their own or their comrades' lives, to protect the safety of the post under their charge or to prevent themselves from being forcibly disarmed.
129. NAI, DT S 11925 A, Attorney General to Defence, 1 February 1940.
130. NAI, DT S 11925 A, Draft of Emergency Powers (No. 28) Order, 1940.
131. MA, PM644, Adjutant General, to O/C, Curragh Command, 5 October 1940.
132. Ó Broin, 5 March, 2003.
133. *United Irishman*, July, 1951.
134. MA, PM644, Adjutant General, to O/C, Curragh Command, 5 October 1940.
135. Transcript of interview with Christy Querney, 17 March 2003 (MA, courtesy of Akajava Ltd.).
136. MA, PM724, Guiney to Provost Marshal, 3 March 1941.
137. MA, PM724, Connolly to Guiney, 1 December 1944.
138. MA, PM724, Guiney to O/C, Curragh Command, 2 February 1944.
139. Ó Broin, 5 March 2003.
140. Ó Broin, 5 March 2003 and McCormack, 21 March 2003.
141. MA, PM651, Bryan to CSO G2 Branch, 18 September 1940.
142. MA, PM651, Bryan to CSO G2 Branch, 22 October 1940.
143. MA, PM651, Memorandum 'Curragh internment camp', 13 September 1940.
144. MA, PM651, Colonel Archer G2, to Adjutant General, Defence Forces, undated.
145. MA, PM651, Bryan to CSO G2, 18 September 1940.
146. MA, PM651, Commandant Cummins to Provost Marshal, 3 October 1940 and Cummins to Provost Marshall, 11 October 1940.
147. MA, PM651, Archer to Adjutant General, Defence Forces, 22 October 1940.
148. MA, PM651, Colonel McNally to Adjutant General, Defence Forces, 22 October 1940.
149. MA, PM651, Colonel McNally to Adjutant General, Defence Forces, 22 October 1940.
150. Ó Broin, 5 March 2003 and Keenan, 13 March 2003.
151. MA, PM651, Colonel McNally, to Adjutant General Defence Forces, 22 October 1940.
152. MA, PM644, Sgt Edward Gill, military police to Commandant, Curragh internment camp, 5 August 1943.
153. MA, PM644, Commandant Guiney, to O/C Curragh Command, 10 August 1943.
154. MA, PM644, Colonel McNally to Provost Marshal, 11 August 1943.
155. MA, C306, Report of Major J.F. Kinneen, 16 December 1940.

156. McCormack, 21 March 2003.
157. MA, C306, Report of Major Kinneen, 16 December 1940.
158. Keenan, 13 March 2003.
159. MA, C306, O/C Curragh Command to C/S Defence Forces, 15 December 1940.
160. MA, C306, Report of Major J.F. Kinneen, 16 December 1940.
161. MA, 2/67589, Fire report, No. 1 internment camp, 2 January 1941. The fire-fighting force in question was supplied by Irish Ropes Ltd.
162. MA, C306, Statement of Commandant Guiney, 16 December 1940.
163. MA, C306, Statement of Commandant Guiney, 16 December 1940.
164. MA, C306, Statement of Commandant Guiney, 16 December 1940; *United Irishman*, June 1951.
165. MA, C306, Statement of Major Kinneen, 16 December 1940; McCormack, 21 March, 2003.
166. *United Irishman*, June 1951.
167. McCormack, 21 March 2003.
168. McCormack, 21 March 2003; Bowyer Bell, *The Secret Army*, p. 179.
169. Ó Drisceoil, *Censorship in Ireland*, p. 239.
170. *United Irishman*, July 1951.
171. McGuffin, *Internment*, p. 54.
172. MA, 2/67589, Staff officer, Department of Defence, to Commandant K. Ryan, Quartermaster, Curragh Command, 29 May 1942.
173. NAI DJ, JUS8/910, Guiney to O/C Curragh Command, 29 April 1943.
174. McCormack, 21 March 2003.
175. Bowyer Bell, *The Secret Army*, pp. 180–1.
176. Keenan, 13 March 2003.
177. Quoted in MacEoin, *The IRA in the Twilight Years*, p. 487.
178. McCormack, 21 March 2003; Bowyer Bell, *The Secret Army*, p. 180.
179. MA [Unnumbered file], Private correspondence, 2 March 1944.
180. Keenan, 13 March 2003.
181. Bowyer Bell, *The Secret Army*, p. 180; MacEoin, *The IRA in the Twilight Years*, p. 469.
182. MacEoin, *The IRA in the Twilight Years*, p. 509; MA [Unnumbered file], Division of internees in camp, Commandant, No. 1 internment camp to Provost Marshal, 16 October 1942; Keenan, 13 March 2003.
183. See MacEoin, *The IRA in the Twilight Years*, p. 509; Keenan, 13 March 2003.
184. MA [Unnumbered file], Division of internees and prisoners, 13 July 1944.
185. MA, CP 204, Guiney to Provost Marshal, Department of Defence, undated.
186. MA, CP 204, Captain D. Sullivan to Provost Marshal, 12 March 1942.
187. MA, CP 204, Sergeant William Callaghan to Guiney, 17 March 1942.
188. MA [Unnumbered file], Hunger-strikes – political prisoners and internees in military custody 1939–1946, undated.
189. MA [Unnumbered file], Division of internees and prisoners at No. 1 internment camp, Commandant, No. 1 internment camp to Provost Marshal, 16 October 1942.
190. MA [Unnumbered file], Division of internees and prisoners, 17 June 1944.
191. According to Pierce Fennell the collapse of the IRA organization within the camp began in the wake of the fire of December 1940. See MacEoin, *The IRA in the Twilight Years*, p. 562.
192. Querney, 17 March 2003.
193. *United Irishman*, August 1951.
194. Ó Broin, 5 March 2003.
195. *Parliamentary Debates, Dáil Éireann*, 4 July 1945, vol. 97, col. 1,881.
196. Ó Broin, 5 March 2003.
197. McCormack, 21 March 2003.
198. NAI, DJ JUS8/944, Tables entitled 'The number of prisoners convicted by (a) the Special Criminal Court and (b) the Military Tribunal' and 'members of unlawful organizations executed from 1935 to date', undated and 'Returns of firearms, ammunition and explosives seized from members of unlawful organizations for years 1939 to 1945', undated; Ó Longaigh, *Emergency Law*, p. 284–5.
199. Coogan, *Ireland in the Twentieth Century*, p. 332; Ó Drisceoil, *Censorship in Ireland*, p. 239; Bowyer Bell, *The Secret Army*, p. 205; English, *Armed Struggle*, p. 57; Ó Longaigh, *Emergency Law*, p. 261–2.
200. Ó Longaigh, *Emergency Law*, p. 261.

201. Ó Drisceoil, *Censorship in Ireland*, p. 241.
202. Ó Drisceoil, *Censorship in Ireland*, pp. 241–2.
203. Michael Farrell, *Northern Ireland: The Orange State* (London: Pluto Press, 1976), p. 151; McGuffin, *Internment*, p. 42.
204. Jonathon Bardon, *A History of Ulster* (Belfast: Blackstaff Press, 1992), pp. 581–2.
205. Bowyer Bell, *The Secret Army*, p. 181. According to Frank McGlade the *Al Rawdah* contained so much barbed wire that 'there was no use wearing any decent clothes'. See McGuffin, *Internment*, p. 69.
206. McGuffin recounts how the ringleaders of this mutiny were dragged out individually from their cells and forced to run the gauntlet between two rows of B–Special officers, who battered them about the head. See McGuffin, *Internment*, p. 71.
207. On this occasion, the Logue family, of Harding Street, whose home abutted the perimeter wall of the prison, were astonished to observe the escapees emerge from a hole that had suddenly appeared in the back garden, dash through the house and make for a parked furniture van across the road. See McGuffin, *Internment*, pp. 71–2
208. Bardon, *A History of Ulster*, pp. 582–3; Farrell, *Northern Ireland*, p. 167.
209. Farrell, *Northern Ireland*, p. 168.
210. Bardon, *A History of Ulster*, p. 583.
211. Farrell, *Northern Ireland*, p. 168.
212. McGuffin, *Internment*, p. 75.

CHAPTER 3

1. *United Irishman*, May 1953.
2. Bowyer Bell, *The Secret Army*, p. 235.
3. *Irish Independent*, 25 May 1945.
4. The Offences Against the State (Amendment) Act, 1940 (Internment Commission) Order, 1945 (No. 182 of 1945) (24 July 1945); *Parliamentary Debates, Dáil Éireann*, 4 July 1945, vol. 97, col. 1,881.
5. NAI, DT S 16274 A, Observations of the government on the application of Gearoid Ó Laighleis and Rory Brady to the European Commission of Human Rights, undated.
6. NAI, DT S 11837 B, Department of Defence memorandum, 3 November 1951.
7. See The Offences Against the State Act, s. 35 (4).
8. NAI, DT S 11837 B, Department of Defence memorandum, 3 November 1951.
9. NAI, DT S 11837 B, Defence memorandum, 3 November 1951 and Defence memorandum, 15 April 1953.
10. NAI, DT S 11837 B, Government minute, 21 April 1953; The Offences Against the State Act, s. 39 (1).
11. James Lydon, *The Making of Ireland: From Ancient Times to the Present* (London: Routledge, 1998), p. 383.
12. Roy Foster, *Modern Ireland: 1600–1972* (London: Allen Lane, 1988), p. 564; The Industrial Relations Act, 1946 (1946 no. 26) (27 August 1946).
13. Maurice Manning, *James Dillon: A Biography* (Dublin: Wolfhound Press, 1999), p. 200.
14. John Horgan, *Noel Browne: Passionate Outsider* (Dublin: Gill & MacMillan, 2000), p. 43. See Manning, *James Dillon*, pp. 210–15 for more on the Locke's Distillery controversy.
15. R. Dudley Edwards, *A New History of Ireland* (Dublin: Gill & MacMillan, 1972), p. 238.
16. Keogh, *Twentieth Century Ireland*, pp. 161–2.
17. Fisk, *In Time of War*, pp. 544–5.
18. Fanning, *Independent Ireland*, p. 161.
19. *Irish Independent*, 15 November 1945.
20. Bowman, *De Valera and the Ulster Question*, p. 258; Eithne MacDermott, *Clann na Poblachta* (Cork: Cork University Press, 1998), p. 1.
21. O'Halpin, *Defending Ireland*, p. 297.
22. Ní Bheachain, 'The lost republicans', p. 45; White, *Ruairí Ó Brádaigh*, p. 38; Ó Longaigh, *Emergency Law*, pp. 267–8; MacEoin, *The IRA in the Twilight Years*, p. 532. According to Tim Pat Coogan: 'Solitary confinement was rendered particularly solitary by having an empty cell on either side, while the warders wore rubber soles so that no sound percolated to the captives, who were not allowed to leave their cells for any reason, even to go to the lavatory.' See Coogan, *Ireland in the Twentieth Century*, p. 336.

23. Seán MacBride Papers [hereafter SMP], (Private Collection), McCaughey inquest, MacBride to Senator James Douglas, 27 May 1946. According to MacBride the authorities had no legal right to impose such punitive conditions as the law only made provision for the prison Visiting Committee to impose solitary confinement for a period of up to fourteen days. In addition, MacBride also claimed that under an old British statute from 1865 an inmate was also entitled to two hours of exercise in the fresh air every day.
24. Coogan, *Ireland in the Twentieth Century*, p. 336.
25. Ní Bheachain, 'The lost republicans', p. 48
26. *Irish Independent*, 29 April 1946.
27. *Irish Press*, 6 to 9 May 1946.
28. *Parliamentary Debates, Dáil Éireann*, 8 May 1946, vol. 100, col. 2,338.
29. *Irish Independent*, 9 and 10 May 1946; Ní Bheachain, 'The lost republicans', p. 49.
30. *Parliamentary Debates, Dáil Éireann*, 8 May 1946, vol. 100, cols 2,322, 2,497.
31. *Irish Independent*, 6–11 May 1946; *Irish Times*, 11 May 1946; Ní Bheachain, 'The lost republicans', p. 51. At the inquest it was found that McCaughey died of cardiac failure caused by 'inanition and dehydration resulting from a lack of food and fluid'.
32. *Irish Times*, 13 May 1946; *Irish Independent*, 13 May 1946. During the course of the inquest there were also a number of irregular practices that were subsequently highlighted by MacBride. Specifically, during the course of the proceedings the coroner openly consulted with the state solicitor. At one stage they left the room together for a period of five to ten minutes. In MacBride's opinion this was for the purpose of consulting with an official from the Department of Justice who was waiting in another room. See SMP, McCaughey Inquest, Notes concerning inquest on Seán McCaughey, undated.
33. *Irish Independent*, 13 May 1946.
34. Ní Bheachain, 'The lost republicans', pp. 39, 52.
35. *Irish Independent*, 22 May 1946; *Belfast Telegraph*, 22 May 1946.
36. *Parliamentary Debates, Dáil Éireann*, 29 May 1946, vol. 101, cols. 1,126, 1,159.
37. NAI, DT S 11515, Political prisoners: treatment of, 18 April 1940.
38. Ó Longaigh, *Emergency Law*, p. 268; *Irish Press*, 27 February 1948.
39. Lee, *Ireland*, p. 293; MacDermott, *Clann na Poblachta*, pp. 29–30.
40. Manning, *James Dillon*, p. 208.
41. MacBride, *That Day's Struggle*, p. 130.
42. MacDermott, *Clann na Poblachta*, p. 13; Colman Tadhg O'Sullivan, 'The IRA takes constitutional action: A history of Clann na Poblachta 1946–65' (MA thesis, National University of Ireland, Galway, 1997), pp. 15–16.
43. David McCullagh, *A Makeshift Majority: The First Inter-party Government, 1948–51* (Dublin: Institute of Public Administration, 1998), p. 65 and Manning, *James Dillon*, p. 208.
44. Lee, *Ireland*, p. 296.
45. Kevin Rafter, *The Clann: The Story of Clann na Poblachta* (Cork: Mercier Press, 1996), p. 32; Keogh, *Twentieth Century Ireland*, p. 175.
46. Fanning, *Independent Ireland*, p. 162; Rafter, *The Clann*, p. 37.
47. MacDermott, *Clann na Poblachta*, p. 14.
48. Keogh, *Twentieth Century Ireland*, p. 175; Fanning, *Independent Ireland*, p. 162.
49. Manning, *James Dillon*, p. 209.
50. MacDermott, *Clann na Poblachta*, p. 57; O'Sullivan, 'The IRA takes constitutional action', pp. 47–9.
51. Lee, *Ireland*, p. 299.
52. In the end the inter-party government collapsed not because of the 'Mother and Child' débâcle, but because it had lost the support of several independents, whose concerns were exclusively agricultural and local. Essentially the government collapsed over the price of milk. See Manning, *James Dillon*, p. 265. For more on the 'Mother and Child scandal' see Lee, *Ireland*, pp. 313–19, Keogh, *Twentieth Century Ireland*, pp. 210–13 and MacDermott, *Clann na Poblachta*, pp. 156–61.
53. O'Sullivan, 'The IRA takes constitutional action', pp. 51–2; Bowyer Bell, *The Secret Army*, pp. 243–4.
54. McCullagh, *A Makeshift Majority*, p. 65.
55. O'Sullivan, 'The IRA takes constitutional action', p. 51.
56. Gerard Hogan, 'The Sinn Féin funds judgment fifty years on', *Bar Review: Journal of the*

Bar of Ireland, vol. 2, no. 9, p. 375; Bernadette Whelan, *United States Foreign Policy and Ireland: From Empire to Independence, 1913–29* (Dublin: Four Courts Press, 2006), p. 523.
57. Hogan, 'The Sinn Féin funds judgment', p. 380; Feeney, *Sinn Féin*, p. 179. In fact the findings in the case were based on a technicality. When de Valera called a meeting in 1923 to try to resurrect Sinn Féin he ignored Sinn Féin's existing officers and Standing Committee, who, under the party's rules, were the only people empowered to call such a meeting.
58. NAI, DJ JUS8/1053, Garda memo, 19 July 1945.
59. NAI, DJ JUS8/1053, Garda memo, 23 April 1945.
60. *An Claidheamh*, vol. 1, no. 1, 1 November 1945.
61. NAI, DJ JUS8/1053, Copy of bulletin issued by coordinating committee of Sinn Féin, 7 July 1945.
62. NAI, DJ JUS8/1053, Garda report: inauguration of President of Ireland – display of black flag at 9 Parnell Square, 25 June 1945.
63. *Irish Independent*, 5 April 1946.
64. O'Halpin, *Defending Ireland*, p. 297.
65. Bowyer Bell, *The Secret Army*, pp. 241–3; Coogan, *The IRA*, p. 254; Edmonds, *The Gun*, p. 183.
66. NAI, DJ JUS8/953, Report of meeting under the auspices of 'Sinn Féin *Cumann* – Seán McCaughey', 18 May 1947.
67. Ó Broin, 5 March 2003.
68. NAI, DJ JUS8/953, Meeting of '*Cumann* – Seán McCaughey', 18 May 1947.
69. Bowyer Bell, *The Secret Army*, p. 242.
70. NAI, DJ JUS8/953, Proposed reissue of '*An Phoblacht*' meeting in 33 Gardiner's Place, 21 June 1947. 1941.
71. Ó Broin, 5 March 2003.
72. NAI, DJ JUS8/953, Copy of *United Irishman*, June 1948; Edmonds, *The Gun*, p. 186. In light of Edmonds' involvement with the IRA and his subsequent internment in 1957, the accuracy of these figures remains to be verified as he produces no evidence to back up his claim.
73. NAI, DJ JUS8/953, Department of Justice memo – 'Seditious utterances published in '*United Irishman*', undated.
74. *United Irishman*, May 1948.
75. Ó Broin, 5 March 2003; Edmonds, *The Gun*, p. 183. Edmonds also argued that this move was a major factor in the reorganization of the IRA, as it appealed 'to all that was idealistic in Irish youth [and concentrated] on the injustice of partition'.
76. *United Irishman*, May and September 1949.
77. Bower Bell, *The Secret Army*, p. 243; NAI, DJ JUS8/953, Garda memo, 27 May, 1947. In fact the RPRA was founded in 1945.
78. NAI, DJ JUS8/953, Garda memo, 27 May 1947.
79. Brian Feeney, *Sinn Féin: A Hundred Turbulent Years* (Dublin: O'Brien Press, 2002), p. 187.
80. Bowyer Bell, *The Secret Army*, p. 246.
81. It was during this Ard Fheis that the IRA also introduced a number of far-reaching amendments to the Sinn Féin constitution, committing the party to the establishment of 'social justice based on Christian principles, by a just distribution and effective control of the Nation's wealth and resources'. See White, *Ruairí Ó Brádaigh*, p. 49.
82. Feeney, *Sinn Féin*, pp. 187–90; Bowyer Bell, *The Secret Army*, p. 246.
83. Smith, *Fighting for Ireland*, p. 66.
84. Sinn Féin, *National Unity and Independence Programme* (private collection, 1952), p. 2.
85. Smith, *Fighting for Ireland*, pp. 66–7.
86. *United Irishman*, July–August, 1949.
87. NAI, DJ JUS8/1053, Garda report of meeting held at Middle Abbey Street, 22 January 1950; *Irish Times*, 17 March 1950; *Belfast Telegraph*, 17 March 1950. In fact the Ministry of Home Affairs dismissed this incident, claiming that spectators did not display 'the slightest interest' in the pamphlets.
88. *Parliamentary Debates, Dáil Éireann*, 24 February 1949, vol. 114, cols 492–501.
89. Enda Staunton, *The Nationalists of Northern Ireland* (Dublin: Columba Press, 2001), p. 162; Rafter, *The Clann*, p. 37.

90. Lee, *Ireland*, p. 301.
91. Keogh, *Twentieth Century Ireland*, pp. 191–2.
92. As a result of this piece of legislation Ireland was to formally leave the Commonwealth as this act vested the powers possessed by the King in the President of Ireland. See The Republic of Ireland Act, 1948 (1948 no. 22) (21 December 1948).
93. *Parliamentary Debates, Dáil Éireann*, 24 November 1948, vol. 113 col. 348.
94. National Archives, UK [hereafter NAUK], Cabinet Office [hereafter CAB] 21/1843, 'The writing on the wall', memorandum, Lord Rugby, November 1948.
95. NAUK, CAB21/1842, Republic of Ireland Bill: Effect on Northern Ireland, 3 December 1948.
96. NAUK, CAB21/1842, Brooke to Attlee, 2 December 1948.
97. NAUK, CAB 21/1842, Minutes of a meeting held at 10 Downing Street, 6 January 1949.
98. Staunton, *The Nationalists of Northern Ireland*, p. 163.
99. NAUK, CAB21/1843, *Aide Memoire* sent to Republic of Ireland, 7 May 1949.
100. Lee, *Ireland*, p. 300.
101. According to Bowyer Bell, while Clann na Poblachta and the Anti-Partition Association remained 'active and ... virile ... they had revealed the evils of a divided Ireland to many who had grown comfortable in the presence of the border. They had, however, devised no means to remove the border. Their methods – pacifism, propaganda and politics – had achieved nothing, no victory only words.' Bowyer Bell, *The Secret Army*, p. 249.
102. McCullagh, *A Makeshift Majority*, pp. 126–7.
103. NAUK, CAB21/1843, Memorandum, 23 February 1949; *Irish Times*, 16 May and 12 June 1950; *Belfast Telegraph*, 16 May and 28 June 1950. The formation of this body was dismissed in an editorial in the *Belfast Telegraph* as something about which Ulster Unionists are not likely 'to worry unduly'.
104. NAI, DEA A/12, G2 report on IRA organization, 27 October 1954 and memo re IRA and similar activities, undated; Bowyer Bell, *The Secret Army*, p. 249; O'Halpin, *Defending Ireland*, p. 298.
105. NAI, DEA A12, Memo re IRA and similar activities, June 1952 and untitled memorandum, undated.
106. White, *Ruairí Ó Brádaigh*, p. 39; R.F. Holland, *European Decolonisation 1918–1981: An Introductory Survey* (London: Macmillan, 1985), pp. 165, 250–2; Raymond F. Betts, *France and Decolonisation: 1900–1960* (London: MacMillan, 1991), p. 103; Eric Hobsbawm, *The Age of Extremes: 1914–1991* (London: Abacus Press, 2003), p. 438.
107. Kevin Hugh McCay, 'The IRA border campaign of 1956–62: A new perspective' (MPhil thesis, Trinity College Dublin, 1992), p. 11.
108. NAI, DEA A12, Memo re IRA and similar activities, June 1952.
109. Bowyer Bell, *The Secret Army*, p. 250; *The Belfast Telegraph*, 6 June 1951.
110. Coogan, *The IRA*, pp. 263–4.
111. *Irish Times*, 6 June 1951.
112. *United Irishman*, June 1951.
113. Coogan, *The IRA*, p. 264; Bowyer Bell, *The Secret Army*, pp. 256–7.
114. *Irish Times*, 28 July 1953.
115. *Irish Times*, 14 August 1953 and 7 October 1953.
116. White, *Ruairí Ó Brádaigh*, p. 47.
117. *Irish Times*, 7 and 8 October 1953; *Irish Press*, 7 October 1953; *Irish Independent*, 7 October 1953.
118. Coogan, *The IRA*, p. 277.
119. Coogan, *The IRA*, p. 278; Federal Bureau of Investigation [hereafter FBI], 61-7606 IRA part 4 of 7, Memorandum from New York to Director, FBI, 14 January 1955.
120. See *United Irishman*, October 1953.
121. NAI, DEA A12, American aid, January 1952.
122. *United Irishman*, January–February 1951; these columns were often titled 'American Notes', and 'For our American Readers'. See also *United Irishman*, April 1951; NAI, DEA A12, American aid for Irish militant organizations, January 1952.
123. *United Irishman*, October 1951.
124. NAI, DEA A12, American aid, January 1952. Prior to this the IRA had already been in receipt of some funding from the United States. In 1950 the sum of £1,000 was conveyed to the republican movement through the medium of a New York GAA delegate who was

attending a GAA convention in Dublin, while in 1952 an undisclosed member of the IRA confirmed that he was in possession of $1,500 which was destined for it.
125. NAI, DEA, A12, American aid, January 1952.
126. NAI, DEA A12, American aid, January 1952.
127. *United Irishman*, January–February and April 1951.
128. Bowyer Bell claims that it occurred in 1948. Bowyer Bell, *The Secret Army*, p. 245.
129. NAI, DEA A12, Memo re IRA and similar organizations, 19 December 1951.
130. *Irish Times*, 5 January 1951.
131. NAI, DEA A12, Memo re IRA and similar organizations, 19 December 1951.
132. NAI, DEA A12, Memo re IRA and similar activities, undated. As part of this agreement the IRA decided to use Arm na Saoirse for the training of some of its new recruits as it was felt that they would be less likely to attract the attention of the authorities than if they were training with the IRA.
133. Patterson, *Politics of Illusion*, p. 79–80.
134. *Parliamentary Debates, Seanad Éireann*, 25 November 1954, vol. 44, col. 368.
135. NAI, AGO GLP, Box No. 1, Observations of the government of Ireland to the Applications of Gearoid Ó Laighleis, undated; *Irish Times*, 28 November 1954.
136. Public Record Office of Northern Ireland [hereafter PRONI], Department of Home Affairs [hereafter HA] /32/1/971, Copy of reply by the leader of the Senate to a private notice question about the raid on Roslea Barracks, undated; *Irish Times*, 29 November 1955.
137. Coogan, *The IRA*, p. 286.
138. *Irish Times*, 29 November 1955.
139. *Parliamentary Debates, Dáil Éireann*, 30 November 1955, vol. 153, cols. 1,336–1,350.
140. *Irish Times*, 28 November 1958.
141. NAI DEA, 98/3/127, Garda memo re Gerard Lawless, 18 December 1958 and Observations of the Irish government on the reply of Gearoid Ó Laighleis (Gerard Lawless) to the submissions made by the said government on his application under article 25 of the European Convention for the Protection of Human Rights and Fundamental Freedoms (ECHR), 25 March 1958.
142. A Fianna Fáil government headed by de Valera assumed power following the collapse of the inter-party government in the wake of the 'Mother and Child' affair in 1951.
143. Manning, *James Dillon*, pp. 290–3.
144. *United Irishman*, May 1953.
145. *Irish Times*, 9 June 1953.
146. *Irish Press*, 16 June 1953.
147. *Irish Times*, 3 July 1953.
148. *Irish Independent*, 12 June 1954.
149. White, *Ruairí Ó Brádaigh*, pp. 47–9; Bowyer Bell, *The Secret Army*, pp. 259–61; Coogan, *The IRA*, p. 264–6; Edmonds, *The Gun*, pp. 184–6; English, *Armed Struggle*, p. 72; *Irish Times*, 14 June 1954; *United Irishman*, July 1954, McGarrity, *Resistance*, pp. 58–9.
150. *Irish Times*, 14 June 1954; *United Irishman*, July 1954.
151. *Irish Times*, 14 June 1954.
152. *United Irishman*, July 1954.
153. *Irish Times*, 14 June 1954.
154. Coogan, *The IRA*, p. 266; Edmonds, *The Gun*, p. 186; O'Halpin, *Defending Ireland*, p. 298.
155. Bowyer Bell, *The Secret Army*, p. 261.
156. McGarrity, *Resistance*, p. 59.
157. Arthur Hezlet, *The 'B' Specials: A History of the Ulster Special Constabulary* (Belfast: Mourne River Press, 1977), pp. 154–5; Bowyer Bell, *The Secret Army*, p. 262; Coogan, *The IRA*, pp. 266–7; NAI, DJ JUS8/1022, Extract from weekly report, 18 October 1954.
158. *Irish Times*, 18 October 1954; NAI, DJ JUS8/1022, Extract from weekly report, 18 October 1954. The wounded raiders were Joe Christle and Joe Mac Liatháin. See White, *Ruairí Ó Brádaigh*, p. 49; Hezlet, *The 'B' Specials*, pp. 155–6; NAI, DJ JUS8/1022, Weekly report 18 October 1954.
159. NAI, DEA 305/14/263, Consulate General, New York to Secretary, Department of External Affairs, 18 October 1954.
160. *Irish Times*, 18 October 1954.

161. *Parliamentary Debates, Dáil Éireann*, 28 October 1954, vol. 147, col. 179.
162. *Irish Times*, 29 October 1954; Bowman, *De Valera and the Ulster Question*, pp. 288–9.
163. NAUK, Admiralty [hereafter ADM] 26778, Memo: precautions against raids by the IRA in England, Scotland and Wales, 12 December 1955.
164. NAUK, ADM/26705, Admiralty to Commander-in-Chief Plymouth, Portsmouth and The Nore, 16 August 1955; WO32/20713, Memo: dogs for security, 17 August 1955. For full details of the security review see NAUK, ADM/26186, ADM/26705, ADM/26711, ADM/26778, AIR2/14478 and WO32/20713.
165. NAUK, Dominions Office [hereafter DO] 35/4984, Note of discussion on IRA activities held at the Home Office, 30 July 1954.
166. NAUK, DO35/4984, Walter Hankinson to A. Strutt, undated.
167. NAUK, DO35/4985, Conversation between Boland and Liesching, 8 November 1954.
168. NAUK, DO35/4985, Record of conversation between the Secretary of State for Commonwealth Relations and Mr. F. Boland, 24 January 1955.
169. NAUK, DO35/4985, Conversation between the Secretary of State for Commonwealth Relations and Boland, 24 January 1955.
170. NAI, DJ JUS8/953, cutting from *United Irishman*, 3 September 1951.
171. O'Halpin, *Defending Ireland*, p. 299.
172. See Ferriter, *Transformation of Ireland*, pp. 488–9; Bowyer Bell, *The Secret Army*, p. 303; Lee, *Ireland*, p. 327; O'Sullivan, 'The IRA takes constitutional action', pp. 115–32.
173. NAI, DEA 2001/43/1440, Memo: Sinn Féin and external relations, 12 March 1953; Sinn Féin, *National Unity and Independence Programme* (undated), p. 5.
174. White, *Ruairí Ó Brádaigh*, pp. 49–50.
175. Staunton, *The Nationalists of Northern Ireland*, pp. 185, 296.
176. NAI, DEA 2001/43/1440, Boland to Nunan, 16 April 1955.
177. White, *Ruairí Ó Brádaigh*, p. 50; *United Irishman*, June 1955.
178. Feeney, *Sinn Féin*, pp. 201–2; White, *Ruairí Ó Brádaigh*, p. 50; *Irish Press*, 12 August 1955.
179. *Irish Press*, 12 and 13 August 1955. In a 90 per cent poll he trebled has majority, winning 30,392 votes.
180. *Re Mid–Ulster Election Petition: Beattie V Mitchell* [1958] NI 143, p. 3.
181. Feeney, *Sinn Féin*, pp. 201–2; White *Ruairí Ó Brádaigh*, p. 50.
182. McKay, 'The IRA border campaign', p. 24.
183. *Irish Times*, 17 August 1955; *Irish Press*, 15 and 16 August 1955; White, *Ruairí Ó Brádaigh*, pp. 52–5; Bowyer Bell, *The Secret Army*, pp. 273–5; Coogan, *The IRA*, p. 268.
184. See NAI DEA, 305/14/263/5.
185. Des Fogerty, *Seán South of Garryowen* (Limerick: FX Press, 2006), p. 50; Seán Scott, 'Training for the border campaign', in Des Long (ed.), *Awakening the Spirit of Freedom* (Limerick: Ryan Printers, 2006), p. 32
186. University College Dublin Archives [hereafter UCDA], John A. Costello Papers [hereafter JACP] P190/763, Review of IRA activities, 19 March 1957.
187. White, *Ruairí Ó Brádaigh*, p. 56.
188. NAI, DJ JUS8/1061, Copy of 'Operation Harvest', undated; McGarrity, *Resistance*, p. 36; *Irish Times*, 18 January 1957; Bowyer Bell, *The Secret Army*, p. 283; McKay, 'The IRA border campaign', pp. 18–19.
189. White, *Ruairí Ó Brádaigh*, pp. 57–60.
190. *Saoirse: Irish Freedom*, January 1997; Staunton, *The Nationalists of Northern Ireland*, p. 185, 296.
191. Bowyer Bell, *The Secret Army*, pp. 284–5

CHAPTER 4

1. McGarrity, *Resistance*, pp. 23–4.
2. *United Irishman Bulletin*, 15 December 1956; White, *Ruairí Ó Brádaigh*, p. 59.
3. Bardon, *A History of Ulster*, p. 605.
4. *Irish Press* 12 and 13 December 1956.
5. McGarrity, *Resistance*, p. 25.
6. *Irish Times*, 13 December 1956; Bowyer Bell, *The Secret Army*, p. 290.

7. *Irish Press*, 12 December 1956.
8. *Irish Times*, 12 and 13 December 1956; *Irish Press*, 12 December 1956; Bowyer Bell, *The Secret Army*, p. 289. It was later reported that the caretaker and his family were taken in a car for three miles before they were released.
9. *Irish Independent*, 13 December 1956.
10. Hezlet, *The 'B' Specials*, p. 163; Bowyer Bell, *The Secret Army*, p. 289; McGarrity, *Resistance*, p. 25; *Irish Times*, 12 and 13 December 1956; *Irish Press*, 12 and 13 December 1956; *Irish Independent*, 13 December 1956.
11. *United Irishman Bulletin*, 15 December 1956; McGarrity, *Resistance*, p. 24.
12. *Irish Times*, 13 December 1956; *Cork Examiner*, 13 December 1956.
13. *Irish Press*, 13 & 14 December 1956.
14. *Irish Times*, 14 December 1956.
15. *Irish Press*, 13 December 1956; *Irish Independent*, 13 December 1956.
16. Seán Garland, 'Memorial to Seán Sabhat, volunteer of the Irish Republican Army, who died at Brookeborough, Co. Fermanagh with his comrade, volunteer Fergal O'Hanlon on 1 January, 1957', in Long, *Awakening the Spirit of Freedom*, p. 90.
17. *Irish Times*, 12 & 13 December 1956; *Irish Press*, 12 & 13 December 1956; *Irish Independent*, 13 December 1956; Bowyer Bell, *The Secret Army*, p. 290.
18. *Irish Press*, 13 December 1956. The raiders in question were twenty-three-year-old Seamus Houston and nineteen-year-old James Oliver Smith. Accused of attempted murder, the charges arose from an incident during the course of their arrest when they exchanged shots with Special Constabulary instructor Joseph McCaughey.
19. McGarrity, *Resistance*, pp. 23–4; *United Irishman Bulletin*, 15 December 1956.
20. Garland, 'Memorial to Seán Sabhat', p. 91.
21. *United Irishman Bulletin*, 15 December 1956.
22. *Irish Times*, 13 December 1956.
23. NAUK, DO35/4984, Dublin embassy to Commonwealth Relations Office, 12 April 1955.
24. Bowyer Bell, *The Secret Army*, p. 289; Hezlet, *The 'B' Specials*, pp. 162–3.
25. *Irish Press*, 13 December 1956; *Belfast Telegraph*, 12 December 1956. Sir Basil Brooke was created Viscount Brookeborough on 1 July 1952.
26. *Irish Times*, 13 December 1956; McKay, 'The IRA border campaign', pp. 29–30.
27. Hezlet, *The 'B' Specials*, p. 163.
28. *Cork Examiner*, 15 December 1956; *Irish Independent*, 15 December 1956; Civil Authorities (Special Powers) Act (Northern Ireland), 1922 (1922 no. 4) (7 April, 1922), s.1 (1); White, *Ruairí Ó Brádaigh*, p. 59.
29. *Irish Independent*, 15 December 1956; *The Times*, 15 December 1956; The National Council for Civil Liberties [hereafter NCCL], *Report of a Commission of Inquiry Appointed to Examine the Purpose and Effect of the Civil Authorities (Special Powers) Acts (Northern Ireland) 1922 & 1933* (London, 1972), p. 19.
30. See The Offences Against the State (Amendment) Act, s. 9.
31. The Civil Authorities (Special Powers) Act (Northern Ireland), §. 23; NCCL, *Report of a commission*, pp. 18–20; Anderson, *Joe Cahill*, pp. 138, 147. In fact the last time the power of internment was technically used in Northern Ireland was during the period 1922–25, when republicans were held in 'the worst possible conditions' on an old hulk, the SS *Argenta*, which was anchored in Larne Harbour. For more see Denise Kleinrichert, *Republican Internment and the Prison Ship "Argenta", 1922* (Dublin: Irish Academic Press, 2001).
32. *The Times*, 14 December 1956; *Irish Press*, 14 December 1956.
33. *Irish Times*, 14 December 1956.
34. McGarrity, *Resistance*, p. 25.
35. Patrick O'Regan, 'Pearse column spearheaded operation harvest', and Garland, 'Memorial to Seán Sabhat', in Long, *Awakening the Spirit of Freedom*, pp. 9, 90.
36. By June 1958 there were 184 republicans detained as 'political internees' within Crumlin Road. See PRONI, HA/32/1/1333, List of persons held as internees in H.M. Prison Belfast, 25 June 1958.
37. PRONI, HA/32/1/1333, Copy of the report of the International Red Cross on a visit to Belfast Prison, 15 July 1958 and List of persons held as internees at H.M. Prison, Belfast, 25 June 1958; Anderson, *Joe Cahill*, p. 147.
38. PRONI, HA/32/1/1333, Whitten to Ministry of Home Affairs, undated. One internee, named 'Doyle' was singled out for keeping his cell in 'spotless order', while another, P.

McGuinness', was criticized for the squalid condition of his cell, owing to his refusal to 'clean or in any way tidy'.
39. PRONI, HA/32/1/1333, Report of Red Cross, 15 July 1958 and Whitten to Ministry of Home Affairs, undated; Anderson, *Joe Cahill*, p. 147.
40. PRONI, HA/32/1/1333, Report of the Red Cross, 15 July 1958.
41. Anderson, *Joe Cahill*, p. 144.
42. PRONI, HA/32/1/1333, Whitten to Ministry of Home Affairs, undated.
43. UCDA, JACP P190/763, Copy of 'The Irish border raids' by Garret FitzGerald, undated.
44. The Suez crisis, which was inaugurated by Gamal Abdul Nasser's nationalisation of the Suez Canal in July 1956 threatened to upset traditional British and French imperial interests in the Middle East. In an attempt to secure international control of the canal, the British and French initiated a combined military strike against Egypt following an Israeli invasion in October 1956. Ostensibly launched in a bid to protect the canal zone, Britain and France continued with their joint military action in the face of a UN Security Council resolution. Only when the USSR threatened to intervene on behalf of Egypt did the British agree to a ceasefire coupled with the promise to create a UN force for the area. Significantly, no international control of the canal was promised or achieved; the affair undermined Britain's ability to operate as a world power and marked a shift in the global balance of power to the United States and the Soviet Union. See Holland, *European Decolonisation*, pp. 191–200; Leon D. Epstein, 'Partisan foreign policy: Britain in the Suez crisis', *World Politic*, vol. 12, no. 2 (January 1960), pp. 201–24.
45. McKay, 'The IRA border campaign', p. 26.
46. *The Times*, 13 December 1956.
47. *Irish Times*, 13 December 1956.
48. *Irish Press*, 14 December 1956.
49. *Irish Times*, 15 December 1956; *Irish Press*, 15 December 1956; *Irish Independent* 15 December 1956; *The Times*, 15 December 1956.
50. *Irish Press*, 15 December 1956.
51. McCay, 'The IRA border campaign', p. 26; *Irish Times*, 20 December 1956.
52. UCDA, JACP P190/73, Brief suggestions re border incidents, undated.
53. *Irish Times*, 17 December 1956; *Irish Press*, 17 December 1956.
54. *Irish Press*, 17 December 1956; *Irish Independent*, 17 December 1956.
55. *Irish Times*, 17 December 1956.
56. *The Times*, 17 December 1956.
57. According to Eunan O'Halpin there is no doubt that the state's initial reaction to the IRA campaign was complicated by Costello's reliance on Clann na Poblachta to maintain his government. See O'Halpin, *Defending Ireland*, p. 299.
58. *Irish Independent*, 31 October 1955.
59. O'Sullivan, 'The IRA takes constitutional action', p. 118.
60. *Irish Independent*, 18 December 1956.
61. *Irish Times*, 18 December 1956; *The Times* 18 December 1956.
62. *The Times*, 18 December 1956; *Irish Press*, 18 December 1956.
63. *Irish Times*, 18 December 1956.
64. *Irish Times*, 19 December 1956; *The Times*, 19 December 1956; McGarrity, *Resistance*, p. 26.
65. NAI, DEA A12/1A, *Aide Memoire*, 18 January 1956 and *Aide Memoire*, 6 February 1956.
66. *Irish Independent*, 19 December 1956; McGarrity, *Resistance*, p. 26.
67. *Irish Press*, 19 December 1956.
68. *The Times*, 20 December 1956.
69. Section 30 provides for the arrest and detention without warrant of any person whom a member of the Gárda Síochána suspects of having committed or being about to commit or being concerned in the commission of any offence under any sub-section of the OASA. See The Offences Against the State Act, s. 30 (1); *Irish Times*, 20 December 1956; *Irish Independent*, 20 December 1956; *Limerick Leader*, 22 December 1956.
70. *Irish Independent*, 19 December 1956; *The Times*, 20 December 1956.
71. *Irish Times*, 21 December 1956.
72. UCDA, JACP P190/763 copy of *aide memoire*, 24 December 1956. The text of this *aide memoire* was widely published in the press. See *Irish Times*, 24 December 1956; *Irish Press*, 24 December 1956; *Irish Independent*, 24 December 1956.

73. White, *Ruairí Ó Brádaigh*, p. 59; The *Times*, 22 December 1956; *Irish Times*, 22 December 1956.
74. NAI, DJ JUS8/1046, Supt., Ballyconnell to Chief Supt., Monaghan, 28 December 1956 and Supt. Division of Sligo/Leitrim, to Commissioner C(3), 31 December 1956.
75. NAI, DEA 98/3/127, Observations of the Irish government, 25 March 1958.
76. See The Civil Authorities (Special Powers) Act, § 1 & 12; *Irish Times*, 22 December 1956.
77. *Irish Independent*, 22 December 1956.
78. *The Times*, 24 December 1956; *Irish Times*, 24 December 1956.
79. Bowyer Bell, *The Secret Army*, p. 295; Garland, 'Memorial to Seán Sabhat', p. 91.
80. *United Irishman Bulletin*, 22 December 1956.
81. According to Joe Cahill, Belfast was the home to the IRA's northern base and had figured largely in republican operations since before the partition of Ireland. See Anderson, *Joe Cahill*, p. 135.
82. Patterson, *Politics of Illusion*, p. 82; McCay, 'The IRA border campaign', p. 20. According to McCay, he spoke to several unnamed republicans who were at pains to point out that Belfast was not targeted over fears that it would 'spark off a sectarian war'.
83. White, *Ruairí Ó Brádaigh*, p. 58.
84. Staunton, *The Nationalists of Northern Ireland*, p. 225. On one occasion an attempt to destroy a transmitter on the Black Mountain had to be abandoned when an RUC party staked out the area.
85. Anderson, *Joe Cahill*, pp. 128–34. In Cahill's opinion the decision to exclude Belfast was incomprehensible to many of the city's volunteers and was viewed by some as an insult.
86. PRONI, HA/32/1/1349, Report of Inspector General, Crime Special Branch, 11 January 1957.
87. *The Times*, 24 December 1956.
88. White, *Ruairí Ó Brádaigh*, p. 59; Bowyer Bell, *The Secret Army*, p. 294.
89. *The Times*, 29 December 1956.
90. *Irish Times*, 27 December 1956. This was simply one of a series of similar incidents. The B-Specials were also involved in shooting at an RUC jeep in error and the shooting of several members of the same family in Tyrone who were making their way home after attending a New Year's Eve party. See *Irish Press*, 2 January 1957; Bowyer Bell, *The Secret Army*, p. 294.
91. *Irish Times*, 29 December 1956; *Irish Press*, 1 January 1957; *The Times*, 1 January 1957.
92. *Irish Times*, 31 December 1956; *Irish Press*, 31 December 1956; *Irish Independent* 31 December 1956; *The Times*, 31 December 1956; Bowyer Bell, *The Secret Army*, pp. 294–7; Hezlet, *The 'B' Specials*, p. 165; White, *Ruairí Ó Brádaigh*, pp. 61–2.
93. *Irish Times*, 31 December 1956.
94. White, *Ruairí Ó Brádaigh*, p. 63.
95. *Irish Times*, 1 January 1957; Bowyer Bell, *The Secret Army*, p. 297. To be accorded prisoner of war status under the Geneva Convention combatants who form a militia or an organized resistance movement must fulfil the following conditions: (a) that of being commanded by a person responsible for his subordinates, (b) that of having a fixed distinctive sign recognizable at a distance, (c) that of carrying arms openly and (d) that of conducting their operations in accordance with the laws and customs of war. In an effort to fulfil these criteria and distinguish themselves from the civilian population, IRA volunteers often wore boiler suits or forms of battledress with distinctive tricolour flashes on their left shoulders. See White, *Ruairí Ó Brádaigh*, p. 59. When the British and Irish governments proceeded to deal with these men under the civil law the IRA accused them of flouting the convention. See The Geneva Convention Relative to the Treatment of Prisoners of War, 12 August 1949, s. 4; *United Irishman*, January 1957.
96. *Irish Times*, 1 January 1957.
97. Fogerty, *Seán South*, p. 97.
98. Interview with Patrick O'Regan, 31 August 2006.
99. O'Regan, 31 August 2006.
100. O'Regan, 31 August 2006.
101. Garland, 'Memorial to Seán Sabhat', p. 92.
102. Ernside (pseudonym), 'The decoy ambush before the Brookebrough raid', in Long, *Awakening the Spirit of Freedom*, pp. 24–8. In this account an unidentified republican, writing under the pseudonym 'Ernside', describes how he and an unnamed associate,

known simply as 'John', had been tasked to take this bomb to a location near Tullynevin, Co. Fermanagh, on the night of 27 December 1957. After trekking cross-country, 'John' slipped and dropped the bomb into a drain full of water. Recognizing that the bomb was now useless, 'John' decided that they should abandon their task and return home. The next day, Ernside was informed by local republican Frank Maguire that the bomb had been intended as a decoy to lure an RUC patrol into an ambush. On 30 December Maguire instructed Ernside to retrieve the bomb and deliver it to Daithí Ó Conaill at an isolated farmhouse in the area. When making the drop, Ernside reported his grave doubts about the effectiveness of the bomb to Ó Conaill who assured him that 'he would check it'.
103. *Irish Times* 2 January 1957; *Irish Press*, 2 January 1957; *Irish Independent*, 2 January 1957; *The Times*, 2 January 1957; Roinn Eolas an Poblachta, *They Kept Faith: In this Tribute to Two Soldiers of Ireland the Full Story of the Brookeborough Attack in which they Lost their Lives is Now Told by their Comrades* (Dublin: Irish Freedom Press, 1957), p. 9; Bowyer Bell, *The Secret Army*, pp. 297–8; Coogan, *The IRA*, pp. 312–15; McGarrity, *Resistance*, p. 31. For a detailed account of the raid and its aftermath see Mainchín Seoighe, *Maraíodh Seán Sabhat Aréir* (Dublin: Sáirséal agus Dill, 1964), pp. 15–21.
104. O'Regan, 31 August 2006.
105. Bowyer Bell, *The Secret Army*, p. 298–9; Roinn Eolas an Poblachta, *They Kept Faith*, p. 11; *Irish Times*, 2 and 3 January 1957; *The Times*, 2 January 1957.
106. *Irish Times*, 4 January 1957. This view was given added credence in later years by Pat O'Regan who visited the disused shed where South and O'Hanlon were left. According to O'Regan, on examining the shed he observed a number of bullet marks on the back wall opposite the entrance. He concluded from this that someone had fired through the open door from the outside. To shoot South and O'Hanlon he would have had to enter the shed while 'continuously emptying a magazine shooting at one man, spray the back wall and then shoot the second man lying on the floor, O'Regan, 31 August 2006; Coogan, *The IRA*, p. 315.
107. Padraigín Ní Mhurchú, 'Fergal O'Hanlon, a young life linked forever with Seán Sabhat', in Long, *Awakening the Spirit of Freedom*, p. 29; *United Irishman*, January 1957.
108. *Limerick Socialist*, January 1977.
109. O'Sullivan, 'The IRA takes constitutional action', p. 127.
110. Roinn Eolas na Poblachta, *They Kept Faith*, p. 6; *Limerick Socialist*, January 1972.
111. *Limerick Socialist*, January 1972; Fogerty, *Seán South*, p. 31. For more on Maria Duce, see Enda Delaney, 'Political Catholicism in post war Ireland: The Revd. Denis Fahey and Maria Duce, 1945–54', *Journal of Ecclesiastical History* vol. 52, no. 3 (July, 2001), pp. 487–511.
112. The *Limerick Leader* published a series of letters outlining South's view on this matter. See: *Limerick Leader*, 3 & 24 January 1949.
113. Fogerty, *Seán South*, p. 51.
114. *Limerick Leader*, 5 January 1957.
115. *Irish Times*, 4 January 1957; *Irish Press*, 4 & 5 January 1957.
116. NAI, DJ JUS8/1043, Chief Supt., Drogheda to Commissioner C(3), 8 January 1957.
117. NAI, DJ JUS8/1043, Drogheda to C(3), 8 January 1957.
118. *Irish Press*, 5 January 1957.
119. *Irish Times*, 5 January 1957.
120. *Limerick Chronicle*, 5 January 1957.
121. NAI, DJ JUS8/1043, Garda report re IRA activities and funeral of late Seán South, 47 Henry Street Limerick, 7 January 1957.
122. *Limerick Chronicle*, 5 January 1957.
123. NAI, DJ JUS8/1043, Funeral of late Seán South, 7 January 1957.
124. English, *Armed Struggle*, p. 74; Bowyer Bell, *The Secret Army*, p. 300; Ferriter, *Transformation of Ireland*, pp. 487–8; Lee, *Ireland*, pp. 222–4.
125. *United Irishman*, January 1957; *Irish Times*, 8 January 1957.
126. Bowman, *De Valera and the Ulster Question*, p. 290; *The Times*, 7 January 1957.
127. *Irish Independent*, 7 January 1957; *Irish Times*, 7 January 1957; *The Times*, 7 January 1957.
128. *Irish Times*, 7 January 1957.
129. Edmonds, *The Gun*, p. 193.
130. More often than not they were either charged under section 21 for being a member of an

unlawful organization or under section 52, for failing to account for their movements. See The Offences Against the State Act, s. 21 & 52.
131. Edmonds, *The Gun*, p. 192; *Irish Times*, 23 January 1957; *Irish Press*, 23 January 1957; *Irish Independent*, 23 January 1957; *Cork Examiner*, 23 January 1957.
132. White, *Ruairí Ó Brádaigh*, pp. 65–70.
133. See The Courts of Justice (District Court) Act, 1946 (1946, no. 21) (29 July 1946) s. 21.
134. UCDA, JACP P190/792, Courts of Justice (District Court) Act, 1946 section 21, report to James Everett, Minister for Justice, 24 February 1957 and addendum to report, 16 March 1957.
135. Manning, *James Dillon*, pp. 306–10.
136. McGarrity, *Resistance*, p. 35; Bowyer Bell, *The Secret Army*, p. 300; *Irish Times*, 9 January 1957.
137. UCDA, JACP P190/763, Mulcahy to Costello, 14 January 1957.
138. *Irish Times*, 18 January 1957; *The Times*, 18 January 1957.
139. NAI, DT S16209 A, G.P. Fitzgerald, Australia, 23 January 1957, Melbourne Telegram, undated, Irish Republican Prisoners Aid Committee, San Francisco branch, 31 January 1957.
140. Writing under the pseudonym 'J. McGarrity', Seán Cronin also expressed this view. See McGarrity, *Resistance*, p. 35.
141. *United Irishman*, February 1957; *The Times*, 19 January 1957; *Irish Times*, 19 January 1957; *Irish Press*, 19 January 1957; McGarrity, *Resistance*, p. 41.
142. Michael Kennedy, *Division and Consensus: The Politics of Irish Cross-border Relations, 1925–1969* (Dublin: Institute of Public Administration, 2000), p. 1.
143. Jason Lane, 'The development of Irish cross–border police co-operation' (PhD thesis, Queen's University Belfast, 1999), p. 146.
144. NAUK, DO121/219, Note of conversation between Swinton and Cosgrave, 4 November 1954.
145. O'Halpin, *Defending Ireland*, pp. 298–9.
146. Sir John Hermon, *Holding the Line: An Autobiography* (Dublin: Gill & MacMillan, 1997), p. 37.
147. O'Sullivan, 'The IRA takes constitutional action', p. 128.
148. *Irish Times*, 10 January 1957.
149. *Irish Times*, 15 January 1957; O'Sullivan, 'The IRA takes constitutional action', p. 129; Bowyer Bell, *The Secret Army*, p. 301.
150. O'Sullivan, 'The IRA takes constitutional action', p. 129; *Irish Times*, 19 January 1957; *Irish Press*, 19 January 1957; Bowyer Bell, *The Secret Army*, p. 301.
151. Bowyer Bell, *The Secret Army*, p. 301.
152. *Irish Times*, 23 January 1957.
153. NAI, DT S 16209 A, Taoiseach's reply to letters from the USA re IRA activities in Ireland, undated.
154. NAI, DT S 16209 A, Copy of reply sent to John Devine, 22 February 1957.
155. NAI, DT S 16209 A, Kearns to Costello, 16 March 1957.
156. NAI, DEA A12/4, Consulate General, New York to External Affairs, 16 February 1957.
157. NAI, DEA A12/4, External Affairs to Consulate General, New York, 16 February 1957.
158. NAI, DEA A12/4, Consulate General, New York to Secretary, External Affairs, undated.
159. O'Sullivan, 'The IRA takes constitutional action', p. 129.
160. Lee, *Ireland*, pp. 326–7; Keogh, *Ireland in the Twentieth Century*, p. 232.
161. O'Sullivan, 'The IRA takes constitutional action', pp. 129, 132; Lee, *Ireland*, p. 327.
162. *Irish Press*, 29 January 1957.
163. *The Times*, 29 January 1957.
164. White, *Ruairí Ó Brádaigh*, p. 74.
165. Manning, *James Dillon*, p. 311.
166. *Irish Times*, 4 February 1957; UCDA, JACP 35c/199, Costello address to Fine Gael Ard Fheis, 6 February 1957.
167. Bowman, *De Valera and the Ulster Question*, pp. 290–1.
168. *Irish Times*, 14 February 1957.
169. *United Irishman*, February and March 1957.
170. *Irish Times*, 13, 15 and 18 February 1957; *Irish Press*, 18 February 1957.
171. In Waterford five men were sentenced to three months' imprisonment on arms charges;

in Dundalk, two individuals were sentenced in Dundalk District Court to four months and two months respectively for offences under the OASA. In Northern Ireland seven Dublin students were detained by the RUC and, in Belfast, seven men arrested in a farm in Co. Down were returned for trial on charges relating to the possession of arms and membership of an illegal organization. See *Irish Times*, 30 January 1957, 31 January 1957, 1 February 1957, 9 February 1957.
172. White, *Ruairí Ó Brádaigh*, p. 70; Bowyer Bell, *The Secret Army*, p. 304.
173. *Irish Times*, 14 & 18 February 1957.
174. *Irish Times*, 4 March 1957; *The Times*, 4 March 1957; Bowyer Bell, *The Secret Army*, p. 302.
175. *The Times*, 6 & 7 March 1957.
176. White, *Ruairí Ó Brádaigh*, p. 75; Bowyer Bell, *The Secret Army*, p. 303; *Irish Times*, 8 March 1957; *Irish Press*, 7 March 1957.
177. Keogh, *Twentieth Century Ireland*, p. 233; *Irish Times*, 8 March 1957; Lee, *Ireland*, p. 327.
178. White, *Ruairí Ó Brádaigh*, p. 75.
179. *United Irishman*, April 1957.
180. Smith, *Fighting for Ireland*, p. 69; Bowyer Bell, *The Secret Army*, p. 304.
181. Bowman, *De Valera and the Ulster Question*, p. 289.
182. Earl of Longford and T.P. O'Neill, *Éamon de Valera* (London: Hutchinson, 1970), p. 444.
183. Bowman, *De Valera and the Ulster Question*, p. 290.
184. *Irish Times*, 9 March 1957.
185. *Parliamentary Debates, Dáil Éireann*, 20 March 1957, vol. 161, col. 25.
186. O' Halpin, *Defending Ireland*, pp. 299–300.

CHAPTER 5

1. *Limerick Leader*, 13 July 1957.
2. *The Northern Whig*, 9 March 1957.
3. *Irish Times*, 9 March 1957.
4. *Parliamentary Debates, Dáil Éireann*, 26 March 1957, vol. 161, cols 92–103.
5. Established in January 1957 by the Inspector General of the RUC, it was presided over by the Deputy Inspector General and consisted of the Army Chief of Staff of the Northern Ireland District, the Commander of 39 Infantry Brigade, the Staff Officer of the Ulster Special Constabulary and two County Inspectors of the RUC headquarters staff.
6. Hezlet, *The 'B' Specials*, pp. 169–170.
7. *The Times*, 7 March 1957.
8. *Irish Times*, 8 March 1957.
9. *Limerick Leader*, 27 February 1957.
10. *Irish Times*, 11 March 1957.
11. *Irish Press*, 12 March, 1957; *Limerick Leader*, 11 March 1957; *The Times*, 12 March 1957.
12. *Irish Times*, 13 March and 1 April 1957; *Irish Press*, 1 April 1957; Hezlet, *The 'B' Specials*, p. 168. The following items were discovered: 300 lbs of gelignite, a quantity of bombs, three revolvers, one German automatic pistol, 150 yards of coil for detonating bombs, one Thompson sub-machine gun, one Mauser automatic pistol, twenty rounds of .303 ammunition, 200 rounds of Thompson sub-machine gun ammunition and 100 rounds of .45 ammunition,
13. Hezlet, *The 'B' Specials*, pp. 169–70. These new regulations emphasized that the assent of the government was needed for every mobilization, and payment could not be made until reports had been received and approved. Moreover, in the event of a sudden emergency, a county commandant was required to obtain the permission of an RUC county inspector, who was required to report to headquarters in Belfast.
14. *Irish Times*, 19 February 1957.
15 *The Times*, 29 March 1957.
16. NAUK, DO35/7810, Lintott to Clutterbuck, 5 April 1957.
17. NAUK, DO35/7810, Londonderry station incident, undated, and Lintott to Clutterbuck, 5 April 1957.

18. NAUK, DO35/7810, Clutterbuck to Commonwealth Relations Office, 15 April 1957.
19. NAUK, DO35/7810, Draft reply, undated.
20. NAI, DJ JUS8/1046, Superintendent's Office, division of Sligo/Leitrim to Commissioner C(3), 31 December 1956.
21. NAUK, DO35/7810, Commonwealth Relations Office to Kimber, Dublin, 21 May 1957 and War Office to Treasury, 22 May 1957.
22. NAI, DJ JUS8/1046, Incident at Scotstown border, Ballyconnell, 10 January 1957.
23. NAI, DJ JUS8/1046, Superintendent's office, Ballyshannon, Co. Donegal, report re: incidents concerning British military at Pettigo border, Co. Donegal, 6 February 1957.
24. NAI, DJ JUS8/1046, Incidents concerning British military at Pettigo, 6 February 1957.
25. NAI, DJ JUS8/1134, Chief Superintendent Downey to Commissioner C3, 31 August 1961.
26. NAI, DJ JUS8/1134, Inspector Brennan to Chief Superintendent, Sligo, 29 August 1961.
27. NAI, DJ JUS8/1134, Aiken to Traynor, 5 September 1961.
28. NAI, DJ JUS8/1134, Note to be handed to Irish Republican Ambassador from CRO, 22 December 1961.
29. NAI, DJ JUS8/1134, Chief Superintendent, Sligo, to Commissioner C3, 4 September 1961.
30. See MacMillan Cabinet Papers [hereafter MCP], CAB 128/31, CC (57) 6, 1 February 1957; CAB 128/31, CC (57) 10, 11 February 1957; CAB 128/31, CC (57) 50, 9 July 1957; CAB 129/85, CC (57) 5, 23 January 1957 in http://www.ampltd.co.uk/online/Macmillan-Cabinet-Papers/index.aspx.
31. Ireland's initial application to join the United Nations in 1945 was vetoed by the Russians on the grounds that the membership of the General Assembly in 1946 was heavily weighted in favour of the United States and the Western bloc. Therefore Ireland's entry was rejected by the Russians in order to prevent any further weakening of its position in the assembly. Russia's veto was finally withdrawn in 1955 when Ireland's membership was accepted as part of a 'package deal' admitting a balanced number of nations from the East and the West. See Norman McQueen, 'Ireland's entry to the United Nations 1946–56', in Tom Gallagher and James O'Connell (eds), *Contemporary Irish Studies* (Manchester: Manchester University Press, 1983), pp. 68–9.
32. Joseph Morrison Skelly, *Irish Diplomacy at the United Nations 1945–65: National Interests and the International Order* (Dublin: Irish Academic Press, 1997), p. 32; NAI, DEA 417/153/2, Government statements on raising question of partition at UN, undated.
33. NAI, DEA 417/153/2, Notice of motion, undated.
34. NAI, DEA 417/153/2, External Affairs to consulate, New York, undated.
35. NAI, DEA 417/153/2, Motion in Dáil Éireann put down by deputies McQuillan and Finucane, undated.
36. O'Brien, *Memoir*, pp. 98, 108, 191.
37. NAI, DEA 417/153/3, Boland to O'Brien, 23 April 1957.
38. NAI, DEA 417/153/3, O'Brien to Boland, undated.
39. NAI, DEA 417/153/3, O'Brien to Belton, 30 April 1957.
40. NAI, DEA 417/153/3, Boland to O'Brien, 28 May 1957.
41. *Irish Times*, 4 April 1957.
42. See Hezlet, *The 'B' Specials*, p. 168.
43. *United Irishman*, May 1957.
44. *United Irishman*, May 1957; Edmonds, *The Gun*, 199.
45. Bowyer Bell, *The Secret Army*, p. 304.
46. *Irish Times*, 4 April 1957.
47. *Irish Times*, 8 April 1957.
48. *Limerick Leader*, 10 April 1957.
49. *Irish Times*, 17 April 1957.
50. Bowyer Bell, *The Secret Army*, p. 316; *United Irishman*, June 1957. As Newry was predominantly a nationalist town the IRA immediately denied all involvement in the affair. In fact, it even went so far as to blame the attack on 'anti-national elements led by the Stormont government'.
51. NAI, DEA 98/3/127, Observations of the Irish government, 25 March 1958.
52. Bowyer Bell, *The Secret Army*, p. 316; *The Times*, 14 May 1957; NAI, DEA 98/3/127, Observations of the Irish government, 25 March 1958.

Notes

53. *Irish Press*, 14 May 1957; *Irish Times*, 14 May 1957; *The Times*, 14 May 1957. One motor vessel, MV *Dundalk*, which was owned by the British and Irish Steam Packet Company, was stranded in the Albert Basin of the canal, just outside of Newry, as a result of the blast.
54. *The Times*, 14 May 1957.
55. Bowyer Bell, *The Secret Army*, p. 305; *Irish Press*, 5 July 1957; *Irish Independent*, 5 July 1957.
56. NAI, DJ JUS8/1051, Telephone message to Garda Headquarters, 5 July 1957; *The Times*, 5 July 1957; *Irish Times*, 5 July 1957. The RUC seemed to intimate that the party consisted of between thirty and forty men, while the Garda believed that it could have consisted of as little as 'one or two'.
57. *Irish Times*, 5 July 1957; *Irish Press*, 5 July 1957; *The Times*, 5 July 1957.
58. *United Irishman*, August 1957.
59. *Irish Times*, 5 July 1957.
60. *The Times*, 5 July 1957; *Irish Press*, 5 July 1957.
61. *Irish Times*, 8 July 1957
62. MCP, CAB 128/31, CC (57) 50, 9 July 1957.
63. NAI, DT S 13710 C62, Cabinet minute, 5 July 1957.
64. *Irish Press*, 8 July 1957.
65. Bowyer Bell, *The Secret Army*, p. 305; *Irish Independent*, 8 July 1957. In fact MacCurtain was detained in Kent station, Cork as he disembarked from a train which had just arrived from Dublin.
66. *The Times*, 8 July 1957; *Limerick Leader*, 8 July 1957.
67. NAI, DT S 13710 B, Copy of 'news item – unofficial', 8 July 1957; *Irish Press*, 9 July 1957.
68. MCP, CAB 128/31, CC (57) 50, 9 July 1957.
69. *The Times*, 9 July 1957.
70. *Limerick Leader*, 13 July 1957.
71. NAI, DT S 16209 A, United Ireland committee, Philadelphia to Department of An Taoiseach, undated.
72. NAI, DT S 16209 A, Internal minute, 27 July 1957.
73. NAI, DT S 16209 A, Clipping from *Herald Tribune*, 2 August 1957.
74. NAI, DT S 16209 A, External Affairs minute from Washington, undated.
75. NAI, DT S 16281 A, Clipping from *Sunday Independent*, 21 July 1957.
76. *United Irishman*, August 1957.
77. UCDA, Éamon de Valera Papers [hereafter DVP] P150/3117, Statement by Minister for Justice, 8 July 1957; *Irish Press*, 8 July 1957.
78. UCDA, DVP P150/3117, Statement by Éamon de Valera, 22 July 1957.
79. UCDA, DVP P150/3117, Copy of statement by de Valera, 25 July 1957.
80. The Offences Against the State (Amendment) Act, s.8 (1) & (2).
81. NAI, DT S 13710 B, Summary of meeting held in Attorney-General's Office, 6 July 1957.
82. The Offences Against the State (Amendment) Act, 1940 (Commission for Inquiring into Detentions) Order, 1957 (1957 no. 157) (16 July 1957).
83. NAI, DJ JUS8/993, Justice to Defence, 18 October 1950 and Defence to Justice, undated.
84. NAI, DJ JUS8/993, Justice to Defence, 17 February 1951 and Arrangements for internment of civilians in event of an emergency, 14 February 1952.
85. Edmonds, *The Gun*, p. 202.
86. O'Regan, 31 August 2006; *Irish Press*, 9 July 1957.
87. *Irish Times*, 9 July 1957
88. *Irish Press*, 9 July 1957; *Irish Independent*, 9 July 1957.
89. *The Times*, 10 July 1957.
90. Interview with Tony Hayde, 31 August 2006; O'Regan, 31 August 2006; Interview with Noel Kavanagh, 12 September 2006. According to Pat O'Regan, thirty-eight people were involved on this occasion.
91. *Irish Times*, 15 July 1957.
92. NAI, DJ JUS8/1056, Report of discussion re: allegations by Sinn Féin, published in *Sunday Independent*, 5 September 1957; NAI, DT S 13785 B, Returns under section 9 of the Offences Against the State (Amendment) Act, 1940, period from 8 July, 1957 to 21 December, 1957, undated, period from 8 July to 1 June 1958, undated, period from 1 June 1958 to 1 November 1958, undated, period from 1 November to 1 March 1959, undated.
93. *The Times*, 10 July 1957.

94. The Offences Against the State (Amendment) Act, 1940, (Detention) Regulations Order, 1957.
95. *Irish Times*, 11 July 1957
96. The Offences Against the State (Amendment) Act, 1940 (Detention) Regulations Order, s. 22, 23, 32, 33, 34 & 35.
97. Hayde, 31 August 2006.
98. Kavanagh, 12 September 2006; Coogan, *The IRA*, p. 313.
99. O'Regan, 31 August 2006. He also recounts how inadequately washed pots, which had been used to prepare his first meal at the Curragh, led to a severe outbreak of food poisoning in his hut on the his first night as an internee.
100. Hayde, 31 August 2006.
101. Kavanagh, 12 September 2006.
102. Hayde, 31 August 2006.
103. Kavanagh, 12 September 2006.
104. Hayde, 31 August 2006.
105. Kavanagh, 12 September 2006.
106. Hayde, 31 August 2006; Kavanagh, 12 September 2006.
107. Coogan, *The IRA*, p. 319.
108. White, *Ruairí Ó Brádaigh*, p. 79.
109. *Irish Times*, 19 August 1957; *Sunday Independent*, 18 August 1957; *United Irishman*, September 1957.
110. NAI, DJ JUS8/1056, Report of discussion held in the Curragh, 18 August 1957.
111. O'Regan, 31 August 2006; NAI, DJ JUS8/1056, Report of discussion held in Curragh, 18 August 1957. In his biography Ó Brádaigh stated that conditions within the camp were 'crowded and cramped' but that the situation was alleviated by the spring of 1958, when the defence forces had finished maintenance works in the compound. See White, *Ruairí Ó Brádaigh*, p. 82.
112. Edmonds, *The Gun*, p. 202; O'Regan, 31 August 2006.
113. O'Regan, 31 August 2006.
114. NAI, DJ JUS8/1056, Report of discussion held in the Curragh, 18 August 1957.
115. Coogan, *The IRA*, p. 319; NAI, DJ JUS8/1056, Report of discussion held in the Curragh, 18 August and Defence to Justice, 5 September 1957.
116. White, *Ruairí Ó Brádaigh*, p. 82.
117. NAI, DJ JUS8/1099, Memo: Curragh detention camp, 26 November 1958.
118. Edmonds, *The Gun*, p. 201. Edmonds recalls this agreeable episode when he notes how the guards' recreation room was equipped with a billiards table, a darts board and a television set 'on which there was very erratic reception from the BBC'.
119. O'Regan, 31 August 2006.
120. Kavanagh, 12 September 2006.
121. White, *Ruairí Ó Brádaigh*, p. 80.
122. Bowyer Bell, *The Secret Army*, p. 323; NAI, DJ JUS8/1101, Sinn Féin publicity committee statement, 25 August 1958.
123. Coogan, *The IRA*, p. 319
124. Bowyer Bell, *The Secret Army*, p. 323.
125. NAI, DT S 13710 B, Government information bureau statement, 19 August 1957; *Irish Times*, 19 August 1957; *The Times*, 19 August 1957.
126. *The Times*, 28 May 1958.
127. *Irish Times*, 27 May 1958; *United Irishman*, June 1958.
128. *Irish Times*, 29 May 1958; *The Times*, 29 May 1958; Coogan, *The IRA*, p. 321
129. White, *Ruairí Ó Brádaigh*, p. 83.
130. Coogan, *The IRA*, p. 321.
131. Kavanagh, 12 December 2006; White, *Ruairí Ó Brádaigh*, pp. 83–4.
132. Coogan, *The IRA*, pp. 321–2; *Irish Times*, 26 September 1958; *The Times*, 26 September 1958.
133. *Irish Press*, 3 December 1958; *The Times*, 3 December 1958; Coogan, *The IRA*, pp. 322–3
134. *Irish Times*, 4 December 1958.
135. Edmonds, *The Gun*, p. 207.
136. NAI, DT S 13710 B, Sinn Féin publicity committee – 'Provocation of Prisoners', 7 January 1959.

137. Bowyer Bell, *The Secret Army*, p. 324–5.
138. White, *Ruairí Ó Brádaigh*, p. 87.
139. See Chapter 6 for more details surrounding the implications of this landmark case.
140. White, *Ruairí Ó Brádaigh*, p. 87; NAI, DT 98/6/490, Moynihan to Berry, 16 January 1959.
141. Bowyer Bell, *The Secret Army*, p. 325; The Offences Against the State Act, s. 52.
142. NAI, CAB 2/19, 17 February 1959.
143. NAI, DEA A12 1A, Report of meeting with British Ambassador, 6 March 1959.
144. *Irish Press*, 7 March 1959.
145. *The Times*, 7 March 1959.
146. NAI, DT S 13710 C/62, Proclamation declaring a cessation of part two of the Offences Against the State (Amendment) Act, 1940.

CHAPTER 6

1. *Report of the committee to review the Offences Against the State Acts*, p. 82; Doolan, *Lawless V Ireland*, p. 220.
2. Ó Longaigh, *Emergency Law*, p. 241; Gerard Hogan, 'The Supreme Court and the reference of the Offences Against the State (Amendment) Bill 1940' in *Irish Jurist*, xxvi (2000), p. 240; Doolan, *Lawless V Ireland*, p. 22. However, the committee to review the Offences Against the State Acts, which was established in 1999, points out that in today's circumstances the Supreme Court would be unlikely to validate the Offences Against the State (Amendment) Act, and would therefore find it to be repugnant to the constitution. See *Report of the committee to review the Offences Against the State Acts*, p. 77
3. Jack Greenberg and Anthony Shalit, 'New horizons for human rights: The European Convention, Court and Commission of Human Rights' *Columbia Law Review*, vol. 63, no. 8 (December, 1963), p. 1,384; MacDermott, *Clann na Poblachta*, p. 134. Other notable foreign policy initiatives pursued by MacBride were the decision to join the Organisation for European Economic Co-operation and the establishment of the Irish News Agency.
4. NAI, AGO GLP Box No. 2, folder entitled 'Document No. 3' – Activities of illegal organisations', 17 February 1958, and folder entitled 'Offences Against the State Commission' – Justice to Attorney-General, 31 January 1958.
5. Anon., 'The Lawless Case,' in *Duke Law Review*, vol. 1962, no. 2 (Spring, 1962), p. 258.
6. *Report of the committee to review the Offences Against the State Acts*, p. 82; Doolan, *Lawless V Ireland*, p. 220.
7. O'Halpin, *Defending Ireland*, p. 300; Bowyer Bell, *The Secret Army*, p. 333.
8. Under section 36 of the OASA, the government has the power to schedule 'offences of any particular class or kind under any particular enactment' for trial by the Special Criminal Court. This has meant that a wide range of offences has been scheduled, including offences under the Malicious Damage Act of 1861, the Conspiracy and Protection of Property Act of 1875, the Explosives Substances Act of 1883 and the Firearms Acts 1925–71. See The Offences Against the State Act, s. 36; John D. Jackson, Katie Quinn and Tom O'Malley, 'The jury system in contemporary Ireland: In the shadow of a troubled past', *Law and Contemporary Problems*, vol. 62, no.2 (Spring 1999), p. 214.
9. White, *Ruairí Ó Brádaigh*, p. 106; Coogan, *The IRA*, p. 325.
10. D.G. Valentine, 'The European Court of Human Rights: the Lawless case', *International and Comparative Law Quarterly*, vol. 10, no. 4 (October 1961), p. 899.
11. NAI, DEA 98/3/127, Part IV, Miscellaneous papers, Garda memorandum, 15 December 1958.
12. Doolan, *Lawless V Ireland*, p. 29.
13. Bowyer Bell, *The Secret Army*, p. 279; NAI, DEA 98/3/127, Garda memorandum, 15 December 1958. It subsequently transpired that Lawless and his colleagues had stolen the weapons in preparation for an unauthorized bank raid in Northern Ireland. When Christle and Kelly learned of this venture they travelled to Donegal where they persuaded the party to abandon the project. On their way back to Dublin Lawless and his comrades were forced to seek accommodation in a disused farmhouse, when their car broke down outside of Drumshambo, Co. Leitrim. They were then arrested when a party of local Garda raided the house.

14. NAI, DEA 98/3/127, Garda memorandum, 15 December 1958.
15. NAI, DEA 98/3/127, Observations to the application of Gerard Lawless, undated. According to the trial judge this could not be conclusively proved with recourse to the oral testimony of the Minister for Justice as well as every Garda superintendent for every police district in the country. See also: NAI, DEA 98/3/127, Observations of the Irish government, 25 March 1958.
16. NAI, DEA 98/3/127, Garda memorandum, 15 December 1958; *Irish Times*, 14 January and 7 May 1957. This proved to be a wholly counter-productive exercise as this Amonel powder, which had been used as a replacement for gelignite during the Second World War, was over sixteen years old and believed to be useless.
17. Doolan, *Lawless V Ireland*, p. 32.
18. NAI, DEA 98/3/127, Observations of the Irish government, 25 March 1958.
19. *Irish Times*, 17 May 1957.
20. NAI, DEA 98/3/127, Statement of complaint and claim 10 December 1957 (Schedule No. 8, Affidavit of Gerard Lawless).
21. *Irish Times*, 17 May 1957.
22. NAI, DEA 98/3/127, Garda memorandum, 18 December 1958.
23. See The Offences Against the State Act, s. 30 (3).
24. NAI, DEA 98/3/127, Statement of complaint and claim, 8 November 1957 (Schedule No. 1, Lawless to Secretary of Government, 8 September 1957, and Moore to Secretary of the Government, 9 September 1957); Edmonds, *The Gun*, p. 204.
25. See The Offences Against the State (Amendment) Act, s. 8.
26. NAI, DEA 98/3/127, Statement of complaint and claim, 8 November 1957 (Schedule No. 1, Ó Nulláin to Moore, 11 September 1957, Moore to Ó Nulláin, 12 September 1957 and Moore to Ó Nulláin, 14 September 1957).
27. NAI, AGO GLP Box No. 2, Folder entitled 'Offences Against the State Commission Papers' – Ó Briaín to unknown recipient, 15 July 1957 and Berry to Traynor, 16 September 1957.
28. *Irish Times*, 18 September 1957.
29. Doolan, *Lawless V Ireland*, p. 51.
30. NAI, AGO GLP Box No.2, 'Offences Against the State Commission Papers' – Chief State Solicitor to Attorney-General, 18 September 1957; *Irish Times*, 19 September 1957.
31. *Re Ó Laighleis* [1960] IR, p. 96.
32. NAI, AGO GLP Box No.2, 'Offences Against the State Commission Papers' – Berry to Traynor, 20 September 1957 and Berry to Registrar of the Commission, 19 September 1957; *Irish Times*, 8 November 1957; Doolan, *Lawless V Ireland*, p. 52.
33. NAI, AGO GLP Box No. 1, Folder entitled 'Original application Lawless and original application Brady' – Order of *Habeas Corpus ad Subjiciendum*, issued by the High Court, 18 September 1957.
34. NAI, AGO GLP Box No.1, 'Original application Lawless and original application Brady' – Order of *Habeas Corpus ad Subjiciendum*, 18 September 1957. In fact several affidavits were lodged in the High Court, including one by Peter Berry, the Secretary of the Department of Justice, and another by Detective-Inspector Philip McMahon. The purpose of these affidavits was simply to show that Lawless was suspected of being a member of the IRA and was therefore detained under the provisions of the Offences Against the State (Amendment) act on that basis. Furthermore, the purpose of Berry's affidavit was to attest to the fact that he had observed the Minister for Justice, Oscar Traynor, actually make out a warrant pursuant to the act, authorizing the internment of Lawless on his authority.
35. *Irish Times*, 9 October 1957.
36. *Re Ó Laighleis* [1960] IR, p. 103.
37. Doolan, *Lawless V Ireland*, p. 54; *Re Ó Laighleis* [1960] IR, p. 125.
38. Specifically his right to liberty and protection from unlawful detention. See The European Convention for the Protection of Human Rights, article 5.
39. Greenberg and Shalit, 'New horizons', p. 1,385; Valentine, 'The European Court', p. 900.
40. NAI, DEA 98/3/127, Statement of complaint and claim, 8 November 1957 (Schedule No. 1 Lawless affidavit, 10 December 1957); Doolan, *Lawless V Ireland*, p. 55.
41. NAI, AGO GLP Box No. 2, 'Offences Against the State Commission Papers' – Memorandum of proceedings before the commission appointed under the Offences Against the State (Amendment) Act, 1940 at the Curragh Camp, 10 December 1957.

Notes

42. NAI DEA 98/3/127, Statement of complaint and claim, 8 November 1957 (Schedule No. 1 Lawless affidavit) 10 December 1957.
43. NAI, AGO GLP Box No. 2, 'Offences Against the State Commission Papers' – Memorandum of proceedings before commission, 10 December 1957.
44. NAI, AGO GLP Box No. 2, 'Offences Against the State Commission Papers' – Moynihan to Detention Commission Registrar, 12 December 1957.
45. Greenberg and Shalit, 'New horizons', p. 1,387; *Irish Times*, 12 December 1957.
46. Doolan, *Lawless V Ireland*, p. 58.
47. NAI, AGO GLP Box No. 2, Folder entitled 'Miscellaneous Papers' – Activities of illegal organizations, 27 February 1958.
48. NAI, AGO GLP Box No. 2, 'Offences Against the State Commission Papers' – Justice to Attorney General, 31 January 1957 and 'Miscellaneous Papers' – Activities of illegal organizations, 27 February 1958.
49. NAI AGO GLP Box No. 2, 'Offences Against the State Commission Papers' – Justice to Attorney General, 31 January 1957 and 'Miscellaneous Papers' – Activities of illegal organizations, 27 February 1958.
50. *Report of the committee to review the Offences Against the State Acts*, p. 82; The Offences Against the State (Amendment) Act, s.3.
51. Anon., 'The Lawless Case', p. 249.
52. The European Convention for the Protection of Human Rights, article 25 (4).
53. Doolan, *Lawless V Ireland*, pp. 8–9.
54. Vincent Berger, *Case Law of the European Court of Human Rights, Vol. I: 1960–87* (Dublin: The Round Hall Press, 1989), p. 2.
55. Anon., 'The Lawless case, pp. 250–2.
56. Brice Dickson, 'The Council of Europe and the European Convention', in Brice Dickson (ed.), *Human rights and the European Convention* (London: Sweet & Maxwell, 1997), p. 11–12.
57. Dickson, 'The Council of Europe and the European Convention', p. 15.
58. Berger, *Case Law of the European Court*, p. 3.
59. NAI, DEA 98/3/127, Statement of complaint and claim, 8 November 1957.
60. The European Convention for the Protection of Human Rights, article 15.
61. NAI, DT S 14921 C, Letter to the Secretary-General, Council of Europe, 20 July 1957; Greenberg and Shalit, 'New horizons', p. 1,387.
62. NAI, DEA 98/3/127, Statement of complaint and claim, 8 November 1957.
63. Doolan, *Lawless V Ireland*, p. 62.
64. White, *Ruairí Ó Brádaigh*, p. 77. Ó Brádaigh's application, which was lodged by his election agent, Mary Delaney, was not pursued with any great vigour and lapsed at a very early stage.
65. NAI, AGO GLP Box No. 1, 'First government reply and schedules' – Observations of the government to the application of Gearoid Ó Laighleis, undated.
66. NAI, AGO GLP Box No. 1, Reply of the complainant to the submissions made by the respondent government, 21 February 1958.
67. NAI, DEA 98/3/127, Part IV, Reply of the complainant to the observations of the respondent government, 12 May 1958.
68. NAI, AGO GLP Box No. 1, Verbatim report of the oral hearing on the admissibility of application No. 332/57, 19 & 20 June 1958.
69. Doolan, *Lawless V Ireland*, p. 83.
70. Berger, *Case Law of the European Court of Human Rights*, p. 2.
71. Doolan, *Lawless V Ireland*, pp. 92–4.
72. NAUK, Foreign Office [hereafter FO] 371/137789, Adair to Foreign Office, 9 October 1958.
73. NAUK, FO371/131022, UK representative to Secretary-General of the Council of Europe, 27 June 1957.
74. NAUK, FO371/137788, Hoare to Cambridge, 14 August 1958.
75. NAUK, FO371/137788, Kimber to Commonwealth Relations Office, 23 September 1958.
76. NAUK, FO371/137789, UK representative, Dublin to Commonwealth Relations Office, 9 December 1959.
77. NAUK, FO371/137788, Adair to Foreign Office, 9 October 1958.
78. NAUK, FO371/137789, Foreign Office to Adair, 24 October 1958.

79. NAI, AGO GLP Box No. 1, Arguments and conclusions, 20 November 1958.
80. Doolan, *Lawless V Ireland*, p. 96.
81. NAI, AGO GLP Box No. 1, Arguments and conclusions, 20 November 1958.
82. NAI, AGO GLP Box No. 1, Counter-memorial of Ireland to the arguments and conclusions, 12 January 1959.
83. NAI, AGO GLP Box No. 1, Decision of the European Commission of Human Rights sub-commission, 25 March 1959.
84. Doolan, *Lawless V Ireland*, p. 108.
85. NAI, DEA 98/3/127, Part IV, Garda memorandum, 15 December 1958.
86. NAI, AGO GLP Box No. 1, Verbatim report of the pleadings held by the sub-commission, 17, 18 & 19 April 1959.
87. Doolan, *Lawless V Ireland*, p. 125.
88. NAI, AGO GLP Box No. 2, Report of the Commission, 19 December 1959; *Irish Independent*, 2 January 1960; *Irish Times*, 5 April 1960; *The Times*, 8 and 21 April 1961; Anon., 'The Lawless case', p. 252.
89. *Kerryman*, 14 June 1958; *Irish Times*, 18 April 1959; *Evening Herald*, 16 April 1959; *Evening Mail*, 16 April 1959.
90. *Irish Times*, 7 April 1960; *The Times*, 8 April 1960.
91. *Daily Express*, 10 April 1961.
92. *The Times*, 21 April 1960.
93. *Daily Express*, 10 April 1961.
94. Doolan, *Lawless V Ireland*, p. 154.
95. Berger, *Case Law of the European Court of Human Rights*, p. 3.
96. Lawless V Ireland, [1961], ECHR, [Online] Available: (http://cmiskp.echr.coe.int) (7 March 2006).
97. *Irish Independent*, 2 January, 1960.
98. Lawless V Ireland, [1961], ECHR.
99. Lawless V Ireland, [1961], ECHR.
100. Berger, *Case Law of the European Court of Human Rights, volume 1, 1960–1987*, pp. 8–9.
101. Doolan, *Lawless V Ireland*, p. 105.
102. NAI, DEA 305/446, Labour party councillor to Department of External Affairs, 5 June 1962.
103. *The Northern Whig*, 4 June 1962.
104. NAI, DEA F100/6/25, clipping from *Sunday Independent*, 9 May 1965.
105. NAI, Military Intelligence [hereafter MI] 2006/161/3, clippings from *Sunday World*, 26 October 1975 & 28 November 1975.

CHAPTER 7

1. *Belfast Telegraph*, 27 February 1962.
2. There were 235 recorded incidents in the first half of 1957, falling to 106 in the second half. McCay, 'The IRA border campaign', p. 57.
3. UCDA, JACP P190/763, Review of IRA organization, 19 March 1957.
4. Bowyer Bell, *The Secret Army*, p. 310.
5. *United Irishman*, July 1957.
6. *Limerick Leader*, 7 August 1957; *Irish Times*, 8 August 1957.
7. *United Irishman*, September 1957.
8. *Irish Independent*, 27 August 1958; NAI, DJ JUS8/1039, Garda report, 26 August 1958.
9. NAI, DJ JUS8/1040, Copy of IRA manifesto, August 1957.
10. Hezlet, *The 'B' Specials*, p. 171; McCay, 'The IRA border campaign', p. 55.
11. *Irish Press*, 14 August 1957.
12. *The Times*, 13 August 1957. In all six people were taken into custody where they were charged with breaches of the curfew before a special sitting of a local resident magistrate on 14 August 1957.
13. *Irish Times*, 14 August, 1957.
14. See Bowyer Bell, *The Secret Army*, p. 311; Hezlet, *The 'B' Specials*, p. 171.
15. *Irish Times*, 14 August 1957.

Notes

16. *Irish Times*, 15 & 16 August 1957.
17. *The Times*, 17 August & 10 September 1957; Hezlet, *The 'B' Specials*, p. 171.
18. *Irish Press*, 10 September 1957.
19. *Irish Times*, 19 August 1957; *The Times*, 19 August 1957; Coogan, *The IRA*, p. 325; Farrell, *Northern Ireland*, p. 217; English, *Armed Struggle*, p. 74.
20. *Irish Times*, 19 August 1957; *Irish Press*, 19 August 1957; *The Times*, 19 August 1957.
21. Coogan, *The IRA*, p. 325.
22. *Irish Times*, 20 & 21 August 1957.
23. *United Irishman*, September 1957.
24. Irish Republican Publicity Bureau [hereafter IRPB], *British Torture in Ireland*, December 1957; Bowyer Bell, *The Secret Army*, p. 311, *Irish Independent*, 6 January 1958.
25. Farrell, *Northern Ireland*, p. 219; Coogan, *The IRA*, pp. 325–6. Already an established Welsh barrister by this stage, Jones was later appointed as the Attorney-General for the United Kingdom.
26. NAI, DT 98/4/488, Clipping from *The Leader*, 11 January 1958.
27. *Irish Times*, 8, 9, 15, 21 January 1958; *Irish Press*, 9 & 15 January 1958; *United Irishman*, January 1958.
28. IRPB, *British Torture*, December 1957.
29. John Hostettler, *Torture Trial in Belfast: Eye Witness Observer Tells the Full Story of Mallon and Talbot whose Acquittal after Murder Trial Shocked the Unionists and Indicted the RUC* (London: Connolly Association, 1958), p. 3.
30. IRPB, *British Torture*, December 1957.
31. Hostettler, *Torture Trial in Belfast*, p. 8.
32. IRPB, *British Torture*, December 1957.
33. NAI, DT 98/4/488, Copy of parliamentary question, 15 January 1958. The amended version read: 'To ask the Taoiseach if he is aware that it is alleged that persons taken up by the RUC and British Military Forces in the six counties are subjected to ill treatment by them and forced to make false impressions, if he has any information to confirm this, and if so, what action he proposes to take in the matter.'
34. NAI, DT 98/4/488, Moynihan to Coyne, 27 January 1958.
35. NAI, DT 98/4/488, Coyne to Garda Commissioner, 27 January 1958.
36. *Parliamentary Debates, Dáil Éireann*, 12 February 1958, vol. 165, col. 2.
37. *Irish Times*, 9 January 1958; IRPB, *British Torture*, December 1957.
38. *Irish Times*, 8, 9 & 15 January 1958.
39. Hostettler, *Torture Trial in Belfast*, p. 3.
40. *Irish Times*, 30 July 1958; Farrell, *Northern Ireland*, p. 218; Hostettler, *Torture Trial in Belfast*, p. 9.
41. *Irish Press*, 1 August 1958
42. *Irish Press*, 6 August 1956.
43. *United Irishman*, September 1958,
44. PRONI, HA/32/1/1337, Report of meeting held at RUC Inspector General's office, 7 August 1958.
45. Farrell, *Northern Ireland*, p. 219. According to Coogan, they did not serve out their full sentences and were freed sometime after the IRA campaign ended in 1962. See Coogan, *The IRA*, p. 326.
46. Hostettler, *Torture Trial in Belfast*, p. 13.
47. NAI, DT 98/6/488, Observations of Irish government to reply of Gerard Lawless, 25 March 1958.
48. Hezlet, *The 'B' Specials*, p. 171; *Irish Times*, 4 September 1957.
49. *The Times*, 27 September 1957.
50. *Irish Independent*, 11 October 1957; *Irish Press*, 11 October 1957.
51. *Irish Times*, 10 & 14 October 1957.
52. Bowyer Bell, *The Secret Army*, p. 313. At this meeting, a new Army Council was elected, which, as expected, confirmed Cronin as C/S and Murphy as A/G.
53. Joseph Bowyer Bell, *The Gun in Politics: An Analysis of the Irish Political Conflict, 1916–1986* (London, 1987), p. 114.
54. *The Times*, 12 November 1957; Bowyer Bell, *The Secret Army*, p. 313; Coogan, *The IRA*, pp. 315–6; English, *Armed Struggle*, p. 74.
55. *United Irishman*, December 1957.

56. NAI, DT 98/6/488, Observations of Irish government, 25 March 1958; Hezlet, *The 'B' Specials*, p. 171.
57. *Irish Press*, 15 January 1958.
58. Bowyer Bell, *The Secret Army*, p. 314. According to Bowyer Bell, much of this success can be attributed to the fact that the Gardaí, on occasion, were tied in to the RUC radio net, thereby allowing them to coordinate counter insurgency operations with their colleagues in Northern Ireland.
59. *United Irishman*, February 1958; UCDA, JACP, P190/763, Review of IRA organization, 19 March 1957.
60. NAI, DT 98/6/488, Observations of Irish government, 25 March 1958. This disparity in numbers is further highlighted by Arthur Hezlet's belief that there were 366 incidents in the first thirteen months of the campaign. The government list reveals 177 for the same period. See Hezlet, *The 'B' Specials*, p. 185.
61. Bowyer Bell, *The Secret Army*, p. 314.
62. *United Irishman*, March 1958.
63. *The Times*, 17 February 1958.
64. *United Irishman*, March 1958.
65. *Irish Times*, 19 February 1958.
66. *Irish Times*, 19 February 1958. Skuse, who was from Cork, first made contact with the IRA in the early 1950s when he was at home on leave from the British army. Providing intelligence on British army installations, Skuse was involved in the Arborfield raid in August 1955. He was transferred to Blandford in 1954. See Bowyer Bell, *The Secret Army*, pp. 268, 272.
67. NAI, DEA A12, Costigan to Coyne, 3 June 1958.
68. NAUK, Air Ministry [hereafter AIR] 2/14478, Group Captain L.G. Brown, Director of Personal Services to Air Officers Commanding-in-Chief, 24 March 1958.
69. NAUK, AIR2/14478, Brown to Air Officers Commanding-in-Chief, 15 December 1958.
70. FBI, 61-7606 IRA part 4 of 7, Memorandum entitled: 'Irish Republican Army (IRA) internal security – Ireland/Great Britain', 13 December 1957.
71. FBI, 61-7606 IRA part 4 of 7, Memorandum: 'Irish Republican Army/Ireland/Great Britain/Registration Act, 15 November 1957 and Memorandum: 'Irish Freedom Committee/Is–Ireland', 6 December 1957.
72. Smith, *Fighting for Ireland*, p. 71.
73. Anderson, *Joe Cahill*, p. 148.
74. PRONI, HA/32/1/1333, Comments by Ministry of Home Affairs on the report of the ICRC 25 June 1958.
75. PRONI, HA/32/1/1333, Topping to Captain T.D. Morrison, British Red Cross Society, 12 May 1958; Anderson, *Joe Cahill*, p. 149. According to Cahill, the men involved were quickly retrieved from the tunnel to avoid punishment, before being rushed down to the shower room 'for a quick wash' before mingling anonymously with the main body of the protesters.
76. PRONI, HA/32/1/1333, Topping to Morrison, 12 May 1958 and Comments on report of ICRC, 25 June 1958; *The Times*, 13 March 1958; *Irish Times* 13 & 15 March 1958.
77. *United Irishman*, April 1958.
78. Anderson, *Joe Cahill*, p. 149–50.
79. PRONI, HA/32/1/1333, Topping to Morrison, 12 May 1958.
80. Farrell, *Northern Ireland*, p. 219.
81. PRONI, HA/32/1/1333, Topping to Morrison, 12 May 1958.
82. *Irish Times*, 18 March 1958.
83. PRONI, HA/32/1/1333, Comments on report of ICRC, 25 June 1958.
84. McCay, 'The IRA border campaign', p. 54.
85. *Irish Times*, 7 & 8 May 1958.
86. *United Irishman*, June 1958.
87. NAI, DT 98/6/489, Hunger strikers in Mountjoy Prison, restoration of privileges, 20 May 1958.
88. *Irish Times*, 22 May 1958.
89. *United Irishman*, June 1958.
90. McCay, 'The IRA border campaign', p. 42.
91. Edmonds, *The Gun*, p. 205. According to Edmonds, the government was certainly aware

of a certain sympathy within the army towards 'republican militants' but did not know the full extent of it.
92. Bowyer Bell, *The Secret Army*, p. 316; Edmonds, *The Gun*, p. 205.
93. *Irish Times*, 4 July 1958; *Irish Press*, 4 July 1957.
94. *The Times*, 3 July 1958; *Irish Times* 3 July 1958; *Irish Press*, 3 July 1958; Farrell, *Northern Ireland*, p. 219.
95. *Irish Times*, 5 & 6 July 1958.
96. Farrell, *Northern Ireland*, p. 220.
97. *Irish Times*, 17 July 1958; *United Irishman*, August 1958.
98. NAI, DT 98/3/493, Justice to Taoiseach, 2 February 1961.
99. *Irish Times*, 26 August 1958; *Irish Press*, 26 August 1958.
100. IRPB, *The Murder of James Crossan*, undated; NAI, DT 98/6/490, Memorandum marked 'For Taoiseach's Information', undated.
101. NAI, DT 98/6/490, 'For Taoiseach's Information', undated.
102. NAI, DT 98/6/490, Parliamentary questions tabled by John Tully, undated.
103. NAI, DT 98/6/490, Justice to Taoiseach, 27 October 1958.
104. Bowyer Bell, *The Secret Army*, p. 315.
105. *Irish Press*, 1 September 1958.
106. *Irish Times*, 3, 6 & 8 September 1958.
107. *Irish Times*, 23 September 1958.
108. Bowyer Bell, *The Secret Army*, p. 322.
109. White, *Ruairí Ó Brádaigh*, pp. 84–6.
110. Coogan, *The IRA*, pp. 323–4, 326.
111. White, *Ruairí Ó Brádaigh*, p. 89.
112. Bowyer Bell, *The Secret Army*, pp. 326–8; White, *Ruairí Ó Brádaigh*, pp. 88–9.
113. *Irish Times*, 17 November 1958 and 27 August 1959; *The Times*, 27 August 1959; Hezlet, *The 'B' Specials*, p. 178. In fact the land rover involved in the Crockada ambush hit a mine placed on the bridge by an IRA ambush party which was lying in wait. The explosion wrecked the bridge and blew the vehicle across the road, before the IRA party opened fire. Both RUC Constable R.F. Robinson and his B-Special colleague W.G. Guy were injured in the incident.
114. Lee, *Ireland*, p. 331; Bardon, *A History of Ulster*, p. 629.
115. John Horgan, *Seán Lemass: The Enigmatic Patriot* (Dublin: Gill & MacMillan, 1999), pp. 189–90.
116. Henry Patterson, 'Seán Lemass and the Ulster question', *Journal of Contemporary History*, vol. 34, no. 1, p. 147.
117. *Irish Times*, 29 August 1959.
118. NAUK, HO284/46, Meeting between Home Secretary and Commonwealth Secretary, 4 September 1959.
119. NAUK, HO284/46, Kimber to Commonwealth Relations Office, 5 September 1959.
120. NAUK, HO284/46, Butler to Brookeborough, 10 September 1959.
121. NAUK, HO284/46, Brookeborough to Butler, 16 September 1959.
122. NAI, DEA A12/1A, Ambassador to Secretary, Department of External Affairs, 18 September 1959.
123. NAUK, HO284/46, Meeting between Campbell and Ulster Members, 17 November 1959.
124. *Irish Times*, 21 November 1959; NAUK, HO284/46, Meeting between Butler, Campbell and Ulster Members, 24 November 1959.
125. *United Irishman*, January 1960.
126. *Irish Times*, 15 December 1959.
127. *Parliamentary Debates, Dáil Éireann*, 10 February 1960, vol. 179, col. 3.
128. White, *Ruairí Ó Brádaigh*, p. 102.
129. *United Irishman*, December 1958.
130. Smith, *Fighting for Ireland*, p. 70.
131. White, *Ruairí Ó Brádaigh*, p. 92.
132. Farrell, *Northern Ireland*, p. 220; Smith, *Fighting for Ireland*, pp. 70–1; Staunton, *Nationalists of Northern Ireland*, pp. 225–6.
133. White, *Ruairí Ó Brádaigh*, p. 92.
134. Bowyer Bell, *The Secret Army*, p. 332.
135. NAUK, HO284/46, Memorandum: 'Terrorism in Northern Ireland', 8 December 1959.

136. Smith, *Fighting for Ireland*, p. 71; Hezlet, *The 'B' Specials*, p. 179.
137. NAUK, HO284/46, 'Terrorism in Northern Ireland', 8 December 1959.
138. *Irish Times*, 27 January 1961; *The Times*, 27 January 1961; *Irish Press*, 28 January 1961.
139. O'Halpin, *Defending Ireland*, p. 300; *Irish Times*, 28 January 1961; *The Times*, 28 January 1961.
140. *United Irishman*, March 1961; White, *Ruairí Ó Brádaigh*, pp. 102–3.
141. *Irish Times*, 28 January 1961.
142. *United Irishman*, March 1961.
143. Bowyer Bell, *The Secret Army*, p. 331.
144. *Parliamentary Debates, Dáil Éireann*, 25 April 1961, vol. 188, cols 1,023–4.
145. Bowyer Bell, *The Secret Army*, p. 331.
146. The Offences Against the State Act, s. 35 (4).
147. NAI, DT S10454 B/63, Department of Defence Memorandum, 26 September 1961.
148. *Irish Press*, 13 November 1961.
149. *The Times*, 13 November 1961.
150. *Irish Times*, 14 November 1961.
151. Ó Longaigh, *Emergency Law*, p. 277; O'Halpin, *Defending Ireland*, p. 300; *Irish Times*, 23 November 1961.
152. *Parliamentary Debates, Dáil Éireann*, 23 November, 1961, vol. 192, cols 839–40.
153. NAI, DT S11837 C/95, Copy of letter from The National Civil Liberties League, undated; NAI, DT S17292/62, Memorandum: persons convicted by the Special Criminal Court, June 1962.
154. McCay, 'The IRA border campaign', p. 58.
155. White, *Ruairí Ó Brádaigh*, p. 106
156. McCay, 'The IRA border campaign', p. 58.
157. White, *Ruairí Ó Brádaigh*, pp. 106–7; Bowyer Bell, *The Secret Army*, p. 334.
158. English, *Armed Struggle*, p. 75.
159. See Smith, *Fighting for Ireland*, p. 72, Bowyer Bell, *The Secret Army*, pp. 334–5.
160. White, *Ruairí Ó Brádaigh*, p. 108.
161. *United Irishman*, March 1962.
162. Smith, *Fighting for Ireland*, p. 72.

CHAPTER 8

1. *Irish Press*, 27 February 1962.
2. *Irish Times*, 27 February 1962.
3. PRONI, HA/32/1/1349, Appreciation of the IRA situation, 13 April 1962.
4. O'Halpin, *Defending Ireland*, p. 302.
5. PRONI, HA/32/1/1349, Appreciation of the IRA situation, 13 April 1962. Some wireless installations were also being dismantled, but it was noted that 'a fairly strong force is being retained at Garda stations along or near the border'.
6. NAI, DT S13706 C/62, Government proclamation, 6 March 1962; The Offences Against the State (Amendment) Act, s 3.
7. NAI, DT S 11387 C/95, Department of Justice Memorandum, September 1962.
8. NAI, DT S 11387, C/95, Lemass to Haughey, 24 September 1962.
9. NAI, DT S 11387, C/95, Message to 'UN, New York', 27 September 1962.
10. NAI, DT S 11387, C/95, Proclamation, 2 October 1962; The Offences Against the State Act, s. 52.
11. *Irish Times*, 3 October 1962.
12. *Report of the Committee to review the Offences Against the State Acts*, p. 215.
13. *United Irishman*, July 1962.
14. Bowyer Bell, *The Secret Army*, pp. 337–9.
15. English, *Armed Struggle*, p. 76.
16. Smith, *Fighting for Ireland*, pp. 72–3.
17. O'Halpin, *Defending Ireland*, p. 300.
18. Kevin J. Kelley, *The Longest War: Northern Ireland and the IRA* (London: Zed Books, 1990), pp. 86–7; Ó Drisceoil, *Peadar O'Donnell*, p. 122.
19. Patterson, *The Politics of Illusion*, p. 88.

20. Kelley, *The Longest War*, p. 87.
21. Patterson, *The Politics of Illusion*, p. 89.
22. Patterson, *The Politics of Illusion*, pp. 90–3.
23. O'Halpin, *Defending Ireland*, p. 301.
24. Anderson, *Joe Cahill*, pp. 153, 158.
25. White, *Ruairí Ó Brádaigh*, p. 121.
26. Ó Drisceoil, *Peadar O'Donnell*, p. 122.
27. Lee, *Ireland 1912–1985*, pp. 432–3
28. O'Halpin, *Defending Ireland*, p. 312.
29. Kelley, *The Longest War*, pp. 154–5.
30. Lee, *Ireland*, p. 437.
31. *Report of the Committee to Review the Offences Against the State Acts*, p. 61; *Irish Times*, 27 May 1972.
32. *Report of the Committee to Review the Offences Against the State Acts*, p. 226. Significantly, it must also be noted that in making this recommendation the Committee stressed the need to keep the operation of the court under constant legislative review.

Appendices

APPENDIX 1: ORGANIZATIONAL STRUCTURE OF THE IRA

IRA ARMY COUNCIL

Usually consists of six members and three officers: Chief of Staff (C/S), Adjutant-General (A/G) and Quartermaster General (QMG)

BATTALION

Consisting of not less than two and not more than six companies. A battalion area should conform as closely as possible to the area of local government administration, e.g. in cities the borough area should be used as the basis of a battalion. Similarly, in large towns where several rural districts exist, the administration of the various county councils would serve to mark geographically the areas of the battalions.

COMPANY

A company at full strength shall consist of not more than six sections and a company staff. In addition a special section should be formed consisting of technicians such as chemists, engineers, wireless operators etc. These may be sympathizers and not necessarily volunteers.

SECTION

Only five men and one leader shall comprise a section and in exceptional cases seven men shall be allowed. In recruiting a section the aim should be to group men who are engaged in similar employment in the same section, i.e. railway workers, electricity workers, road transport workers etc.

APPENDIX 2.1: VARIATION IN THE NUMBER OF INTERNEES, MAY 1940 – FEBRUARY 1946

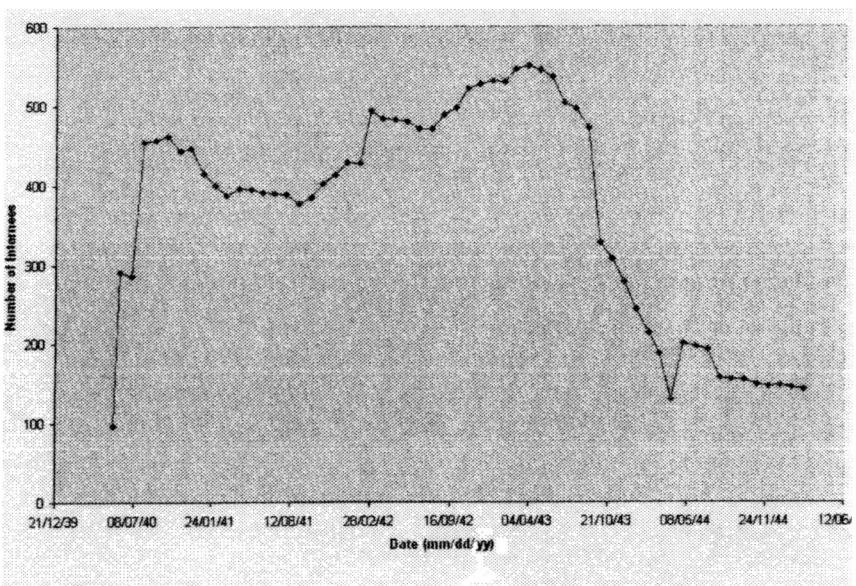

APPENDIX 2.2: PRISONERS AND INTERNEES IN MILITARY CUSTODY ON HUNGER STRIKE, 1939–1946

Year	No. on hunger strike
1939	4
1940	10
1941	0
1942	16
1943	13
1944	0
1945	0
1946	0

cont

APPENDIX 2.2 cont

Individual	Strike commenced	Strike terminated	No. of days on strike
1939			
Seán Lynch	16/10/39	18/11/39	32
Jeremiah Daly	16/10/39	11/11/39	26
Charles McCarthy	16/09/39	12/10/39	28
Richard McCarthy	16/10/39	18/11/39	32
1940			
Jeremiah Cronin	12/03/40	05/04/40	24
Jeremiah Crowley	14/03/40	05/04/40	22
Tony D'Arcy	25/02/40	16/04/40	52 (Died)
Seán McNeela	25/02/40	19/04/40	55 (Died)
Thomas Grogan	25/02/40	19/04/40	55
Thomas McCurtain	25/02/40	19/04/40	55
John Plunkett	25/02/40	19/04/40	55
Michael Traynor	25/02/40	19/04/40	55
Seamus P. Byrne	16/09/40	03/10/40	17
Patrick Moloney	24/10/40	28/10/40	4
1942			
Jeremiah Daly	10/03/42	19/03/42	10
John Lordan	10/03/42	19/03/42	10
Cornelius Donovan	10/03/42	19/03/42	10
James Ronayne	10/03/42	19/03/42	10
Charles Murphy	10/03/42	19/03/42	10
Patrick Lynch	10/03/42	19/03/42	10
Patrick Muldoon	10/03/42	19/03/42	10
John Varian	10/03/42	19/03/42	10
Thomas Murphy	10/03/42	19/03/42	10
Patrick J. McGann	10/03/42	19/03/42	10
Thomas Griffin	10/03/42	19/03/42	10
Timothy O'Connell	10/03/42	19/03/42	10
Michael O'Sullivan	10/03/42	19/03/42	10
Timothy Aherne	10/03/42	19/03/42	10
Thomas McSweeney	10/03/42	19/03/42	10
Patrick Fitzpatrick	10/03/42	19/03/42	10

APPENDIX 2.2 cont

Individual	Strike commenced	Strike terminated	No. of days on strike
1943			
Seán McCool	22/05/43	11/07/43	50
Seán Maxwell	22/05/43	28/06/43	37
Peadar Houston	22/05/43	24/06/43	33
John Gerard O'Doherty	22/05/43	11/07/43	50
Gerard Bohan	22/05/43	02/06/43	11
Terence McLoughlin	22/05/43	11/07/43	50
John Curran	22/05/43	13/06/43	22
Andrew Boland	14/07/43	25/07/43	11
John Francis Doyle	14/07/43	05/08/43	22
Florence Moynihan	14/07/43	30/07/43	16
James Keating	24/08/43	26/08/43	2
Patrick Shannon	01/09/43	05/09/43	4

APPENDIX 3: ACTIVITIES IN NORTHERN IRELAND,
1 DECEMBER 1956 – 3 MARCH 1958

DECEMBER 1956

11–12/12/56: Police patrol fired at near Ballycastle, Co. Antrim. BBC station at Derry badly damaged by explosives. Twelve men, disguised as police, set fire to Magherafelt Courthouse. Police patrol fired on from motor van at Armagh. Explosives left at wall of Armagh military barracks and sentry fired upon. Police drill hall at Newry burned. Lady Brooke and Carry bridges at Enniskillen damaged by explosion. Quarry magazine near Enniskillen broken into and 300 lbs of explosives stolen.

14/12/56: Police barracks attacked at Lisnaskea and Derrylin. Bridges blown up and telephone poles cut down in Co. Fermanagh.

18/12/58: Police patrol ambushed in Co. Fermanagh – constable wounded.

19/12/56: Gelignite found in British army hut at Enniskillen.

21/12/56: Bomb blast damaged police hut near Roslea.

22/12/56: Fifty men arrested by police.

23/12/56: Thirty men arrested by police.

24/12/56: Shots fired at two police barracks in Co. Derry. More arrests by police.

30/12/56: Occupants of motor car wounded when fired on by police at Caledon, Co. Tyrone.

31/12/56: Derrylin police barracks attacked by explosives and gunfire. Constable killed. Telephone poles and trees cut down. Three men arrested in Co. Tyrone.

JANUARY 1957

01/01/57: Widespread hunt for Derrylin attackers. Car fired on by police – five wounded in Co. Tyrone

02/01/57: Attack on police barracks at Brookeborough – two attackers (F. O'Hanlon and S. South) killed and four wounded. Police drill hut at Newry blown up.

04/01/57: Big manhunt in Co. Fermanagh. Inquest on men killed. Seven men arrested in Newry.

05/01/57: Arms found in Rostrevor. Exhausted men arrested at Belfast Airport.

15/01/57: Police hut blown up in Derry. Spikes removed from cross border road.

17/01/57: Bomb explosion damaged transformer at Eglington, Derry.

18/01/57: Single-handed bomb attack on power station at Altnagelvin, Co. Derry.
19/01/57: British army territorial barracks at Dungannon extensively damaged by explosion. Car commandeered by raiders.
22/01/57: Police hut damaged by bomb at Claudy, Co. Derry. Bridge damaged at Glenshane, Co. Derry, by explosion.
25/01/57: British army officer's home burned at Omagh.
26/01/57: Shots at Crossmaglen. Police fired on men in field.
28/01/57: Taxi owner held prisoner in Lifford by armed men. Unoccupied mansion burned near Newtownbutler.
31/01/57: Shots fired at Ballymena – men ran away.

FEBRUARY 1957
08/02/57: Two transformers damaged by explosion in Co. Derry. Derry mansion destroyed by fire – had been used as government store.
11/02/57: Bridge damaged by explosives in Co. Antrim.
12/02/57: Pump house at Tyrone aerodrome blown up. Transformer damaged at Lisnaskea.
15/02/57: Twice during the night of 15–16/2/57, shots were exchanged at Duncreggan army camp, Co. Derry.
18/02/57: Two bridges blown up in Co. Tyrone. GNR main line cut. Shots at army camp in Coleraine.
21/02/57: Arms found by police in haystack in Co. Tyrone.
22/02/57: Newry army hut blown up. Transformer damaged by explosives at Maghera.
27/02/57: Bridges and telephone kiosk damaged by explosions in Cos Tyrone, Derry and Down – telegraph poles cut – transformers blown up.

MARCH 1957
01/03/57: Booby trap discovered in Newry house. Telegraph poles cut down in Co. Tyrone.
02/03/57: GNR goods office in Derry burned. Bomb thrown but did not explode.
07/03/57: Derrylin police barracks fired upon – policeman wounded. Newry recruiting centre blown up. Bomb thrown into electricity board's premises in Newry, but failed to explode.
10/03/57: Road bridge at Derryneece, Roslea, damaged by explosion.
12/03/57: Unsuccessful attempt to rescue internee from Belfast hospital – two men detained.
15/03/57: Two transformers damaged in Co. Derry. Newry telephone kiosks put out of action.

16/03/57: Explosion in Co. Derry – transformer blown up at Gulladuff.

18/03/57: Police fired on car near Belfast Prison. Electric cable poles cut down at Moy and Killyman, Co. Tyrone.

21/03/57: Unoccupied mansion destroyed by fire at Carra, Newtownbutler.

22/03/57: Border hostel damaged by fire at Clonfad, Newtownbutler. Co. Antrim telephone exchange damaged by explosion. Underground telephone cable cut near Ballymena.

24/03/57: Gelignite found on island in Lough Erne by police.

29/03/57: Water house filter blown up at Altadeavin, Clougher, Co. Tyrone.

30/03/57: Five buses and a lorry destroyed by fire at Ulster Transport Authority garage in Dungiven, Co. Derry. Damage estimated at £30,000. Intruders approached Duncreggan army camp – fled when challenged.

31/03/57: Arms and explosives found in unoccupied house in Derry – 100 houses searched – twenty-three men detained – 300 lbs of gelignite found.

APRIL 1957

01/04/57: Arms and explosives found in Derry sports club premises.

02/04/57: Arms dump found in Co. Derry farmhouse by police.

03/04/57: Two bombs hurled at police barracks at Coalisland, Co. Tyrone. One failed to go off. No one injured.

06/04/57: Casement memorial damaged in Co. Antrim.

08/04/57: Explosion at British Royal Air Force radar station at Torr Head, Co. Antrim. Water supply cut off.

10/04/57: Two transformers damaged by explosion in Derry. Waterworks damaged by explosion at Loughmore, Clogher, Co. Tyrone.

11/04/57: Attempt to burn down Orange hall at Annaloiste, Lurgan.

13/04/57: Three explosions wrecked one telephone exchange and damaged two others at Dunloy, Co. Antrim, and Co. Derry.

14/04/57: Time bomb found in telephone exchange in Co. Antrim. Police removed and dismantled it.

15/04/57: Bridge at Carrickwater severely damaged by explosion. Transformer at Plumbridge, Co. Antrim, destroyed by bomb. Explosion outside army recruiting office in Derry.

22/04/57: Policeman injured by booby trap bomb at Clontone. Antrim cyclist wounded by policeman. Customs post set on fire in Derry. Petrol bomb thrown at electric station in Derry.

Appendices

23/04/57: Ancient Order of Hibernians hall burned down in Newtownbutler.
23/04/57: GNR bridge at Alallogue, Goraghwood, damaged by explosion. Trains stopped.
24/04/57: Fire bombs thrown into airfield hut near Cookstown. Unoccupied shooting lodge burned in Co. Derry. Road blocked at Rostreavor – phone kiosk damaged.
25/04/57: Gelignite found beneath Co. Fermanagh bridge.
26/04/57: Blast damaged railway line near Lurgan – three explosions.
27/04/57: Explosion damaged bridge in Co. Down.
29/04/57: Armed men held up bus in Co. Tyrone.

MAY 1957
02/05/57: Three explosions in Co. Antrim – railway bridge and post office damaged.
04/05/57: Three telephone kiosks demolished by explosions in south Armagh.
06/05/57: Attempt to kill police chief – time bomb found in boat.
07/05/57: Road bridge at Derrytesk, Coalisland, damaged by explosion.
14/05/57: Newry canal lock blown up by raiders.
16/05/57: Police hall burned by explosion at Coalisland.
18/05/57: Signal cabin at Dunloy, Co. Antrim, blown up.
25/05/57: Derry blacked out by explosion – transformer blown up. Attempt to blow up Derry harbour installations foiled by woman police sergeant – two youths arrested.
27/05/57: Sluice gate blown up on Clady River at Innisrush, Co. Antrim. Kiosk blown up at Mayogall, Co. Derry. Bombs and ammunition found in car after border chase.
31/05/57: Double explosion destroyed bridge at Creggan, Co. Armagh.

JUNE 1957
01/06/57: Explosion destroyed pump house at Cavankerran, Pomeroy.
04/06/57: Bid to blow up bridge failed – 120 sticks of gelignite found.
10/06/57: Police fired on car near border in Co. Armagh – Belfast woman wounded.
12/06/57: Mine exploded in Dungannon – set off by dog.
13/06/57: Four bomb explosions in Co. Tyrone signal cabin – telephone kiosk, electric transformer and bridge damaged.
25/06/57: Police drill hall blown up at Eskra, Fintona, Co. Tyrone.
27/06/57: Fire destroyed Derry British Air Force Club.

JULY 1957

04/07/57: Bomb wrecks police hut at Dernawilt, Roslea. Ambush at Forkhill – policeman killed – another wounded – box of gelignite found on road.

05/07/57: Bomb in post box in Strabane – disconnected.

06/07/57: Attempt to burn bus at Coagh, Co. Tyrone. Gelignite in telephone kiosk. Explosion near Sion Mills police station.

11/07/57: About fifty rifles found by police in Derry.

23/07/57: Attempt to burn Orange hall at Brackey, Co. Tyrone.

27/07/57: Four masked men set fire to army lorry in Newry.

AUGUST, 1957

05/08/57: Explosion fails to damage transformer at Dunloy.

10/08/57: Attack on police barracks at Swartagh, Co. Derry. Customs hut blown up at Mullan, Co. Fermanagh.

12/08/57: Attack on police barracks at Cranagh, Co. Tyrone – shots exchanged. Bomb damaged Newry electricity offices. Post office garage burned at Newry – cars destroyed.

13/08/57: Curfew imposed in Newry – clashes with police – arrests. Dredger sunk by explosives in Lough Neagh.

15/08/57: Four machine-guns and parcel of gelignite found by police at Blackaville, Coalisland, Co. Tyrone.

19/08/57: Police sergeant killed and two constables and a soldier injured at Brackaville, Co. Tyrone. Booby trap in unoccupied house.

26/08/57: Post office garage in Derry set on fire – vehicles damaged. Customs hut at Strabane blown up.

30/08/57: Telephone exchange wrecked by explosion at Brookhall, Derry.

SEPTEMBER 1957

02/09/57: Transformer damaged by explosion at Newcastle, Co. Down. Girl Guides camp damaged.

04/09/57: Attack on patrol near Clogher, Co. Tyrone. Policeman wounded. Rifle fire across border.

09/09/57: Seven telegraph poles sawn down in Co. Tyrone.

14/09/57: Derry bomb explosion. British RAF building damaged.

18/09/57: Unexploded bomb found near telephone exchange, Newry.

23/09/57: Motorist shot by police patrol at Lisnaskea, Co. Fermanagh.

24/09/57: Road damaged by explosions near Belcoo – ammunition found.

25/09/57: Police drill hall damaged by explosion at Tullintrain, Derry.

27/09/57: Customs hut blown up at Clontivrin. Bomb attempt on police officers' car. Explosive under car of County Inspector A.H. Kennedy, Deputy Commissioner, Belfast City Police.

OCTOBER, 1957

01/10/57: Bomb and gun attack on police barracks in Armagh. Cathedral windows damaged.

09/10/57: Bridge damaged by explosion at Mullaghmore, Co. Tyrone.

11/10/57: Attack on Roslea police barracks, mine explosions and gun fire. Police lorry damaged, policeman injured by mine. Armed men set fire to Armagh Transport Depot.

14/10/57: Enniskillen post office garage damaged by explosion. Attempt to set fire to Coalisland labour exchange.

17/10/57: Shots fired at police patrol in Derry. Police find booby trap near Coalisland.

23/10/57: Three explosions in Cos Derry and Antrim. Bridge at Clady damaged and phone kiosk at Gortahease destroyed. Electricity transformer at Creagh damaged.

25/10/57: Blockhouse blown up at Magillan Point, Lough Foyle. Police drill huts at Kilkeel damaged by explosion.

28/10/57: Booby trap near Coalisland.

29/10/57: Armed men take car near Newry – police patrol stop car – Men escape in darkness.

NOVEMBER, 1957

02/11/57: Bomb scare near Derrylin – box on road. Men searched going to work.

04/11/57: Explosion damaged police hut at Ballinahinch.

09/11/57: Two explosions in Enniskillen – transformer damaged – wall of police depot damaged – time bomb dismantled.

15/11/57: Unexploded canister bomb found at bridge near Coalisland.

30/11/57: Two policemen disarmed in Armagh. Sten guns and revolver seized by five armed men.

DECEMBER 1957

02/12/57: Police patrol car escapes land mine near Kinawley.

06/12/57: Two telegraph poles cut down near Stewartstown.

07/12/57: British customs hut blown up at Beleek. Three armed men hold up officials.

08/12/57: Explosion damaged bridge at Havies, Enniskillen.

21/12/57: Two masked and armed men held up taxi driver at Newry.

23/12/57: British customs patrol car fired upon at Cullamore, Co. Tyrone. No one injured.

31/12/57: Explosion wrecked police hall at Derrylin.

JANUARY 1958

04/01/58: Three explosions damaged transformers in Newry – four men charged with causing explosions. Telegraph pole sawn down near Enniskillen.

06/01/58: Three roads damaged by explosives in Co. Fermanagh. Gelignite found.

14/01/58: Explosion destroyed store at Strabane. Windows smashed.

15/01/58: Police barracks at Swartagh attacked. Policeman wounded. two bridges damaged – one at Curran, Co. Derry and the other, Ranahan Bridge, at Glenshale Pass. Electricity transformer at Rashakin, Co. Antrim, blown up. Electricity transformer at Brodge Street, Strabane, wrecked by explosion.

16/01/58: Customs hut at Upper Fathon, Co. Armagh, burned down.

18/01/58: Customs hut at Molenan, Co. Derry wrecked by explosion. Customs hut at Killea, Co. Derry damaged by explosion.

21/01/58: Running gun battle near border at Killeen – gelignite found. Bridge on Castlewellan–Rathfriland Road, Co. Down, damaged by explosion.

31/01/58: British observation corps hut at Mounthamilton, Co. Antrim, wrecked by explosion.

FEBRUARY 1958

02/02/58: Telephone exchange at Loughguile post office near Ballymoney, Co. Antrim, wrecked by explosion.

05/02/58: Small concrete hut at Culhane near Strabane used by Royal Observer Corps destroyed by explosion.

06/02/58: Arms dump of sub-machine guns, revolvers etc. found by police at Strabane, Co. Tyrone.

17/02/58: Middletown (Co. Armagh) police barracks attacked by armed men, who escaped. Armed attack on Beleek, Co. Fermanagh, police barracks attackers escaped. Police patrol car fired on by armed men on the Rostreavor–Hilltown Road, Co. Down.

22/02/58: Electricity transformer 100 yards from the border at Clady badly damaged by explosion.

MARCH 1958

03/03/58: Police land rover ambushed and damaged by land mine at Coovagurt, near Roslea. Two policemen slightly injured.

Bibliography

PRIMARY SOURCES

Film Interviews
Christy Querney (Courtesy of Akajava Productions Ltd.)
Dan Keating (Courtesy of Akajava Productions Ltd.)
Eddie Keenan (Courtesy of Akajava Productions Ltd.)
John L. McCormack (Courtesy of Akajava Productions Ltd.)
Tomás Ó Broin (Courtesy of Akajava Productions Ltd.)

Personal Interviews
Noel Kavanagh (12 September 2006)
Patrick O'Regan (31 August 2006)
Tony Hayde (31 August 2006)

Newspapers
Belfast Telegraph
Cork Examiner
Evening Herald
The Times
Irish Independent
Irish Press
Irish Times
Limerick Leader
Limerick Socialist
The United Irishman

Official Records
Military Archives
Civilian Internees in Military Custody (Provost Marshal files, 1940–45)

National Archives of Ireland
Cabinet Minutes
Department of External Affairs
Department of Justice
Department of An Taoiseach
Military Intelligence
Office of the Attorney General

Public Record Office, London
Admiralty
Air Ministry
Cabinet Office
Dominions Office
Foreign Office
Home Office
Northern Ireland Office
Prime Minister's Office
Security Services
War Office

Public Record Office of Northern Ireland
Cabinet Conclusions
Ministry of Home Affairs
Prime Minister's Office

Special Collections Library, University of Limerick
Leonard Collection

United States National Archives, Washington
Federal Bureau of Investigation

Parliamentary and Official Publications, Legislation and Statutory Instruments
Buckley and others (Sinn Féin) V Attorney General [1950] IR

Bunreacht na hÉireann
The Civil Authority (Special Powers) Act (Northern Ireland), 1922 (1922 no. 4) (7 April 1922)
The Constitution Amendment (No. 17) Act, 1931 (1931 no. 37) (17 October 1931)

Dáil Debates
The Defence of the Realm Act, 1914 4 & 5 Geo. V, c. 29 [U.K.] (8 August 1914)
The Emergency Powers Act, 1939 (1939 no. 28) (3 September 1939)
The European Convention for the Protection of Human Rights and Fundamental Freedoms (4 November 1950)
The Geneva Convention Relative to the Treatment of Prisoners of War (12 August 1949)
The National Council for Civil Liberties, *Report of a commission of inquiry appointed to examine the purpose and effect of the Civil Authorities (Special Powers) Acts (Northern Ireland) 1922 and 1933* (London, 1972)
The Public Safety (Emergency Powers) Act, 1924 (1924 no. 1) (31 June 1924)
The Public Safety (Emergency Powers) Act, 1926 (1926 no. 42) (19 November 1926)
The Public Safety (Emergency Powers) Act, 1927 (1927 no. 31) (11 August 1927)
Report of the committee to review the Offences Against the State Acts, 1939–1998 and related matters, [R.I.] (Dublin, 2002)

Seanad Debates
The Offences Against the State Act (1939 no. 13) (14 June 1939)
The Offences Against the State (Amendment) Act (1940 no. 2) (9 February 1940)
The Offences Against the State (Amendment) Act, 1940 (Internment Commission) Order, 1945 (1945 no. 182) (24 July 1945)
The Offences Against the State (Amendment) Act, 1940 (Detention) Regulations, 1957 (1957 no. 146) (10 July 1957)
Re article twenty-six of the Constitution and the Offences Against the State (Amendment) Bill, 1940 [1940] IR
Re Ó Laighleis [1960] IR
Re Mid-Ulster election petition: Beattie V Mitchell [1958] NI 143
The State (Burke) V Lennon and the Attorney General [1940] IR

Pamphlets
Bean Ui Bhuachalla, M., *Sinn Féin 1905–1956: A Proud History Gives Confidence of Victory* (Dublin, 1956) – National Library of Ireland
Hostettler, John, *Torture trial in Belfast: Eye Witness Observer Tells the Full Story of Mallon and Talbot whose Acquittal after Murder Trial Shocked the Unionists and Indicted the RUC* (London, 1958) – British Library, London

McGarrity, Joe (pseudonym), *Resistance: The Story of the Struggle in British occupied Ireland* (Dublin: Irish Freedom Press, 1957) – Private Collection

O'Higgins, Brian, *Martyrs for Ireland: The story of McCormick and Barnes* (Dublin, 1940) – National Library of Ireland

Roinn Eolas na Poblachta, *They Kept Faith: In this Tribute to Two Soldiers of Ireland the Full Story of the Brookeborough Attack in which they Lost their Lives is Now told by their Comrades* (Dublin, 1957) – Special Collections Library, University of Limerick

Private Papers
John A. Costello (University College Dublin Archives)
Éamon de Valera (University College Dublin Archives)
Seán MacBride (Private Collection, Property of Caitriona Lawlor)

SECONDARY SOURCES

Books and Articles
Anderson, Brendan, *Joe Cahill: A life in the IRA* (Dublin: O'Brien Press, 2002)

Anon., 'The Lawless case', *Duke Law Review*, vol. 1962, no. 2 (Spring 1962)

Augusteijn, Joost, *From Public Defiance to Guerrilla Warfare: The Experience of the Ordinary Volunteers in the Irish War of Independence 1916–1921* (Dublin: Irish Academic Press, 1998)

Bardon, Jonathon, *A History of Ulster* (Belfast: Blackstaff Press, 1992)

Barton, Brian, *Brookeborough: The Making of a Prime Minister* (Belfast: Institute of Irish Studies, Queen's University Belfast, 1998)

Berger, Vincent, *Case Law of the European Court of Human Rights, volume I: 1960–1987* (Dublin: The Roundhall Press, 1989)

Betts, Raymond F., *France and decolonisation: 1900–1960* (London: MacMillan, 1991)

Bowman, John, *De Valera and the Ulster Question 1917–1973* (Oxford: Oxford University Press, 1982)

Bowyer Bell, Joseph, 'Contemporary revolutionary organisations', *International Organisation*, vol. 25, no. 3 (1971)

Bowyer Bell, Joseph, *The Gun in Politics: An Analysis of the Irish Political Conflict, 1916–1986* (London: Transaction Books, 1987).

Bowyer Bell, Joseph, *The Secret Army: The IRA* (Dublin: Poolbeg, 1990)

Boyce, D. George, *Nationalism in Ireland* (London: Croom Helm, 1982)

Browne, Noel, *Against the Tide* (Dublin: Gill & Macmillan, 1986)

Campbell, Colm, *Emergency Law in Ireland, 1918–1925* (Oxford: Clarendon Press, 1994)

Carter, Carolle, J., *The Shamrock and the Swastika: German Espionage in Ireland in World War II* (Palo Alto: Pacific Books, 1977)

Caulfield, Max, *The Easter Rebellion* (Dublin:Gill & Macmillan, 1995)

Comerford, R.V., *The Fenians in Context: Irish Politics and Society 1848–1882* (Dublin: Wolfhound, 1998)

Coogan, Tim Pat, *Ireland in the Twentieth Century* (London: Random House, 2003)

Coogan, Tim Pat, *The IRA* (London: Harper Collins, 2000)

Costello, Francis, *Years of Revolt: The Irish Revolution and its Aftermath, 1916–1923* (Dublin: Irish Academic Press, 2003)

Costello, Kevin, *The Law of Habeas Corpus in Ireland: The History, Scope of Review and Practice under Article 40.4.2 of the Irish Constitution* (Dublin: Four Courts Press, 2006)

Cronin, Seán, *Irish Nationalism: A History of its Roots and Ideology* (Dublin: Academy Press, 1980)

Cronin, Seán, *The McGarrity Papers: Revelations of the Irish Revolutionary Movement in Ireland and America 1900–1940* (Tralee: Anvil Books, 1972)

Curtin, Nancy J., *The United Irishmen: Popular Politics in Ulster and Dublin 1791–1798* (Oxford: Clarendon Press, 1998)

Delaney, Enda, 'Political Catholicism in Post-War Ireland: The Revd. Denis Fahey and Maria Duce, 1945–54', *Journal of Ecclesiastical History*, vol. 52, no. 3 (2001)

Dickson, Brice, 'The Council of Europe and the European Convention', in Dickson, Brice (ed.), *Human Rights and the European Convention* (London: Sweet and Maxwell, 1997)

Dickson, David, *New foundations: Ireland 1660–1800* (Dublin: Irish Academic Press, 2000)

Doherty, Gabriel and Keogh, Dermot (eds), *1916: The Long Revolution* (Cork: Mercier Press, 2007)

Donohue, Laura K, 'Civil liberties, terrorism and liberal democracy: Lessons from the United Kingdom', Belfer Centre for Science and International Affairs Discussion Paper (John F. Kennedy School of Government: Harvard University, 2000)

Donohue, Laura K, 'Regulating Northern Ireland: The Special Powers Acts 1922–1972', *Historical Journal*, vol. 41, no. 4 (1998)

Doolan, Brian, *Lawless V Ireland (1957–1961): The first case before the European Court of Human Rights, An international miscarriage of Justice?* (Dartmouth: Ashgate, 2001)

Duggan, Lieut.-Col. John, *Herr Hempel at the German Legation in Dublin 1937–1945* (Dublin: Irish Academic Press, 2002)

Dunphy, Richard, *The Making of Fianna Fáil Power in Ireland, 1923–1948* (Oxford: Oxford University Press, 1995)

Edmonds, Seán, *The Gun, the Law and the Irish People: From 1912 to the Aftermath of the Arms Trial 1970* (Tralee: Anvil Books, 1971)

Edwards, Owen Dudley, Rhys Evans, Ioan and MacDiarmid, Hugh, *Celtic Nationalism* (London: Routledge and Kegan Paul, 1968)

Edwards, Robin Dudley, *A New History of Ireland* (Dublin: Gill & Macmillan, 1972)

Edwards, Ruth Dudley, *Patrick Pearse: The Triumph of Failure* (Dublin: Poolbeg, 1990)

Elliott, Marianne, *Robert Emmet: The Making of a Legend* (London: Profile Books, 2004)

Elliott, Marianne, *The Catholics of Ulster: A History* (London: Allen Lane, 2000)

English, Richard, *Armed Struggle. A History of the IRA* (London: Macmillan, 2003)

English, Richard, *Ernie O'Malley: IRA Intellectual* (Oxford: Oxford University Press, 1998)

English, Richard, *Radicals and the Republic: Socialist Republicanism in the Irish Free State, 1925–1937* (Oxford: Oxford University Press, 1995)

Epstein, Leon D., 'Partisan foreign policy: Britain in the Suez crisis', *World Politics*, vol. 12, no. 2 (January 1960)

Fanning, Ronan, *Independent Ireland* (Dublin: Helicon, 1983)

Fanning, Ronan, '"The rule of order": De Valera and the IRA, 1923–40', in O'Carroll, John P. and Murphy, John A., *De Valera and his Times* (Cork: Cork University Press, 1983)

Farrell, Michael, *The Apparatus of Repression* (Derry: Field Day, 1986)

Farrell, Michael, *Northern Ireland: The Orange State* (London: Pluto Press, 1992)

Feeney, Brian, *Sinn Féin: A Hundred Turbulent Years* (Dublin: O'Brien Press, 2002)

Ferriter, Diarmaid, *The Transformation of Ireland 1900–2000* (London: Profile Books, 2004)

Fisk, Robert, *In Time of War: Ireland, Ulster and the Price of Neutrality 1939–45* (Dublin: Gill & Macmillan, 1983)

Fitzpatrick, David, *Harry Boland's Irish Revolution 1887–1922* (Cork: Cork University Press, 2003)

Fitzpatrick, David, *Politics and Irish Life 1913–21: Provisional Experience of War and Revolution* (Dublin: Gill & Macmillan, 1977)

Fitzpatrick, David, 'The geography of Irish nationalism 1910–1921', *Past and Present*, no. 78 (1978)

Fitzpatrick, David, *The Two Irelands 1912–1939* (Oxford: Oxford University Press, 1998)

Fogerty, Des, *Seán South of Garryowen* (Limerick: FX Press, 2006)

Foley, Conor, *Legion of the Rearguard: Republicanism, Nationalism and the Irish* (London: Pluto Press, 1992)

Foster, Roy, *Modern Ireland 1600–1972* (London: Allen Lane, 1989)

Garvin, Tom, *Nationalist Revolutionaries in Ireland 1858–1928* (Oxford: Oxford University Press, 1987)

Geoghegan, Patrick M., *Robert Emmet: A Life* (Dublin: Gill & Macmillan, 2002)

Girvin, Brian, *The Emergency: Neutral Ireland, 1939–45* (London: Macmillan, 2006)

Greenberg, Jack and Shalit, Anthony, 'New horizons for human rights: The European Convention, Court and Commission of Human Rights', *Columbia Law Review*, vol. 63, no. 8 (December 1963)

Harkness, David, *Ireland in the Twentieth Century: Divided Island* (London: Basingstoke, 1996)

Hanley, Brian, '"Oh here's to Adolph Hitler"? The IRA and the Nazis', *History Ireland*, vol. 13, no. 3 (May/June 2005)

Hanley, Brian, *The IRA: 1926–1936* (Dublin: Four Courts Press, 2002)

Hart, Peter, *Kilmichael: The False Surrender – A Discussion* (Milstreet: Aubane Historical Society, 1999)

Hart, Peter, '"Operations abroad": The IRA in Britain, 1919–23', *English Historical Review*, vol. 115, no. 460 (2000)

Hart, Peter, *The IRA and its Enemies: Violence and Community in Cork, 1916–1923* (Oxford: Oxford University Press, 1999)

Hart, Peter, *The IRA at War: 1916–1923* (Oxford: Oxford University Press, 2003)

Hermon, Sir John, *Holding the Line: An Autobiography* (Dublin: Gill & Macmillan, 1997)

Hezlet, Sir Arthur, *The 'B' Specials: A History of the Ulster Special Constabulary* (Belfast: Mourne River Press, 1997)

Hoar, Adrian, *In Green and Red: The Lives of Frank Ryan* (London: Brandon Press, 2004)

Hobsbawm, Eric, *The Age of Extremes: 1914–1991* (London: Abacus Press, 2003)

Hogan, Gerard, 'The Sinn Féin funds judgment fifty years on', *Bar Review: The Journal of the Bar of Ireland*, vol. 2, no. 9 (2005)

Hogan, Gerard, 'The supreme court and the reference of the Offences Against the State (Amendment) Bill 1940', *Irish Jurist*, XXXV (2000)

Hogan, Gerard and Walker, Clive, *Political Violence and the Law in Ireland* (Manchester: Manchester University Press, 1989)

Holland, R.F., *European Decolonisation 1918–1981: An Introductory Survey* (London: MacMillan, 1985)

Hopkinson, Michael, *The Irish War of Independence* (Dublin: Gill & Macmillan, 2002)

Horgan, John, *Noel Browne: Passionate Outsider* (Dublin: Gill & Macmillan, 2000)

Hull, Mark, *Irish Secrets: German Espionage in Ireland, 1939–1945* (Dublin: Irish Academic Press, 2003)

Inglis, Brian, *Roger Casement* (London: Penguin Books, 2002)

Jackson, Alvin, *Ireland 1798–1998* (Oxford: Blackwell, 1999)

Jackson, John D., Quinn, Katie and O'Malley, Tom, 'The jury system in contemporary Ireland: In the shadow of a troubled past', *Law and Contemporary Problems*, vol. 62, no. 2 (1999)

Jordan, Anthony, *Seán MacBride* (Dublin: Blackwater Press, 1993)

Kelley, Kevin J., *The Longest War: Northern Ireland and the IRA* (London: Zed Books, 1990)

Kennedy, Michael, *Division and Consensus: The Politics of Irish Cross-border Relations, 1925–1969* (Dublin: Institute of Public Administration, 2001)

Kennedy, Michael, 'Towards co-operation: Seán Lemass and north/south economic relations 1956–65', *Irish Economic and Social History*, XXIV (1997)

Kee, Robert, *The Green Flag: A History of Irish Nationalism* (London: Penguin, 2000)

Keogh, Dermot, *Twentieth Century Ireland: Nation and State* (Dublin: Gill & Macmillan, 1995)

Kleinrichert, Denise, *Republican Internment and the Prison Ship Argenta 1922* (Dublin: Irish Academic Press, 2001)

Lee, J.J., *Ireland 1912–1985: Politics and Society* (Cambridge: Cambridge University Press, 2001)

Long, Des (ed.), *Awakening the Spirit of Freedom* (Limerick: Ryan Printers, 2006)

Longford, Earl of, and O'Neill, T.P., *Éamon de Valera* (Wales: Hutchinson, 1987)

Lydon, James, *The Making of Ireland: From Ancient Times to the Present* (London: Routledge, 1998)
Lyons, F.S.L., *Charles Stewart Parnell* (Suffolk: Fontana, 1978)
MacAtasney, Gerard, *Seán MacDiarmada: The Mind of the Revolution* (Manorhamilton: Drumlin Press, 2004)
MacBride, Seán [Caitriona Lawlor (ed.)], *That Day's Struggle: A Memoir 1904–1951* (Dublin: Currach Press, 2005)
MacDermott, Eithne, *Clann na Poblachta* (Cork: Cork University Press, 1998)
MacEoin, Uniseann, *The IRA in the Twilight Years* (Dublin: Argenta Publications, 1997)
Manning, Maurice, *James Dillon: A Biography* (Dublin: Wolfhound Press, 1999)
Manning, Maurice, *The Blueshirts* (Dublin: Gill & Macmillan, 1988)
McClelland, J.S., *A History of Western Political Thought* (London: Routledge, 2000)
McConville, Seán, *Irish Political Prisoners, 1984–1922: Theatres of War* (London: Routledge, 2005)
McCullagh, David, *A makeshift majority: The First Inter-Party Government 1948–51* (Dublin: Institute of Public Administration, 1998)
McGarry, Fearghal, 'Introduction', in McGarry, Fearghal (ed.), *Republicanism in Modern Ireland* (Dublin: University College Dublin Press, 2003)
McGladdery, Gary, *The Provisional IRA in England: The Bombing Campaign, 1973–1997* (Dublin: Irish Academic Press, 2006)
McGuffin, John, *Internment!* (Tralee: Anvil Books, 1973)
McQueen, Norman, 'Ireland's entry to the United Nations 1946–56', in Gallagher, Tom and O'Connell, James (eds), *Contemporary Irish Studies* (Manchester: Manchester University Press, 1983)
Moran, Seán Farrell, 'Patrick Pearse and the European revolt against reason', *Journal of the History of Ideas*, vol. 50, no. 4 (1989)
Noone, Michael F. and Alexander, Yonah (eds), *Cases and material on terrorism: Three nations' response* (London: Martinus Nijhoff Publishers, 1997)
O'Brien, Conor Cruise, *Memoir: My life and Themes* (Dublin: Poolbeg Press, 1998)
O'Donnell, Ruán, *1798 Diary* (Dublin: Irish Times Books, 1998)
O'Donnell, Ruán, *The Rebellion in Wicklow, 1798* (Dublin: Irish Academic Press, 1998)
O'Donnell, Ruán, *Robert Emmet and the Rising of 1798* (Dublin: Irish Academic Press, 2003)

O'Donnell, Ruán, *Robert Emmet and the Rising of 1803* (Dublin: Irish Academic Press, 2003)

Ó Drisceoil, Donal, *Censorship in Ireland 1939–1945: Neutrality, Politics and Society* (Cork: Cork University Press, 1996)

Ó Drisceoil, Donal, *Peadar O'Donnell* (Cork: Cork University Press, 2001)

O'Halpin, Eunan, *Defending Ireland: The Irish State and its Enemies since 1922* (Oxford: Oxford University Press, 2000)

O'Halpin, Eunan (ed.), *MI5 and Ireland 1939–1945: The Official History* (Dublin: Irish Academic Press, 2002)

Ó Longaigh, Seosamh, 'Emergency law in action 1939-45', in Keogh, Dermot and O'Driscoll, Mervyn (eds), *Ireland in World War Two: Neutrality and Survival* (Cork: Mercier Press, 2004)

Ó Longaigh, Seosamh, *Emergency Law in Independent Ireland, 1922–1948* (Dublin: Four Courts Press, 2006)

Ó Longaigh, Seosamh, 'Preparing law for an emergency: 1938–1939', in Keogh, Dermot and O'Driscoll, Mervyn (eds), *Ireland in World War Two: Neutrality and Survival* (Cork: Mercier Press, 2004)

O'Malley, Ernie, *On Another Man's Wound* (Dublin: Anvil Books, 2002)

O'Malley, Ernie, *The Singing Flame* (Dublin: Anvil Books, 1978)

O'Neill, Michael S., 'In time of "war": Irish domestic security legislation 1939–45', *Irish History: A Research Yearbook*, vol. 2 (2003)

Patterson, Henry, 'Seán Lemass and the Ulster question', *Journal of Contemporary History*, vol. 34, no. 1 (1999)

Patterson, Henry, *The Politics of Illusion: Republicanism and Socialism in Modern Ireland* (London: Hutchinson Radius, 1989)

Rafter, Kevin, *The Clann: The Story of Clann na Poblachta* (Dublin: Mercier Press, 1996)

Regan, John M., *The Irish Counter Revolution 1921–1936* (Dublin: Gill & Macmillan, 1999)

Ryan, Meda, *Tom Barry: IRA Freedom Fighter* (Cork: Mercier Press, 2003)

Salmon, Trevor C., *Unneutral Ireland: An Ambivalent and Unique Security Policy* (Oxford: Clarendon Press, 1989)

Seoighe, Mainchin, *Maraiodh Seán Sabhat aréir* (Dublin: Sairseal agus Dill, 1964)

Skelly, Joseph Morrison, *Irish diplomacy at the United Nations 1945–65: National Interests and the International Order* (Dublin: Irish Academic Press, 1997)

Smith, M.L.R., *Fighting for Ireland? The Military Strategy of the Irish Republican Movement* (London: Routledge, 1997)

Smyth, Jim, *The Men of No Property: Irish Radicals and Popular Politics in the Late Eighteenth Century* (Dublin: Gill & Macmillan, 1992)

Staunton, Enda, *The Nationalists of Northern Ireland 1918–1973* (Dublin: Columba Press, 2001)

Stewart, A.T.Q., *The Narrow Ground: Aspects of Ulster 1609–1969* (Belfast: Blackstaff Press, 1997)

Sweeney, George, 'Self-immolation in Ireland: Hungerstrikes and political confrontation', *Anthropology Today*, vol. 9, no. 5 (1993)

Tanner, Marcus, *Ireland's Holy Wars: The Struggle for a Nation's Soul 1500–2000* (Reading: Yale University Press, 2003)

Townshend, Charles, *Easter 1916: The Irish Rebellion* (London: Allen Lane, 2005)

Townshend, Charles, *Ireland: The Twentieth Century* (London: Arnold, 1999)

Townshend, Charles, *Political Violence in Ireland: Government and Resistance in Ireland since 1848* (Oxford: Clarendon Press, 1983)

Townshend, Charles, *The British Campaign in Ireland* (Oxford: Oxford University Press, 1975)

Valentine, D.G., 'The European Court of Human Rights: The Lawless case', *International and Comparative Quarterly*, vol. 10, no. 4 (October, 1961)

Whelan, Bernadette, *United States Foreign Policy and Ireland: From Empire to Independence, 1913–29* (Dublin: Four Courts Press, 2006)

White, Robert W., *Ruairí Ó Brádaigh: The Life and Politics of an Irish Revolutionary* (Bloomington: Indiana University Press, 2006)

Wilson, Robert, 'Questions relating to Irish neutrality', *American Journal of International Law*, vol. 36, no. 2 (1942)

Wilson, Tom, *Ulster: Conflict and Consent* (Oxford: Basil Blackwell, 1989)

Theses

Lane, Jason, 'The development of Irish cross-border police co-operation' (PhD thesis, Queen's University Belfast, 1999)

McCay, Kevin Hugh, 'The IRA border campaign of 1956–62: A new perspective' (MPhil Thesis, Trinity College Dublin, 1992)

Ní Bheachain, Caoilfhionn, 'The lost republicans: Seán McCaughey and the disruption of the Free State narrative' (MA thesis, National University of Ireland, Galway, 1997)

O'Sullivan, Colman Tadhg, 'The IRA takes constitutional action: A history of Clann na Poblachta 1946–65' (MA thesis, University College Dublin, 1995)

Woods, Jane Cole, '"To blow and burn England from her moorings": The Irish republican army and the English bombing campaign of 1939' (PhD Thesis, University of Kentucky, 1995)

Web-based Material

Lawless V Ireland [1961], European Court of Human Rights (http://cmiskp.echr.coe.int) (7 March 2006)

Macmillan Cabinet Papers, 1957–63, Cabinet Office (http://www.ampltd.co.uk/online/Macmillan-Cabinet-Papers/index.aspx) (8 March 2006)

Index

abstentionism, parliamentary, 80, 113, 115, 206
Adams, Lieut.-Col. Joseph, 199
Aiken, Frank, 66, 121–2, 123, 142
Al Rawdah prison ship, 52
Algeria, 69
All-Ireland Anti-Partition League (APL), 56
American League for an Undivided Ireland, 110
An Claidheamh (Sinn Féin newsletter), 62
An Dé (Sinn Féin newsletter), 62
An Fórsa Cosanta Áitiúil (FCA), 145
An Gath (republican magazine), 103
Andersen, Constable, 197–8
Anglo-Irish trade talks (early 1960s), 195, 196
Anglo-Irish Treaty (December 1921), 9–10
Arborfield army depot raid (1955), 81–2
Arbour Hill military barracks, 27, 30, 34, 49
Archer, Colonel, 42
Arm na Saoirse, 72
arms raids, IRA (1951-5), 1, 69–70, 75–7, 80, 81–2
Army (Emergency Powers) Resolution (1922), 11
army, British, 70, 77, 95, 96–7, 120–1, 181
  Arborfield depot raid (1955), 81–2
  Blandford Camp attack (February 1958), 184–5
  Gough barracks attacks, 75–6, 77, 86–7, 192
  Territorial Army barracks, 69, 75, 85, 109, 113, 118
army, Irish, 11, 28, 52, 93–4, 145, 189–90
  republican reserve (launched 1934), 15, 21
Army Comrades Association (ACA, Blueshirts), 15–16, 21
Army Council, IRA
  1930s, 15, 22, 23
  1939–45:, 32, 38, 48–9, 50–1, 53
  1947–56:, 62, 63, 64, 68, 69, 71, 73, 74, 75
  'border campaign' and, 82–4, 98, 99, 110, 114, 126, 130, 173, 186, 201
  Curragh camp and, 48–9, 138, 140
  Curragh dispute (split), 138–41, 193–4, 203–4, 209
  Serpentine Avenue safe house, 68, 192–3
Arriba (Spanish periodical), 77
Attlee, Clement, 67
Australia, 108
'Auxiliaries', the, 9

Bacon, Sergeant William, 86
Ballycastle RUC barracks (Co. Antrim), 86
Bardon, Jonathon, 53
Barnes, Peter, 24–5
Barrett, Patrick, 121
Barry, Mrs. Leslie, 137
Barry, Tom, 22–3, 137
Beattie, Charles, 81
Beggar's Bush barracks (Dublin), 11

Behan, Brendan, 35, 40
Belfast, 'border campaign' and, 98–9
Bellaghy RUC station attack (1958), 192
Bennett, Colonel Francis, 20, 55, 199
Berry, Peter, 131, 151, 202
Black, Lord Justice, 180
'Black and Tans', 9
Blandford Army Camp attack (February 1958), 184–5
Blueshirts, 15–16, 21
Bodenstown (Co. Kildare), 63, 66, 173–4
Boland, Frederick, 78–9, 80, 124, 125
Boland, Gerald, 16, 18, 26–7, 53, 54, 114
  hunger strikes and, 31–2, 57, 58
  internment and, 27, 28–9, 33, 38
'border campaign' of IRA (1956-62), 1–2, 85–116, 125–30, 174–201
  ambushes, 127–8, 194, 195, 199
  assassination attempts, 181, 197–8
  Belfast and, 98–9
  booby trap bombs, 176–7
  British army barracks/camps attacks, 86–7, 109, 113, 118, 184–5, 192
  British state and, 91–2, 93, 95, 109, 171, 184–5
  Christmas suspension (1956), 98, 99, 100
  commencement of (December 1956), 85–9
  communications systems, attacks on, 89, 97, 118, 181, 192
  John A. Costello and, 80, 91, 92, 93, 94, 95, 96, 101, 105–6
  de Valera and, 105, 106, 115–16, 117, 128–9, 182, 192
  decline of, 181–6, 189, 197
  Derry arrests (March 1957), 118
  Derry railway station attack (March 1957), 114, 119
  economic consequences, 97, 118–20
  Edentubber explosion (November 1957), 182
  ending of (February 1962), 2, 4, 5, 201, 202
  explosives/ordnance, 85, 86–7, 101–2, 109, 127, 173
  internment and, 3–5, 88, 89–91, 128–42, 173, 183–6, 192–3
  see also Lawless, Gerard
  IRA fatalities, 1, 101, 102–4, 105, 115, 182, 190
  IRA funerals, 103–4, 182, 190
  Kinawley Orange hall attack (September 1958), 192
  Newry attacks (1957), 118, 127
  Operation Harvest documents, 82, 100, 108–9, 110, 146
  Pettigo village confrontations (February 1957), 120–1
  planning for, 82–4

RUC barracks/station attacks, 1, 73, 89, 98, 126, 175, 181, 182–3, 192, 194
  see also Brookeborough RUC barracks; Derrylin RUC barracks attacks
Special Criminal Court and, 144, 200–1
Torr Head radar station attack (April 1957), 126
transport network, attacks on, 85, 89, 113–14, 118, 127, 181, 183, 192, 198
United Nations and, 122–5
USA and, 110–11
  see also Irish Republican Army (IRA); Royal Ulster Constabulary (RUC): 'border campaign'
border crossings, closures of, 96–7
Breathnach, Diarmaid, 35
Breathnach, Fionan, 94, 111–12
Bridewell prison, 110, 132, 147
British Embassy (Dublin), 72, 175–6
British state
  'border campaign' and, 91–2, 93, 95, 109, 171, 184–5
  ECHR and, 162, 163, 167
  Embassy (Dublin), 72, 175–6
  Felsted barracks raid (July 1953), 70, 75
  IRA and, 2, 74–5, 78–9
  Ireland (1797-1922), 6–10
  Ireland Act (1949), 1, 67–8, 95
  Irish state and, 1–2, 3, 119–22, 128–9, 171, 185, 195–6, 199
  Lawless case and, 161–3
  Republic of Ireland Act and, 67
  S-Plan bombing campaign, 21–5, 26
British Torture in Ireland (IRPB pamphlet), 178, 179
Brocket, Lord, 195
Brookeborough, Lord Basil (Sir Basil Brooke), 67, 73, 88, 92, 95, 118, 119, 195, 196
  Irish state and, 88, 93, 94, 127, 129
Brookeborough RUC barracks, 1, 100, 101–6
'Broy Harriers', 15, 21
Bryan, Colonel Dan, 40–1
B-Specials, the, 52, 85, 87, 89, 99, 118, 176, 181, 183
  mobilisation, 88, 117, 119
Buckley, Margaret, 65
Bunracht na hÉireann (1937), 2, 18–19, 21, 26
Burke, James, 28, 29, 143
Burke, Liam, 36, 38
Butler, Richard, 195–6
Byrne, Col. James H., 199

Cahill, Joe, 91, 98–9, 187, 206
Campbell, David, 195
Campbell, Senator Seán, 31
Canning, Manus, 70, 196
capital punishment, 11, 13, 14, 24–5, 34, 40, 50, 51, 52, 53
  Easter Rising and, 7–8
Carroll, James, 160, 163
Carroll, P., 152–3, 154, 155
Carter, Frank, 115
Casement, Sir Roger, 7
Casey, Barney, 45, 46, 47
Cashel (Co. Fermanagh), 96–7
Catholic Church, 16, 103
censorship, 4, 26–7, 30, 34, 46, 55, 57

Chicago Daily Tribune, 77
Chichester-Clarke, Robin, 119
Christle, Joseph, 73, 83, 127, 145–8, 159, 165–6, 172, 174
Churchill, Winston, 11
Civil Authorities (Special Powers) Act (SPA, 1922), 12
  'border campaign' and, 88, 89, 96, 97, 180–1
Civil War, the, 2, 11, 33, 34, 61
Clan na nGael, 22, 70–2, 200
Clann na Poblachta, 56, 59–62, 72–3, 79–80, 191–2
  John A. Costello and, 91, 94, 107, 108, 109, 111–13
  electoral support, 60, 74, 114
  inter-party government (1948-51), 60–1, 66, 79, 103
  inter-party government (1954-7) and, 107, 108, 109, 111–13
Clann na Talmhan, 60, 179
Clarke, Kathleen, 31
Clarke, O.M., 136
Clarke, Philip, 77, 80–1
Clutterbuck, Sir Alexander, 95, 119, 142
Coalisland RUC barracks attack (April 1957), 126
Cold War, 4
Collins, Michael, 10, 11
Common Market, 194, 201, 206
Commonwealth, the, 67
communications systems, attacks on, 89, 97, 118, 181, 192
compensation issues, 'border campaign', 119–20
Conlon, Vincent, 101, 139
Connolly, James, 13
Connolly, Thomas J., 149, 160
Constitution (Amendment No. 17) Act (1931), 14–15
Constitution, Irish (Bunracht na hÉireann, 1937), 2, 18–19, 21, 26
Constitutional (Special Powers) Tribunal, 14, 16, 18, 19, 20
Conway, Michael, 62, 64
Cooney, Anthony, 86
Cork military barracks, 34
coronation of Queen Elizabeth II (1953), 74–5
Cosgrave, W.T., 12
Costello, John A., 2, 60–1, 67, 72, 74, 110, 122–3
  'border campaign' and, 80, 91, 92, 93, 94, 95, 96, 101, 105–6
  Clann na Poblachta and, 91, 94, 107, 108, 109, 111–13
  general election (March 1957), 112
  IRA and, 73, 74, 77–8, 79–80
  Radio Éireann broadcast (6 January 1957), 105–6, 109, 111
Costello, Seamus, 85
Coughlan, Anthony, 204–5
Council of Europe, 56, 122, 152, 156–7, 158, 167, 168
Committee of Ministers, 157, 158, 160, 163
Council of State, 29
Coventry bombing (August 1939), 24–5, 26
Cowan, Peadar, 59, 68
Coyne, Thomas, 160, 179
Craig, William, 202
Craven, Oliver, 182
Criminal Investigation Department (CID), 10, 63

Criminal Law and Procedure (Ireland) Act (1887), 7
Crockada Bridge ambush (August 1959), 194
Cronin, Seán, 82, 87, 108, 126, 140, 173, 182, 184, 192, 194
Crosbie, James, 161, 166
Crossan, James, 190–2
Crumlin Road Prison (Belfast), 52, 89–91, 186–8, 207–8
Cumann na nGaedheal, 15–16
Cummins, M.J., 41
Curragh camp
  1950s regime, 4, 6, 133–41
  arson at (December 1940), 44–6, 47
  closure (1945), 54
  closure (1959), 4, 5, 141–2, 143, 144, 170, 193, 203
  conditions at (WW2), 35–7, 43–4, 47, 50
  escape attempts, 38–9, 42–5, 46, 138–41, 193
  internee releases (1943-5), 49–50, 54, 57
  internees' 'camp staff', 40–2, 47–9, 135
  IRA disunity at (WW2), 47–9, 50
  Gerard Lawless and, 148, 151, 155, 163
  ostracization at, 37–8, 41–2, 47–8
  reconstruction of (1939-40), 34–5
  reopening (1957), 130, 131–4
  shootings of internees, 45–6
  WW2 and, 3, 6, 33, 34–50, 131, 137–8, 208
Curragh dispute (IRA split), 138–41, 193–4, 203–4, 209
Curragh military barracks, 34, 149
Cyprus, 69, 125, 162

Dáil Éireann, 9, 10, 13, 28, 57, 94, 96, 123
Daily Express, 168
Daly, Jeremiah, 48
D'Arcy, Tony, 30–1
de Valera, Eamon
  becomes Prime Minister (1932), 15
  Blueshirts and, 15, 16
  British state and, 119, 206
  Constitutional Tribunal, 15, 16
  Dáil Éireann and, 9, 13, 15
  ECHR and, 162–3
  Fianna Fáil, founding of (1926), 13
  general election defeat (1948), 60
  general election (March 1957), 114, 115
  hunger strikes and, 28, 30–2, 33, 57–8
  internment and, 29, 53, 128–9, 136, 142, 172
  IRA and, 15, 17–18, 20, 21, 25–6, 28, 54, 77, 125–6, 142, 205
  IRA 'border campaign' and, 105, 106, 115–16, 117, 128–9, 182, 192
  partition and, 56, 66, 68, 106, 116, 129
  President, election as (1959), 194
  Sinn Féin and, 9, 13, 129–30
  United Nations and, 55–6
  WW2 and, 3, 25–6, 28, 29, 30–3, 53
Defence Conference (1940), 33
Defence of the Realm Acts (DORA, 1914-18), 7, 8
derogation, right of (from ECHR), 158–9, 160, 163–4, 169–70, 171
Derry, 52, 69, 114, 118, 119
Derrylin RUC barracks attacks, 89, 100–1, 106–7, 118
Detention Commission, 27, 29, 130–1

Lawless case, 144, 148–51, 152–4, 170
  procedure, 148–50, 152–6, 170
Devereux, Michael, 51
Devlin, Colonel Felix, 27, 55, 199
Dillon, James, 112
discrimination in Northern Ireland, 69, 124, 126
Doherty, J., 196
Dolan, Joe, 47
Dolan, Lieutenant Patrick, 189–90
Donegal Democrat, 121
Donnellan, Michael, 179
Doolan, Brian, 171
Doran, Tom, 36, 48
Dowling, Seamus, 48
Doyle, James, 63
Doyle, Joseph, 82
Doyle, Paddy, 98
Doyle, Seamus, 72
Doyle, Thomas, 128
drilling with arms, IRA, 63, 66, 69, 79, 82
Driver, Frank, 63
Duane, D.J., 58
Dublin transport dispute (1935), 17
Duffy, Justice Gavin, 28, 29
Duffy, Patrick, 108
Duggan, Seán, 173
Duke, Henry, 9
Duncreggan camp attack (February 1957), 113
Dungannon barracks attacks (1957), 109, 118

Easter Rising (1916), 7–8
Ebrington TA barracks raid (June 1951), 69, 75
economy, Irish, 1, 3, 55, 107, 111, 113, 194, 205–6
Eden, Sir Anthony, 91–2, 95, 96
Edentubber explosion (November 1957), 182
Edgeworthstown (County Longford), 17–18
Edmonds, Seán, 126
Egan, John, 18
elections, British, 9, 80–1, 113, 196–7
elections, Irish
  by-elections, 60, 80, 107, 108, 111
  general election (March 1957), 2, 80, 112–16
  general elections, 59, 60, 74, 197
  local, 80
  presidential (1945), 59
elections, Northern Ireland, 67
Electoral Amendment Act (1927), 13
electricity supply, attacks on, 24, 113, 126, 175, 181
Emergency Powers Act (EPA, 1939), 26, 28–9, 34, 50, 54
escape attempts from internment, 42–5, 46, 138–41, 193
  lethal force orders, 38–9
  Northern Ireland, 52, 186–7
European Commission of Human Rights, 141, 152, 155, 156–67, 170
European Convention on Human Rights (ECHR), 143, 144, 151–2, 156–72, 197, 198
European Court of Human Rights, 5, 143, 144, 152, 157, 158, 167–70, 171, 173, 208
Everett, James, 76
Explosives Act (1875), 14
explosives/ordnance, IRA, 85, 86–7, 101–2, 109, 127, 173

External Relations Act, 66
extradition requests to Irish state, 109, 185

Faulkner, Brian, 202, 207–8
Felsted barracks raid (July 1953), 70, 75
Ferguson, Constable William John, 94
Fermanagh and South Tyrone constituency, 80–1, 113
Fianna Fáil
  administration (1957-73), 117, 123, 125–6
  'border campaign' and, 105
  economic policies, 194, 205–6
  electoral support, 13, 59, 60, 74, 107–8, 111, 114
  first administration (elected 1932), 15
  founding of (1926), 13
  general election (March 1957), 2, 113, 114–15
  IRA and, 15–20, 21, 54, 69, 115–16, 117, 128–9
  Lemass administration, 194–201
Fianna Uladh, 72–3, 92
Fine Gael, 2, 59, 103, 114, 117
  see also Costello, John A.; inter-party government
Finucane, Patrick, 123
Firearms Act (1925), 14, 100
Fitzpatrick, Michael, 59
Fleming, Patrick, 62
Fleming Fireclay Company (Athy), 146, 147, 153, 154, 165
Forkhill ambush (4 July 1957), 127–8
Frongoch prisoner-of-war camp (Wales), 8
funerals, IRA, 58, 66, 103–4, 182, 190, 191

Gaelic Athletic Association (GAA), 97
Gaelic League, 97
Gallipoli film robbery (1933), 16
Garda Síochána
  border patrols, 106, 109, 116, 182, 183, 197
  'Broy Harriers', 15, 21
  fatalities, 34, 51
  formation of (1922), 10
  Gerard Lawless and, 146, 147, 149, 150, 152–6, 165
  internment and, 33, 128, 132
  IRA and, 33, 34, 50–1, 92–4, 104
  IRA arrests, 26, 62, 96, 100–1, 102, 106, 128, 192–3
  powers of, 2, 12, 14, 19, 26
  RUC and, 96, 109–10, 116, 120–2, 182, 191–2
  see also Special Branch
Garland, Seán, 75, 86–7, 101, 200
Geraghty, Seán, 145, 146, 147, 165
Germany, 8
  Nazi, 3, 22, 25, 33
Gill, Thomas, 134
Gilmore, George, 13
Good Friday Agreement (1998), 209
Goold-Verschoyle, Neil, 35
Görtz, Herman, 25, 33
Goss, Richard, 34
Gough barracks raids, 75–6, 77, 86–7, 192
Goulding, Cathal, 62, 70, 194, 204–5, 206, 207
Green, Connie, 73
Gregg, Constable Cecil, 127
Grogan, Thomas, 30, 35, 43–4, 47, 192
Grosvenor, Lieutenant-Colonel R.G., 81, 195
Guiney, Captain James, 35, 38, 39, 40, 43–5, 46, 48

Habeas Corpus Suspension Act (1797), 6
Halligan, Constable Robert, 127
Hamilton, R.T., 177
Hand, Aloysius, 190
Hannigan, James, 59
Hare, John, 92
Harte, Tom, 34
Hartnett, Noel, 22, 59
Haugh, Kevin, 38
Haughey, Charles, 144, 202
Hayde, Tony, 133, 134, 135
Hayes, Stephen, 26, 50, 56
Hederman, Anthony, 160
Heffernan, Myles, 27
Herald Tribune, 129
Hornibrook, Jasper, 72
Hughes, James, 134
hunger strikes, 28, 30–3, 189
  Seán McCaughey (1946), 56–8, 59, 62
Hunter, William, 199

Imperial Chemical Industries (Moorestown), 145
Industrial Relations Act (1946), 55
Insurrection Act (1796), 7
internment
  'border campaign' and, 3–5, 88, 89–91, 128–42, 173, 183–6, 192–3
  Civil War, 2, 33, 34
  Crumlin Road Prison (Belfast), 52, 89–91, 186–8
  historical context (1797-1922), 6–10
  internee releases (1943-8), 49–50, 54, 57, 58, 61
  Irish state legislation, 2, 11–12, 19–20
    see also Offences Against the State Act (OASA, 1939); Special Criminal Court
  legal challenges to, 28, 29, 143, 159
    see also Lawless, Gerard legislation (1797–1922), 6–10
  Northern Ireland (1957-61), 1, 88, 89–91, 186–8
  Northern Ireland (1971-5), 207–8
  Northern Ireland legislation, 12, 88
  Northern Ireland (WW2), 51–3
  release mechanisms, 37–8, 41, 47, 91, 117, 148
  Republic of Ireland (1950s), 1, 3–4, 5, 6, 203, 208–9
  WW1 and, 8–9
  WW2 and, 3, 4, 6, 26, 27–50, 137–8, 208
    see also Curragh camp
inter-party government
  1948–51:, 60–1, 66–7, 74, 79–80, 103
  1954–7:, 74, 80, 107–8, 109, 111–13, 122–3
Ireland Act (1949), 1, 67–8, 95
Iris Oifigiúil, 131
Irish Association for Civil Liberties, 137
Irish Free State, 2, 10–20, 21
Irish Independent, 57
Irish Press, 57, 178
Irish Republican Army (IRA)
  1919–23:, 5, 9–12
  ACA and, 15–16
  Arborfield army depot raid (1955), 81–2
  arms and munitions, 28, 50, 66, 110–11, 118, 173, 182
  arms raids (1951-5), 1, 69–70, 75–7, 80, 81–2
  assassinations, 13, 17–18
  British state and, 2, 74–5, 78–9
  Bunracht na hÉireann (1937), 18–19, 21

Index

ceasefire (May 1923), 11
cessation in Irish state (1948), 65
Christle's splinter group, 73, 83, 127, 145–8, 159, 165–6, 172, 174
Clan na nGael and, 22, 70–2
Clann na Poblachta and, 79–80
Constitution (Special Powers) Tribunal, 16, 18
Curragh dispute (split), 138–41, 193–4, 203–4, 209
Curragh disunity (WW2), 47–9, 50
de Valera and, 15, 17–18, 20, 21, 25–6, 28, 54, 77, 142, 205
drilling with arms, 63, 66, 69, 79, 82
Ebrington barracks raid (June 1951), 69, 75
electricity supply, attacks on, 24, 113, 126, 175, 181
Felsted barracks raid (July 1953), 70, 75
Fianna Fáil and, 15–20, 21, 54, 69, 115–16, 117, 128–9
fundraising, 22, 25, 68, 70–2, 186, 200, 207, 208
funerals, 58, 66, 103–4, 182, 190, 191
Gallipoli film robbery (1933), 16
Garda Síochána and, 33, 34, 50–1, 92–4, 104
Garda Síochána arrests, 26, 62, 96, 100–1, 102, 106, 128, 192–3
Gough barracks raid (June 1954), 75–6, 77
ideology, 5, 14, 16, 21, 22, 35, 71, 204–7
Irish army and, 189–90
Seán Lemass and, 199
magazine fort raid (December 1939), 28
Nazi Germany and, 3, 22, 25, 33
Northern Ireland, 51–3, 65–6, 69, 75–7, 117–18, 173
Omagh barracks raid (1954), 77
prison activities, 27–8, 30–3, 56–8, 186–9
prisoner releases (1957), 125–6
proscription of, 18, 20, 25
recruitment, 68–9, 76
reorganisation and revival (1948-56), 6, 60–1, 62–6, 68–72, 74–80, 81–4
Republic of Ireland and, 1–2, 73, 74, 77–80
RUC and (pre 'border campaign'), 52, 58, 76, 77
Sinn Féin and, 61, 63, 64–6, 72, 115, 135, 196
socialism and, 13–14, 16–17, 21, 22, 35, 71, 204–7
S-Plan bombing campaign and, 2, 21–5, 26
split (1970), 2, 207
splits (1949-56), 72–3
strategic review (early 1960s), 2
The United Irishman and, 64, 66
USA and, 22, 25, 207, 208
WW2 and, 3, 4, 6, 25, 26–53, 54
see also Army Council, IRA; 'border campaign' of IRA (1956-62)
Irish Republican Brotherhood (IRB, 1951 IRA rival), 72
Irish Republican Brotherhood (IRB) rising (1867), 7
Irish Republican Publicity Bureau (IRPB), 178, 179, 185, 189, 191, 197–8, 202
Irish state
British state and, 1–2, 3, 119–22, 128–9, 171, 185, 195–6, 199
Bunracht na hÉireann (1937), 2, 18–19, 21, 26
economy, 1, 3, 55, 107, 111, 113, 194, 205–6
IRA cessation (1948), 65
Ireland Act (1949) and, 1, 67–8, 95

Irish Free State, 2, 10–20, 21
WW2 and, 2–3, 20, 25–53, 55–6
see also Republic of Ireland
Irish Times, the, 76, 77, 93–4, 132, 174, 177, 178, 198, 202, 203
Irish Volunteers, 9
Irish Workers League, 71

Johnston, Roy, 204–5
Jones, Elwyn (QC), 178, 180
Jonesborough ambush (November 1961), 199
Joyce, Colonel John Vincent, 20, 131
Juries (Protection) Act (1929), 14

Kavanagh, Noel, 100, 108, 134, 135, 140
Keegan, George, 182
Keenan, Eddie, 37, 48
Kelly, John, 139
Kelly, Liam, 72–3, 92, 99, 127, 145, 165, 190, 192
Kelly, Pearse, 47
Kenna, Raymond, 72
Kennedy, Albert, 181
Kenya, 69, 162
Kerins, Charles, 40, 51, 53
Killeen, Jim, 18
Kimber, Gurth, 162–3, 195
Kinawley Orange hall attack (September 1958), 192
Kinneen, Major, 35, 44
Knights of the Red Branch, 110
Korea, 125

Labour Party, 59, 60, 79, 107, 114, 176
Larkin, James, 107
Lawless, Gerard
  criminal trials, 145–7
  Detention Commission and, 144, 148–51, 152–4, 170
  ECHR and, 151–2, 156–72, 197, 198
  European Commission of Human Rights and, 141, 152, 155, 156, 157–67
  European Court of Human Rights and, 5, 167–70, 173, 208
  Garda Síochána and, 146, 147, 149, 150, 152–6, 165
  internment of, 148–56
  IRA and, 145, 146, 147, 152, 159, 160, 165–6, 169, 172
  later life, 172
  legal challenge to internment, 4–5, 6, 143–4, 148–72, 209
  OASA and, 147–8, 154–5
  Saor Uladh and, 145, 165
Lawlor, Mrs. George, 31–2
Leader, The, 178
Leddy, Liam, 47, 48, 49
Lee, Joe, 115
Legion of Mary, 103
Lehane, Con, 59, 111–12
Lemass, Seán, administration of, 194–201, 205–6
Lennon, District Justice Michael, 106–7
Lennon, Thomas, 118
Liesching, Percivale, 78–9
Liggett, W.J., 191
Lintott, Sir Henry, 122
Lisnaskea RUC barracks attack (1956), 89, 98

Locke's distillery, 55
London bombings (1939), 24
Lords Lieutenant, 6, 7
Louth by-election (1954), 80
Lynch, Jack, 208
Lynch, Jeremiah, 28
Lynch, Liam, 10, 11
Lynch, Tadhg, 47

Mac Giolla, Tomás, 203
Mac Stiofáin, Seán (Seán Stephenson), 70, 207
MacBride, Seán, 14, 18, 22, 28, 32, 58, 122, 202
  'border campaign' and, 96
  Clann na Poblachta and, 59, 72, 74, 79–80
  ECHR and, 143, 151, 158–60, 161, 164
  general election (March 1957), 114
  Gerard Lawless and, 143, 149, 150–4, 158–60, 161, 162, 164, 165
  inter-party government (1954-7) and, 80, 107–8, 111–12
  Mallon and Talbot affair, 178
  Minister for External Affairs, 61, 66, 124
MacCartan, Dr. Patrick, 59
MacCurtain, Tomás, 30, 56–7, 109–10, 128
  Curragh camp and, 134, 135, 137, 138–40, 141, 192, 204
  IRA Army Council, 64, 83, 193–4
MacEntee, Seán, 114
MacEoin, Seán, 59, 61, 66, 115
Macken, Richard, 34
MacMillan, Harold, 142
MacNeela, Seán, 23
Magan, Anthony, 62, 109–10, 128, 204
  Curragh camp and, 138, 140, 141, 192, 193–4
  IRA C/S, 64, 72, 82, 83, 98–9
Maghera RUC station attack (1958), 192
Magherafelt court house, 85
Maginess, Brian, 106
Maguire, Ben, 115
Maguire, C.J., 151–2
Maidstone prison ship, 208
Mallon, Kevin, 177, 178–81
Maria Duce, 103
Martin, Patrick, 40
McAteer, Hugh, 51–2
McCann, Éamonn, 172
McCarthy, Charles, 28
McCarthy, Gerard, 134
McCarthy, Michael, 192
McCarthy, Richard, 28
McCaughey, Seán, 50, 56–8, 59, 62
McCool, Seán, 49, 60, 63
McCormack, John, 36, 46
McCormick, James, 24–5
McEldowney, Michael, 200
McGann, Hugh, 27, 122
McGann, P., 136
McGarrity, Joseph, 22
McGarry, Fearghal, 5
McGirl, John Joe, 62, 115, 182
McGrath, Patrick, 28, 34
McGuinness, Willie, 62, 64
McKenna, Colonel Daniel, 20
McKeown, Malcolm, 85
McLeod, Scott, 186
McLogan, Patrick, 63, 64, 65, 128, 196

McMahon, Philip, 146–7, 165, 166
McManus, Patrick, 190
McMonagle, Thomas, 71, 173–4
McNair, Lord, 167–8
McNally, Colonel T., 42, 44
McNeela, Jack, 30, 31, 32
McNulty, A.B., 167
McQuillan, Jack, 117, 123, 125
McRory, Cardinal, 30
Mid-Ulster constituency, 80–1, 113
military courts, 11, 13, 14, 19, 34, 50, 54
military police corps, 34, 38–40, 44–6, 47, 137–8
Mitchell, Thomas, 77, 80–1, 189, 196, 202
Moore, Justice Kingsmill, 61
Moore, P.C., 148, 149
Morrissey, Seán, 160
mother and child scandal (1951), 60
Mountjoy Prison, 27, 30, 31–2, 114, 126, 132, 134, 188–9
Moynihan, Maurice, 131, 179
Mulcahy, Richard, 108
Mulligan, William, 41
munitions, IRA, 173
Murphy, Charlie, 65, 138, 139, 141, 173, 182
  Curragh dispute (split), 138, 141, 193–4
  Patrick Dolan and, 189–90
Murphy, Donal, 82
Murphy, James, 82
'Murphy, Paul', 185
Murphy, Seamus, 35
Murray, James, 183

Na Fianna Éireann, 104, 145, 165
National Unity and Independence Programme (Sinn Féin), 65, 80
Nationalist Party, 80, 81, 197
New York consulate, Irish, 110–11, 129
New York Times, 77
Newry, 75, 118, 127, 175
  curfew (August 1957), 175, 176
North Atlantic Treaty Organisation (NATO), 66
Northern Ireland
  Anglo-Irish Treaty and, 10
  'border campaign' and, 85–116, 125, 126
  'border campaign' economic issues, 118–20
  discrimination in, 69, 124, 126
  Ebrington barracks raid (June 1951), 69, 75
  internee releases (1961), 188
  internment (1957-61), 1, 88, 89–91, 186–8
  internment (1971-5), 207–8
  internment (WW2), 51–3
  internment legislation, 12, 88
  IRA and, 51–3, 65–6, 69, 75–7, 117–18, 173
  see also 'border campaign' of IRA (1956-62)
  Mallon and Talbot affair, 177, 178–81
  Newry curfew (August 1957), 175, 176
  partition and, 67
  Saor Uladh and, 73
  Special Powers Act, 12, 88, 89, 96, 97, 180–1
  WW2 and, 51–3

Ó Brádaigh, Ruairí, 83, 98, 115, 159, 194
  'border campaign' attacks, 81–2, 100–1, 106–7
  Curragh camp and, 134, 137, 139–40
  IRA C/S, 193, 200–1, 206
Ó Briain, Donnachadh, 179

Ó Briain, Judge Barra, 131, 148–9, 150, 154, 156
Ó Broin, Tomás, 39, 63
Ó Cadhain, Martin, 37
Ó Caoimh, Aindrias, 130–1, 153–4, 160
Ó Conaill, Daithí, 101, 139–40
Ó Dubhghaill, Tomás, 114
O'Brien, Conor Cruise, 124–5
O'Brien, Sergeant Denis, 51
O'Donnell, Peadar, 13–14, 16–17, 21, 204, 205
O'Donoghue, Dermot, 104
O'Donovan, Donogh, 160
O'Donovan, Seamus, 23
O'Farrell, Richard More, 17–18
Offences Against the State Act (OASA, 1939), 2, 19–20, 26, 27, 58, 62, 117, 141, 209
  'border campaign' and, 94, 96, 106–7, 110
  Gerard Lawless and, 147–8, 154–5
  legal challenges, 28, 29
  see also Lawless, Gerard
  Special Criminal Court and, 144, 199, 200
Offences Against the State Act (OASA) Amendment Act (1940), 29, 88, 130–1, 156, 158, 208
  internment provisions, 54, 128, 132–3, 148, 151
  internment provisions, deactivation of (1962), 142, 156, 202–3
Official IRA, 207
Óglaigh na hÉireann, 64
  see also Irish Republican Army (IRA)
O'Hanlon, Lieutenant-Colonel, 136
O'Hanlon, Éighneachán, 115
O'Hanlon, Fergal, 1, 102–4, 105, 115, 190
O'Hare, Father John, 31, 32
O'Higgins, Kevin, 13
Oireachtas (Irish Parliament), 2, 26, 66, 151, 152
  Dáil Éireann, 9, 10, 13, 28, 57, 94, 96, 123
  internment and, 26, 29, 88
O'Kane, Canice, 96
O'Kelly, James, 63
O'Kelly, Seán T., 59, 62
Omagh barracks raid (1954), 77
O'Mahoney, Patrick, 71
O'Malley, Ernie, 10
O'Neill, Captain Terence, 194
O'Neill, Cristoir, 66
O'Neill, Maurice, 34
'Operation Harvest' *see* 'border campaign' of IRA (1956–62)
ordnance/explosives, IRA, 85, 86–7, 101–2, 109, 127, 173
O'Regan, Patrick, 101, 134
O'Reilly, Gerard, 71
Orr, William, 92
ostracization at Curragh camp, 37–8, 41–2, 47–8
O'Sullivan, Carl, 133, 136, 151
O'Toole, Seán, 139
Ovens, Sergeant Arthur, 126, 176–7, 178–81

Parle, Patrick, 182
partition issue, 1, 56, 66–7, 94, 96, 111, 112, 124–5
  de Valera and, 56, 66, 68, 106, 116, 129
  Ireland Act and, 67–8
  Lemass and, 194
  use of force and, 68, 105, 106, 110, 124, 129, 189
Patterson, Henry, 194
Pettigo village confrontations (February 1957), 120–1
Plant, George, 34, 51
Plunkett, John, 30
Portlaoise Prison, 30, 33, 56–8
Powers, Johnny, 35
Prevention of Violence (Temporary Provisions) Act (1939), 24, 25
Price, Michael, 17
prisons
  conditions in, 58, 90–1
  IRA and, 27–8, 30–3, 56–8, 90, 186–9
Provisional IRA, 207, 208
Public Safety Acts (1920s), 2, 11–12, 13, 19

Querney, Christopher, 35, 39
Quin, H., 126

Radio Éireann, 105–6, 109, 111
Radio Free Europe, 167
Rea, Lieut.-Col. William, 199
Red Cross, the, 90–1, 137
Reddin, District Justice Kenneth, 107, 108
release mechanisms, internment, 37–8, 41, 47, 91, 117, 148
Representation of the People Act (1949), 81
Republic of Ireland
  'border campaign' and, 91–6, 99–101, 103–16
  British army border crossings, 120–1
  British Embassy bomb scare (August 1957), 175–6
  British state and, 2, 119, 120–2, 128–9, 171, 185, 195–6, 199
  counter-insurgency policy, 1, 4, 5, 6, 144, 170
  see also internment
  derogation, right of, 158–9, 160, 163–4, 169–70, 171
  ECHR and, 151–2, 156–61, 162–72
  economic crises, 1, 107, 111, 113, 194
  economic policies, 107, 194, 205–6
  Fianna Fáil administration (1957-73), 117, 123, 125–6
  internment (1950s), 1, 3–4, 5, 6, 128–42, 203
  inter-party government (1948-51), 60–1, 66–7, 74, 79–80, 103
  inter-party government (1954-7), 74, 80, 107–8, 109, 111–13, 122–3
  IRA and, 1–2, 73, 77–80
  Lemass administration, 194–201
  Mallon and Talbot affair, 178, 179
  Northern Ireland policy, 68, 124–5
  see also partition issue
  United Nations and, 122–5
  see also Irish state
Republic of Ireland Act (1948), 66–8
Republican Congress, 17, 205
Republican Prisoners Release Association (RPRA), 64
Restoration of Order in Ireland Act (ROIA, 1920), 9
Rice, John Joe, 115
right to silence, 19
Roslea RUC barracks attacks, 73, 181, 194
Ross, Albert, 24
Royal Irish Constabulary (RIC), 9
Royal Ulster Constabulary (RUC)
  'border campaign' and, 87, 88, 96–7, 99, 109–10, 116, 126, 191–2
  'border campaign' engagements, 86, 89, 94–5, 100, 175, 181–2, 194, 195, 199

border crossings of, 120, 121–2
Brookeborough barracks, 1, 100, 101–6
casualties/fatalities, 52, 85, 94, 100, 127, 176–7, 197, 199
James Crossan shooting (August 1958), 190–2
Derrylin barracks, 89, 100–1, 106–7, 118
Forkhill ambush and, 127–8
Garda Síochána and, 96, 109–10, 116, 120–2, 182, 191–2
IRA (pre 'border campaign') and, 52, 58, 76, 77
Lisnaskea barracks, 89, 98
Mallon and Talbot affair, 177, 178–81
powers of, 12
reserve platoons, 117–18, 187
Roslea barracks, 73, 181, 194
Swatragh barracks, 175, 182–3
see also B-Specials, the
Rugby, Lord, 67, 68
Russell, Robert, 108
Russell, Seán, 22–5
Ryan, District Justice Edward, 131

Saor Éire, 13–14, 16, 205
Saor Uladh, 72–3, 83, 99, 127, 145, 165, 190
Saunderson, Maria, 17
Scally, John, 100, 101
Scotstown (Co. Monaghan), 93–4
Seadairí na Saoirse, 103
Sealy, James, 120
Seanad Éireann, 57, 72
Serpentine Avenue safe house (Dublin), 68, 192–3
Sheil, Justice J., 81
Sinn Féin
  abstentionism, parliamentary, 80, 113, 115, 206
  'border campaign' and, 98, 99, 103–4
  Civil War split, 61
  Curragh camp and, 135–6
  de Valera and, 9, 13, 129–30
  electoral support, 9, 80–1, 113, 115, 196–7
  Germany and, 8
  internment and, 128, 129–30, 186
  IRA and, 61, 63, 64–6, 72, 115, 135, 196
  National Unity and Independence Programme, 65, 80
  proscription of in Northern Ireland (1956), 99, 196
  reorganisation (1945), 61–2
  WW1 and, 8
Sinn Féin Bulletin, 62
Skuse, Frank, 185
Smith, Paul, 182
socialism, 13–14, 16–17, 21, 22, 35, 71, 204–7
Somerfield, Henry Boyle, 18
Sorahan, Seamus, 149, 160
South, Seán, 1, 101, 102–4, 105, 115, 190
Special Branch, 78, 182
  IRA and, 61, 62–3, 64, 93, 109–10, 128, 132, 192
  Gerard Lawless and, 146, 165, 166
Special Criminal Court, 18, 19, 26, 27, 28, 34, 46, 50, 51
  bombing of headquarters (1943), 33
  dissolution of (October 1962), 203
  membership, 20
  post-WW2 abeyance, 54–5
  reconstitution (1961), 4, 55, 144, 198–201
  reconstitution (1972), 144, 203, 208, 209

Special Powers Act (SPA, 1922) *see* Civil Authorities (Special Powers) Act (SPA, 1922)
S-Plan bombing campaign, 21–5, 26
Stack, Mrs. Austin, 31–2
Stephenson, Col. Seán (Seán Mac Stiofáin), 70, 207
Suez crisis, 91–2
Sunday World, 172
Suppression of Disturbances Act (1833), 7
Supreme Court, 28, 29, 151, 152
Swatragh RUC barracks attacks, 175, 182–3
Sweetman, Gerard, 107

Talbot, Francis Patrick, 177, 178–81
Teevan, Justice Thomas, 107
Territorial Army barracks, 69, 75, 85, 109, 113, 118
Times, The, 114, 128–9, 168
Timmons, Richard, 72
Topping, Col. W.W.B., 95, 106, 110, 119, 125, 192
  Forkhill ambush and, 127–8
  Newry curfew and, 175, 176
Torr Head radar station attack (April 1957), 126
torture allegations, RUC, 178–81
Touhy, Major Michael, 27
transport network, attacks on, 85, 89, 113–14, 118, 127, 181, 183, 192, 198
Traynor, Michael, 30, 126, 128
Traynor, Oscar, 38, 117, 148, 198
Treasonable Offences Act (1925), 14, 19
Treason-Felony Act (1848), 77
Tribunal, Constitutional, 14, 16, 18, 19, 20
Tuite, Major Patrick, 20
Tully, John, 191–2
Twomey, Moss, 14, 18

Ulster Unionist Party (UUP), 92, 95, 119, 195
United Ireland Committee, 110
United Irishman, The, 63–4, 66, 69, 70, 71, 76, 79
  'border campaign' and, 87, 98, 128, 174, 177, 183, 192, 198
  Mallon and Talbot affair, 178, 180–1
United Irishmen, 6
United Nations (UN), 55–6, 122–5
United States of America (USA), 108, 110–11, 129, 173–4
  IRA fundraising and, 22, 25, 70–2, 186, 200, 207, 208

Wakehurst, Lord, 75
Waldock, C.H.M., 160, 161, 166
Walsh, Brian, 160
Walsh, Liam, 40
War of Independence (1919-21), 9, 22
Watters, Michael, 182
Whelan, Major Cornelius, 20
Williams, Tom, 52
Wolfe Tone commemoration (Bodenstown), 63, 66, 173–4
Wolfe Tone Society, 205
World Health Organisation (WHO), 55
World War One (WW1), 7, 8–9
World War Two (WW2), 2–3, 6, 25–53
  cessation of, 54–6
  internment, 3, 4, 6, 33, 34–50, 131, 137–8
  IRA violence during, 33, 51–3

Young Ireland rising (1847), 7